Dictators and Democracy in African Development

What are the conditions for good governance in Africa, and why do many democracies still struggle with persistent poverty? Drawing on a historical study of Nigeria since independence, this book argues that the structure of the policy-making process explains variations in government performance better than other commonly cited factors, such as oil, colonialism, ethnic diversity, foreign debt, and dictatorships. The author links the political structure of the policy process to patterns of government performance over half a century to show that the key factor is not simply the status of the regime as a dictatorship or a democracy, but rather it is the structure of the policy-making process by which different policy demands are included or excluded. By identifying political actors with the leverage to prevent policy change and extract concessions, empirical tests demonstrate how these "veto players" systematically affect the performance of two broad categories of public policy. But the number of veto players impacts these categories in different ways, generating a Madisonian dilemma that has important implications for African countries struggling with the institutional trade-offs presented by different regimes.

A. Carl LeVan is Assistant Professor in the School of International Service at American University in Washington, D.C.

African Studies

The African Studies Series, founded in 1968, is a prestigious series of monographs, general surveys, and textbooks on Africa covering history, political science, anthropology, economics, and ecological and environmental issues. The series seeks to publish work by senior scholars as well as the best new research.

A list of books in this series will be found at the end of this volume.

Dictators and Democracy in African Development

The Political Economy of Good Governance in Nigeria

A. CARL LEVAN
American University

CAMBRIDGE
UNIVERSITY PRESS

CAMBRIDGE
UNIVERSITY PRESS

32 Avenue of the Americas, New York NY 10013-2473, USA

Cambridge University Press is part of the University of Cambridge.

It furthers the University's mission by disseminating knowledge in the pursuit of education, learning and research at the highest international levels of excellence.

www.cambridge.org
Information on this title: www.cambridge.org/9781107081147

First published 2015

A catalogue record for this publication is available from the British Library

Library of Congress Cataloguing in Publication data
LeVan, A. Carl.
Dictators and democracy in African development : the political economy of good governance in Nigeria / A. Carl LeVan (American University).
    pages   cm. – (African studies series ; 130)
Includes bibliographical references and index.
ISBN 978-1-107-08114-7 (hardback)
1. Nigeria – Politics and government.   2. Dictatorship – Nigeria.   3. Democracy – Nigeria.   4. Economic development – Political aspects – Nigeria.   5. Nigeria – Economic conditions.   I. Title.
JQ3090.L48   2015
320.9669–dc23   2014026675

ISBN 978-1-107-08114-7 Hardback
ISBN 978-1-107-44095-1 Paperback

For Monisola, my muse

Contents

List of Tables		*page* x
List of Figures		xi
Preface		xiii
Acknowledgments		xvii
	Introduction	1
1	A Theory of Institutions, Preferences, and Performance	32
2	Veto Players in Nigeria's Political History since Independence	55
3	The Impact of Nigeria's Veto Players on Local and National Collective Goods	120
4	Analytic Equivalents in Ghana and Zimbabwe	176
5	Madison's Model Unbound	211
	Appendix 1 Possible Measurement Error in the Clearance *Variable*	239
	Appendix 2 Descriptive Statistics for Variables	241
	References	243
	Index	275

Tables

2.1. Election Results by Party in the Southwest Geopolitical
      "Zone," 1999   *page* 97
2.2. Distribution of Seats in National Assembly   107
2.3. List of Veto Players   113
3.1. Impact of Veto Players on National Collective Goods,
      1961–2007   146
3.2. Impact of Veto Players on Local Collective Goods,
      1961–2007   150
4.1. Ghana's Governments, 1956–Present   184
A2.1. Descriptive Statistics   241

Figures

3.1. The *fedbudget* variable, 1961–2007   *page* 126
3.2. The *inflation* variable, 1961–2007   127
3.3. The *clearance* variable, 1960–1987   130
3.4. Government consumption as a share of GDP, 1961–2007   137

Preface

After more than sixteen years of dictatorship and instability, Nigeria transitioned back to democracy in 1999, electing a new president, legislature, and governors. The new constitution closely resembled the founding document of the failed Second Republic (1979–1983) in that it established a bicameral legislature, a strong president, and a federal political system. Within months of the government's taking office, ethnic riots shook the northern city of Kano, rebels in the Niger Delta took oil workers hostage, and communal clashes rocked the commercial capital of Lagos. Security forces responded to the kidnapping of police officers in the state of Bayelsa by razing the village of Odi with bombs and heavy artillery. The disproportionate response raised questions about whether civilians really controlled the military, and human rights organizations accused the government of genocide.

The new government's plans to promote school construction, macroeconomic stability, and poverty reduction suddenly seemed secondary to the question of whether the country could hold together. Equally unclear was whether the National Assembly could provide an adequate check on the power of the new president, former military dictator Olusegun Obasanjo. The legislature deadlocked with the executive over the federal budget and a sweeping anticorruption bill. It fumbled its response to the provocative decision by a dozen state legislatures to implement Islamic criminal codes, and it was paralyzed by debates over a national fuel subsidy and a federal minimum wage. Nigeria's two previous failed attempts at democracy loomed large in the national memory.

One early morning in June 2000, it seemed as though history was about to repeat itself. A member of the National Assembly called me at home in a panic because President Obasanjo had ordered the police to surround the home of Senate President Chuba Okadigbo with armored vehicles. Over the previous week, Obasanjo and the Senate had bickered over a supplemental appropriations bill and a proposal to form a Niger Delta Development Commission (NDDC), a government agency to coordinate development efforts in the country's oil-producing region. The Senate president infuriated Obasanjo by adjourning the Senate for a scheduled recess and taking the mace – the ceremonial staff symbolizing the parliamentary sovereignty that was needed to convene the Senate – home with him. Obasanjo's supporters unsuccessfully tried to convene the Senate without Okadigbo.[1] When Senator Okadigbo formally reconvened the upper chamber a week later, he led votes to override Obasanjo's veto on the NDDC legislation (due to concerns about its funding mechanism) and demand additional details about the president's supplemental spending plans.

Reflecting on that incident, and the decade since Nigeria's tumultuous transition to democracy, a former top adviser to Senator Okadigbo told me there has been a "significant transformation" and a shift toward "genuine democratic governance." Now–Deputy Speaker of the House of Representatives Emeka Ihedioha said, "The separation of powers doctrine today is observed. The executive tries of course to encroach upon the functions of the legislature, but it is met this time with civilized resistance."[2] His comment stands out for its institutional imagery: The balance of authority is granted by the constitution but actualized only through its use; rules by themselves do not guarantee the capacity to exercise authority.

This book draws upon interviews, newspapers, government documents, and information gathered during field research that began in 2003 and continued with recurring visits since then. I trace fifty years of Nigeria's history from independence in 1960 to the end of President Obasanjo's second term in 2007, linking changes in political authority to public policy performance. For readers unfamiliar with Nigeria, this political narrative also provides an introduction to Africa's most populous country and one of the world's biggest oil producers. Though constitutions and formalities provide a road map to Nigeria's "veto players," I see them as institutional expressions of social and historical conditions

[1] Sufuyan Ojeifo, "The Deal, the Plot That Nailed Okadigbo," *Vanguard*, August 12, 2000.
[2] Interview with Emeka Ihedioha, March 17, 2010. Abuja.

that acquire meaning through recurring behavior and norms. To put it in Honorable Ihedioha's terms, the Federal Constitution of 1999 designated the legislature as a separate institution, but it is "civilized resistance" to executive overreach that actually makes the National Assembly an independent body capable of exercising power.

I use the concept of veto players to show how a variety of political actors successfully (or unsuccessfully) assert such authority. This concept from political science transcends the American origins of the term "veto." I demonstrate through a mixed-methods analysis that the number of veto players reliably predicts government performance in Nigeria between 1961 and 2007. But their effects on local and national collective goods are different, meaning there is no simple answer regarding the optimal number of veto players. This analysis recasts the conditions for good governance in Africa as a dilemma shaped by the structure of policy making. Influential traditional chiefs, stubborn military officials, ambitious civilian politicians, and principled democratic activists are all part of what makes these structures real. I explore their preferences and capabilities for collective action and argue for their ability to shape and enforce political institutions. This offers a new basis for comparative thinking about Africa. But I also hope that readers will see in this casual story an appreciation for the Nigerian people's struggle for dignity and development, and an insistence that any resolution of the nation's policy performance dilemmas ultimately reside with them.

Acknowledgments

This book would not have been possible without the encouragement and ongoing support of many people. The Political Science Faculty at the University of Ibadan graciously hosted me during my initial field research. Eghosa Osaghae, Ademola Ariyo, Oye Oyediran, Kunle Amuwo, Alex Gboyega, and Yinka Atoyebi all provided constructive feedback and important correctives to my early work. Adigun Agbaje, Victor A. Isumonah, Bayo Adekanye, and my generous faculty sponsor, Rotimi Suberu, all did the same – often around the dinner table. I would not have found my way to U of I in the first place without the intervention of Richard Sklar and Larry Diamond. During my year there, I was also lucky enough to assemble an amazing research team with Josiah Olubowale, Nike Okotete, Idowu Kareem, and Olumide Famuyiwa. The National Archives, the Nigerian Institute for Social and Economic Research, the Kenneth Dike Library, the *Nigerian Tribune* archives, and the private library of Professor Ajayi all opened their doors to us. Chris Bankole's cooking provided a home away from home every Sunday. Claire Christian, Amarachi Utah, Jillian Emerson, Edward Whitney, Katie Mattern, Andrew Doty, and Yoonbin Ha continued and expanded the research after I returned from the field.

In Abuja, Jibrin Ibrahim at the Centre for Democracy and Development and Jacqueline Farris at the Yar'Adua Centre provided contacts and context. Richard Akinnola at the Center for Free Speech, Emeka Iheme at the Libertarian Institute, Yinka Lawal at the Constitutional Rights Project, Aaron Gana at AFRIGOV, and Innocent Chukwuma at CLEEN provided invaluable insights about the darkest years of the democratization struggle. The help of Dahiru Mohammed Abba, C. J. Osman, Farouk Adejoh-Audu, and Ngozi Nkemdirim was invaluable, and Suleiman Alhaji Garba facilitated access to the assembly's archives. I will never be able to thank all of the "honourables" and senators who helped me over the years, Peter Adeyemo, Ghali Na'Abba, Ibrahim Mantu, Emeka Ihedioha, Lynda Chuba-Ikpeazu, and Ken Nnamani among them. I am especially grateful for the help and friendship of Chidu Duru and Farouk Lawan. For the many individuals whom I cannot thank, it is worth recalling Alexis de Tocqueville's introduction to *Democracy in America*: "A stranger often hears important truths at his host's fireside, truths which he might not divulge to his friends; it is a relief to break a constrained silence with a stranger whose short stay guarantees his discretion." To this end, I seek to honor the trust of those who confided unpleasant truths in me.

When the day was done, Ben Agande, Rotimi Fadeyi, Idowu Bakare, Lateef Ibrahim, Rotimi Ajayi, Sunday Fase, Henry Umoru, and Jackson Ogbonna helped me navigate Abuja's politics – and its nightlife. On these excursions I was fortunate enough to have the company of Valentine Eke, Abuja's most knowledgeable driver. My field research was made possible by a State Department Fulbright Grant, an award from the Institute for International Area and Comparative Studies, and an International Faculty Travel Award from American University.

This book grew out of my Ph.D. work at the University of California – San Diego, and I owe a great debt to many professors and mentors there. Clark Gibson, Karen Ferree, Phil Roeder, Ivan Evans, and Matthew Shugart ushered the project through its dissertation stage with tireless patience. Gary Cox, Alan Houston, Kaare Strøm, Craig Macintosh, Arend Lijphart, and Nora Gordon provided guidance on key conceptual issues. After my arrival at American University, Clarence Lusane, Lou Goodman, Patrick Ukata, Randy Persaud, Michelle Egan, Jim Goldgeier, and (the late) Robert Pastor all provided support and encouragement at critical moments. I am also grateful to Marcus Raskin and Emira Woods at the Institute for Policy Studies for their unwavering faith in my research.

While I was writing the manuscript, the students in my African Political Institutions course helped me polish the Introduction, as did Joseph Oleyinka Fashagba. Chapter 1 benefited from feedback from Nic Cheeseman and Don Horowitz, as well as presentations at the Working Group on African Political Economy organized by Daniel Posner in 2005 and at the International Studies Association Annual Meeting in 2006.

Steve Burgess, Jessica Piombo, Staffan Lindberg, and many members of the African Politics Conference Group also lent their critical eyes to early drafts. Ebere Onwudiwe identified critical gaps in Chapter 2. Some of the research in that chapter appeared in *Commonwealth and Comparative Politics* as an essay, "Analytic Authoritarianism and Nigeria" (Vol. 52, no. 2, 2014). Todd Eisenstadt, Gina Lambright, Deborah Brautigam, Rachel Sullivan Robinson, Jeff Colgan, and participants on a panel at the Midwest Political Science Association 2011 Annual Meeting offered careful critiques of the empirical analysis in Chapter 3, while Assen Assenov deserves special thanks for his many statistical tutorials. Richard Asante, Alexander Frempong, Karuti Kanyinga, and participants on a panel at the African Studies Association 2010 Annual Meeting offered helpful feedback on Ghana and Zimbabwe material now included in Chapter 4. For all things Nigeria, including the finer points of history, I am fortunate enough to have access to an incredible network including Paul Lubeck, Darren Kew, Peter Lewis, John Paden, Pauline Baker, Deirdre LePin, Judy Asuni, John Campbell, Howard Jeter, Robin Sanders, Ryan McCannell, Sarah Pray, Jennifer Cooke, and Matthew Page. Liz Goldberg's editing expertise clarified my prose.

At Cambridge University Press, Eric Crahan provided early guidance about the manuscript's structure and focus, and Will Hammell saw it through to the end. Three anonymous reviewers provided invaluable, detailed feedback. I wish to extend a special thanks to Shari Bryan, Chris Fomunyoh, and Ken Wallach from the National Democratic Institute for International Affairs, who introduced me to Nigeria in 1999. Fran Farmer, Wayne Propst, and Christine Owre opened their homes to me, while Sandra Omali, Deji Olaore, Tunde Durosenmi-Etti, and Boderin Adebo cultivated my *oyinbo* curiosity and my first friendships. Sadly, my mother did not live to see me return from the field, and my father could not hold on long enough to see this book. But it would not have been possible without the encouragement and unwavering support from them, my sisters, and my beloved wife, "Monisola."

Introduction

As decolonization neared its end in the 1950s, a wave of optimism swept across Sub-Saharan Africa. In Nigeria, the jewel of Britain's African colonies, citizens anxiously embraced the promise of political sovereignty. At his inauguration as governor-general in 1960, Nigeria's great nationalist Nnamdi Azikiwe, recited a poem by the African American author Langston Hughes, describing the promising future for Africa's new generation of young leaders. Hughes sat in the audience with thousands of Nigerians, all welcoming a new dawn.[1] The incoming government promised massive investment in education and socioeconomic development. Voters had peacefully exercised their rights at the polls, foreign investment was pouring in, and the economy was expanding.

When a new political generation gathered in the capital half a century later to commemorate that momentous day, militants detonated two bombs near President Goodluck Jonathan, killing a dozen people. Only minutes before, Jonathan had cautiously reflected on Nigeria's previous five decades, declaring, "There is certainly much to celebrate: our freedom, our strength, our unity and our resilience." One newspaper called the 2010 bombing "perhaps one of the most unfortunate incidents in the 50 years of Nigeria's post-independence history."[2] Another Nigerian commentary bluntly asked, "Has Nigeria achieved the greatness it was clamoring for at independence? Or is Nigeria a fool at fifty?"[3]

---

[1] "Zik Becomes His Excellency," *West Africa*, November 19, 1960.
[2] Abba Gana Shettima, "Nigeria: Abuja Bomb Blasts – Agony of a Confused Nation," *Daily Trust*, October 8, 2010.
[3] Lawan Yakubu, "A Requiem for Nigeria?" *Daily Trust*, October 8, 2010.

Readers responding to these questions with cynicism will be disappointed, while optimists will be challenged. It is true that the United Nations counts Nigeria among the world's most underdeveloped nations, where approximately 90 percent of the population lives on less than two dollars per day, and the average life expectancy is less than forty-eight years. Economic growth since the transition to democracy in 1999 masks significant governance failures, including increases in economic inequality and extreme poverty (United Nations Development Programme 2009). The country also has little to show for the estimated US$300 billion it has earned from oil exports since the 1970s. When Transparency International, a global nongovernmental organization that monitors corruption, ranked Nigeria just ahead of low achievers such as Zimbabwe and Mauritania in a 2010 report, an editorial in one of Nigeria's leading newspapers lamented, "The fight against corruption has remained a problematic one, with sloganeering by successive governments and very little else to show for it."[4]

But President Jonathan's optimistic reflections on the 50th anniversary of independence were not unfounded. After all, Nigeria survived one of Africa's most brutal civil wars and five military coups. It emerged from this violence to become an important regional and global leader in peacekeeping and diplomacy. The youth literacy rate stands at 87 percent, up from 65 percent in 1985. In the early years after independence, only 5 percent of the nation's children were enrolled in primary school; enrollment rates now reach 100 percent in some parts of the country. In contrast to the high inflation that crippled Nigeria's booming oil economy in the 1970s and the heavy foreign borrowing during the subsequent era of harsh economic reform, consumers today face more predictable prices and the government has rid itself of almost all foreign debt.

Nigeria's record seems to validate the claim that development occurs through good public policy. Increased literacy and school enrollment owe much to policies instituted in the 1970s, when the federal government called education the "greatest investment that a nation can make for the development of its economic, political, sociological and human resources."[5] Federal budget deficits and inflation became less volatile after a reform-minded public finance team renegotiated or paid off the

[4] Editorial, "The Transparency International Corruption Report," *Daily Trust*, November 1, 2010.
[5] Editorial, "Hard Road for Education," *West Africa*, May 21, 1979.

country's debts in 2006. Nigeria's many failings must be viewed alongside successful policies that punctuate its postcolonial history.

The question that drives this book is, How does the distribution of political authority affect the Nigerian government's ability to formulate and deliver policies conducive to development? Polices are binding decisions about public resources, and good government performance means that policy outputs serve a greater common good over the long term. Comparative studies often blame ethnic diversity, foreign debt, authoritarianism, or an economy dependent on natural resource exploitation for policy failures in the developing world. Research on Africa very often adds colonial legacies to this list. Nigeria possesses many of the qualities associated with policy failure, including a string of dictatorships, high foreign debt, tremendous ethnic diversity, and a robust oil economy. While these characteristics are certainly relevant to understanding Nigeria, none of them adequately explains the tremendous variation in policy outcomes over time.

I study these outcomes using variables that the development literature associates with long-term economic development. I distinguish between national collective goods, nonexcludable public policies that inherently benefit the country on the whole, and local collective goods that are more particularistic and might be targeted to specific communities or interests. Excessive increases in spending on local collective goods are a sign of patronage or misappropriation of these policy outputs with excludable benefits. I proxy for local collective goods with different measures of federal government spending per capita, and I operationalize national collective goods with variables measuring fiscal discipline, inflation, education outputs, and judicial efficiency.

Drawing on a historical study of Nigeria since independence, I argue that the structure of the policy-making process explains variation in government performance as measured by these two broad categories of public policy. To capture the underlying structure of policy-making authority that drives patterns of performance over time, I use the concept of "veto players," which are political actors operating in both formal and informal political settings with the leverage to block policy change and extract concessions. They can be rooted in institutions such as legislatures or military ruling councils, or they can emerge from alternative centers of power manifest in military factions, cohesive political parties, or broad regional coalitions. Using data gathered during extensive field research, I identify Nigeria's veto players between 1961 and 2007. Through quantitative and qualitative analyses, I empirically link the number of veto players to patterns in government performance over time. Even after taking into account intervening variables for dictatorship, debt, economic conditions, and oil revenue, I show that the number of veto players systematically explains Nigerian government performance over time.

However, the number of veto players has different effects on the two types of public policy in Nigeria: An increase in veto players contributes to bigger budget deficits, higher rates of inflation, larger student-teacher ratios, and slower courts, but these regimes are also better at restraining government spending characteristic of patronage. This leads to an important insight: Conditions that impair the delivery of national collective goods also tend to improve the delivery of local collective goods. Good government performance, as understood by this study, requires the delivery of both national and local collective goods. Nigeria therefore faces what I refer to as a "Madisonian dilemma," since it has to balance contradictory effects implicit in the structure of the policy process.

Resolving this dilemma remains a perennial challenge since Nigeria, like many African countries, faces cultural and demographic pressures to make the policy process representative and include additional political actors. James Madison's writings inspired my choice of terminology because he eloquently argued that dividing political wills would enhance accountability, ensuring that no single branch of government would dominate. But he also knew that separating powers could contribute to stalemates preventing policy change. Veto players in contemporary political science liberate the "veto" from its association with American government and presidential systems, formulating veto authority in broad conceptual terms that promote comparison across regimes and in different contexts.

In what follows, I summarize the conventional wisdom about government performance and associate each explanation with common approaches to Nigeria. Studying one case over time provides a natural experiment that controls for variables associated with some of these explanations, such as ethnic diversity or colonial legacy. I then advance my alternative explanation rooted in veto players, and describe how this approach contributes to new ways of thinking about the causes of suboptimal government performance in Africa and beyond. Veto players transcend blunt distinctions between democracy and dictatorship, helping to disentangle the relationship between democratization and economic development. By focusing on political actors with leverage, rather than levels of political freedom, veto player analyses also contribute to emerging literature on authoritarianism and introduce new comparative approaches to informal institutions. My application of veto player theory contributes to research on federalism, too, by linking successful collective action by subnational units to broad national policy outcomes. Finally, by exploring how veto players impose accountability on each other, I return to core Madisonian principles and ultimately claim that political leverage can be used to limit patronage rather than demand it. This places one of my main empirical findings – about the relationship between the number of veto players and the overall level of local collective goods – at the center of debates in African politics over the causes of distributional distortions.

Government Performance in the Literature

In order to situate this book's central argument about veto player theory in a proper context, it is important to review four standard explanations for poor government performance in Africa. Each of these explanations faces limitations. I begin with a discussion of modernization theory, which argues that economic and social progress lead to democratization. This theory has experienced a revival over the last decade, although the persistence of illiberal regimes in a surprising number of countries across the developing world has kept the debate over modernization theory's explanatory value alive. A second, common explanation attributes performance failures to the relative wealth of the state. Governments with little income have weak capacity due to few resources to enact good public policies, while governments with substantial revenue from natural resources perform poorly because citizens lack political leverage to hold government accountable. In this construction, Africa's poor countries are doomed either way. A third explanation blames ethnic diversity for breeding parochialism and clientelism, outcomes that distort the distribution of resources and ultimately undermine long-term economic growth. Finally, there is the bad leadership explanation. Political commentators, casual observers, and scholars often attribute governance successes or failures to leaders' personal qualities. There is reason to be skeptical of this formulation. As Tanzania's first president, Julius Nyerere, said in 1968, "Leadership cannot replace democracy" (Nyerere 1973, 62). This blunt assessment of leadership still rings true, affirming the possibilities of comparative politics by emphasizing the need to understand the systemic factors that impact decision making by individuals. "For policies to be effective," writes a leading Nigerian political scientist, "the process through which they are made and executed has to be rational, sequential and deliberative" (Jega 2007, 105).

The Regime Type Explanation: Does Democracy Deliver?

When European colonial powers withdrew from Africa in the 1950s, many Africans hoped that independence would lead to political development and economic self-sufficiency. The developed world promised assistance to ease the transition from colonialism to independence, and the new nationalist governments enjoyed enormous popular support. Decolonization coincided with democratization. Nationalist movements in Kenya, Tanzania, and elsewhere were reborn as political parties, and citizens embraced new forms of political participation as the franchise quickly expanded. By the end of the 1960s, though, a number of African countries, including Nigeria and Ghana, had experienced violent coups and fallen prey to a cycle of instability and corruption. Continuing violence sowed doubts about the possibility for true democracy. Events in the developing world, including the cold war and ambiguous outcome of the third wave of democratization, further clouded the picture in Africa.

Support for illiberal politics in the name of stability and prosperity remains common in Africa. Rwanda's middle class often rationalizes away President Paul Kagame's poor human rights record, saying, "it's necessary to have a little repression here to keep the lid on" in order to obtain economic development (Kinzer 2007, 23–26). Similarly, President Yoweri Museveni in Uganda has tightened his grip on power by suppressing civil society and harassing opposition. As the country's combined score for political and civil rights by the nongovernmental organization Freedom House dropped from 11 in 2000, to 9 (out of 14) in 2004, the economy grew at a rate of 5.4 percent. Jeffrey Sachs notes that dictators in Prussia, Japan, and China all historically created conditions conducive to economic growth (Sachs 2012). This evidence presents the question, Does democracy deliver? Is the existence of a democratic government linked to positive performance outcomes?

Research on the linkages between regime type and government performance has its origins in modernization theory. Early cross-national studies noted a correlation between development and democracy – certain socioeconomic conditions contributed to particular political outcomes (Lipset 1959; Deutsch 1961). Modernization theorists argued that democratization occurs when an educated middle class develops an expectation of political influence and a willingness to exercise political moderation. Samuel Huntington led a group of scholars who took the argument one step further, arguing that building a middle class and achieving economic growth in the developing world would require limiting popular participation in the short term until political institutions consolidated. In his view, limits on democracy were a necessary and temporary sacrifice to achieve long-term economic growth and contain communism (Huntington 1968).

"Bureaucratic authoritarian" models of development from Latin America seemed to confirm the claim. Military regimes governed by unelected technocrats adopted politically unpopular but economically rational public policies conducive to growth (O'Donnell 1973; Collier 1979). Chile emerged as a favorite example, where the dictator Augusto Pinochet recruited American economists to liberalize the economy. Growth in East Asia also seemed to confirm democracy's disadvantages, as governments maintained high growth rates through corporatism (Wade 1992) and "soft authoritarianism" (Johnson 1987, 136–164).

This reasoning had strong appeal in Africa. In 1979, reflecting on progress made under his military government, Olusegun Obasanjo defended dictatorship's ability to promote growth through sound public policies. He credited his outgoing government with a fourteenfold increase in economic output, the establishment of free primary education, and reduced inflation.[6] General Ibrahim Babangida, four years into his dictatorship in 1989, similarly praised the Nigerian military's contribution to stability and progress. He claimed credit for rescuing the nation from the "serious economic crisis arising from the mismanagement of the political era."[7] Some scholars claim that for all their flaws, these military regimes still contributed positively to the country's development (Iwayemi 1979, 47–72; Ohiorhenuan 1988, 141–162). One of Babangida's civilian governors (who later went on to chair the political party still ruling today) praises the government of the late 1980s for its policies on rural development, economic liberalization, and infrastructure expansion. Drawing a comparison to the pragmatism of U.S. President Barack Obama, he says, Babangida ran a "task oriented" cabinet full of experts.[8]

Democratization since the 1990s has challenged modernization's causal claims in both directions. First, affirming a famous critique by Rustow (1970) contemporary examples across Latin America and Africa

---

[6] "A Budget for Civilian Rule," *West Africa*, April 19, 1979.
[7] Address by General Imbrahim Babangida on the Occasion of the Inauguration of the Armed Forces Consultative Assembly (Government Monograph), June 5, 1989.
[8] Interview with Okwesilieze Nwodo, March 8, 2010. Abuja.

suggest there are no socioeconomic preconditions for democracy (Wood 2000; Lindberg 2006). Democratic transitions can occur at any point in a country's development, although democracy is more likely to survive the further along a country is on the development continuum (Przeworski et al. 2000). Second, a thriving postdemocratization literature explores the unexpected persistence of hybrid regimes nestled somewhere between dictatorship and democracy (Levitsky and Way 2010; Zinecker 2009; Art 2012). Breaking with modernization's linear philosophy, which sees illiberal polities as moving inexorably toward democracy, this new research explores the possibility of *authoritarian* consolidation – not just stalled democratization (Brownlee 2007; Tripp 2010). The North African revolutions of 2011 notwithstanding, Freedom House classifies a third of the world's 194 countries as only "partly free." As if taking a cue from Aristotle, who explains in *The Politics* that tyrants extend their rule by giving the appearance of limited royal authority, these intermediate regimes mask oppression in a veneer of freedom. With great skill, a surprising number of governments thus manage to hold formal elections while suppressing competition and popular participation (Schedler 2006; Bunce and Wolchik 2010).

In terms of the impact of democracy on policy performance, a robust literature on governance and growth generally concludes that democracies perform better than autocracies. But there are important layers of nuance. For example, dictators may invest in productive economic policies when they do not fear for their future. Relative political stability and institutional longevity extend the time horizon with which rulers judge the political benefits (or costs) of public policies. To borrow Mancur Olson's famous analogy, these regimes may behave as "stationary" rather than "roving" bandits and are thus able to promote long-term growth by enforcing contracts (Olson 2000), protecting property rights (Clague et al. 1997), and investing in social policies such as education and health care (Glaeser et al. 2004). Theoretical models also claim that oligarchs may adopt policies to enhance productivity because they can efficiently overcome organizational obstacles and face potentially greater potential returns on investments (Gorodinichenko and Grygorenko 2008). Countless articles document the link between natural resources and corruption, but dictators with revenue streams from natural resources also face less political uncertainty, and this can create incentives to pursue productive policies (Boix 2003).

Democracy's defenders continue to argue that political freedom and competition deliver clear benefits through several mechanisms.

Democracy resolves the problem of short-term, self-interested thinking by politicians by creating an institutional incentive for leaders to supply the type of good governance that voters demand. This arrangement is meant to bind the short-term interests of politicians to the long-term economic and political development of the nation (North and Weingast 1989). Democracy also addresses the succession problem that plagues all autocrats from Mubarak to Mugabe. An institutionalized, recurring method of leadership selection reduces uncertainty about the future (Brownlee 2002; Hirschman 1970). Finally, democracy's defenders argue that by creating a credible threat of replacement, democracy incentivizes politicians to provide public goods and resist "temptations for politically opportunistic behavior that is economically damaging" (Alence 2004, 178). Even poor democracies face electoral pressures to provide services such as education that benefit society as a whole (Brown and Hunter 1999; Halperin, Siegle, and Weinstein 2010).

Extensive cross-national research concludes that citizens of democratic countries live longer, happier, and healthier lives (Halperin, Siegle, and Weinstein 2010; Przeworski et al. 2000). Precisely how democracy leads to these outcomes remains a subject of considerable debate. Democracy may directly alter governmental spending priorities. Studies from newly democratized Latin American countries report shifts from government consumption to social welfare (Ames 1987; Looney and Frederiksen 1987), as well as increases in the absolute amount of resources devoted to social services (Brown and Hunter 1999). Research from Africa shows that democracy leads to increased spending on education (Stasavage 2005a) and access to education (Stasavage 2005b). On a global level, the evidence is more mixed: Democratic and authoritarian regimes typically fund social services (such as pension and welfare) at comparable levels (Mulligan, Gil, and Sala-i-Martin 2004).

However, democracy's most important effects on policy performance may actually be indirect. A broad range of studies refute modernization theory's claims about the developmental advantages of dictatorship, but they also fail to find a specific causal link between democracy and economic growth (Feng 2003; Bueno de Mesquita et al. 2001; Mainwaring and Perez-Linan 2003; Norris 2008). A metaanalysis of the democracy-development link reviewing 483 sets of statistical results from 84 studies concludes that democracy's direct impact on government performance is indeterminate and that its primary benefits are indirect (Doucouliagos and Ulubasoglu 2008). This is reinforced by studies showing that democracies are more likely to promote human capital formation by investing in health care and education. The effects of such policies are indirect in that the benefits become clear over time, as the labor force becomes healthier, better educated, and more productive (Schultz 1999; Baldacci et al. 2008).

But the direct and indirect benefits of democracy are both predicated on the existence of viable political competition. This caveat possibly explains the ambiguous effects of African experiments with democracy in the 1990s (Olivier de Sardan 1999; van de Walle 2001). Without competition, party turnover, and a broader political environment of freedom and transparency, governments lack accountability. This has complicated assessments of African democracy because democratic institutions seem to coexist with corruption, inflation, and economic mismanagement. Notwithstanding the significant economic development in a number of African countries, Lewis (2008), for example, points to the problematic phenomenon in Africa today of "growth without prosperity." Governance decisions generate wealth and improve macroeconomic performance, but the poor are ignored and disempowered.

A disadvantage of focusing on regime type (democracy versus dictatorship) is that it glosses over important variations among democracies and dictatorships, both in terms of how they govern and in terms of how they perform. For every Zimbabwe or Cameroon, where authoritarianism has led to economic catastrophe, there is a Uganda or Rwanda, where illiberal regimes have created laudable development. For every Ghana, where democracy has contributed to economic gains, there is a Benin, where democracy reigns but the population remains poor. Perhaps the most comprehensive multicountry study of African development to date concludes that regime type was less important to explaining growth than overregulation, war, shortsighted policy making, or distribution of resources along ethnoregional lines. Combining cross-national analyses with country case studies, the authors argue that countries can at least partially overcome unfavorable structural conditions such as landlocked geography or exploitative colonial pasts by adopting growth-enhancing policies (Ndulu et al. 2008). A recent global study makes a similar case for inclusive political institutions, arguing that economies that incentivize innovation and punish expropriation can break the low-growth poverty traps that impede prosperity (Acemoglu and Robinson 2012). Bracketing the question of whether countries are democratizing or not therefore allows us to focus on other factors and institutional arrangements that affect the policy-making environment.

State Wealth: Poor States, Poor Performance?

Another common set of explanations for government performance focuses on levels of government income. In one version, scholars argue that governments with little income have less capacity and fewer resources to direct toward good public policies (Przeworski et al. 2000). Countries are developmentally poor because the state is poor and spending largely depends on revenue (Please 1967). Moreover, revenue fluctuations from global commodity price changes adversely impact African public policy spending (Ekpo 1996). Exposure to exogenous economic conditions is a perennial issue for Africa's largely undiversified economies (Ake 1996). Another version of the economic argument blames surplus rather than scarcity for government performance failures. In particular, governments that receive a great deal of income from natural resources tend to perform poorly. Resource-rich countries have low levels of taxation, and this condition deprives citizens of a powerful source of leverage they can use to hold government accountable (Jensen and Wantchekon 2004; Ulfelder 2007). In the long run, this so-called resource curse weakens state capacity as public officials see politics primarily as a redistributive game (Karl 1997; Robinson, Torvik, and Verdier 2006).

Together, these two sides of the economic coin suggest that African countries are at risk when the state is too rich or too poor. Africa's economies are susceptible to exogenous shocks, and natural resource revenue has fueled violence, corruption, and clientelism. Mineral-rich countries like Angola and the Democratic Republic of the Congo are mired in corruption and patronage, while revenue-poor countries such as Benin and Togo cannot afford to make the human capital investments necessary for economic growth. These challenges remain prevalent today, and they lie at the center of "poor state, poor performance" explanations.

Subsequent chapters will examine the political circumstances that contribute to the economic problems facing African governments. Recent oil discoveries in several African countries point to an urgent need to rethink the resource curse hypothesis since extraction will have begun *after* democratic transitions (unlike dictatorships that benefited from oil discoveries in the 1970s). Ghana, for example, expected to earn $400 million from its first year of oil production in 2011, boosting economic growth from an already respectable 5 percent to nearly 12 percent.[9] Since countries that

---

[9] Will Connors, "Ghana Is Set to Start Pumping Oil," *Wall Street Journal*, December 15, 2010.

have a record of human capital investment appear to be better equipped to absorb such income and technology shocks (Kurtz and Brooks 2011), Ghana's democracy just might manage to turn the curse into a blessing.

Nigeria offers an especially useful case study in this regard, since Nigeria has fallen into both categories at various points in its history – it has suffered from both too little and "too much" income. Since oil exports took off in 1970, the country has earned more than US$400 billion in oil revenue. In considering the effects of a sudden influx of dollars, most studies have focused on how Nigeria's oil booms undermined governance by enabling corruption and creating economic distortions (Ikein, Alamieyeseigha, and Azaiki 2008; Ahmad Khan 1994). There is little reason to question this relationship, but it is important to acknowledge that increased revenues impact other aspects of performance as well. For example, the initial rise of oil revenues in Nigeria in the early 1970s also prompted huge investments in education and infrastructure (Odetola 1982; Onyejekwe 1981).

The problem for Nigeria really occurred when subsequent governments encountered reduced oil revenues (Asiodu 2000, 7–10). Faced with the daunting task of collecting taxes in a poor country with weak property rights and political instability, governments instead cut social spending and, like many African countries, borrowed liberally from abroad. Across the continent, African debts to foreign creditors accumulated at an astonishing pace during the 1970s and 1980s. In the early 1980s, Africa's foreign debt to export ratio increased more than fivefold. By the end of the 1990s, the average African country was spending 15 percent of all export earnings paying off debts (DeLancey 2001, 117). These loans had helped stabilize recalcitrant dictators, and the long-term costs were passed on to fragile new democratic governments during the third wave of democratization. When Nigeria transitioned to democracy in 1999, it had more debt in absolute dollars than any other country in Africa: 15 percent of the continent's total. For nearly seventeen years, creditors provided generous loans to a succession of Nigerian dictators, oblivious to the damage the practice was doing to political reformers by propping up autocrats (Chevillard 2001).

Africa's debts affected government performance by diverting scarce revenue into loan repayments rather than human capital and infrastructure investments (Tordoff 2002), which undermined economic growth (Pattillo, Poirson, and Ricci 2004; Mohamed 2005). Without the debt burden, some models predict that growth in thirty-five African countries would have been as much as 50 percent higher (Fosu 1999). But like the relationship between development and democracy, the relationship between debt and government performance is complex. With regard to growth, the amount of debt is clearly significant, since modest loans invested productively actually tend to stimulate growth (Ayadi and Ayadi 2008; Moore and Thomas 2010). In terms of diverting money from the social sector, there is some evidence that anticipated future debt rather than the actual payments may be to blame for adverse effects on government policy (Fosu 2007). Debt thus influences policy priorities, but it offers only a partial explanation for performance. We can better understand how revenue and spending impact policy performance by including the early 1960s, an era when neither oil nor debt significantly shaped Nigeria's policy planning environment. A longitudinal study such as this one therefore offers a natural experiment. My findings suggest that the structure of the policy making had a more systematic impact on government performance than these other factors.

Ethnicity Explanations: Primordialism and Parochialism

A third account blames social heterogeneity for poor policy performance and a broad range of other outcomes summarized in an influential literature review by Chandra (2012). At the far end of the spectrum, ethnicity is seen as the root of civil war – and the conflicts in Yugoslavia and Rwanda would seem to bear this out. Scholars in this tradition argue that people reflexively turn to primordial identities in moments of uncertainty or tension and allow these emotional attachments to spur violence. Even when ethnic identity does not lead to war, some scholars see diversity as a threat to political stability and democratic consolidation; this operates on assumptions about the willingness of incumbent elites to exclude some groups permanently. Finally, several studies link ethnic diversity to poor government performance across different types of public policies.

At the most basic level, social heterogeneity is seen as a possible impediment to collective action. Compelling empirical research shows that ethnic fractionalization contributes to low growth, low school enrollment, and federal budget deficits (Easterly and Levine 1997, 1203–1250). Coordinating interests across socially diverse constituencies is simply more difficult as a result of mistrust or memories of marginalization among ethnic groups. And even if they do not harbor hard feelings that inspire retaliation, it can still be difficult to communicate across communities with different cultural values. Corruption increases and the quality of policy making declines for similar reasons (Alesina et al. 2003, 155–194). Tests in 130 countries using the broad concept of "social diversity," which incorporates multiple expressions of ethnicity, arrive at similar conclusions about economic performance (Okediji 2011).

Recent groundbreaking microlevel research complements these large-N studies by offering an explanation for how diversity can undermine public policy. "Ethnically homogeneous communities have an advantage in providing public goods because ethnic groups possess both norms and networks that facilitate the sanctioning of community members who fail to contribute to collective endeavors" (Habyarimana et al. 2007, 722). Extreme ethnic heterogeneity, such as Nigeria's, therefore supposedly generates collective action problems that impede the delivery of public goods with broad, national-level benefits. Other scholars link ethnicity to distributional distortions. Without other meaningful political cleavages based on ideology or class, ethnic differences breed the kind of mistrust conducive to patronage. This argument is especially compelling with regard to Africa because colonial authorities purposefully exacerbated ethnic tensions among groups in order to divide and conquer. Both the direct and indirect forms of colonial rule favored some groups over others in order to maximize imperial efficiency and minimize costs (Mamdani 1996).

Nigeria's governance failures could therefore be rooted in its diversity. After all, the North is largely Muslim, the South is largely Christian, and hundreds of languages (5 percent of the world's total) are spoken in Nigeria's four-hundred- square-mile territory. This hyperdiversity could conceivably create countless possibilities for primordialism and parochialism. The British famously adopted a sympathetic view toward the Hausa and Fulani in the North, which undermined national integration and generated lasting resentments. This tension climaxed with a brutal civil war from 1967 to 1970, which killed more than a million people. Simply put, scholars writing in this tradition argue, quite reasonably, that politicians will serve their own ethnoregional communities at the expense of others. This ethnic patrimonialism depends on access to the so-called national cake, the figurative and literal resource wealth controlled by the center. Nnoli, for example, blames ethnicity for Nigeria's failure to allocate these resources, for intragroup bourgeois competition, and for religious conflict (Nnoli 1995). A core problem in governing ethnically diverse countries is limiting politicians' ability or incentive to serve their own ethnoreligious communities at the expense of others. This has been described as a problem of "prebendalism" (Joseph 1991) in Nigeria, whereby public office itself serves as a patronage payment to ethnic or kinship circles.

Nigerians discuss this diversity through the discourse of the "national question." For ordinary citizens, this involves reconciling your identity as a citizen of the modern state with your ethnic and cultural affinities (Amuwo et al. 2000; Suberu 2001). Successive governments experimented with various solutions since the 1950s, including building strong regional governments, imposing ethnic quotas on the bureaucracy and the military, and sharing power among various ethnic groups.

Like a variety of recent research (Fish and Brooks 2004; Collier 2003), I argue that the standard view of ethnicity overestimates the likelihood that diversity will undermine government performance. As noted, even in ethnically divided societies, a government's performance record significantly shapes citizens' voting preferences (Gibson and Long 2009; Bratton and Kimenyi 2008; Weghorst and Lindberg 2011). Patronage politics remain common in Africa. But voters increasingly seem to weigh those benefits against other objectives, including more programmatic national policies, and clientelist relationships are not necessarily based on ethnicity (Wantchekon 2003). The political salience of ethnicity may be conditional on a range of factors including demography and the relative size of ethnic groups (Posner 2004), political institutions such as electoral systems (Brambor, Clark, and Golder 2007), and colonial legacies (Berman, Dickson, and Kymlicka 2004; Basedau et al. 2011). In the end, ethnicity is no more likely to be activated than any other type of identity, even though it is relatively more visible. It therefore does not have the sort of unique causal status often ascribed to it in the literature (Chandra 2009).

By focusing on a single country over time, the research design of this book, as described in Chapters 2 and 3, provides a natural experiment to measure the impact of ethnic diversity on government performance because the outcomes vary but the number of ethnic groups in Nigeria does not. The factors shaping whether different social distinctions become politicized change, for example, through the creation of new states, some of which reinforce ethnic identity, and some of which do not by drawing political boundaries through groups. Other political and social incentives influence ethnic self-identification too. Surveys shortly after the 1999 democratic transition showed Nigerians having stronger ethnic self-identification than almost any other Africans (Afrobarometer 2002). This was perhaps a consequence of people's searching for reassurance amid a new government with an uncertain future. Since then, ethnic and religious self-identification have varied locally over time (Lewis 2007b). Clearly, ethnic heterogeneity alone cannot explain the vicissitudes of government performance. I argue that Nigeria's political differences between North and South remain the most important, and that institutional consolidation depends upon balancing or transcending these regional cleavages. This was dramatically illustrated in 2010, when a president from the North, Umaru Yar'Adua, died in office and a succession battle erupted because Vice President Goodluck Jonathan was from the South. Jonathan eventually became president. I claim in the book's Conclusion that his presidential election win the following year constitutes a historic turning point because it suggests that Nigerians are joining other African voters, who increasingly value policy performance when evaluating politicians (Bratton, Bhavnani, and Chen 2011; Ferree 2011).

Leadership

The last explanation for government performance commonly invoked by scholars, officials, and casual observers is the quality of leadership. Ideas about the centrality of a leader's personal characteristics arose during the anticolonial struggles that featured towering personalities such as Jomo Kenyatta in Kenya, Léopold Sédar Senghor in Senegal, and Kwame Nkrumah in Ghana. Patrick Chabal refers to "failure of leadership" as the standard explanation for Africa's postcolonial disappointments (Chabal 2009, 118), and it emerged again after Africa's redemocratization in the 1990s. "The effective study of leadership is enjoying a period of resurgence across the globe," wrote Joseph Ayee in an assessment of Ghana's leadership since the 1993 transition to democracy. Leadership entails formulating a vision for the future, developing a rational strategy for realizing that vision, and enlisting the support of political actors who can help. Politics is based on a "leader-follower" relationship that is purposeful, interactive, and capable of causation (Ayee 2007, 166). Kwame Boafo-Arthur, drawing on the work of the former British prime minister Tony Blair, the World Bank, and the New Partnership for Africa's Development, argues that there is a recent convergence of views about the importance of good leadership in mobilizing economic resources, limiting political failures, and adopting good policies (Boafo-Arthur 2007). "Leadership, in other words, is an essential element in the process of nation-building," concludes one diagnosis of postcolonialism. "The history of nation-states and civilizations have clearly shown that well-focused, transparent, and visionary leaders have played strategic roles ... above all, changing the destiny of their countries" (Abubakar 2004, 154).

In this view, good governance requires leaders like Plato's philosopher-king, possessed of noble virtue. When Chukwuma Nzeogu began discreetly planning Nigeria's first coup in late 1965, he and his coconspirators blamed selfish politicians and weak leadership for "moving the nation steadily but surely into self-destruction." They dreamed that military discipline would lead the country into social revolution, or at least unify a nation that democracy had divided (Obasanjo 2004, 82). Praise for selfless personal character routinely leads to romanticizing of Asia's soft authoritarianism. Kwaku Tsikata writes that what distinguishes the Asian success stories from many African cases is "strong and enlightened visionaries at the helm" who provided "developmental leadership" (Tsikata 2007, 82). Ayee also attributes Africa's stalled development to a lack of "transformational" leadership of the kind that benefited the Asian dragons (Ayee 2007, 165). A current deputy governor of Nigeria's Central Bank argues, "All great transformations in modern history have been driven by strong leadership – from China under Deng Xiaoping to Malaysia under Mahtir Mohamad, and Singapore under Lee Kuan Yew and many others. Leadership is everything" (Moghalu 2013, 108). Nigeria's former dictator, Yakubu Gowon, agrees, "I wish we had the fortune of Singapore's or Malaysia's leadership.... When one got to know them and see how they [were] doing things, that was what we wanted to achieve."[10] A senior Nigerian senator comments, "When you have a very energetic and visionary president, things change. And Nigeria has not been blessed with one so far. If you look at Asian countries, there comes a time when a president comes and changes everything." Speaking in 2010, during the most dramatic constitutional leadership crisis since the 1999 transition, he said, "Nigeria has a bright future, provided that we are lucky to have the right leadership. Just like in America or any other country, you see that the fortunes of those countries change when they have good leadership."[11]

Scholars blame Nigeria's flawed leaders for a variety of developmental problems, including widespread corruption (Balogun 2009; Aluko 2009). One of Nigeria's leading political scientists and the current chair of the electoral commission, Attahiru Jega, writes that the country faces a "crisis of leadership." Transparency, accountability, and good governance all originate in "the mind-set of the leaders," he says (Jega 2007, 171). "There is a near consensus that almost all of Nigeria's problems are traceable to poor leadership," says another scholar. "In no sphere of life is this debacle being more universally felt than the economy.... Policy

[10] Interview with General Yakubu Gowon, March 16, 2010. Abuja.
[11] Interview with Senator Abiola Ajimobi, March 15, 2010, Ibadan.

uncertainty, executive arbitrariness, unsustainable expansionary spending and wastage are the defining characteristics of what could pass for monetary and fiscal policies" (Tukur 2004, 244). Joseph's classic work on the short-lived Second Republic argues that democracy collapsed as a result of bad leadership rather than any inherent institutional flaws (Joseph 1987, 129). An analyst of the current Fourth Republic writes, "Most politicians, statesmen and business leaders have not been practicing the politics of virtue." Nigeria's leaders therefore need to display loyalty, respect, fairness, compassion, and self-discipline. This "hero in history" model builds from counterfactuals, arguing that desirable outcomes would have been lacking without the influence of individual leaders possessed of strong moral character (Dike 2003, 44).

Capturing the cultural mood on the question of national stewardship, one of Nigeria's most famous authors, the late Chinua Achebe, writes, "The trouble with Nigeria is simply and squarely a problem of leadership." Studies of African governance frequently refer to this quote from *The Trouble with Nigeria* (Achebe 19831983, 1). For example, an introductory chapter to the 2010 edition of *Democratization in Africa* says it "sums up the opinion of many contemporary Africans about the underlying cause of their perennial national crises of bad governance and underdevelopment" (Prempeh 2010, 22). Achebe, however, puts this conclusion in important contexts. First, he says, "It is totally false to suggest, as we are apt to do, that Nigerians are fundamentally different from any other people in the world" (Achebe 1983, 38). This is important because it responds to claims of African exceptionalism. Political science spent much of the last decade revisiting debates over area studies, methodology, and positivism with surprising contentiousness.[12] Achebe's view affirms the possibilities of informed comparison. Second, Achebe probes his compatriots to think about deeper explanations and alternatives, writing, "Nigerians are corrupt because the system under which they live today makes corruption easy and profitable.... They will cease to be corrupt when corruption is made difficult and inconvenient" (Achebe 19831983, 38). In this formulation, enlightened citizens are more important than enlightened leaders. When some of Nigeria's reformers argued in the late 1990s that their best hope lay in the hands of the brutal dictator Sani Abacha, a dissident colonel offered a stringent critique: "To continue to

---

[12] See, for example, the symposium, "Perestroika in Political Science: Past, Present, and Future," *PS: Political Science and Politics* 43, 4 (October 2010), 725–754.

predicate the future of this country on the existence of one man, I think will be very dangerous. What happens when the man is gone?"[13]

A new generation of political thinkers now links the quality of leaders to the political processes that choose them. Suggesting that Achebe's oft-used quotation represented postcolonial hero worship and Weberian ideas of charismatic authority, Eghosa Osaghae says that democratization taught Africans one thing: "The best form of leadership was that restrained by institutional checks" (Osaghae 2010, 420). Liberian President and Nobel Prize in Peace Laureate Ellen Johnson Sirleaf similarly concludes, "Good leadership is only partly about the individual people in leadership positions. Much more important is how these leaders are chosen and how they are held accountable by citizens" (Radelet 2010, 5).

Clearly, leadership matters for something. Rising to power in 1994 after 27 years in prison, Nelson Mandela demonstrated a willingness to protect the rights and property of South Africa's white minority that constituted a monumental act of forgiveness, which also helped preserve the country's engines of growth. And as Seymour Martin Lipset reminds us of George Washington, nothing exemplifies "self-sacrificing heroism" like the former general's willingness to return gracefully to private life after the Revolutionary War and then do so again after serving two terms as president. England's stunned King George commented that this made Washington "the greatest character of the age" (Lipset 1998, 24). James Madison himself asked, during the Virginia Convention, "Is there no virtue among us? If there be not, we are in a wretched situation. No theoretical checks – no form of government can render us secure" (Madison 2006b, 157). However, Madison ultimately argued for the dangers of relying on political will and placing hope in individual leaders. "A nation of philosophers is as little to be expected as the philosophical race of kings wished for by Plato," he writes in "Federalist Number 49" (Hamilton et al. 2008, 251).

The danger of embracing leadership as a causal explanation is that it discounts institutions, social forces, and other types of postcolonial agency. By resigning history to randomness, it falsely separates a leader's decisions from the social reality and political systems in which they are made. Like structural determinism, the leadership explanation asks citizens to accept governance failures as the result of forces beyond their control. African nationalists in fact discarded colonial constitutions with

[13] Danlami Nmodu, "What If He Is No More?" *TELL*, February 23, 1998.

surprising swiftness after independence. And while many postcolonial policies had failed by the 1970s, evidence increasingly demonstrates that excessive voluntarism is too stochastic to account for empirical patterns of government performance in the decades since then (Alence 2004; Ndulu et al. 2008). African agency operates within a finite universe of opportunity constraints; Africans are not locked fatalistically into path dependency in which neither politicians nor citizens have control over their destiny. Veto player theory can help illuminate these contexts and constraints.

An Alternative Explanation

An enduring, hard reality, Madison writes in the *Federalist Papers*, is that "enlightened statesmen will not always be at the helm." Governance always entails confrontations among hostile factions, and "it is in vain to say that enlightened statesmen will be able to adjust to these clashing interests, and render them subservient to the public good" (Hamilton et al. 2008, 51). He argues that the causes of factions, which include above all the unequal distribution of property, cannot be removed. Therefore, "controlling the effects" of factions is among the principal tasks of government. "Each department should have a will of its own," he explains, famously arguing that "ambition must be made to counter ambition" (Hamilton et al. 2008, 256–257). Since the 1990s, political scientists have used this central insight as the basis for veto player theory, developing it as a tool for identifying the different interests and institutions that divide wills and compete to shape policy. Yet Madison's foundational legacy is largely taken for granted and the literature rarely mentions him. In one sense, this is unsurprising because veto player theory is intended to operate in a comparative framework, and overt references to Madison could be misinterpreted as narrowing its scope to just the American experience. In a broader sense, though, veto player theory and even comparative politics more generally have unpaid debts to Madison (Samuels and Shugart 2010).

George Tsebelis has advanced a contemporary theory of "veto players" as a comparative tool of regime analysis, arguing that conventional categories such as presidential/parliamentary, unicameral/bicameral, or majoritarian/proportional often defy clear demarcation. Policy making is better understood in terms of a continuum reflecting the number and type of divided interests. These veto players are thus "individual or collective actors whose agreement is required for a change of the status quo"

(Tsebelis 1995, 289). Despite innumerable national differences, this theory allows meaningful comparisons between political actors, who often exercise effective vetoes over policy, even though they formally lack such authority. The important point about regimes is not their form, but rather the number of political actors with the capacity to advance their preferences, and arguably the ideological distance among those preferences.

His work has spawned dozens of studies over the last fifteen years that have tested this general framework on various outcomes. Most veto player studies focus on explaining policy stability and change (Konig, Tsebelis, and Debus 2010). For example, regimes with too many veto players can lock in high rates of inflation or other problematic macroeconomic policies (Schiavon 2000; Tsebelis 2002). One study finds that strong interest groups can act as veto players, and this potential makes such policies difficult to change (Gelbach and Malesky 2010). At the same time, regimes with too few veto players have trouble generating credibility about existing policy, since it could suddenly change. This discourages foreign direct investment and other conditions conducive to long-term economic growth by creating a perception of uncertainty about the future (Henisz 2000). One influential formulation of policy stability gauges the impact of veto players on the level of "commitment" or "resoluteness" with regard to the status quo (Haggard and McCubbins 2001).

This focus on policy stability is unnecessarily narrow, since some literature does link veto players to other types of outcomes. Research on power-sharing agreements, for example, suggests that additional veto players increase the likelihood of renewed political violence; either their vast disagreements form barriers to cooperation, or they collude with each other to postpone lasting solutions to the violence (Cheeseman and Tendi 2010). More importantly, another stream of the research argues that if veto players have the ability to block policy change, then they should also have the ability to demand targetable policy outputs that function as side payments to political allies (Cox and McCubbins 2001; Lyne 2008). Indeed, one study looking at institutional actors in seventy-eight countries found that as the number of "veto points" increases, governments embark on more costly "white elephant" infrastructure projects that benefit narrow constituencies (Henisz and Zelner 2006). The literature explores how veto players limit opportunities for selfish behavior, but the lens of policy stability remains central to theory. Accountability is framed as a safeguard against impetuous policy shifts driven by a small number of cohesive political actors.

Madison recognized the risks of making policy too difficult to change through the proliferation of interests, or making policy too easy to change with the concentration of authority in one set of institutions. But accountability was also central to his vision of government. For example, he argued for a strong, bicameral legislature as a safeguard against sudden policy shifts. The division of the legislature was intended as a form of horizontal monitoring – separate and sovereign authorities to create checks and balances within and across government. Contemporary veto player studies also find the capacity for such horizontal accountability in influential militaries or strong judiciaries with the ability to shape policy choice and drive accountability (Tsebelis 2002; Andrews and Montinola 2004). Though he was no populist, Madison also visualized accountability with a vertical dimension – between citizens and the government. He feared that inadequate control of authority delegated to the government would disenfranchise the poor majority or enable the executive to spend recklessly. Contemporary veto players literature incorporates these principles of vertical accountability by recognizing the possibility that strong unions or other organized interests can constrain public authority.

In this book I move such actors closer to the heart of veto player theory. An analysis rooted in these foundational principles advances the study of Africa, where nationalists won their freedom in the 1960s, where social movements were often effective in building capacity for vertical accountability in the 1980s, and where restraining executive authority stands out as perhaps the central problem of institutional consolidation today (Barkan 2009; Diamond and Plattner 2010). I build upon veto player theory by integrating the social bases of authority into the analysis of elite behavior. My findings suggest that the number of veto players not only impacts policy stability, the usual focus of veto player studies, but also has differential effects on local and nationally oriented public policy outputs.

This book also contributes to veto player theory by exploring its applications in a developing country. With a few notable exceptions,[14] virtually all of the research has focused on wealthy cases. "It may be that there is much less faith in institutional approaches among those who do not work on developing countries," explains a recent literature review on veto players, an unfortunate trend in light of the theory's "proven use" (Hallerberg 2010, 35). While veto player theory has formed the basis of a highly integrated niche literature on the developed world, it has been

---

[14] See, for example, Cheesman and Tendi (2010) and MacIntyre (2001).

less convenient to apply in regions where key concepts are difficult to measure and quantify. If veto players are more than numbers on a chart, and they represent some implicit social contract concerning the distribution of political authority, operationalizing this idea in the developing world has been a challenge.

Most veto player studies also focus on democracies. By applying this approach to the study of an African case with a long history of dictatorships, this book also aims to contribute to emerging comparative scholarship about authoritarianism. This research, which now complements democratization as a significant field of inquiry, strives to disaggregate authoritarian regimes in order to understand how they govern. By examining alternative bases of accountability, policy control, and civic participation, this literature has exposed how seemingly different regimes face surprisingly similar pressures to represent societal interests. For example, twenty-nine years into his tenure as president of the Ivory Coast, Félix Houphouët-Boigny asserted, "There is no number two, three or four ... In Côte d'Ivoire there is only a number one: that's me and I don't share my decisions" (Meredith 2011, 379). The emerging comparative authoritarian literature questions this kind of excessive bravado (LeVan 2014). It explores how political institutions such as legislatures or mass political parties can and do constrain dictators (Wright 2008; Brownlee 2007; Frantz and Ezrow 2011). Autocrats govern through a variety of collective decision-making mechanisms, challenging the myth of the "solitary autocrat" (Gandhi 2008, 2008). Even repression has its limits because autocrats face "audience costs," which increase the political risks of coercion compared to co-optation (Weeks 2008). Burkina Faso's dictator, for example, has survived several waves of mass protests since gaining power in 1987 by employing strategies of conciliation rather than coercion.[15] Unlike much of the democratization literature, which uses a wide array of ideal types to analyze illiberal regimes, veto player theory advances comparative analysis by conceptualizing political authority on a continuum and identifying checks on a surprising range of nondemocratic rulers.

There is a pressing need to understand authoritarianism better because two decades after the "third wave" of democratization reached Africa's shores, democracies across the continent are in a precarious condition and illiberal politics retain a significant allure. The Economist Intelligence

---

[15] Adam Nossiter, "In Burkina Faso, Leader Keeps Cool under Fire," *New York Times*, May 10, 2011.

Unit declared in 2010 that "democracy is in retreat. The dominant pattern in all regions over the past two years has been backsliding on previously attained progress." In Sub-Saharan Africa, democratization "is grinding to a halt and in some cases is being reversed" (Economist Intelligence Unit 2010, 2). Freedom House reported similarly discouraging findings in 2013 when it announced that freedom on a global level had declined for the seventh consecutive year.

Surveys carried out by Afrobarometer show that, since the project began in 1999, demand for democracy has increased across Africa and that majorities reject alternatives to democracy (understood as one-man rule, one-party rule, or military rule). Still, fewer than half (47 percent) of respondents in 2008 indicated a demand for democracy, with significant variation across countries. More alarmingly, among the 20 most politically liberal countries in Africa, nowhere do a majority of respondents see democracy as consolidated – and in several cases a majority describe a consolidation of autocracy (Bratton and Mattes 2009). Citizens also express strong doubts about the quality of democracy. Vertical accountability and government responsiveness are low, indicating a deficiency in "extending the link between citizens and government beyond regular elections and formal constitutional protections to the day-to-day realm of policy-making and implementation" (Logan and Mattes 2010, 11). And even in countries where citizens do prefer democracy, impatience with its ability to deliver on desired policies creates a restlessness that coup plotters have historically exploited.

In Nigeria, evidence suggests that citizens still clearly prefer democracy, but their commitment to the democratic process is weak. According to statistically sampled nationwide surveys, there has been decline in patience with democracy since 2000, due to the government's performance record. In 2005, nearly 40 percent of Nigerians said that they would "consider other political options" if democratic performance does not improve (Afrobarometer 2006, 13). Even before the corrupt elections of 2007, polls revealed growing cynicism about democracy. And after the elections, less than one-third of those interviewed were either "fairly satisfied" or "very satisfied" with the way democracy works in Nigeria. Nigeria's youthful population, roughly half of whom had never lived under a democracy at the time of the transition, expressed frustration. One retired military colonel who had risked his life to move the democratic transition forward in Nigeria complained in 2004, "This democracy that we have made so many sacrifices to bring about and invested so much hope in, has not delivered the expected dividends....

This system has not promoted good governance."[16] For his generation, such sentiments evoke memories of the period before the 1983 coup, a surprisingly popular regime change that ushered in sixteen dark years of dictatorship. Olusegun Obasanjo, who stepped aside in 1979 to allow a democratic transition, perhaps best expressed the nation's enigmatic attitude toward democracy. Commenting after a 1985 coup that ordinary citizens are more concerned with the substance of government than its form, he said, "[Nigerians] are interested in the ability to deliver, the ability to perform, rather than the means by which the government is brought about."[17]

Obasanjo's view that good governance is defined by government performance, rather than the procedures that generate policies or choose rulers, reflects a perspective that was widespread in Africa during the 1970s and 1980s. By presenting an analytical framework centered on political leverage, rather than the level of political freedom, a key implication of this book's argument is that democratic disappointments are at least partly a function of the distribution of policy-making authority. Neither dictators nor democrats will be able to resolve today's simmering frustrations fully through performance legitimation; they also need to confront core questions of interest aggregation. Regimes need to reflect a range of interests while limiting the bargaining problems stimulated by broad inclusion. This difficult choice resides at the core of the veto players model I introduce in the chapters that follow.

In sum, this book contributes to comparative politics by engaging core debates about public policy performance in Africa. Carrying out a detailed longitudinal study of one country over time facilitates a natural experiment, whereby I am able to hold constant factors such as colonial history and the level of ethnic diversity that are often blamed for bad governance. The rentier literature suggests that Nigeria's performance could be undermined by oil revenues, the modernization literature blames low levels of economic development, and research on foreign debt points the finger at international pressure from lenders. I control for all of these factors and still find statistically significant patterns of performance across a broad range of variables measuring national and local collective goods. I therefore also dismiss explanations for government performance centered on the virtues of leaders as too stochastic. Though my time series

[16] Abubakar Umar, "Why I Am Angry," *Vanguard*, April 5, 2004.
[17] "Obasanjo Breaks His Silence," *West Africa*, August 12, 1985; "Which Way Forward?" *West Africa*, August 19, 1985.

analysis uses a proxy variable for local collective goods, my results have important implications for efforts to understand the conditions conducive to patronage since I find that the addition of new political actors to the policy process limits the opportunities for such payoffs.

My alternative explanation contributes to other important areas of comparative politics research. Veto players transcend blunt distinctions between democracy and dictatorship, shifting the analytical focus to the number of political actors with leverage over policy. This departs from the democratization literature's emphasis on the level of political freedom and helps account for varieties of government performance in illiberal regimes, which now constitute a significant area of research. In this regard, my causal explanation also contributes to research on comparative authoritarianism by exploring how institutional, individual, and collective actors can advance their policy preferences and hold each other accountable. By showing how these actors sometimes construct authority through coalitions outside formal institutions, or through factions within them, my formulation of veto player theory contributes to two other areas of research. One relates to informal institutions, since my model offers a way of operationalizing them. The other concerns federalism, since I link successful collective action by subnational units (Nigeria's states and geopolitical "zones") to public policy outcomes. Finally, I contribute to veto player theory by applying it to a developing country with a history of authoritarianism, and by invoking some of James Madison's foundational ideas to test for empirical relationships across a broad range of outcomes beyond policy stability.

The Structure of the Book

During the 1990s, a new dictator sent Obasanjo to prison, where the retired general changed his mind about democracy, abandoning the view he articulated in his 1985 interview. After he was released, Obasanjo became the first democratically elected president after the 1999 transition. During his eight years in office, he clashed continually with the National Assembly, which tried to impeach him numerous times, oversaw two flawed elections, and witnessed the rise of Islamic law in the North and new violent rebellions in the South. He also increased social spending, oversaw economic reforms, paid off the country's foreign debts, and restored Nigeria's international reputation. What does this decidedly mixed record teach us about the factors that determine government performance? This book digs beneath the standard political and cultural formulations to understand the underlying structural dynamics that guided policy making in Nigeria from 1960 through 2007. I show how veto players capture essential elements of this structure, and how the number of veto players impacts two broad categories of public policy.

The first chapter develops veto player theory as an alternative explanation for government performance. Before making any reference to Nigeria, which forms the focus of my study, I detail criteria for identifying veto players. In my formulation, political actors possess veto authority when they have motives to challenge the status quo, the organizational means to coordinate preferences internally, and they demonstrably block policy in one major area such as federal budgets or constitutional reform. Most veto players are collective, meaning that they must meet some internal decision rule in order to exercise authority; the literature describes dictators and strong presidents as individual veto players. Veto players are typically associated with formal institutions, including legislative chambers or presidencies whose assent is necessary for a bill to become law. The literature also identifies cohesive political parties as "partisan" veto players that can emerge from within the legislature. I incorporate informal institutions into my model in two ways: First, I draw upon scholars who explore how authority coalescing from the bottom up can form alternative centers of power with veto authority. In Nigeria, this leads to "regional" vetoes exercised by visible political coalitions constructed across either one of the country's two broadest sociocultural cleavages. Second, I discuss how factions within military ruling councils can possess veto authority. I link them to Madison's formulation of factions in general terms, and I compare them operationally to partisan veto players in the existing literature.

Highlighting a tension between two different traditions in the literature, I then argue that the conditions that increase policy stability and credibility also make it more difficult for political actors to coordinate their interests. An increase in the number of veto players should therefore undermine the delivery of policies with nonexcludable benefits at the national level since it is more difficult for veto players to agree that their interests are better served by these broad, collective policies. At the same time, an increase in the number of veto players should also theoretically impact the overall levels of more particularistic goods since each actor can use its leverage to demand payoffs. These goods with more excludable benefits are characteristic of patronage. Throughout the book I describe these two distinct dependent variables as national collective goods and local collective goods, respectively. A "coordination" hypothesis predicts that an increase in the number of veto players will exacerbate coordination problems that impede the delivery of national collective goods. A "logroll" hypothesis predicts that additional veto players will correspond with significant increases in the overall level of local collective goods. Before testing these hypotheses, I undertake the task of coding the study's independent variable.

Chapter 2 therefore counts the number of veto players in each Nigerian regime between independence in October 1960 and the end of President Olusegun Obasanjo's second term in May 2007. Defining a regime as a distinct configuration of veto players, I identify 14 distinct regimes, each one with between one and four veto players. Anecdotes from interviews and a variety of primary sources vividly illustrate why regimes with more veto players face coordination problems. I explain how authority develops, sometimes from the top down through military factions, and sometimes from the ground up through regional vetoes exercised by political coalitions constructed across either the northern or the southern region of Nigeria. I pay special attention to policy actors who have gained power since Nigeria's 1999 transition, the country's longest experience with democracy since independence. I argue that violent agitation for Islamic law in the North and militant demands for control over oil resources in the South stem from efforts to maintain a federal bargain between two distinct geopolitical regions. This analysis roots macrolevel political leverage in geography, culture, and history, and it explores the endogenous factors that shape institutions.

In Chapter 3, I define government performance, specify different variables for measuring my dependent variable, and perform two sets of statistical tests. I elaborate on distinctions between national and local collective goods, drawing upon public goods theory to explain that what distinguishes them is how they are consumed (not the fact that governments often provide these goods). With regard to national collective goods, it is costly to exclude some citizens from enjoying their benefits. I operationalize these variables with original empirical data on budgetary policy, inflation, education, and judicial resolution of property rights cases in Nigeria. With respect to local collective goods, it theoretically is possible to target delivery and exclude some constituencies, making them prone to patronage. I operationalize these variables with original data on capital and recurrent spending as a share of gross domestic product per capita. All of the variables, with the exception of the judicial data (for reasons I explain), measure aggregated outcomes at the federal level between 1961 and 2007. Baum and Lake (2003) point out that even if the government is not a direct provider of the goods and services in question, it still regulates them and monitors performance. This is an important point since jurisdiction over some policy is shared with states or other implementers. Working with federal-level data means that we can only infer evidence of patronage from the tests with local collective goods, if there are exorbitant levels of spending, and we cannot identify "who got what." However, my models offer the benefit of being able to identify patterns of performance systematically and objectively over time. I also draw upon speeches and government documents to show that these performance indicators all reflect recurring government policy priorities.

Statistical tests of the coordination hypothesis show that an increase in the number of veto players contributes to bigger budget deficits, higher rates of inflation, larger student/teacher ratios, and less efficient judicial resolution of property rights cases. In a practical sense, having more veto players makes it more difficult to enact policies at a national level because it is difficult for veto players to agree on broad, collective policies. Tests of the logroll hypothesis show that an increase in the number of veto players helps restrain overall levels of government spending. This is contrary to my predictions that patronage would increase as each veto player uses her political leverage to demand payoffs. I attribute this result to the improved monitoring generated by additional veto players, much as Madison anticipated. All of these results remain robust after including controls for the conventional explanations for government performance. I conclude that Nigeria faces a "Madisonian dilemma," since the conditions that contribute to coordination problems simultaneously foster accountability.

A succinct qualitative analysis then complements the statistical tests. Rather than attempting to link specific veto players to explicit policy preferences, this analysis associates particular veto player regimes with patterns of performance. I identify statistical outliers and some inconsistencies within each cluster of variables measuring local and national collective goods. By showing *which* veto player regimes struggled to deliver national collective goods, and which ones successfully limited policy logrolls, this chapter specifies the effects of Nigeria's Madisonian dilemma at different points in time. The chapter also offers a check against my sample's modest size, since none of the variables has more than 47 years of data.

To probe the comparative potential of the model beyond Nigeria, Chapter 4 investigates the individual, collective, and institutional factors guiding the policy process in two other African cases, Ghana and Zimbabwe. Rather than attempting to identify veto players explicitly, the narratives search for their "analytical equivalents" by focusing on historical junctures when the policy process expanded or contracted. In this regard, the chapter serves the comparative goal of concept validation, to see how my model could be applied elsewhere. The study of Ghana focuses on a period of institutional consolidation in the 1980s when the country showed signs of breaking with postindependence patterns of impetuous economic policy making. This transformation reduced corruption and improved macroeconomic performance, even before democratization took root. Three critical junctures emerge in the narrative: a policy reversal in 1969 that led to the formation of new economic coalitions opposed to austerity, a 1979 coup that unleashed a populist wave of anger against corruption, and a debate over economic policy in the 1980s that dispersed political authority across society.

The Zimbabwe narrative in Chapter 4 traces the path to the 2008 power-sharing agreement and identifies the sources of political reconfigurations in economic liberalization, coalitions for institutional reform, and new electoral challenges. By the time the country arrived at this critical historical juncture, institutions capable of arbitrating among different political factions had been weakened, and the regime was beholden to a variety of independent-minded allies. Though poverty remains serious, economic performance improved and the emergence of these analytic equivalents of veto players reined in a particularly controversial form of patronage. Unlike in Ghana, these institutions remain in flux.

The final chapter, "Madison's Model Unbound," explains how this study advances comparative analysis of Africa. For starters, it adds to our understanding of informal institutions and federalism. Even during regimes that formally limited states' power, subnational actors sometimes constructed authority from the ground up through sustained political coalitions. Conversely, sometimes institutions designed to counterbalance interests failed to exercise this power. This study also adds to our understanding of authoritarian governance by analyzing the distribution of authority through veto players, rather than focusing on the level of political freedom, which is a common focus of the democratization literature. The analysis further contributes to an emerging literature on authoritarian institutions that argues for the collective nature of nondemocratic governance. Next, I point out how my empirical tests raise important questions about distributional politics in Africa because democratic governance by itself explains little about the conditions that either enable patronage or undermine broad public policies for the common good. The weak significance of foreign debt on Nigeria's public policy performance over time speaks to the ability of African countries to overcome colonial atavisms, and the limited impact of oil revenue on key categories of government performance suggests that natural resources are not necessarily a curse. Similarly, the weak association between the level of development and my government performance indicators challenges core ideas of modernization theory.

The chapter also identifies factors that potentially limit the model's generalizability. For example, Nigeria differs from many countries in its minimal dependence on foreign aid. The analytic narratives of Ghana and Zimbabwe in Chapter 4 similarly suggest that veto player models may need to do more to integrate some international factors that were less influential in Nigeria. In addition, many cases do not share Nigeria's political equilibrium between the northern and southern regions at the heart of its federal system, and this could make it more difficult to include informal institutions.

Militant movements demanding "resource control" in the oil-rich Niger Delta, and Islamic movements such as Boko Haram in the Northeast, are straining the historical North/South bargain at the core of Nigeria's nationhood, which marked its centennial in 2014. However, there are positive signs that Nigeria's political system is becoming more broadly accessible and that its institutions are creating incentives for political organizing that cut across the highly sensitive North/South regional cleavage. This may be leading the country toward a more stable resolution of its Madisonian dilemma by balancing representation and accountability. Many southerners rose to defend presidential term limits in 2006, even though a southern politician stood to gain from constitutional modifications that would have allowed him to stay in office. Similarly, when a succession crisis ensued after the death of President Umaru Yar'Adua, a northerner, in 2010, the presidency peacefully shifted to a southerner, Vice President Goodluck Jonathan. I explain how the resolution to the crisis demonstrated a commitment to constitutional terms of separate sovereignty, public authority grounded in distinct branches of government, and protection of national interests that cut across regional concerns. In these and other examples, Nigerians strengthened their political institutions by defending them, and politicians and civil society activists continue to fortify them in ways that demonstrate creativity and hope.

I

A Theory of Institutions, Preferences, and Performance

The term "veto" is most commonly used to describe a chief executive's ability to block legislation in a presidential democracy. America's founders, who aimed to avoid having another king, were persuaded by Montesquieu that "when the legislative and executive powers are united in the same person, or in the same body of magistrates, there can be no liberty" (Montesquieu et al. 1989, 154). In his reflections on Montesquieu, Madison agreed, noting, "The accumulation of all powers legislative, executive, and judiciary in the same hands, whether of one, a few or many, and whether hereditary, self-appointed or elective, may justly be pronounced the very definition of tyranny" (Hamilton et al. 2008, 239). Madison therefore sought to prevent the concentration of authority in any single institution or office by dividing political wills. Independently constituted institutions would have their own interests and an autonomous capacity to resist encroachment by the others.

The premise of contemporary veto player theory is that these underlying principles of checks and balances operate in a wide variety of political regimes, not just in presidential systems or in democracies. This chapter provides an introduction to the terminology and logic of veto player theory. It explores how this analytical tool can be productively applied to policy making in Nigeria and contemporary African politics more broadly. For example, veto player theory provides new ways to examine different sources of policy control in authoritarian regimes. A growing literature on comparative authoritarianism argues that from Chile to China, dictators rarely govern unilaterally. Veto player theory can help us understand how collective ruling bodies and other institutions constrain rulers' behavior and shape the bargaining environment.

This means that dictatorships do not necessarily have fewer veto players than democracies. Veto player theory also accommodates informal actors as potential vetoes, thereby engaging a core debate in African studies about the feasibility of comparative analysis where "formal" institutions might merely be a mask for those who wield power behind the scenes. Most importantly, the theory generates new explanations relevant to our examination of government performance in Nigeria over time. Rather than comparing democracy with dictatorship to analyze the structure of authority, the number of political actors with the ability to prevent a change in the status quo policy systematically captures the underlying regime characteristics that affect policy performance.

This chapter does not yet identify Nigeria's veto players, and it does not test to see how they impact government performance. Instead, I define key concepts, develop criteria for operationalizing them, explain how existing research expects veto players to impact two broad types of public policy, and formulate two testable hypotheses. First, I discuss the basic categories of analysis in veto player theory, which distinguish between *individual* and *collective* actors as well as between *institutional* and *partisan* actors. For the sake of this study, a political actor is only considered a veto player if it possesses a motive to challenge the status quo, has the organizational means to coordinate preferences, and demonstrably blocks a major policy initiative. While setting a high threshold for being counted as a veto player, these criteria also allow the inclusion of a wide range of political actors including military factions, powerful individuals, legislatures, and political parties. In the case of Nigeria, these criteria also accommodate inclusion of the North and South as broad regional actors with distinct cultural histories and colonial experiences. If subnational political actors across either region overcome collective action problems, they can mobilize a "regional veto" that enforces the fundamental federal bargain that drew the two regions together a hundred years ago. My model therefore strives to capture the potential for constructing authority from below, rather than simply through constitutional structures and formal institutions. Madison, who deserves more credit as an intellectual inspiration for contemporary veto player theory, argued for such necessary connections between civic life and public authority.

Second, I analyze how existing theory expects veto players to impact government performance. Some analyses suggest that ideological distance among veto players and their internal "cohesion" matter; however, I side with scholars who claim that the number of veto players is the most important trait. An existing literature, which I group under a "credible commitment" tradition of research, overwhelmingly focuses on explaining policy stability in developed democracies. This focus is unfortunate because veto player models could advance our understanding of policy making in the developing world, and it overlooks other potential effects of veto players. Specifically, a "distributional" research tradition suggests that political actors capable of preventing a change in policy theoretically have the ability to extract self-interested benefits as well.

In the chapter's final section, I explain how veto players in each of these traditions should logically impact the two broad categories of public policy that I will use in empirical testing. Building on the credible commitment tradition, I formulate a "coordination" hypothesis that posits that regimes with more veto players face coordination problems that impede the delivery of indivisible public policies enjoyed at the national level. Building on the distributional tradition, I then formulate a "logroll" hypothesis that posits that regimes with more veto players face demands for excessive spending on targetable policies enjoyed at the local level. These policies with excludable benefits are characteristic of patronage.

Veto Player Theory: Defining the Terms

Veto player theory liberates the term "veto" from its American associations and its relationship to presidential democracy. Developed by George Tsebelis in the 1990s, it facilitates broad comparative analysis by transcending conventional institutional categories and greatly expanding the definition of veto power. Whether examining presidential or parliamentary governments, proportional or majoritarian electoral systems, democratic or authoritarian regimes, the theory coheres around a central claim that diverse institutions have similar aggregate effects on the policy process by channeling interests and shaping the bargaining environment. While cross-national studies using veto player analysis tend to focus on formal institutions, the theory is also capable of integrating informal political authority. This means that institutions do not have to be divorced from the historical contexts that create them or the social frames in which they operate.

Two brief examples illustrate this last point. Mexico's Chamber of Deputies, the lower house, formally possesses broad powers over the federal budget. In practice, though, the president exercises tremendous influence over budget proposals, and once the budget is passed, the president frequently departs from the official spending plan (Weldon 2002). Under single party rule from 1929 to 2000, the president managed to do this through his powerful role in the political party by creating strong incentives for legislators to fall in line (Casar 2002, 134–140). In effect, the lower house does not have a veto despite constitutional provisions that suggest otherwise. Similarly, in Ghana, the National Assembly has "formal authority in terms of legislation, policy direction, nominations, budgeting improving the conditions of service and providing oversight," but "the executive is for the most part unconstrained by the legislature" (Lindberg and Zhou 2009, 157–159). The career paths of politicians in both cases undermine any institutional incentive to challenge the president: Mexico's legislators can only serve one term, making them dependent upon party loyalty for a future job (Ugalde 2000). And in Ghana legislators can simultaneously serve in the cabinet and the legislature, an arrangement that encourages them to pander to the president (Sakyi 2010). A similar "fusion" of political offices exists in several other African countries with the same debilitating effects on legislative autonomy and authority (van Cranenburgh 2009). In such examples, applying the conventional understanding of a veto or relying solely on constitutional provisions to define authority would leave one with an incomplete and inaccurate understanding of the realities of the policy-making process. Veto player theory embraces a broader definition of veto in order to accommodate these issues and facilitate rich comparisons across institutional contexts.

A Typology of Veto Players and Criteria for Identifying Them

Veto player theory addresses the issues raised by cases such as Mexico and Ghana by describing the policy-making process in terms of relative leverage among veto players. Veto players, according to Tsebelis, are "individual or collective actors whose agreement is required for a change of the status quo" (Tsebelis 1995, 289). Most veto players are *collective*, such as a legislative chamber whose consent is necessary for a bill to become law. To exercise authority, a collective veto player must first satisfy an internal decision rule such as a majority, unanimity, or a qualified majority. In contrast to collective actors, *individual* veto players are unencumbered by these internal decision rules either because either their authority is exercised through one person or the preferences of the collective body in question substantially overlap. Examples of the former include presidents who have a legislative veto and most autocrats. In terms of the latter, Tsebelis (2002) points out that organizations with internally overlapping preferences either must make decisions by unanimous agreement or must have majorities that are monolithic, as in a totalitarian political system. These conditions are rare, and veto player theory does not presume that dictators hold the only veto in authoritarian regimes.

Veto players also differ according to the source of their political authority. *Institutional* veto players derive their authority from constitutions or other legal statutes. In presidential systems, for example, executives and lower legislative chambers each have the codified ability to prevent policy proposals from moving forward. But defining collective players strictly in institutional terms would fail to capture how political leverage is exercised. It is often difficult for organizations that contain a multiplicity of preferences and have few mechanisms for aggregating them to exercise their institutional authority. They may have the formal authority to exercise a veto, but not the collective will. In order to act upon their preferences, collective actors must possess an "organizational basis" for reducing transaction costs associated with collective action (Strøm 2000).

Subgroups within an institution that can exercise a controlling set of preferences are known as *partisan* veto players. The concept of partisan veto players recognizes that power derives not just from institutional rights, but from a collective organization's role (and ability to exert power) within an institution. For example, in a parliamentary system with a tightly disciplined majority party, it would be a mistake to say that the parliament holds an institutional veto, since only the majority party can effectively exercise that authority. In this case, the majority party is itself a partisan veto player and its members have a strong incentive to stick together because they want to avoid having to form a new cabinet and government.[1] Alternatively, if no political party holds a majority and passing legislation depends on forming a coalition, then each party in the coalition has a partisan veto. This means that these parties must agree in order to change policy. Partisan veto players are significant because they embed political leverage within an institution, rather than attributing authority to the institution itself. Even in an organization where only one majority is likely, veto authority rests not with the formal institution but with the specific partisan player within it. Using these two sets of characteristics – individual or collective, institutional or partisan – veto player analysis attempts to describe and tally accurately the number of

---

[1] For an authoritative discussion of these incentives, see Strøm, Müller, and Bergman (2003).

political actors who can assert their preferences as part of the policy-making process.

But before we can count veto players, several other issues must be considered. First, each political actor's veto power is influenced by the number of other political actors who share the same set of policy preferences. In other words, if a political actor's policy preference is already well represented in a particular debate by another political actor, the addition of the second actor to the debate does not impact policy stability (Tsebelis 2002, 28). Known as the "absorption rule" in the veto player literature, this means that political actors whose preferences substantially resemble those of other actors should be eliminated from the veto player analysis because their consent is not required. The absorption rule, in effect, makes an important distinction between having a policy preference and having the ability to assert that preference successfully in the policy realm. This leads to another critical rule in tabulating veto players. Preferences should not be counted as vetoes just because they differ from other interests. Kaare Strøm argues that "a credible veto player must have both opportunity and motive" (Strøm 2000, 280). As the cases of Ghana and Mexico suggest, political actors who have the right to exercise veto authority may not act as veto players if proper disincentives exist.

These insights culminate in the three operational principles that guide the identification of veto players in this study. To be considered a veto player, a political actor must (1) have a motive based on distinct preferences for challenging policy; (2) have a mechanism for coordinating common interests and reducing information costs through an organization or institution, if the political actor is collective; and (3) prevail on at least one major policy issue. For purposes of this study, each configuration of veto players constitutes a regime, coded on a yearly basis over the 47 years in my sample.

Informal Institutions and Veto Power through Military Factions and Regional Vetoes

Identifying veto players in dictatorships poses additional challenges. While the current literature on authoritarianism questions the idea that dictators always have the first and final word, might we identify multiple veto players even in harshly repressive regimes? Do the rules stated in a military decree actually matter? Consider, for example, Chile under General Augusto Pinochet from 1973 to 1990. Amnesty International reported that when Pinochet ascended to power he displayed "astonishing savagery" that led to a "death toll of victims ... unprecedented in recent Latin American history" (Amnesty International 1974). Decrees and various rules specified that the military junta had legislative powers and was required to operate according to unanimous agreement. Arturo Valenzuela writes that this arrangement was comparable to "one man rule" and describes a process whereby Pinochet used his veto to keep rebellious military service chiefs in check (Valenzuela 1991). It is difficult, at first, to imagine a role for veto players under the early years of Pinochet.

However, by shifting the analytical focus away from the level of freedom and focusing instead on the ability of different actors to exercise political leverage, veto player theory generates four insights into the operation of authoritarian regimes. First, it acknowledges the fact that leadership – even dictatorship – is not a one-man show. "Power corresponds to the human ability not just to act but to act in concert," Hannah Arendt wrote in her classic study of dictatorships. "Power is never the property of an individual; it belongs to a group and remains in existence only so long as the group keeps together" (Arendt 1969, 44). Revisionist interpretations of the Pinochet regime embrace the collective nature of public authority, pointing out that the requirement for unanimous agreement empowered competing centers of authority – similar to veto players within Pinochet's military junta. This onerous decision rule actually resulted from demands by leaders in the navy and air force for increased policy-making authority. This element of forced pluralism ultimately limited Pinochet's policy options (Barros 2003). In the end, this same set of veto players rebuffed Pinochet's efforts to stay in power and played a central role in arranging the 1989 plebiscite that finally drove out Pinochet (Schneider 1995). The situation was not so different in Argentina, Brazil, and Uruguay, where despite the appearance of personalism, military regimes governed collectively (Chehabi and Linz 1998). One recent cross-national study of authoritarian regimes since 1946 similarly found that ruling coalitions are the norm (Slovik 2012), while another goes so far as to argue that the image of the solitary "stereotypical autocrat" is not accurate since all dictators face some endogenous constraints on authority (Weeks 2008). In other words, dictators rarely rule alone.

These findings are consistent with key insights from veto player theory. "While non-democratic regimes are generally considered to be single veto player regimes," writes Tsebelis, "close analysis may reveal the existence of multiple veto players" (Tsebelis 2002, 90). Veto player theory does not equate the absence of elections or prevalence of state-sponsored violence with a single policy actor of monolithic preferences. One of the few studies to apply veto player theory to authoritarian regimes explicitly concludes that all of the regimes it examined have some collective decision making body. Only in the most extreme cases of charismatic leadership can one ruler successfully dominate a regime's collective actors (Frantz and Ezrow 2011).

The second way that veto player analysis provides insights into authoritarian regimes is that it moves away from a traditional comparative strategy of classifying regimes according to shared characteristics and ideal types. This has produced a surfeit of categories such as "semi-authoritarianism" (Ottaway 2003) or "hybrid regimes" (Morlino 2009; Shevtsova 2001), each associated with a different configuration of regime characteristics. These studies have advanced our understanding of dictatorships, but as an analytical tool this approach has limitations. Jennifer Gandhi, for example, argues that common terms such as "developmental dictatorships" are problematic because the definition is linked to outcomes, creating a tautological problem if one is trying to test for causal relationships. Another problem is that using lists of attributes such as "low political mobilization" or the presence of a "guiding ideology" to analyze authoritarianism often leads to proposing regimes that exist only in theory, due to their particular combination of characteristics. Moreover, descriptive attributes such as the "distinctive mentality" of the ruler are ambiguous and subjective (Gandhi 2008, 7–9). Other common concepts based on attributes, such as "electoral authoritarianism," suffer from the opposite problem in that they now arguably constitute residual categories since they apply to so many cases (Edozie 2009). A recent CATO Institute study noted, for example, that "even the most despotic of African leaders wish to have their leadership affirmed by elections" (Leon 2010, 1). Similarly, the term "neopatrimonialism" has been applied to nearly every African country (Pitcher, Moran, and Johnston 2009, 132). At least one veto player study borrows from an established regime typology and associates different labels with the number of veto players and other characteristics (Frantz and Ezrow 2011). This may be a reasonable approach for a cross-national study. But in a longitudinal analysis, such as the one utilized in this book, the reader gains important information regarding the identity of relevant actors and the contexts that create them that is otherwise sacrificed in such classifications.

Third, veto player analysis allows for a more nuanced understanding of power centers in authoritarian regimes by exploring whether formal institutions actually matter for the policy process. For example, legislatures, once considered mere rubber stamps for unelected executives, shape policy choice in some surprising cases. In Vietnam, the legislature includes numerous delegates outside the ruler's inner circle who have different professional and geographical backgrounds and can advance their constituents' preferences (Malesky and Schuler 2010). Similarly, political parties are more than propaganda machines for tyrannical dictators. Parties resolve conflicts among elites and facilitate recruitment, activities that are either too time consuming or too risky for dictators to perform (Geddes 2003; Levitsky and Way 2010). Parties also help prolong authoritarian rule because they institutionalize the resolution of disputes that arise during regime formation (Brownlee 2007; Magaloni 2008).

Finally, veto player theory improves our ability to analyze and operationalize the impact of authority occasionally exercised through bureaucracies, military factions, economic elites, or other interest groups in authoritarian regimes. There are at least two strategies for incorporating informal institutions. One approach claims that the behavior of such actors is "ultimately mediated through formal veto structures" (MacIntyre 2001, 90). For example, elites in the former Soviet republics allied with bureaucrats and various nonstate interests to generate reciprocal accountability among "tiers" of government (Roeder 1994). We could label this the "institutional mediation" approach since it supposes that informal authority is ultimately expressed through formal institutions of some sort. It operates on reasonable assumptions since most preferences either are absorbed by existing veto players or fail to gain traction.

However, if veto player authority emerges from the bottom up or is created outside formal institutions, this requires another analytical strategy, which we could call a "constructed" approach to informal institutions. This enables us to locate veto players grounded in popular forces or sustained state/society coalitions. Even Madison's formulation anticipated this possibility: "The partitions and internal checks of power" are not the most important guardians of liberty, he wrote in 1792. "The people who are the authors of this blessing must also be its guardians" (Madison 2006c, 212–213). The power of institutions cannot be divorced from "the people" who create and comply with them. This approach is also consistent with recent comparative research. Rod Alence's study of African government performance explains that veto players originate from historical bargains between competing interests and that violating these compacts generates risks and costs (Alence 2004). Jason Browlee's (2007) study of Egypt, the Philippines, Iran, and Malaysia focuses on elites' political constituencies and the structural factors that limit their agency. In Nigeria and Indonesia, Peter Lewis (2007a) juxtaposes policy makers and popular organizations that form "counterpart coalitions." Guillermo O'Donnell similarly discusses "societal accountability" in Latin America as a nonelectoral mechanism for controlling political authority through institutional and noninstitutional means (O'Donnell 2003, 47–48). In sum, the emerging comparative authoritarian literature understands political leverage as contingent upon the social and historical context, reflecting the constructed approach to informal authority.

The theory proposed here links this comparative work to the handful of qualitative veto players analyses that use primary sources and other data to unpack the internal dynamics of political parties or key pressure groups (Cheeseman and Tendi 2010). This is visible in my operational formulation of veto players in two ways. First, I set out to identify specific subgroups that control the power of broader political institutions or collective political actors, much like partisan veto players. For example, a faction might dominate a military ruling council, or a balance of power between two factions might emerge. Madison describes a faction as "a number of citizens, whether amounting to a majority or minority of the whole, who are united and actuated by some common impulse or passion, or of interest, adverse to the rights of other citizens, or to the permanent and aggregate interests of the community" (Hamilton et al. 2008, 49).

There has been some terrific scholarship dedicated to critiquing Madison's understanding of faction.[2] For the purposes of this book, though, I use the concept of "faction" simply to refer to a cohesive subgroup of interests with sufficient political leverage to insist upon their preferences in the policy-making process successfully. Like partisan veto players, they emerge from within institutional actors such as legislatures or ruling military councils, even though they often draw upon alliances

---

[2] Garry Wills (citing Robert Dahl) famously criticizes this definition for biasing the status quo and leaving the common good undefined. He also argues that it focuses on differences between citizens and elites – rather than among the factions themselves (Wills 1981, 193–197). Colleen Sheehan suggests that one of Madison's main goals here was to raise concerns about the danger of *majority* faction, which might trample on the minority's rights (Sheehan 2009, 7). Madison feared that the fragmentation of the democratic polity could give rise to dictatorship. He told the Virginia Convention in 1788, "On a candid examination of history, turbulence, violence and the abuse of power, by the majority trampling on the rights of the minority, have produced factions and commotions, which, in republics, have more frequently than any other cause produced despotism" (Madison 2006a, 144).

with elites or other nonstate actors to consolidate their influence. And like partisan veto players, factions are identifiable, meaning that it should typically be possible to name them. Factions are thus neither abstract nor arbitrary, and their identifiability is an essential part of their authority. For simplicity's sake, one might think of factions as an adaptation of the partisan veto player terminology for regimes that do not have political parties or the typical manifestations of "partisanship." Factions serve the same analytical function, though, in that they are a controlling subset of preferences; they just happen to operate within institutions such as military ruling councils.

The second way that my operational formulation of veto players relates to the internal dynamics of collective actors is through constructed informal authority by cohesive political actors that emerge mainly outside formal institutions, rather than from within them. Nigeria's geopolitical structure, as a balancing act between its northern and southern regions, forms the basis for such sustainable and substantial informal authority. A prevailing norm of politics since independence is the idea that political institutions and elites must honor this equilibrium between the North and the South. These two regions constitute the broadest subnational distinction within Nigeria, and when their interests are threatened, I claim that a "regional veto" can emerge. Regional vetoes still require satisfying all of the criteria outlined previously for the other types of veto players, meaning they must have a motive, prevail on at least one policy issue, and possess some mechanism for coordinating their interests. In Nigeria's case, such coordination occurs through distinct social structures of federalism, including coalitions across states. Regional vetoes are historically rare since they require extensive and sustained coordination across each ethnically and politically diverse region, and not just simply within part of it. This means that smaller blocs of states by themselves, such as Nigeria's six "geopolitical zones" composed of six states each, are unable to meet this high threshold for coding as regional vetoes.

An underlying political balance between large regions is not unusual in comparative federalism (Watts 1999; Gana and Egwu 2003), so the concept of a "regional veto" should not be taken as unique. In Nigeria's case, the cultural and political differences between its two regions are largely due to the imperial origins of a unified Nigerian state. Britain imposed colonial rule in 1861 after conquering the coastal city of Lagos and began establishing agreements with emirs across the North. In the South, decentralized societies and the topographies of equatorial forests and the tributaries of the Niger River (forming the Niger Delta) presented additional challenges; half a century later, many peoples were still completely unaware of the British presence (Uchendu 1965). The expansion of Christianity across the South accented the region's differences with the Muslim North, where missionary activity was formally prohibited. These two distinct regions thus had little in common when the British decided to join them in 1914 and under indirect rule soon thereafter. The British subdivided the South into eastern and western regions in 1939, creating a lasting imprint on Nigerian politics that manifests itself in voting behavior, ethnic organizing, and other phenomena even today. Due to the role of such an outside power, the 1914 amalgamation constitutes what scholars describe as "putting together" federalism, in contrast to cases (such as Australia or the United States) that "come together" to unite against an external threat (Stepan 1999). One of Nigeria's most famous nationalists, Obafemi Awolowo, famously referred to the country as a "mere geographical expression" for these reasons (Awolowo 1966, 47). And as it approached its 100th anniversary, polemics about "the mistake of 1914" peppered media commentaries, expressing a strong sense of regional identity.[3] Nigeria's North/South distinctions are thus rooted in colonialism's troublesome legacy, and regional vetoes are collective political actors that enforce the terms of the underlying federal bargain at the heart of the country's existence. In relation to broader veto player theory, regional veto players are consistent with innovative efforts (by Cheeseman and Tendi, for example) to incorporate actors nestled between formal and informal politics that emerge from social and historical conditions, and that become institutionalized through observed behavioral regularities.

In Chapter 2, I use the aforementioned criteria and definitions to identify Nigeria's veto players over the last half-century. This includes collective institutional actors such as legislatures and military ruling councils, and individual actors such as presidents and military dictators. It also includes collective actors that possess partisan veto authority such as disciplined political parties in a multiparty coalition or factions within military ruling councils with informal but demonstrable veto power. Regional vetoes arise through visible coalitions across a large majority of states within either the North or the South, for example when governors form alliances with traditional rulers or when civil society bridges state and society. Complaints about regionalism are a part of everyday

---

[3] Adisa Adeleye, "Amalgamation: Was It a Mistake?" *Vanguard*, May 18, 2012; "Don't Celebrate 1914 Amalgamation," *The Punch*, August 19, 2012.

political discourse, but the ability to act upon these shared preferences turns out to be relatively rare. Even though I have slightly departed from standard veto player terminology by introducing factions and regional veto players, both of these actors must satisfy the same criteria in order to be coded as veto players: They must have a motive for challenging policy and a mechanism for coordinating common interests, and they must prevail on one major issue. But before moving on to test the impact of veto players, it is first necessary to consider the kinds of effects we would expect from changes in the number of veto players, or perhaps other qualities about them. In the next section, I review the main ideas from the literature and generate causal propositions and hypotheses about how the number of veto players impacts policy.

The Policy Consequences of Veto Players

As noted, much of the previous scholarship on veto player theory has focused on policy stability. This is surprising because the philosophical basis for divided public power stems from a desire to limit public authority. Madison wanted to protect against both the revival of a despotic monarch and tyranny by the majority. And while he acknowledged the possibility that factional disagreements could paralyze the policy process, he prioritized creating a system in which representatives remained accountable.

In what follows, I draw these ideas together to formulate two hypotheses that I will later test on Nigeria. First, I briefly address literature that claims that the internal cohesion of veto players, as well as the degree to which their preferences differ, influences the effects of veto players. I then explain why this study is nevertheless able to concentrate on the number of veto players as an independent variable. Second, I highlight how the capacity to prevent policy change also has implications for different types of policy outcomes, not just stability. As the number of veto players increases, so do the transaction costs of coordinating preferences. This means that when more veto players are involved, the probability of enacting national policies with broad nonexcludable benefits declines. At the same time, more veto players involved means more demands for narrow policy benefits consumed at the local level. Third, I formulate two hypotheses that reflect these different logics. Since good government performance entails delivery of both types of public policies, which I refer to throughout this study as national and local collective goods, I characterize this tension as a "Madisonian dilemma."

Factors Determining Veto Player Impact

The existing literature discusses three factors that could shape veto players' impact on policy. I discuss each of these and explain why the number of veto players is the most important characteristic of a regime. First, the efficacy of collective veto players arguably depends on their level of internal cohesion. Organizations such as legislatures, political parties, or military councils are constrained by their own internal decision rules, whether they demand a majority, plurality, or unanimity. Tsebelis (2002, 49) offers logical proofs but does not test his "conjectures" about cohesion of collective players since even in Europe and the United States, the data just are not good enough. Many veto player studies do not include this factor. I address the issue by establishing a minimum threshold for cohesion: A collective player must remain demonstrably cohesive over time and with respect to multiple policy issues. This also increases the likelihood of visibility, which is especially important for the practical task of identifying informal political actors such as military factions. I therefore do not include a separate variable measuring internal cohesion in my empirical tests.

Second, some scholars claim that efficacy also depends on the degree to which veto player preferences differ from one another. A scenario where distinct players have radically different preferences means that it is more difficult to reach a compromise over policy (Tsebelis 1995; Treisman 2000). This is easy to visualize with a spatial model of bargaining in which policy actors sit at opposing ends of a continuum. The positions of actors with very different preferences are polarized because the ideological distance between them is significant and they are reluctant to compromise on strongly held beliefs. In this one-dimensional spatial model, bargaining continues until a winning coalition converges to promote a moderate view, which is illustrated by single peak at the median (Downs 1957).[4]

This is a matter of ideology, and many studies operationally simplify bargaining by representing preferences on an ideological left-right continuum (Pavão 2010). Regardless of whether we are thinking in one or more policy dimensions, though, measuring this is problematic. In fact Tsebelis's data set does not even include the United States because "no method has been able to place the President in these ideological continuums"

---

[4] But political life is rarely so simple. When politics is modeled as a multidimensional phenomenon instead, equilibrium solutions do not exist and a compromise on the middle ground may be elusive. An opposition that is always trying to defeat the status quo and some coalition can always do so, at least theoretically (Riker 1962). Veto player theory

(Tsebelis 2010, 13). The practical point for this study is that the relevant political cleavages in Africa are typically not ideological (Bleck and van de Walle 2011). Observers regularly lament African political parties' lack of ideology or programmatic appeal (Salih 2003). With regard to veto players, a number of studies cast doubt on whether ideological distance matters at all (Crepaz and Moser 2004; Andrews and Montinola 2004). In other words, veto player theory does not strictly require spatial modeling of ideological distance between veto players, and such an approach would make little sense anyway in Africa, where preferences are based on other concerns or power is sought for its own sake.

Third and most important, the literature agrees that total number of veto players matters. When more veto players are present in the regime, a larger number of preferences must be taken into account. On the one hand, the policy stability that results from a crowded political stage can be beneficial when the government in power lacks credibility. In new democracies, for example, governments struggle to attract investment if the policy process seems arbitrary or there is a perceived risk of sudden policy change. This was the situation in Ghana until the 1990s, when economic policy stability finally reassured the private sector and investment started to return. "Today is the opportune time for investors to come in and make profits," the deputy finance minister confidently said at the time.[5] On the other hand, having too many veto players can be a burden since they can potentially block needed policy change (Haggard and McCubbins 2001). When Kenya formed a multiparty coalition in order to mitigate the sense of exclusion that had stimulated electoral violence, it also burdened the government with new executive offices conducive to gridlock (LeVan 2011). A balance must be struck between these extremes: "Having more than one veto player helps to reduce the likelihood of policy volatility, but there is some point of inflexion after which additional veto players become unwelcome, serving only to increase the likelihood of policy rigidity" (MacIntyre 2001, 88). The idea that having more veto players is "better" is therefore too simplistic – just as the earlier discussion explained why having fewer veto players cannot necessarily be equated with dictatorship. Veto player regimes present trade-offs.

---

offers an advantage over other bargaining models for precisely this reason. Intransigence on one issue does not exclude compromises on others; veto players may not care about each policy issue equally (Conley and Bekafigo 2010).

[5] "Ghana: We Need to Sing Our Song Louder," *African Business*, January 2006.

In sum, some research incorporates the internal cohesion of and the ideological distance between veto players into empirical models. But there is broader agreement in the literature that changes in the number of veto players have predictable effects, and there is good reason to leave out ideology entirely. These predictions largely focus on policy stability, and the next section explains why we should also be able to test for other types of consequences when the number of veto players changes.

Formulating Hypotheses from the "Distributional" and "Commitment" Traditions

In this study of Nigeria, I maintain that the number of veto players can be used to identify patterns of government performance over time, as measured by two broad categories of public policy. In what follows, I outline how a "credible commitment" tradition in the literature associates veto players with policy stability. But an increase in the number of political actors with the capacity to defend the status quo also implies the ability to generate coordination problems that impair the delivery of national collective goods, which are policies with nonexcludable benefits consumed at the national level. This is a basic insight of public goods research (Olson 1965; Habyarimana et al. 2009). Next, I outline how a "distributional" tradition in the literature expects the number of veto players to impact government performance by increasing demands for local collective goods. Because their consumption is excludable, they can theoretically be denied to some citizens or segments of society. Formulating hypotheses to test the impact of veto players on both types of public policies will give us a more complete picture of government performance in Nigeria. Taken together, they can identify the conditions conducive to patronage as well as those that promote broadly beneficial national policies.

As already noted, most empirical veto player studies test how the number of players affects policy stability (Konig, Tsebelis, and Debus 2010). This credible commitment tradition in the literature links veto players to several types of outcomes. For example, regimes with multiple veto players are known to lock in place high rates of inflation or other problematic macroeconomic policies (Schiavon 2000; Tsebelis 2002). If such regimes also have strong interest groups, they face a lower likelihood of political reform due to a strong commitment to current policies (Gelbach and Malesky 2010). Policy commitment, regardless of the substantive elements, reduces uncertainty about future economic and political conditions, reassures private investors, and restrains public spenders. For this reason, a perception of credibility is supposedly conducive to economic growth over the long term (Henisz 2000). Without commitment, this literature claims that policy makers indulge in government consumption and adopt unsustainable economic policies, advancing their short-term interests through "intertemporal transfers" that borrow from future revenue (Collier and Gunning 2008). But if commitment reduces uncertainty, should not that impact other aspects of government performance as well, not just policy stability? After all, Cameron's seminal study of veto authority (in the American context) points out that the capacity to veto does not just block proposals; it also shapes their content (Cameron 2000, 9).

Other scholars thus focus on how the number of veto players and their relative capacities to exert leverage can have profound consequences for the distribution of resources. This "distributional" tradition in the literature asks, If policy actors have sufficient bargaining power to prevent a change in policy, then do they also have the ability to extract payoffs that exclude other actors? "Each veto player will be able to demand, and receive, such side payments in the form of narrowly targeted policies," argue Cox and McCubbins (2001, 28). Indeed, there is evidence that subnational governments with veto authority can successfully press for narrowly targeted fiscal transfers (Treisman 2000, 839–840; Crepaz and Moser 2004). The provision of excludable benefits such as "fiscal pork," rents benefiting narrow interests, or geographically targetable projects should increase spending levels overall, since providing side payments to a large numbers of policy actors is costly. However, very few empirical studies actually test Cox and McCubbins's intuition (Lyne 2008). This is especially unfortunate with regard to Africa, where patronage and clientelism are recurring features of government performance that undermine good governance (Tripp 2010; Basedau, Erdmann, and Mehler 2007; Berman 1998).

As the number of veto players increases, I claim that these two traditions in the literature generate quite different predictions with regard to local and national collective goods. The distributional tradition implies at least two possible public policy outcomes. One outcome is increased provision of broad national collective goods because political actors realize that allocating individual side payments to each one of them cumulatively becomes expensive. Side payments are inefficient, according to this logic, because of diminishing returns to each actor as new veto players are included. Theoretical studies on the selectorate, referring to the pool of potential political rulers, make a similar claim: Regimes with large ruling coalitions should provide more public goods as a strategy for avoiding expensive transfers to each of the various constituencies that compose the coalition (Bueno de Mesquita et al. 2003; Heger and Salehyan 2007). Within the veto player literature, there is also some evidence that additional vetoes moderate the influence of interest groups and fragmented constituencies that demand economically inefficient and geographically targetable investments (Henisz and Zelner 2006). As the number of veto players increases, we can represent the underlying logic as follows:

Proposition 1(a): larger number of payoffs → incentives for coordination → delivery of national collective goods increases

Although it may be rational to deliver broad public policies, governments may not opt to do so. Rather than *coordinating* to deliver nationally oriented policies, veto players might *collude* to distribute targetable benefits among themselves. This suggests a second, alternative outcome in which policy "logrolls" multiply the number of particularistic payoffs in order to satisfy each actor involved in passing policy (Strøm, Müller, and Bergman 2003). This course is especially attractive in regimes with relatively few political actors because each one will receive a larger payoff as the relative gains of redistribution increase. Ethnicity is often a proxy for these parochial interests in African studies, since it provides a convenient basis for explaining why policy benefits are denied to some segment of society (Collier and Gunning 2008, 218–219). Such proxies are unnecessary with the carefully coded veto players used in this study, which make the same inferential point about redistribution: When policy making depends upon a large number of political actors capable of extracting payoffs, limiting those side payments is difficult and the result is an expensive policy logroll. This effect of an increase in the number of veto players is represented as follows:

Proposition 1(b): larger number of payoffs → incentives for collusion → policy logrolls increase overall levels of local collective goods

Both sets of outcomes depend on the assumption that transaction costs are low. Under these circumstances, actors will theoretically bargain to an efficient allocation of resources (Coase 1960). Low transaction costs explain why coordination in proposition 1(a) is relatively easy, and why veto players have weak incentives to hold each other accountable in proposition 1(b), which would limit the overall level narrow policy benefits. However, there are a variety of reasons to assume instead that interaction among veto players does generate transaction costs. For example, new institutional economics research demonstrates that exchanges between actors do generate transaction costs, meaning that enforcement and information are costly, and that Adam Smith's "invisible hand" of the free market exists only in the abstract (North 1990). Coalition bargaining theory also argues that transaction costs increase with the number of political actors, contributing to information uncertainties and the structural complexity of coordination (Lupia and Strøm 2008, 66–77). In sum, transaction costs increase the likelihood that neither cooperation to deliver national collective goods nor collusion for payoffs through the delivery of local collective goods is likely in regimes with the greatest number of veto players. Policy making thus entails constant trade-offs between the benefits of cooperation and the costs of transactions with more political actors (Cooter 2000).

This logic is expressed by the distributional tradition in the veto player literature: If political actors have the capacity to impose a veto on the policy process, then they also have the ability to hold other actors accountable. This means that an increase in the number of veto players should reduce opportunities for collusion to share narrow policy benefits (Haggard and McCubbins 2001). Additional veto players introduce new checks and balances (Andrews and Montinola 2004). This idea is already inherent in some of the commitment literature, which attributes credibility to checks on the arbitrary exercise of power (Keefer and Stasavage 2003). This means that different political actors with similar capacities to impose transaction costs possess incentives to monitor the behavior of others, rather than collude with them. This harkens back to Madison's foundational principle: "It is to be hoped, do the two governments possess each the means of preventing or correcting unconstitutional encroachments of the other" (Madison 2006c, 212). This idea associates veto players' political leverage with the capacity to generate accountability – much as the theory's philosophical roots intended. This new proposition about the effects of an increase in the number of veto players can be stated as

Proposition 2(a): increased transaction costs → more accountability → less logrolling of local collective goods

The corollary to this proposition suggests that delivering nationally oriented policies is actually less likely as the number of political actors increases. Additional veto players mean more preferences to accommodate and greater coordination problems because the opportunities for disagreement multiply. This can be stated as:

Proposition 2(b): increased transaction costs → less coordination → fewer national collective goods

Does an increase in the number of veto players facilitate the delivery of national collective goods through the logic represented in proposition 1(a)? Or does it lead to collusion and excessive payoffs through local collective goods represented in proposition 1(b)? If policy outcomes coincide with neither scenario, this would mean that regimes with more veto players are not necessarily better, and regimes with few veto players are not necessarily worse. Such outcomes would also validate intuitions about the effects of transaction costs on bargaining. Good government performance would therefore entail a difficult balancing act that constantly weighs the benefits of additional veto players with their drawbacks. I will characterize these difficult choices as a "Madisonian dilemma," since it evokes the necessity for both accountability and coordination.

The commitment and distributional traditions in the literature generate different predictions about how the number of veto players should impact the two broad categories of public policy used in this study. The next step is to translate the causal processes implied by each tradition into hypotheses that will be tested in the next chapter. The credible commitment tradition generates what I label a "coordination" hypothesis. It predicts that an increase in the number of veto players impedes the delivery of national collective goods – nonexcludable public policies. Confirmation of this hypothesis would mean that regimes with more veto players have more trouble reaching agreement for the reasons identified by the bargaining literature and new institutional economics. Rejection of this hypothesis would imply that these regimes do in fact bargain to efficient public policy outcomes, as envisioned by selectorate theory and research that assumes low transaction costs.

The distributional tradition generates what I label the "logroll" hypothesis. It predicts that an increase in the number of veto players will lead to excessive spending on local collective goods. Confirmation of this hypothesis would mean that each veto player uses its political leverage to demand excludable, targetable policies characteristic of patronage in Africa. Rejection of this hypothesis would imply that veto players in these regimes live up to Madison's expectations by holding each other accountable, whereby "ambition counters ambition." To test these hypotheses in Chapter 3, I will operationalize government performance with variables that reflect Nigerian government policy priorities and that clearly capture the conceptual distinctions between national and local collective goods. Statistical models also control for factors (such as oil revenue, democracy, economic conditions, and foreign debt) that could shape the political environment or offer alternative explanations for Nigeria's government performance over time. The tests validate Madison's core principles by showing that regimes with more veto players have the checks and balances he hoped for, as well as the potential for gridlock he worried about.

Conclusion

This chapter showed how veto player theory enables new modes of comparative analysis by liberating the "veto" from its American origins, while making the case that it has unpaid debts to Madison. Veto players are individual or collective actors whose agreement is needed to change the status quo, and I defined a regime as a set of veto players. I noted some disagreements within the literature about the importance of the internal cohesion of collective actors and the ideological differences among veto players. I then asserted that the key causal claims follow from the number of veto players, rather than these other traits. To set clear criteria for counting veto players in Nigeria, I said political actors must (1) have a motive for challenging policy based on distinct preferences; (2) have a mechanism for coordinating common interests and reducing information costs if the actor is collective; and (3) prevail on at least one major policy issue.

Applying these criteria, this study will identify 14 distinct veto player regimes in Nigeria between 1961 and 2007. They include institutional veto players such as legislatures and ruling military councils, whose authority is formally defined in the regime's rules, and partisan players such as political parties, whose leverage emerges from within such institutions. Some military factions count as veto players because they meet all of my criteria; like partisan veto players they operate as a cohesive and enduring set of preferences within an institution. I also claim that Nigeria's northern and southern regions, which constitute the broadest basis of identity and collective interest, can each enforce a regional veto under rare circumstances. This requires extensive coordination among subnational actors and occurs only when existing institutions have inadequately accommodated their interests. Nigeria's unity has entailed a geopolitical balancing act between the two regions ever since their amalgamation a century ago under British colonial rule, which ethnonationalists today sometimes refer to as "the mistake of 1914." While the concept of regional veto players potentially limits comparative applications of my model, it is based on a simple symmetry of political units that federalism research points out is not so unusual.

Since independence in 1960, dictators have governed Nigeria for a total of 29 years, and this could present obstacles to identifying veto players. Nigeria's longest serving dictator, General Yakubu Gowon, once remarked to me: "Oxford says one thing, Cambridge says that, but Sandhurst decides," implying that civilian policy makers are always trumped by what the officers (trained in Britain's military academy at Sandhurst) have to say. His government's record, explored in the following chapters, tells a more nuanced story in which political authority is not quite so arbitrary. Military rulers do attempt to dominate politics, but like his successors, Gowon understood that the use of force expends political capital and jeopardizes whatever legitimacy the government might possess. Counting veto players in dictatorships is challenging but within the realm of existing veto player theory, and doing so valuably contributes to an emerging literature on comparative authoritarianism in several ways. It challenges colloquial characterizations of dictators as all-powerful unitary rulers, offers an alternative to elaborate regime typologies, and helps clarify links between informal institutions and the policy process.

The final task of this chapter was to formulate predictions about how veto players should empirically impact government performance, drawing upon two different schools of thought in the theoretical literature. A distributional tradition suggests that a political actor with the ability to impose a veto also possesses the capacity to demand excludable benefits. As a result, an increase in the number of veto players either will improve the overall level of national collective goods as these political actors realize this is cheaper than each one of them receiving a payoff, or they will distribute such payments to each other through logrolls, increasing aggregate spending on local collective goods to levels characteristic of patronage. The first outcome reflects successful coordination among veto players. The second entails collusion, which I state as a logroll hypothesis. A credible commitment tradition in the literature anticipates a different pair of outcomes: Since transaction costs increase with the number of veto players, an increase in the number of veto players should actually limit logrolling of collective goods because veto players seek to hold each other accountable. The literatures on coalition bargaining and new institutional economics suggest that such regimes should also face greater coordination problems. If so, then an increase in the number of veto players should impede the delivery of national collective goods. I state this as a coordination hypothesis.

How does an increase in the number of veto players actually impact different types of public policy over time? After systematically coding Nigeria's veto players in Chapter 2, I empirically examine these questions in Chapter 3. Drawing on 50 years of government performance data gathered during extensive field research in Nigeria, I develop one set of variables that measure national collective goods with indivisible benefits and another set of variables to measure local collective goods with excludable and targetable benefits. Statistical tests show that an increase in number of veto players has two effects: First, the delivery of national collective goods declines, confirming my coordination hypothesis, and second, overall spending levels on local collective goods also declines, rejecting my logroll hypothesis. Taken together, these results imply that the conditions conducive to accountability simultaneously undermine coordination. I argue that this creates a Madisonian dilemma because governments must both provide national collective goods *and* limit logrolling manifest in excessive spending on local collective goods. Thus a major challenge for Nigeria and many African countries is how to achieve an appropriate balance between these different types of public policy outcomes.

2

Veto Players in Nigeria's Political History since Independence

In this chapter I trace Nigeria's history from independence in 1960 to the end of President Olusegun Obasanjo's second term in 2007. Drawing upon newspapers, books, interviews, and various primary sources, I identify the veto players in each regime by applying the criteria established in the previous chapter. These political actors may be individual or collective, institutional or partisan, and they sometimes operate in the realm of informal politics, but they are all political actors who could not be ignored during policy making. This analysis will familiarize readers with Nigeria's recent political past, but the underlying purpose is to code the independent variable to be used in empirical tests in Chapter 3.

The veto players identified in this chapter all meet three conditions: They have (1) a motive for challenging policy, (2) a mechanism for coordinating common interests and reducing information costs if they are collective, and (3) they prevailed on at least one major policy issue. These criteria set a high standard. To emphasize this point, I document several instances in which powerful military factions or regional coalitions attempted to exercise a veto but ultimately failed to do so. I pay special attention to this during treatment of authoritarian regimes since it is probably more difficult to persuade the reader that a veto player successfully challenged a dictator than it is to demonstrate that the dictator himself possessed a veto. This also separates mere disagreements from the successful exercise of a veto; the veto players literature is careful to differentiate between actors with distinct preferences from those with the actual ability to impose those preferences on others. This also means that veto players are more than just temporary coalitions that converge on a single issue: they constitute structural characteristics of the policy-making process. Each set of veto players in this chapter constitutes a different veto player regime. While "regime" commonly refers to whether a country is a dictatorship or a democracy, the term here thus invokes its more precise meaning in comparative politics referring to the allocation and limitation of public authority.

In order to identify Nigeria's veto players, I sift through debates over federal budgets, proposed regime transitions, and constitutional questions such as the creation of new states or the role of religion in governance. This focus necessarily means that many interesting and well-known political debates are neglected, but it also weaves a coherent narrative thread through Nigeria's numerous regimes. I chose these particular issues because their frequent recurrence over time enables me to apply my coding criteria consistently to similar policy questions, and they all have the potential to alter the overall allocation of political authority significantly. For example, if a regime with two veto players finds that it can no longer make decisions on federal spending without accommodating a third political actor, this new veto player signals that a fundamentally different regime has emerged (even if the same constitution or the same ruler is in place). This understanding of regimes also therefore assumes an element of transitivity: The *capacity* to impose a veto on one issue also exists with regard to others; it does not assume a motivation to do so. I mention this because it is important to clarify that the policy issues examined in the following in order to locate veto authority are different from the policy outcomes used in the next chapter to measure the dependent variable. This chapter is thus essential to understanding the institutional environment that shapes public policy outputs, but I am not yet providing an analysis of government performance in Nigeria. Chapter 3 will perform that task by statistically linking the number of veto players to the delivery of local and national collective goods, and then connecting particular regimes with outcomes on the dependent variable through a succinct qualitative analysis. Thus while Nigeria's economy does inform part of the analysis that follows, it does so in order to determine the structures of political authority manifest in Nigeria's veto player regimes. This approach is consistent with the veto player literature, which distinguishes between the preferences of political actors, and their actual ability to make policy demands.

Between 1960 and 2007, I examine these issues and apply the preceding coding criteria to identify 14 distinct regimes in Nigeria with between one and four veto players. Tables at the end of the chapter provide a complete list. While this might seem to be a small number, it is comparable to other veto player studies already cited. It may also be worth recalling that institutions very often end up mediating other interests, meaning that these actors are aggregations of interests. Nigeria's regimes over this period include democratic and military heads of state, three partisan veto players created by multiparty coalitions, five distinct factions within military regimes, and three regional vetoes. They also include institutional veto players such as the legislature and several ruling military councils. The simplest way to understand the importance of these different actors over time is to read what follows as a chronicle of policy processes that expand and contract on the basis of number of veto players. This recasts Nigerian politics as a struggle over inclusion and exclusion rather than merely over democracy and dictatorship, utilizing veto players as a novel means of conceptualizing the factors driving government performance.

Two Veto Players in the First Republic's First Government (1960–1964)

Among the 17 African countries that gained independence in 1960, Nigeria stood out for its large population, comparatively peaceful transition, and national ambitions. One authoritative study of the First Republic describes Nigeria as falling prey to a "conspiracy of optimism" (Diamond 1988). During this period, realism was brushed aside in favor of lofty aspirations and grand plans. Although the British had enacted a series of legal reforms in the 1950s designed to enfranchise Nigerians and turn authority over to "natives" gradually, Awolowo and the incoming national leadership inherited a country with very low literacy rates in the North, poor infrastructure in the East and other remote areas, and stark economic inequalities everywhere. The British left behind a Westminster-style parliamentary system and three strong regional governments, each dominated by one of the largest ethnic groups: the Yoruba in the West, the Igbo in the East, and the Hausa-Fulani in the North. Reflecting on the gradual unraveling during this hopeful period, a character in the hugely successful Nigerian novel *Half of a Yellow Sun* laments,

> The real tragedy of our postcolonial world is not that the majority of people had no say in whether or not they wanted this new world; rather it is that the majority have not been given the tools to *negotiate* this new world. (Adichie 2006, 129)

A shift from a unitary to a federal system left unresolved the question of how to represent hundreds of minorities beyond the three largest ethnic groups. Numerous studies document the political instability and ethnic violence that soon followed (Diamond 1988; Sklar 2002). Our task here is not to debate why the First Republic ultimately collapsed in 1966. Instead, it is to identify veto players by using the criteria established in the previous chapter and without doing injustice to the intricate details of Nigeria's complex history. The First Republic encompassed two distinct veto player regimes: The first featured two partisan veto players who governed through a coalition government in a Westminster system until parliamentary elections in December 1964. When the Northern People's Congress (NPC) emerged with an outright majority of parliamentary seats, a single veto player regime formed because it dropped its coalition partner. It did not last long.

The NPC, a regionally based party dominated by Hausa and Fulani elites in the North, emerged from the 1959 elections just short of the 157 seats it needed in the House of Representatives in order to form a majority government. The National Council of Nigeria and the Cameroons (NCNC), the largest party in the predominantly Igbo East, won 58 of the 73 parliamentary seats from the region. The Action Group (AG) won a slim majority of the seats in the western region dominated by the Yorubas (Federal Government of Nigeria 1960). These election results underscored the strong regional basis of the respective parties in Nigeria at the time: The NPC captured 134 of 174 available federal seats in the North and won no seat in the South. They also meant that no party could form a government without reaching across regional divides.

The NPC leadership indicated that it would accept opposition status if the NCNC and the AG, the two largest parties in the South, formed an alliance. But after some initial jockeying among all the parties, the NPC agreed to give the NCNC key portfolios such as finance and foreign affairs.[1] The result was a parliamentary coalition in which each party exercised a partisan veto and cemented an alliance between the North and the East. The government, led by NPC founder Prime Minister Abubakar Tafawa Balewa, consisted of 23 cabinet positions; 8 of those went to the NCNC (and several seats went to ministers with no party affiliation). The AG seemed to accept its opposition status as a natural consequence of the democratic process. AG's party leader wrote to the country's new figurehead president, Nnamdi Azikiwe, who was head of the NCNC, pledging to cooperate and respect political differences peacefully.[2]

[1] "Face-Lifting the NPC," *West Africa*, May 28, 1960.
[2] "Race Prejudice an Unfriendly Act," *The London Times*, November 17, 1960.

The NCNC and NPC differed on several major policy questions and the leaders had little in common now that the British were gone, but the coalition government operated under clear conditions of mutual dependence. Even after a row over radical rhetoric used by NCNC's foreign minister, calling for liberation from imperialism across the continent, prominent newspaper reports saw "no reason why the NPC-NCNC Coalition should not last until the elections in 1964."[3] The two parties colluded in parliament in 1963 to create a fourth region, the Midwest, with the intended effect of empowering minority groups in the western region and therefore undermining the AG's influence. This became clear even during the debates, when the outspoken N. A. Ezonbodor, an Ijaw member of parliament, called for the creation of a Rivers State within three years in exchange for supporting the Midwest – and then proceeded to threaten that the AG "not come into our area to confuse the people. My people are not cowards," he warned.[4] The following month, the coalition government rammed through a declaration of a State of Emergency. With no opportunity to read provisions, which the government said had already taken effect, Awolowo called the motion "the height of unfairness" in parliament. His colleague, Chief Enahoro, further protested, "What kind of country are we building when we seek powers to detain persons, to ask them to report, to restrict their movements?"[5] The AG lost the lopsided vote, and instability in the West would ultimately undermine the young democracy.

A split over foreign policy caused one of the first major rifts between the parties in the ruling coalition. The NCNC advocated nonalignment with the Western powers, a position that would have moved it closer to Pan-Africanists in Ghana and elsewhere who hoped to redraw the map of Africa, while the NPC called for neutrality. (The AG proposed openly supporting the West during the cold war.) In addition, the federal government accepted a loan from Israel, even though the NPC orchestrated a nonbinding resolution in the House opposing it, driving the ideological wedge deeper (Sklar 2004, 510). The NPC also lost a fight over the Anglo-Nigerian Defense Pact, which made formal arrangements for ongoing British military training of Nigerian soldiers (Otubanjo 1989).

---

[3] "Nigerian Foreign Minister Attacked," *West Africa*, December 2, 1961; "Minister from Idoma," *West Africa*, March 3, 1962.

[4] Parliamentary Debates, First Parliament (3rd Session), 1962–1963, House of Representatives, Vol. 2, April 17, 1962, pp. 1898–1902.

[5] Parliamentary Debates, First Parliament (3rd Session), 1962–1963, House of Representatives, Vol. 2, May 29, 1962, pp. 2212–2214.

The NPC and the NCNC needed each other to govern but increasing strains were apparent.

The NPC was more successful advancing its position on civil service reforms. When Nigeria won independence, Yorubas received a disproportionate share of positions within the bureaucracy for the simple reason that literacy rates were much higher in the West, where missionaries had been most active. This meant northerners were now at a distinct disadvantage in competing for civil service jobs. During the constitutional conference leading up to the transfer of power, northern leaders had obtained guarantees that "Nigerianization" of the civil service would essentially mean "northernization." Between 1960 and 1965, educational requirements were loosened, new scholarships and training opportunities for young northerners were established, and staff were transferred from the regional to the federal civil service. As a result, northerners disproportionately obtained new civil service jobs during the republic's early years. The NPC took steps to share the wealth with Igbos in the East to satisfy its coalition partner, the NCNC.

Discrimination by the coalition government against Yorubas in the West, however, contributed to an explosive split within the AG (Gboyega 1989, 173–175). Already engaged in a heated internal debate about the role of socialism in the party's platform, the AG finally splintered over the issue of whether its leader in the federal parliament had authority over the leader of the regional parliament. Among other things, this had implications for whether the AG would join the coalition cabinet at the federal level, if given the chance. The acrimonious feud climaxed when party leaders expelled the western regional government's premier, Chief Samuel Akintola, from the party in 1962.[6] Akintola responded by forming a splinter party that drew Yorubas away from the AG, the NCNC, and two other minor parties in the western regional government.[7]

The NPC seized this opportunity to undermine the AG further at the federal level. Conservative Hausa-Fulani elites protective of their new political power feared an alliance between the AG and some progressive populist parties in the North; NCNC anger simmered over criticism of its eastern members who wanted to remain aligned with the NPC. When the western regional parliament descended into violence, the two coalition

---

[6] "Action Group Split at Jos," *West Africa*, February 10, 1962; "Awolowo versus Akintola," *West Africa*, May 19, 1962; "Chief Akintola Dismissed," *West Africa*, May 26, 1962; Machet's Diary, *West Africa*, June 30, 1962.

[7] "New Party in W. Nigeria," *West Africa*, March 14, 1964.

partners colluded to declare a State of Emergency in the western region (Diamond 1988, 96–103). The federal government even jailed the leader of the AG opposition in parliament, Obafemi Awolowo, on subversion charges (Sklar 2002). A central plank of the AG platform had included the creation of new states within each region in order to represent ethnic minorities better and weaken the stranglehold of the three largest groups (Igbo, Yoruba, and Hausa-Fulani). "The reorganization was part of a vindictive campaign," writes Nigeria's leading scholar of federalism about the selective creation of a new region. It was waged by the coalition government "to destroy the base of the main federal opposition party" (Suberu 2000, 281).

But if their shared animosity toward the AG had created a détente between the NCNC and the NPC, the two veto players began growing apart over disagreements regarding the census count. Initial census figures released in 1962 showed implausibly large population gains in the North, suggesting that even more seats would be allocated in NPC strongholds in the upcoming elections. Another count, done in 1963, also gave the North a substantial edge. The NPC-affiliated prime minister insisted on the validity of these preliminary results, and the redistricting commission charged with redrawing parliamentary constituency boundaries opted to move forward, even though it conceded that the provisional figures were questionable and noted that the "situation rendered some areas for consideration as border line cases" (Constituency Delimitation Commission 1964). Foreseeing huge setbacks for easterners in the 1964 elections, the NCNC protested. The prime minister supposedly told the NCNC ministers to accept the results or resign, saying, "My acceptance and publications of the figures is final." He later denied making the comment, but the NPC national spokesperson sent the same message when he said, "The NPC will rule the Federation forever."[8]

Such comments set off alarm bells throughout the South. The fragile coalition suffered another blow when the NPC offered newly created cabinet positions to Akintola's splinter group, the Nigerian National Democratic Party (NNDP), instead of to the NCNC. Igbo leaders began complaining about discrimination, saying that northernization of the civil service had gone too far and invoking memories of historic ethnic violence against Igbos in the North. To build its case, the NCNC published a list of expensive development projects that benefited the North at the

---

[8] "The State of the Nigerian Parties," *West Africa*, January 25, 1964; "Census Result in Nigeria," *West Africa*, February 29, 1964.

expense of the eastern region (Diamond 1988, 142–143). In 1964, labor unions (which were sympathetic to the AG's democratic socialist tendencies) launched a general strike, protesting wage inequality, rising inflation, and elite corruption. The same year that the government, which employed 54 percent of all wage earners, was debilitated by the strike (Diamond 1988, 179–188), the NCNC premier of the eastern region reached out to the AG in order to build solidarity against the NPC.[9] Combined, these events laid the groundwork for a possible new political coalition based on class interests rather than ethnic alliances just as the country prepared for the upcoming elections.

Coalition Collapse and the First Republic under a Single Veto Player (1965)

This alternative alignment collapsed almost immediately. In the months leading up to the 1965 election, Nigerian politics became increasingly divided along regional lines (Dudley 1971). Abandoning the NCNC, the NPC campaigned with the NNDP under the banner of the Nigerian National Alliance (NNA). Meanwhile, the NCNC and AG formed the United Progressive Grand Alliance (UGPA), drawing progressive populists in the North into the fold alongside ethnic minority groups in the "middle belt," an area on the southern edge of the North that had been plagued by communal violence. As a gesture of solidarity, the NCNC demanded the release of Awolowo, the former AG party leader still jailed by the NPC. The southern parties based in the East, the West, and the Midwest stood united in their anger over the census, which created the possibility of permanent northern domination, as well as their support for the creation of additional regions to represent ethnic minority groups (Suberu 2001).[10]

But instead of distributing power more broadly, the 1964 federal elections consolidated power in the hands of a single veto player; in a surprise result, the NPC secured an outright majority with 162 House seats. This meant that with a moderate degree of cohesion, it could survive a parliamentary confidence challenge. Moreover, with the NPC's victories limited to the North, it could expect challenges from opponents in the South.

---

[9] "Dr. Okpara on the Move," *West Africa*, June 13, 1964.
[10] "Nigeria's Election Eve 1," *West Africa*, August 22, 1964. The term "states" replaced "regions" after 1967.

The NPC initially failed to include any NNDP politicians in the cabinet, offending its campaign partner, who had secured huge victories against the AG in the West, and surprising even NPC Prime Minister Balewa himself.[11] In April 1965, the NPC moderated its stance, announcing that 7 of the federal government's 32 cabinet positions would be held by NCNC ministers. He excluded the AG from the government, and the AG stated its continued loyalty to UPGA.[12] It soon became clear that NPC gestures to the South were insincere and that the party aimed to dominate national politics (Diamond 1988, 224; Osaghae 1989, 144).

When the NNDP swept regional elections in the West, the UPGA alleged fraud. The Federal Electoral Commission confirmed massive election fraud had occurred, sparking protests that paralyzed the West. The NNDP government responded with large-scale violent repression (Diamond 1988). Fanning the flames of frustration, new corruption charges surfaced as Nigeria's first attempt at democracy swiftly crumbled. Olusegun Obasanjo, who would later rule Nigeria as a military dictator and then an elected president, reflected, "It was the mishandling of the elections in the Western region, and the subsequent total breakdown of law and order which resulted in the complete insecurity of life and property, that was the last straw." Electoral politics had inspired "tribal bias" and regionalism, he said. "A rescue operation was thought to be desirable and necessary" (Obasanjo 2004, 78–79).

The Aguiyi-Ironsi Regime: A Dictator's Ambitions Checked by a Regional Veto (1966)

Neither the people nor the politicians could resist Obasanjo's logic. Chukwuma Nzeogwu, a promising young Igbo military officer, agreed. In January 1966, he led a group of mostly Igbo majors in a bloody coup attempt against the democratic regime. Nzeogwu's forces killed the prime minister while the figurehead president, Nnamdi Azikiwe, was overseas, sending the government into chaos. So dispirited and divided were regional leaders at this point that the UPGA in the East issued a statement after the coup had begun, saying this "will pass into the history of our great republic as the day when we first achieved true liberty." The

---

[11] "The Calm before the Storm?" *West Africa*, March 6, 1965; "The Last Interview," *West Africa*, January 29, 1966.

[12] "Nigeria's New Government," *West Africa*, April 10, 1965.

Zikist movement, a youth organization inspired by Azikiwe's nationalist philosophy, commented that "the widespread anarchy and disillusion of the masses made this revolution necessary" (Kapuscinski 2001, 103).[13] Even Yoruba chiefs in the West offered support, calling the coup an "act of God."[14] A new dictator, General Johnson Thomas Umunnakwe Aguiyi-Ironsi, quickly took over. But despite his best efforts to consolidate authority in a single veto, he faced countervailing power from a regional veto composed of northerners opposed to his constitutional restructuring.

Aguiyi-Ironsi negotiated his way to power after a meeting with the federal cabinet produced an "invitation" from the Senate president for the military to govern. Announcing that the Council of Ministers had willingly decided to hand over power to the military, the acting president acceded to martial rule (Achike 1980).[15] Aguiyi-Ironsi assured Nzeogwu's safety, then promptly betrayed him and threw him in prison (Ademoyega 1981).

In private letters he wrote to Obasanjo from prison, Nzeogwu disavowed having any ethnic agenda, but many observers understood the coup attempt in precisely those terms (Obasanjo 2004). An Igbo from the East, Aguiyi-Ironsi attempted to counteract that perception by extending a hand to the northern elites who had been ousted by the coup. He sought the advice and support of northern chiefs. The emir of Kano publicly mused that military rule might improve political stability, and the emir of Zaria urged citizens to support the new military rulers. In June, the sultan of Sokoto said that his "fears and anxieties" about Aguiyi-Ironsi had been allayed.[16]

These civilian endorsements enabled Aguiyi-Ironsi to try to solidify his status as a single veto player by fusing executive and legislative powers. In his infamous Decree Number 1, he claimed vast legislative authority for himself; any decree signed by the head of the federal military government would be considered law. He also created an ineffective Federal

---

[13] On the origins and meaning of Zikism, see Sklar (2004, 72–83).

[14] "Nigeria Settles Down," *West Africa*, February 5, 1966; "Nigeria's Critical Areas," *West Africa*, June 25, 1966.

[15] The 1963 Constitution made no provision for a temporary suspension of democracy, but subsequent military regimes seized upon the deal as a basis for legitimacy. The military successfully argued to the Supreme Court in the infamous *Lakanmi* (1970) case that the Gowon regime derived its authority from the civilian constitution (Ojo 1987, 124–126).

[16] "Report from Sokoto," *New Nigerian*, February 9, 1966; "Report from Kano," *New Nigerian*, March 4, 1966.

Executive Council (FEC) to manage the ministries and a Supreme Military Council (SMC) to act as the highest governing body. As it turned out, the SMC would attempt to challenge Aguiyi-Ironsi's single-veto-player status by opposing military promotions for his Igbo kinsmen and approving a trial for Nzeogwu, the leader of the failed coup (Muhammadu and Haruna 1979). The SMC also challenged Aguiyi-Ironsi on his handling of anti-Igbo riots in the North (Luckham 1971a), but the challenge was unsuccessful.

Instead, Aguiyi-Ironsi's ambitions were ultimately checked by a regional veto from the North. Several issues catalyzed northern resistance. First, Decree Number 1 undermined the federal balance that was widely understood as the basis for Nigeria's national unity. It eviscerated the authority of the regional governments and handed over all regional authority to the military governors. Aguiyi-Ironsi belittled the regions by referring to them as "areas" requiring governance from the center.[17] He humiliated senior regional officials from the First Republic by employing them as advisers to his military regime (Dent 1971). Second, northerners began to view the Aguiyi-Ironsi regime as ethnically biased when Yoruba and Hausa officers were excluded from military promotions. He tried to push through a set of civil service reforms to remove the Hausa language requirement, which had been imposed to ensure that northerners were proportionately represented in the federal bureaucracy (Dudley 1973). Because of the North's educational disadvantage this seemingly minor policy shift had huge implications for the civil service. Setting aside the class-based complaints prevalent in the North during the First Republic, the Hausa-Fulani began mobilizing and articulating grievances along broad regional lines (Kirk-Greene 1971).

Aguiyi-Ironsi's attack on the federal structure culminated in May 1966 when he tried to create a unitary state and drop the word "federal" from the government's name. In the face of this provocation, a powerful opposition movement arose in the North, made up largely of military officers, regional NPC elites, and bureaucrats. They managed to coordinate activities, fund visible protests, and successfully block civil service reforms (Dent 1971; Dudley 1973). Aguiyi-Ironsi lost the confidence of western elites when he imprisoned the Yoruba opposition leader of the ousted regional parliament. By June, Yoruba politicians were boycotting policy planning meetings (Dudley 1971). Asked when a transition from military

---

[17] "Nigeria Settles Down," *West Africa*, February 5, 1966; "Major-General Ironsi Appoints Three Study Groups," *New Nigerian*, March 2, 1966.

rule would take place, Aguiyi-Ironsi said, it "depends on how long it takes for life to return to normal."[18]

The regime lasted barely six months. The northern opposition had managed to block Aguiyi-Ironsi's civil service and constitutional reforms. Regime change soon followed in July 1966, when he was easily routed in a coup led by northern military officers looking to restore regional power. The conspirators quickly named General Yakubu Gowon head of the new military regime. Gowon restored federalism by creating new states, but it was too late. The East had already begun its descent into civil war.

Yakubu Gowon Contends with a Military Council Veto (1966–1975)

"The idea of a unitary system of governance was the major fear of all the regions at the time," said Gowon, reflecting years later on the pernicious regionalism that had taken hold in 1966.[19] In an effort to defuse the situation, he restructured the federal system, doing away with the regions and creating nine new states, for a total of twelve. This unfortunately failed to reassure the Igbos in the East, who launched a war of secession soon thereafter. Between June 1967 and January 1970, more than one million Nigerians died as a result of the civil war, many of starvation.

The Gowon regime survived this bloody war of secession and subsequently oversaw a period of political change and major economic transformation. Surging revenues from oil exports bankrolled a sweeping postwar reconstruction effort. Contentious debates over federalism, finance, and fealty to the nation of Nigeria continued to play out through two veto players, Gowon and a veto institutionally grounded in the Supreme Military Council (SMC) that often prevented Gowon from acting unilaterally. In fact, the SMC's consultative process significantly slowed decision making across the government, recalls one retired general.[20]

One group that fortified the SMC's capacity to challenge Gowon was the Federal Executive Council (FEC), made up of technocrats. Gaining power with little government experience, Gowon relied heavily on these senior bureaucrats to give policy advice and confer legitimacy. While the law formally stipulated that the FEC could only "exercise such functions as may be delegated to it by the Supreme Military Council,"[21] three

[18] "The First Weeks of Military Rule," *West Africa*, January 29, 1966.
[19] Interview with Yakubu Gowon, March 16, 2010. Abuja.
[20] Interview with General Josiah Laoye, March 13, 2010. Ibadan.
[21] Constitution (Suspension and Modification) Decree No. 8, 1967, Section 6.

conditions allowed senior FEC bureaucrats to acquire enormous sway over the policy-making process successfully. First, they used the FEC's institutional position to establish back channels between them and the SMC's permanent secretaries. And because the ministerial duties of the SMC and the FEC were not formally codified, these senior bureaucrats realized they could operate with considerable latitude concerning day-to-day activities (Luckham 1971a, 256). Second, the military regime explicitly banned political parties and politicians from the outset. Senior bureaucrats amassed power by filling the void, capitalizing in effect on the absence of a parliament (Asiodu 1979, 73–95). The cabinet met almost weekly, making decisions with the FEC according to a logic of collective responsibility. Third, the percentage of federal revenue from oil exports increased from single digits to more than 75 percent between 1966 and 1975, adding to the bureaucrats' influence; the military commanders relied on economists and accountants to manage the new financial issues and the ministries suddenly commanded huge budgets. Even without explicit legal or political authority, senior bureaucrats began attending meetings of the FEC alongside the ministers. This created a "military–civil service coalition government" (Olugbemi 1979). Certain so-called super-permanent secretaries, bureaucratic advisers to the ministers, were able to overturn key Gowon administration decisions, such as the appointment of an oil minister (Othman 1989, 122). Olusegun Obasanjo, who later ruled as dictator from 1976 to 1979, commented that "what [the civil service] ordained and what they wished would happen in most cases, no matter the pronouncement or desire of government."[22]

Another factor that fortified the SMC's effective check on Gowon's power was the state governors. It was clear from the start that the military governors felt little pressure to kowtow to Gowon. Unlike later military ruling councils, they in fact sat on the SMC. An Igbo governor from the East boycotted the SMC's maiden meeting, declaring, "Gowon is not my superior and the question of acknowledging him does not arise."[23] The Yorubas also successfully rebuffed Gowon during his campaign to expand the number of states. Fearing a reduction of western political influence at the national level, they rejected his proposed boundaries for Lagos and Ogun states.[24] And Gowon was ultimately forced to bow to northern demands regarding a flawed 1973 census. A charged political

[22] Cited in Adamolekun (1987), p. 366.
[23] "Military Governors to Meet Soon," *West Africa*, October 15, 1966.
[24] Interview with Yakubu Gowon, March 16, 2010, Abuja.

issue since the First Republic, the census became even more sensitive with the increase of oil revenues because the windfall was distributed by the federal government largely on the basis of demographic data (Adebayo 1993). Northern military governors had rigged the 1973 census in their favor and forced Gowon to publish the flawed results (Suberu 2001, 150–154).

The power of the governors emerged as a major grievance among northern traditional rulers, whom Gowon consulted infrequently and who resented having inexperienced young officers appointed to positions of authority (Vaughan 2000, 126–127).[25] The purchase and sale of chieftaincy titles had cheapened traditional authority; possibly as many as 90 percent of those holding titles in the 1980s had bought them during the Gowon regime.[26] Gowon's principal rival, Murtala Mohammed, who had played a key role in putting Gowon in power, also complained about the governors' usual level of influence (Othman 1989, 113–144). By 1974, the governors were publicly discredited, but the SMC was incapable of removing this large bloc of votes from its membership; since the abolition of federalism preceded the civil war, states' rights remained a highly sensitive issue. Amid widespread charges of corruption in 1970, Gowon was able to dismiss only one governor.[27] Through their positions on the SMC, the other governors thwarted his ability to make reappointments. Over the course of his nearly eight years in office, he successfully dismissed only two governors despite several other attempts.[28]

During his final months in office, Gowon had trouble advancing his policy agenda and made a series of strategic political errors. In October 1974, he reneged on a promise to lift the ban on politics, greatly damaging the government's credibility and agitating civilian politicians who had been planning to occupy new positions. Then in 1975 he pulled the plug on plans that had been under way for four years to transition to democracy. "It would indeed amount to a betrayal of trust to adhere rigidly to that target date," he said, declaring that the general ban on politics would continue indefinitely. He restated the message in February 1975, complaining that the public should not "keep on talking about 1976," which had been the expected transfer date. These comments drew fire

[25] "Nigeria: A Pride of Governors," *Africa Confidential*, July 18, 1975.
[26] "Men of the People or Relics of the Past?" *Concord Weekly*, August 24, 1984.
[27] "New Governor for West," *Nigerian Tribune*, December 28, 1970; "Who's Who in the West," *West Africa*, November 19, 1971.
[28] "Gowon will Reshuffle Governors," *West Africa*, May 26, 1975.

from his ministers.[29] Gowon tried to buy support from those in favor of a transition by swiftly replacing the military ministers with civilians.[30] But this failed to placate political elites who were supportive of a democratic transition and who felt that Gowon had become inaccessible and self-centered.[31]

Gowon feared that civilian politicians, like the former AG leader Obafemi Awolowo, were simply trying to get their hands on oil revenues that were booming in the wake of the 1973 Arab-Israeli War and believed they were stirring up the same ethnonationalism that had caused the civil war. Behind the scenes in the SMC, Gowon argued that completing implementation of the five-year national development plan before turning over power would offer the best chance for peace by creating incentives for politicians to protect Nigeria's prosperity. "I had to review my claim that we will return the country to civilian rule in 1976, and I said it is more important to see the economic take-off do well," Gowon explained in an interview in 2010. That way, he said, "It will not matter who comes into power: military, civilian, or whoever."[32]

Mohammed/Obasanjo: Three Veto Players and an Unexpected Succession (1975–1979)

Gowon did not get the opportunity to transfer power at all. On July 29, 1975, a group of generals staged another coup and swiftly installed a new regime, naming Murtala Mohammed the head of state. They made a clean break from the Gowon regime, dismissing all the governors and firing eleven thousand civil servants en masse. "They castrated all the civil servants and those who were able to give you honest advice," said Gowon of his successors.[33] Secret cables from the U.S. Embassy in Nigeria described Mohammed as an "impetuous, ruthless man indelibly identified with the Nigerian north."[34]

---

[29] "Gowon Wants Peace Not Politics," *West Africa*, February 11, 1975; "Army Will Stay after 1976," *West Africa*, October 7, 1974.

[30] "19-Man Federal Cabinet Named," *Nigerian Tribune*, January 25, 1975; "Gowon Picks His Men," *West Africa*, February 3, 1975.

[31] "Mohammed Speaks to the Nation," *West Africa*, August 4, 1975.

[32] Interview with Yakubu Gowon, March 16, 2010, Abuja.

[33] Interview with Yakubu Gowon, March 16, 2010, Abuja.

[34] Cable from U.S. Embassy Lagos to Secretary of State, "Nigeria's New Leaders," July 30, 1975 (declassified 2006); Cable from U.S. Embassy Lagos to Secretary of State, "Appraisal of Mohammed's July 30 and 31 TV Appearances," August 1, 1975 (declassified 2006).

Indeed, the new regime again remade the political order. Between 1975 and the transition to democracy in 1979, vetoes were held by the head of state, the chief of staff of supreme headquarters, and the Supreme Military Council. Presciently, the regime established succession rules within the SMC in the event that the head of state be overthrown or killed (Ojo 1987). Barely six months into the new regime, a group of officers angry about biased military promotions killed Mohammed in a failed 1976 coup attempt. The regime's succession rules were implemented and its policy-making structures survived intact. According to firsthand accounts of an emergency SMC meeting after Mohammed's murder, Obasanjo, who had barely escaped death in the coup attempt, adamantly refused to take over as head of state. A top air force official agreed, insisting that the office should remain with the North, even though northerners were to blame for the bloody coup attempt. But pushing the Obasanjo candidacy, Army Chief of Staff T. Y. Danjuma argued that the country needed someone with "the full support of the whole council" and resolved the impasse by proposing that a powerful northerner be appointed alongside him to provide checks and balances. The SMC elected Obasanjo head of state and Shehu Musa Yar'Adua the new chief of staff of supreme headquarters, a position with considerable responsibility over the military and major policy questions (Farris and Bomoi 2004, 122–123).

Obasanjo retained all the same members of government, declaring, "All policies of the Federal Military Government continue as before."[35] This included formation of a National Council of States that nominally represented, but effectively weakened, the governors. Mohammed and Obasanjo had hoped that positioning this council between the FEC and the SMC would undermine the technocrats who had grown powerful under Gowon. The Council of States' authority was contingent upon SMC approval and supervision (Othman 1989; Ojo 1987). The government also excluded senior bureaucrats from the SMC, ending the mechanism through which the technocrats had previously coordinated and gained access to the higher-ups in government. The regime had learned from Gowon's mistakes and worked to prevent challenges from the state level as well. When the government decreed the creation of seven new states, it successfully resisted complaints originating from eastern Igbos and even from northerners in Kaduna. Obasanjo fired state government officials who disagreed with his efforts, and the SMC shut down constitutional reformers agitating for four additional states. In contrast to

---

[35] "No Policy Change in Nigeria," *West Africa*, February 23, 1976.

his predecessors, there is evidence that Obasanjo actually wanted the democratic transition to succeed. The government departed surprisingly little from Mohammed's initial timetable, allowed Gowon to return safely to the country after the coup, and lifted a twelve-year ban on politics.

Yar'Adua balanced the interests of northerners against Obasanjo's powerful southern allies, who controlled much of the private sector. He guided key elements of the transition, including an inclusive public discussion about the new constitution. Yar'Adua was backed by the Kaduna Mafia, a powerful northern group of elites made up of educated northern technocrats, military officers, and politicians who were increasingly impatient with the conservatism of the Muslim emirates. A tight knit and secretive group, the Kaduna Mafia rose to power outside traditional channels (Olukoshi 1995). Northerners threatened to derail the entire constitutional reform process until they were assured that a core demand would be met: the incorporation into the constitution of a judicial appeals process that followed Islamic law. Obasanjo, a southern Christian, attempted unsuccessfully to veto these reforms (Falola and Heaton 2008; Laitin 1982), having become "something of a 'hostage' head of state whose degree of freedom was limited" (Osaghae 1998, 89). He made some changes to the draft constitution, but, according to a key senator in the National Assembly leadership after the transition, Obasanjo's contributions were not very substantial. The SMC deliberated on the major changes to the final draft of the constitution (Gboyega 1979).

With his strong base of regional support, Yar'Adua guided SMC initiatives on local government reform that led to the election of new local government councils.[36] These reforms served to exclude traditional leaders from a range of local governance matters and limited their control over property rights (Vaughan 2000; Oyediran and Gboyega 1979). The effort raised Yar'Adua's profile and added to his power within the regime. He assumed key roles in the day-to-day operations of government, including leading a massive macroeconomic effort to boost food production and supporting foreign policies to fund African resistance movements engaged in guerrilla warfare against apartheid South Africa's cold war allies (Farris and Bomoi 2004, 126–137).

---

[36] "The General's Vision of Nigeria," *West Africa*, November 1, 1976; "The Brigadier and the Guidelines," *West Africa*, November 1, 1976; "Nigeria: A Transitional Regime?" *Africa Confidential*, September 26, 1975.

Partisan and Presidential Veto Players during the Second Republic (1979–1981)

True to its word, the Obasanjo government oversaw a transition to a democracy in October 1979. But no sooner had the ballots been counted than storm clouds gathered over Nigeria's Second Republic. While the new constitution adopted a presidential system modeled after the United States', Article 126 included the provision that a presidential candidate had to satisfy two criteria in order to claim victory: He had to win a plurality of the vote nationwide and 25 percent of the vote in at least two-thirds of the states. No candidate emerged from the election satisfying both of these criteria. Moreover, the constitution included neither a clear contingency plan nor a short-term strategy for governing in the interim.

After 13 years of military rule the country was on edge. In a controversial decision, the Supreme Court interpreted "two-thirds" of the country's 19 states to mean 12 2/3, rather than 13 (Falola and Ihonvbere 1985, 69–73). The decision made Shehu Shagari president, thereby returning executive power to a northerner once again, relegating Awolowo and other Yoruba politicians to their familiar place in the opposition.

While the structure of the constitution suggested three institutional veto players would emerge (president, Senate, and House of Representatives), the electoral dispute left Shagari with a fragile popular mandate, compounded by the fact that his National Party of Nigeria (NPN) lacked a majority in either chamber of the National Assembly. The NPN, like its cousin, the NPC in the First Republic, also failed to unify the North in the face of intraregional ethnic tensions and turmoil over the proper role of traditional rulers in the modern Nigerian state (Omoruyi 1989, 199–200). Lacking a legislative majority, the NPN opted to form a coalition with the Nigerian People's Party (NPP), a splinter party that attracted support in the Middle Belt states on the edge of the North, and among Igbos in the East. The result was government with two partisan veto players who maintained sufficient – if short lived – party discipline to challenge the president on the federal budget and other major policy issues.

NPP participation restored a southern (and largely eastern Igbo) voice to power, inviting comparisons to the coalition government of the First Republic. In the House, the coalition consisted of 168 NPN and 78 NPP members, totaling 246 of 450 seats. In the Senate, the agreement brought together 36 NPN and 16 NPP senators, for a total of 52 of 95 seats. Published details of the accord were vague, but the Senate president later said that the agreement involved specific quid pro quos: The NPP received ten leadership positions, including the House speakership, the deputy Senate presidency, and numerous cabinet positions.[37] Rules were put in place to "zone" the top offices, meaning different geopolitical regions would have control over important portfolios. The public purpose was to foster interethnic collaboration, but zoning also served as a way to share the national riches popularly known as the "national cake" (Joseph 1987, 138–150). After the 1970s oil boom, the cake had in fact grown substantially.

The NPN-NPP coalition was productive at first, suggesting that party discipline was sufficient to keep veto power within the parties rather than in the institutions of the House and Senate. Between October 1979 and July 1980, the Senate passed seventeen bills and ninety-two motions, including important legislation such as the 1980 appropriations bill. Interestingly, all of the bills that passed were introduced by the president, suggesting a high degree of cooperation between President Shagari and the National Assembly leadership. When the opposition parties brought a motion to deny the president's supplemental appropriations bill in 1980, only five members of the NPN-NPP coalition voted with the opposition.[38] NPN and NPP leaders even conspired together (with the speaker of the House) to try to circumvent the rules governing consideration of appropriations bills (Babatope 2001, 60–61). Clearly, the parties had firm control of the agenda and the internal cohesion required of partisan veto players.[39]

The NPN-NPP coalition began to show signs of strain later that year. The NPN was dismayed by the fact that all five senators who had voted with the opposition on the supplemental bill were NPP members and that the opposition's motion on the bill passed by a single vote. For its part, the NPP was irked by revelations that the NPN had secretly agreed to more than doubling the amount being funneled into a contingency fund to pay off military debts to the states.[40] Igbos in the NPP were furious about the president's choice of cabinet nominees from the East – politicians who were derided by their brethren for lacking credibility at the grassroots level. Igbo elites noted the slight, pointing out the NPP had carried

[37] "Details of the Proposed NPN/PRP Accord," *Daily Sketch*, February 23, 1981.
[38] "Senate Proceedings," *Daily Times*, April 1, 1980.
[39] "House of Reps Proceedings," *Daily Times*, March 18, 1980; "Senate Passes 17 Bills," *Daily Sketch*, July 24, 1980.
[40] Amma Ogan, "The Picture as Senate Goes on Easter Recess," *Daily Times*, March 31, 1980.

the two largest Igbo states by overwhelming margins in the House and Senate elections.

The underlying problem, as scholars have pointed out, was that nothing "tied the president to the party or the winning coalition after the election since he could act independently in the choice of his cabinet and in the performance of his activities once elected" (Omoruyi 1989, 217). Comparatively speaking, multiparty legislative coalitions occur about 40 percent of the time in presidential political systems.[41] But the separate sovereignty of legislative and executive elections weakens incentives for party discipline. In the absence of a confidence relationship between the cabinet and the legislature, politicians have few reasons to remain loyal to the coalition after an election (Shugart and Carey 1992; Oyugi 2006).

In January 1981, NPP members voted against an NPN proposal to reform the country's revenue allocation system. To retaliate, the NPN refused to ratify ambassadorial nominees and rejected a number of other NPP-proposed political appointees (Joseph 1987; Falola and Ihonvbere 1985). The chairman of the NPP accused NPN members of "bare-faced rape" of the coalition agreement. The NPN retorted that the NPP had been "an unfaithful wife" in politics.[42] The assignment of "presidential liaison officers" (PLOs) to the National Assembly further contributed to tension within the coalition. Since the NPN controlled the presidency, the NPP (and many of the opposition party politicians) saw the officers as spies. Harsh political attacks by the NPN-dominated legislature in Kaduna State against Governor Balarable Musa finally doomed the national coalition. Musa belonged to the radical People's Redemption Party (PRP), which enjoyed widespread support among Hausa commoners in the North. These *talakawa*, as they were known in Hausa, posed a challenge to the conservative authority of the emirate and were seen as a threat to elites within the NPN. The NPN formed a secret committee spearheaded by the Senate president to support Musa's impeachment. Whether they were aware of the conspiracy or not, the opposition parties seized the opportunity to attack the NPN. Meanwhile, progressives in the NPP were furious with the NPN's reactionary opposition to Governor Musa's moderate socialism.

---

[41] If no party secures a majority, coalitions are actually slightly *more* likely under presidential than parliamentary systems (Cheibub 2007).

[42] Femi Johnson, "NPP Ready for Divorce," *Daily Sketch*, January 27, 1981; "Break NPN/NPP Accord Now," *Daily Sketch*, February 2, 1981.

The tension between the parties reached a climax in July, when the NPP announced it would withdraw from the coalition in six months. Azikiwe, the aging nationalist from the First Republic now preparing to run for the presidency, gambled that the threat would extract additional concessions from the NPN and thereby strengthen the Igbos' position vis-à-vis the Yoruba (Omoruyi 1989, 205–206). Four NPP cabinet ministers resigned, alleging undue presidential pressure. But the NPP strategy backfired when the NPN called its partner's bluff and demanded immediate termination of the coalition.[43] The collapse heightened tensions between Nigeria's northern and southern regions to such an extent that the U.S. vice president, George H. W. Bush, flew to Nigeria to meet with the Senate leadership to urge them to support a strong president in order to preserve national unity.[44] The country held together, but democracy was in doubt.

Three Institutional Veto Players and the Second Republic's Swift Decline (1982–1983)

After the collapse of the NPN-NPP coalition, the number of veto players remained the same (three) but shifted from partisan to institutional vetoes grounded in the House and Senate; the presidency similarly retained its veto. When the NPN and NPP had enough internal cohesion to function as partisan veto players, policy preferences sometimes transcended institutional (and regional) cleavages. But without that cohesion, a realignment of authority occurred along institutional lines.

The wedge between the executive and legislature, already palpable from the PLO scandal, grew wider. One-third of all bills now originated from within the House or Senate (Babatope 2001, 83), and the legislature felt emboldened to defeat the president's supplemental appropriation bill in 1982. The Senate specifically objected to efforts by the executive to allow states to make foreign loans without the approval of the legislature.[45] While the assembly had delegated emergency authority to the president in the event of an economic crisis, such as a debilitating labor strike, lawmakers objected when the president deemed it unnecessary to ask for renewal of this authority after it expired. As one legislator recalls, when the president finally showed up, he was accompanied by fifty-five staff

---

[43] "Four Ministers Resign," *West Africa*, July 27, 1981.
[44] Interview with a former senator, May 29, 2004, Abuja.
[45] John Uyakonwu, "Senate Says 'No' to Shagari," *The Punch*, October 22, 1982.

members, "defiled parliamentary privileges, disregarded rules of procedure of the House, and violated protocol" (Babatope 2001, 80).

The end of the coalition also sparked a revival of the pernicious regionalism that had undermined Nigeria's first attempt at democracy in the 1960s. In the 1979 elections, the NPN had outperformed the other parties in two important southern states, Rivers and Cross Rivers, winning governorships and large shares of the vote in the legislative and presidential elections. Thus, unlike the NPC in 1959 or 1964, the NPN had some claim to national support, just as the connected plurality provisions in the electoral system intended. But when the NPP defected from the coalition, it explicitly aligned itself with the opposition parties, the main one being the United Party of Nigeria (UPN), led by the aging nationalist, Awolowo. The UPN was dominant in the Southwest, where it held all four governorships, all 24 of the seats representing the predominantly Yoruba states in the National Assembly, and 71 of the 85 seats in the House of Representatives. The defection of the NPP, along with the UPN's consolidation of the power in the West, planted the seeds of familiar regionalist tendencies.

The NPN secured majorities in the National Assembly during the 1983 election, winning 264 of 450 House Seats and 61 of 95 Senate seats. This removed any impetus the NPN had to find a coalition partner, and the results therefore ignited generalized fear that a government based in the North would discriminate and dominate. The election also diminished hopes that the national parties would serve as instruments of interethnic cooperation across regions. Quite the opposite occurred. The NPN consolidated its support in the North, capturing thirteen governorships (out of nineteen states), while the Southwest remained almost completely dominated by the UPN. The elections in the House of Representatives were so acrimonious that results from Ondo and Oyo States were never finalized, and defeated candidates immediately overwhelmed the courts with complaints.

The NPN had to cope with internal tensions between the Kaduna Mafia and other organized interests that supported President Shagari, but the main leaders of the party cohered around a conservative ideology that included plans to extend sharia from the regional to the federal level, declare Azikiwe (the Igbo politician) ineligible for the presidency because of his role in the First Republic, and restore a majoritarian parliamentary system that the NPN could dominate. Party leaders went so far as to question the autonomy of the ten northern states created in 1976 openly (Omoruyi 1989, 201–203). Electoral violence soon followed in late 1983 and Nigeria's second democratic experiment collapsed in December.

A Veto from Buhari, a Veto from Idiagbon (1984–1985)

Brigadier Sani Abacha (who would take over a decade later) announced the overthrow of Nigeria's Second Republic. Outlining the reasons for the coup on behalf of the new federal military government, he said, "Our economy has been hopelessly mismanaged," leading to increased debt and high food prices. "Health services are in shambles," and "our educational system is deteriorating at an alarming rate." The new head of state, General Muhammadu Buhari, promised to save the nation from "imminent collapse" (Akinnola 2000, 66–67). At the time, the coup was welcomed with widespread public support. The *National Concord* wrote, "At no other time in the history of the country had corruption been so deep-seated and widespread," calling the coup "the verdict of the people." Another newspaper, *The Guardian,* noted, "Nigerians had had enough." And *The Punch* called the coup "a welcome change notwithstanding the excruciating experience" with previous military regimes (Akinnola 2000, 71–72). Any relief the citizens of Nigeria felt was short lived, as the country began a sixteen-year stretch of authoritarianism.

The new regime governed via two veto players, Head of State Muhammadu Buhari and his deputy, Tunde Idiagbon, while repeated efforts by Army Chief of Staff Ibrahim Babangida to influence debates on neoliberal economic reform and other issues failed, thus preventing a third veto from emerging. The political structures formally resembled the Mohammed/Obasanjo regime in several ways. First, Buhari's founding proclamation, Decree Number 1, stipulated a similar governing structure. But Buhari's executive authority formally required consultation with the Supreme Military Council (Ojo 1987). The SMC was "the final arbiter on all the national issues" with the power to "overrule any decision or action of any individual or institution."[46] Second, the regime substantially weakened the powers of the governors, starting with the arrest of fifteen civilian governors (and four hundred other politicians) after the coup.[47] The Council of State played an entirely consultative role and, in a new encroachment on subnational authority, the SMC actually

[46] "Military Rule in Nigeria Part 1: Building a New Framework," *West Africa*, March 26, 1984.
[47] "400 Detained," *The Punch*, January 20, 1984.

dictated the composition of the ministries within the states.[48] Third, just as Mohammed had done in 1975, the new government swiftly moved to undermine senior bureaucrats (Oyediran 1979). It dismissed seventeen permanent secretaries and reduced the number of federal ministries from twenty-six to eighteen. Tens of thousands of federal and state civil servants went with them. All of this occurred on the heels of mass firings of virtually all of the senior police commissioners and inspectors. In a gambit for public legitimacy, eleven of the eighteen new ministers were civilians.[49]

Despite these formal resemblances to the three-veto-player regime of 1975–1979, the new policy-making apparatus cohered around only two veto players. Buhari served as the head of state and commander in chief. He boasted some Fulani heritage and enjoyed political backing of the Kaduna Mafia, but he had contradictory relationships with northern leaders. For example, he expressed support for Islamic law but traditional rulers could not agree on how to implement sharia. A campaign for pannorthern solidarity orchestrated by the governors flopped (Othman 1989, 137). He was unable to pacify Islamic radicals in Yobe State, and when tensions boiled over, riots there caused five thousand deaths (Ibrahim 1997, 427–447).[50]

Fractionalization in the North notwithstanding, the Buhari regime was still perceived as operating with northern bias, in no small part because a large majority of SMC members were northerners (Ikoku 1985).[51] The regime enforced the mandatory retirement of 185 senior ranking army officers, the majority of whom were southwestern Yorubas and only 10 of whom were northern Hausas.[52] Anticorruption prosecutions under Buhari also smacked of selective enforcement; northern governors from Kaduna and Sokoto were acquitted and former president Shehu Shagari received a mild house arrest (Kukah 2003, 166–170). By contrast, Shagari's former vice president from the South languished in jail. Prosecution of members of now-banned opposition parties also fell more

---

[48] Taiwo Okutubo, "SMC Drops Netimah as Rivers Governor," *Daily Times*, January 10, 1984; "19 Governors Named," *Daily Times*, January 4, 1984; "Rivers Governor Charged," *West Africa*, January 16, 1984.

[49] "17 Federal Permsecs Retired," *Daily Times*, January 27, 1984; "Axe Falls on 34 Police Chiefs," *Daily Times*, January 25, 1984; Sola Oyeneyin, "SMC Names Ministers," *The Punch*, January 18, 1984.

[50] "Maitatsine et al.: Undercurrents in the North," *Africa Confidential*, March 14, 1984.

[51] Banji Adeyanju, "The 'Federal Character' Serenade," *Concord Weekly*, January 28, 1985.

[52] "The Fallen Officers," *Africa Confidential*, January 30, 1985.

heavily on southern-based figures from the United Party of Nigeria and the Nigerian People's Party. All of this fueled perceptions that NPN elites were cozy with the SMC (Osaghae 1998).[53]

Buhari's chief of staff, Idiagbon, gave regional balance to this complex political equation. Though he was hardly a southern partisan, his official biography lists him as Yoruba and he claimed a blood relationship to the emir of Ilorin, a southwestern city historically and culturally linked to Muslim Yorubas (Ikoku 1985).[54] It was separated from the heart of contemporary Yorubaland only by political boundaries inherited from the colonial era, which aimed to weaken the saliency of religious cleavages in the area (Laitin 1986, 156–158). The Yoruba had fallen just short of capturing the presidency in 1979 and again in 1983, so a second in command from the Southwest provided a measure of legitimacy in the eyes of this wary region.

In substantive terms, Idiagbon managed the regime's most significant and controversial policy initiative: the War on Indiscipline (WAI). The purpose of WAI was supposedly to root out corruption, but it relied on extrajudicial means that were easily manipulated to suit political interests (Diamond, Oyediran, and Kirk-Greene and others 1997). Idiagbon also managed the new internal security apparatus, the National Security Organization (NSO), which the population and senior officials alike soon dreaded (Othman 1989, 113–144). Significantly, Buhari tried but failed to limit the NSO's reach. It is possible that Buhari did not put his full effort behind curtailing the NSO because he feared it might strengthen his and Idiagbon's mutual rival, Army Chief of Staff General Ibrahim Babangida, whom the coup plotters had only narrowly rejected to lead the state. The NSO was also useful because it helped keep the government informed.[55]

At the subnational level, Buhari made some attempts to co-opt governors and traditional rulers. He publicly reached out to the sultan of Sokoto in the Northwest and chiefs from Benue State and pushed reforms that granted traditional rulers expanded powers over local government policy, referring to them as "an informal second tier of authority"

---

[53] Onyema Ugochukwu, "A Parade of Gubernatorial Convicts," *West Africa*, July 2, 1984; "Nigeria: Alienation," *Africa Confidential*, June 6, 1984; "Nigeria: Balancing Act," *Africa Confidential*, October 31, 1984.

[54] "Nigeria: The Inevitable," January 4, 1984; "Nigeria: The General's Grip," *Africa Confidential*, January 30, 1985.

[55] "Nigeria: Deadly Serious," *Africa Confidential*, March 14, 1984; "Nigeria: The General's Grip," *Africa Confidential*, January 30, 1985.

(Vaughan 2000, 195). But there is evidence that the regime also worked to marginalize the traditional rulers, contributing to tension between the center and the states. When a group of chiefs offered to cooperate with the military and requested a monthly stipend in return, Buhari's military governors rebuffed their request. Buhari dethroned several *obas* (traditional rulers) in Yorubaland in the Southwest. In the North, when Kano State's military governor then asked the local emir to resign, protesters seized the symbols of government and killed the governor's top adviser.[56] The administration also punished the emir for traveling to Israel with the *oni* of Ife, a high Yoruba chief. Chiefs resented the fact that many governors were not indigenes of their appointed states and saw the governors as loyal to the center rather than the state. The Niger State governor exposed his disdain for traditional rulers when he said, mockingly, that they should live in "mud huts."[57] The reality was that the states ran massive deficits and were dependent on the central leadership to provide public benefits. When a few states tried to impose additional taxes to raise revenue, they faced massive rebellion.[58] Buhari looked away as the governors were left to bear the political costs of this increased taxation.

Amid unpopular budget cuts, support for the regime waned quickly. General Babangida had unsuccessfully opposed nearly every major government initiative, including the treatment of the detained politicians, industrialization plans, and a deflationary monetary policy without neoliberal reforms (Othman 1989).[59] Deprived of a veto within the regime, his faction set out to mold a new regime entirely, which turned out not to be very difficult after twenty months of mounting frustrations at the elite and popular levels. Babangida thus found it easy to recruit support for a coup and pledged a speedy transition to democracy – a promise the Nigerian people had heard before.

A Triumvirate of Veto Players during Babangida's Early Years (1985–1990)

Shortly after the August 1985 coup, Babangida released hundreds of political prisoners, annulled unpopular and repressive decrees, and embarked

---

[56] "The Uncertain Reign of Traditional Rulers," *Concord Weekly*, August 24, 1984.
[57] "Nigeria: Deadly Serious," *Africa Confidential*, March 14, 1984; "Nigeria: The General's Grip," *Africa Confidential*, January 30, 1985; "Nigeria: Shadows of the Mafia," *Africa Confidential*, February 1984.
[58] Dare Babarinsa, "Averting Battle of the Goats," *Newswatch*, March 18, 1985.
[59] "IMF Should Review Loan Terms – Buhari," *Daily Times*, January 25, 1984.

on the economic liberalization that his predecessor had avoided. Babangida used his criticism of the unpopular War on Indiscipline to signal how his policies would differ from Buhari's and to increase his government's credibility with the populace (Olanrewaju 1992). A special panel of judges reviewed more than a thousand pending cases, releasing most of the detained politicians and referring the rest to the judiciary (Federal Military Government 1986). The government pardoned prominent newspaper editors and others detained under Buhari's decrees and legalized large civil society organizations such as the National Medical Association and the National Association of Nigerian Students.[60]

Between 1986 and 1989, Nigeria was ruled by a triumvirate of veto players: Babangida and key northern allies, the collective Armed Forces Ruling Council (AFRC), and a faction of regime soft-liners. Other factions rooted in the bureaucracy asserted themselves but ultimately failed to exercise a veto. Departing from previous regimes, Decree Number 17 endowed Babangida with the exclusive authority to hire or fire his top deputy, and he engaged in frequent cabinet shuffles. When he welcomed the new national council of ministers, he emphasized the contingent nature of the cabinet's authority, explaining, "I shall not hesitate to remove from office any of you found wanting on grounds of incompetence, impropriety and disloyalty to me in any capacity" (cited in Othman 1989, 142). Babangida appointed his first cabinet in September 1985, announced a reshuffle in January 1986, changed the ministers in March 1989, changed them again later that year when a new AFRC was formed, and sacked ten ministers in 1992.[61]

Some scholars therefore argue that Babangida was an all-powerful autocrat, citing evidence that decrees emanated directly from Babangida and never went through the AFRC (Osaghae 1998, 192–193). Decree Number 17, for example, eliminated the AFRC's power to appoint the armed service chiefs. But he faced powerful and high-ranking military officials on the AFRC, and the regime's constituting rules vested the AFRC with important collective authority relating to taxation and spending, declaring a state of emergency, and making laws. Until March 1989, any change in policy required the collective consent of the AFRC, and Babangida succeeded in making only minor changes in the AFRC's

[60] "President Pardons Thompson, Irabor," *The Guardian*, January 7, 1986. See also Osaghae (1998), pp. 190–191.
[61] "New Ministers in Lagos," *West Africa*, September 16, 1985; "President Babangida Re-Shuffles," *West Africa*, January 27, 1986; A. Adelegan, "IBB Drops 10 Ministers," *The Punch*, January 14, 1992.

composition. The AFRC's preferences also prevailed on significant policy questions such as state creation. For example, in September 1987 the administration announced the creation of two new states and declared the issue closed. A rancorous response from Igbos in the East and minorities in the South forced the administration to revisit the issue through the National Council of State, which was supposed to have only consultative status within the AFRC. Eventually, nine more states were created in 1991 to accommodate the uproar. A government White Paper on state creation leaked a few years later confirmed the regime's internal divisions on state creation and other issues (Diamond, Oyediran, and Kirk-Greene 1997). This evidence thus contradicts the portrait of a feeble ruling council and instead argues for the AFRC's veto capacity.

Finally, a government-created Political Bureau, made up of well-known political activists and former military officers, carved out political space for a faction of soft-liners who became the regime's third veto player. The bureau was established to develop recommendations for political reforms to promote the transition to democracy. Once formed, it managed to expand its membership and its mandate, despite resistance from the bureaucracy and military officials (Oyediran 1997). In January 1987, several members of the bureau, including a former military governor who had been army chief of staff, accused the government of northern bias. That same month, the recently retired General Obasanjo published a sympathetic biography of the leader of Nigeria's first coup, Nzeogwu. The government was already alert to Obasanjo's seemingly anti-Babangida inclinations: Just two weeks before Babangida overthrew the Buhari/Idiagbon regime, Obasanjo "commended" key policies of the Buhari government.[62] Obasanjo went on to criticize the Babangida government's economic policy openly and denounced proposals to delay the transition to democracy, cementing his reputation among Babangida's faithful as a cantankerous critic (Adekanye 1997, 55–80). But by the end of the 1980s, Babangida had to reverse course and repackage key elements of his budget plans that were fueling critics such as Obasanjo and emboldening soft-liners.

This opened the gate for other reform-minded military figures, including Shehu Musa Yar'Adua (the top deputy in the Obasanjo regime), Chukwuemeka Ojukwu (the former leader of the defeated Biafran secessionist movement), and General Yakubu Gowon (the former dictator), all

---

[62] "Which Way Forward?" *West Africa*, August 19, 1985. Obasanjo's book was about Chukwuma Nzeogwu (Obasanjo 2004).

of whom openly nursed political ambitions for national office after the scheduled transition. Other retired military officials also began pressing their ideas for reform and the transition. The soft-liners' influence grew sufficiently widespread that Babangida attempted to ban their activities in 1987. Yet the ban failed to reign in many of the government's harshest critics, including elite ministers and SMC members who had served in previous military governments (Adekanye 1999). By evading the ban on politics and then pushing the government to change course on critical issues concerning the constitutional authorities of the states and the transition timeline, the soft-liner faction could not be ignored and successfully asserted their collective strength.

Pressure Builds for a Transition and a Fourth Veto Player Emerges (1990–1993)

Babangida's final years in office offer a conflicting picture of government authority. On the one hand, Babangida worked at the end of 1989 to undermine the AFRC and curtail its jurisdiction. He took over the powerful minister of defense post and abolished the National Security Organization, replacing it with new security organizations that reported directly to him.[63] He also threw scores of political activists into jail for protesting his administration's economic reforms and demanding democratization. These changes suggest that Babangida was consolidating his authority at the expense of other potential veto players. On the other hand, though, new challenges from military elites, fragmentation within the regime's institutions, and large-scale political reform contributed to a dispersion of political authority. After Babangida's government lifted the ban on politics in 1989, new state governments were elected and the influence of regional governors once again increased. One state politician recalls that the governors routinely circumvented their own state assemblies' authority on spending. A new National Assembly was also elected, ushering in a Third Republic in preparation for a full transition to democracy. The assembly had only limited influence over national policy, but, like the new state-level institutions and the outgoing Political Bureau, it opened political space for civilian politicians to criticize and mobilize against the regime.

---

[63] "New Ruling Council Announced," *Africa Research Bulletin*, March 15, 1989; "Sweeping Cabinet Reshuffle," *Africa Research Bulletin*, February 15, 1990.

In this complex political environment, Babangida's authority faced challenges from three distinct veto players. After the regime crackdown, the AFRC split into two factions, each of which constituted a powerful new coalition of interests with a veto. One faction was made up of army personnel and led by Sani Abacha, who had served under Buhari and Babangida, and another faction was made up of the political soft-liners within the government. The regime's fourth veto emerged in the South, where Babangida faced coordinated resistance from labor unions and new civil society coalitions demanding democratic reform.

Abacha, the young army chief who had announced the coup in August 1985 and who helped foil a coup attempt against Babangida in December 1985,[64] had tried to keep the army united ever since. He continued to play the loyalist role after a failed putsch in April 1990. Abacha was among a small number of untouchable officials who survived all of Babangida's cabinet shuffles.[65] But as Babangida worked to undermine the AFRC as a collective player, Abacha's authority increased. He beat out a navy commodore for the chairmanship of the Joint Chiefs of Staff. Before an AFRC meeting in 1992, Abacha allegedly approached commanding officers in strategically placed military divisions with the idea of replacing Babangida. Someone tipped off Babangida, who discreetly preempted the issue in the meeting, but Abacha was neither purged nor punished.[66] Emboldened, Abacha began working with a clique known as the "Lagos Group" and encouraged defection of Babangida loyalists. The faction eventually prevailed over a competing group led by David Mark and other generals resisting the 1993 transition discussed later (Omoruyi 1999).

The other faction with a veto formed around soft-liners based in the Langtang Mafia, a coalition consisting mostly of Christian army officers, including the prominent Major General Domkat Bali. Like Abacha, Bali had helped put Babangida in power and helped foil the December 1985 coup attempt against him. Babangida continued to feel indebted to both men.[67] The Langtang Mafia particularly drew support from the Southwest, where Yorubas felt they had been denied the presidency in both the First and the Second Republics. When Bali, as the most senior

---

[64] Juilyeme Ukabiala, "Abacha Defrosts Coup Plot Freeze in Barraks," *The Guardian*, January 7, 1986.
[65] Muyiwa Akintudne, "The Untouchables," *Newswatch*, January 18, 1993.
[66] Dele Agekameh, "A Game of Danger and Blackmail," *TELL*, December 14, 1998.
[67] "Coup Plot Verdicts," *West Africa*, March 3, 1986.

and longest-serving army general, publicly protested a change in his portfolio, the Langtang Mafia and a group of powerful officers backed him up. The "Bali Affair," as it became known, exposed the limits of the regime's centralization. "He was not part of the regime that took over," said one retired general. "But they still needed his fatherly support."[68] Babangida backed down and promoted General Bali and other southern army officials (Adekanye 1997) in order to placate the Langtang Mafia and a heavy-hitting group of retired generals, including Gowon, Obasanjo, and Yar'Adua.

In addition to these military factions, Babangida faced a challenge from the South, which coalesced after 1990 to mount a regional veto. Three issues had catalyzed this resistance and facilitated coordination across the diverse region. First, the regime's decision to join the Organization of Islamic Countries (OIC) in 1986 created a cause célèbre in the overwhelmingly christian South. It mobilized the Christian Association of Nigeria and generated widespread skepticism about the regime's commitment to ethnic balancing (Kukah 1999). Babangida was pressured into suspending OIC membership. This was apparently not enough, as many participants in the 1990 coup attempt against Babangida were Christians from the southern and Middle Belt regions.[69] The financier of the 1990 coup later claimed that, despite its failure, the coup attempt restrained Babangida's excesses and pressured him to exit.[70] Second, the 1989 reshuffling of the AFRC left Muslims in charge of the armed services and the presidency. This was unacceptable to a military that for a generation now had used a principle known as "federal character," which took ethnicity into consideration for political appointments. It was a key reason for General Bali's risky and very public dissent. It is also a clear example of a cautious policy reversal as regional actors from the South flexed their muscle.

Third, the prodemocracy movement had its roots in the South, drawing particularly militant support in Lagos and the Southwest, where most of the industry and civil society groups were located. When the planned transition to democracy appeared that it might falter, southern organizers prepared to take on the regime. The Nigerian Labour Congress regrouped after suffering for their opposition to structural adjustment in the 1980s. In the Niger Delta, where most of the federal government's oil revenues

---

[68] Interview with General Josiah Laoye, March 13, 2010, Ibadan.
[69] "Coup Attempt Foiled," *Africa Research Bulletin*, May 15, 1990.
[70] "The Godfather," *TELL*, July 2000.

originated, militant oil workers lined up alongside minorities in the East on strategic issues (Osaghae 1998).

In the days before the election on June 12, 1993, retired military officers gathered at former ruler Obasanjo's farm to strategize about how to neutralize groups working to derail the transition.[71] A partial release of election results indicated that a Yoruba candidate, Moshood Kashimawo Olawale Abiola, won the presidential election. He declared, "Thank God we got what looks like a major national mandate."[72] The western chapter of the defeated party conceded Abiola's victory, but shadowy front groups backed by officials who stood to lose power through a transition obtained court injunctions to delay a formal declaration of the election results.[73] In the East, the Igbos had mixed attitudes about Abiola. Some Igbos felt they should have a turn at power, while others insisted that a democratic transition required honoring the June 12 results. With the support of Babangida, the Senate became embroiled in the impeachment of the Senate president, who insisted that the results should be respected. Senators from the eastern part of the country initially opposed the effort, but the administration's machinations eventually won out and the Senate impeached its president on a vote of 55 to 25.[74]

After weeks of protest and procrastination, Babangida annulled the elections, creating what became known as the "June 12 crisis." The international community responded with sanctions and strong diplomatic censures. Sharp political divisions formed, with most prodemocracy groups pushing to install Abiola and others demanding new elections. Some members of the losing party worked to awaken sectarian regional concerns. "We were selfish and without foresight," admits a member of the National Republican Congress (NRC) who supported the annulment. NRC governors entered an alliance of convenience with hardliners who sought to extend military rule to prevent the North's loss of power.[75] Regional politics took over as northerners once supportive of Abiola began organizing against a southern politician's assuming the

---

[71] Camillus Eboh, "Aikhomu Alleges Hidden Agenda by Democracy Groups," *The Guardian*, June 5, 1993.

[72] Osaretin Imahiyereobo, "Abiola, in Lagos, Envisages Victory," *The Guardian*, June 15, 1993.

[73] "NRC's Leaders Okay Conduct of Election," *The Guardian*, June 17, 1993; Edetaen Ojo and Benedict Hart, "Courts Order Prompt Release of Poll's Result," *The Guardian*, June 18, 1993.

[74] Remi Ibitola, "Plot to Impeach Ayu Uncovered," *The Punch*, July 10, 1993; Chekwuemeka Gahia, "Grace to Grass," *Newswatch*, November 15, 1993.

[75] Nats Agbo, "Deadlock," *Newswatch*, August 1993, 2.

presidency. Within the AFRC, Abacha and the Lagos group encouraged criticism of Abiola and managed to block Babangida's access to his top advisers.[76]

Southern frustration over the 1993 election annulment is no surprise. One might make the case, though, that the North might coordinate a regional veto. In fact, Abacha discreetly worked to rally northern elders against Abiola, hoping to present a united front (if not a fait accompli) to Babangida; the sultan of Sokoto and other traditional rulers in the North were reportedly receptive to the strategy (Omoruyi 1999, 165–168). In addition, though Babangida hailed from a northern state, he had an ambiguous relationship with the region's traditional rulers. He also deliberately distanced himself from the Kaduna Mafia, which offered an organizational alternative to the sultanates. In his first administration, only four of the twenty-eight members in the initial AFRC were considered sons of the northern establishment, and only two were ethnically Hausa-Fulani. In the cabinet, only seven of the twenty-four members claimed northern roots. But when the government joined the OIC, it backed out under southern pressure.

More importantly, government policies had undermined the solidarity across states and ethnicities necessary for a northern regional veto in at least three ways. First, the creation of new states pitted Northeast, North-Central, and Northwest interests against each other. When new states were created in 1987, the North only gained one new one. Then when additional requests for states were rejected in 1991, riots broke out in Kano and Sokoto states – but the government stood firm against any further state creation. Second, northerners formed a "Committee of Elders" within the Political Bureau, recruiting elites across the region in an effort to coordinate solidarity on key issues. They presented a united front on the question of sharia and opposed customary court reforms (Vaughan 1997, 413–434). But the bureau itself divided, with some elements expressing hostility to the emirs' requests and the government accepted the bureau's recommendation to limit traditional rulers' authority to local affairs (Diamond, Oyediran, and Kirk-Greene 1997). In the end northern victories on local government reforms, sharia, and judicial reforms were limited. When the Committee of Elders later doubted that the 1993 transition would serve northern interests, Babangida sternly

[76] Adetunji Olurii, "The Abacha-Babangida Showdown," *TELL*, December 14, 1998; Dele Agekameh, "A Game of Dagger and Blackmail," *TELL*, December 14, 1998.

rebutted them in a speech at the National War College. Third, Babangida had controversially engineered the replacement of the sultan of Sokoto with Ibrahim Dasuki, rejecting the more conservative candidate favored by local elites. The Hausa-Fulani kingmakers resented Dasuki for building an independent base over the years through national level politics, rather than cultivating support from within the caliphate (Paden 2005, 17–37). The government's director of military intelligence later reflected that these confrontations with the North contributed to Babangida's failures (Alli 2001). Dasuki, a few months after his installation, lined up sixty-three traditional rulers behind Babangida to condemn the 1990 coup attempt. For all these reasons, the North did not successfully coordinate to form a regional veto.

Babangida surrendered power in August 1993 after two months of political upheaval precipitated by the June 12 election annulment that made the country virtually ungovernable. An interim national government led by Ernest Shonekan, a southwestern business leader, inherited an extraordinarily volatile political situation. He freed political activists from prison, pardoned politicians, and lifted restrictions on the press. A newly formed Northern Consultative Group that comprised NRC and SDP elites complained that the government contained too many incumbent holdovers. A group of elders from the Middle Belt states (on the edge of the North) similarly complained that the government was not actually replacing the administration "but would rather extend it."[77] Three months into his tenure, Shonekan was invited by several military leaders to their barracks to express their concern about "the general uneasiness in the country and the apparent lack of stability." They warned him of "the restiveness of the rank and file in the military."[78]

Later that month, Shonekan stepped down, in part blaming agitation by June 12 sympathizers for the collapse of the interim government. Sani Abacha quickly stepped in to fill the void, promising to put the transition back on track and restore order. Many generals later argued that Abacha's support for the idea of transition was a ruse – an effort to avoid turning power over to the South via Abiola or a Machiavellian plot to assume power through an interim government designed to fail. Either way, the nascent Third Republic was dead on arrival.

---

[77] Tunde Olafintila, "Interim Govt: Northern Elders Seek Exclusion of Serving Officers," *The Guardian*, August 16, 1993.
[78] "Why I Stepped Out," *Newswatch*, November 29, 1993.

Abacha after the Failed Transition: From Two Veto Players to One (1993–1998)

Abacha's takeover precipitated a protracted struggle over the transition to democracy. As the issue of the annulled June 12 election dragged on, some agitated for a constitutional conference, a proposal adamantly opposed by many northerners. Though there is some evidence that Abacha was not strictly opposed to honoring the June 12 results, he manipulated widespread fear in the North about a regional shift of power to the South implied by an Abiola victory. For the next several years, a June 12 faction and Abacha operated as the regime's two veto players

Abacha quickly tried to consolidate his authority by announcing the dissolution of the interim national government, all legislative assemblies, the two political parties that competed in 1993, and "any consultative committee by whatever name."[79] This effort was complicated by the fact that Babangida had officially "stepped aside" and had arguably not been toppled in a coup. When Abacha took the reins, he led a government and a bureaucracy full of Babangida allies who had accumulated influence and power over eight years of military rule. Abacha slowly weeded out Babangida's loyalists and reversed many of Babangida's last-minute military promotions. He issued a decree creating a new Provisional Ruling Council (PRC) to pass legislation that did not have a single member with ties to Babangida.[80] Abacha dismissed the army chief of staff two months into his regime, doubting his allegiance to the new government. Some of the "IBB Boys," as the Babangida loyalists were called, had their passports confiscated to prevent them from traveling,[81] and several officials from Babangida's AFRC died under mysterious circumstances.

For all his efforts to rid the government of Babangida supporters, Abacha could not change the fact that there was still broad disagreement within the government and across Nigeria over how to resolve the June 12 crisis. Members of the interim government had themselves remained deadlocked over whether to install Abiola, the alleged winner of the June election, and, if not, how to proceed with new elections (Emelifeonwu 1997, 193–216). In the face of such deep disagreement and uncertainty, Abacha appointed a broadly inclusive cabinet to signal (or perhaps to

---

[79] Decree No. 13: Constitution (Suspension and Modification) (Amendment) (No. 2) Decree 1994; "A Child of Necessity," *Newswatch*, November 29, 1993.

[80] Ima Niboro, "Caging in the Turks," *TELL*, September 4, 1995.

[81] "Armed Forces Reshuffle," *Africa Research Bulletin*, September 30, 1993, p. 1141.

create the illusion) that the transition was still on track and the divisive regional tensions would be negotiated. Known as the "rainbow cabinet," it included prominent members of the June 12 movement, including major Abiola sympathizers and members of his party (the SDP). It also included Abiola's vice presidential running mate, Baba Gana Kingibe, who was among only four ministers who sat on the twelve-member PRC.[82] (Kingibe was also implicated in forcing Babangida aside, since he apparently believed the incoming generals would reverse the 1993 annulment.) Even Abiola himself was given powerful influence within the government, as Abacha consulted him regularly on cabinet appointments. The Abacha government did not want to trigger another state of economic paralysis such as that which followed the election annulment. So, as long as the June 12 faction remained strong, policy making required its participation (Alli 2001). This faction managed to maintain veto power for the next three years.

The June 12 faction included the chief of naval staff, Allison Madueke, and the top intelligence official, Chris Alli, the latter of whom had worked closely on the transition plan that Babangida discarded. The most prominent member of the June 12 faction, though, was Lieutenant General Oladipo Diya, a Yoruba who shared the Southwest's frustration with the annulled election. He held the powerful post of vice chairman of the PRC (Babatope 2000). Colonel Abubakar Dangiwa Umar, the former military governor of Kaduna State, spoke for the most radical elements of the June 12 faction. He ultimately resigned his commission and publicly informed the military government that he would not command his subordinates "to put down any civil disturbance that may arise" in support of the June 12 mandate.[83] Such statements lent credence to the view within the upper echelons of the regime that there was a conspiracy afoot to install Abiola by force (Alli 2001, 291–292). Umar posed a particular political threat to the junta since his roots in the northern Sokoto caliphate positioned him as a principled advocate for a democratic transition that would turn power over to a southerner; he mobilized northerners sympathetic to the June 12 cause through the Movement for Unity and Progress.[84] As further evidence of the June 12 faction's leverage, the regime's innermost circle, the "Abacha caucus," unanimously agreed that Diya and Abacha

---

[82] Muyiwa Akintunde, "Firming Up," *Newswatch*, December 6, 1993.
[83] Nats Agbo, "Coup Report Is Rubbish," *Newswatch*, November 8, 1993.
[84] Osa Director, "Umar on Trial," *TELL*, February 10, 1997; Danlami Nmodu, "In Search of Justice," *TELL*, December 8, 1997.

should be the only two members of the PRC with political positions (Alli 2001).

Abacha co-opted allies and elites from the SDP by promising them government positions in exchange for moderating their stance on the June 12 matter (Lewis 1994, 323–340). Despite including them in the regime, the SDP members were constantly accused of being spies for the National Democratic Coalition (NADECO), a civil society network agitating for the June 12 cause. In 1995, several of these soft-liners were convicted of plotting a coup against Abacha, a coup that the military administrator for Kaduna State (where the plot supposedly unfolded) says was a total fabrication.[85] By the end of 1996, Nigeria's Civil Liberties Organization tallied eighty-seven purges directed at this faction (Amuwo 2001, 1–56), including Abacha's decision to arrest former head of state Obasanjo and other critics. The repressive sweep extended to traditional leaders in the Southwest, including the octogenarian chief of the pan-Yoruba group, Afenifere.[86] The victims of these government attacks later recounted how their prison interrogators drilled them on Abiola and June 12.[87]

Abacha's efforts to subvert the June 12 faction did not succeed immediately. When the PRC underwent a major reshuffling in October 1996, for example, Diya and other June 12 sympathizers survived. It is also notable that until then, all three military chiefs were southern Christians, part of an apparent effort by the government to obtain legitimacy (Sklar 2001, 265–266). But after the purges, the June 12 faction members apparently made a tactical decision to avoid direct ties with civilian elites and groups like NADECO. As a former governor explained, many people in government were upset with Abacha but supported the democracy activists quietly, fearing that "by supporting them we were exposing them."[88] Ironically, this created a distance between the elite and the grassroots members of the June 12 coalition that weakened Diya's leverage.

In 1997, Abacha surprised the nation when he declared that he would run in the upcoming elections. The June 12 faction tried to mount an attack against Abacah's "self-succession" bid. Tensions grew within the PRC. In May, one minister ordered government officials to refrain from supporting any presidential candidate, and a huge scandal erupted when

---

[85] Interview with General Lawal Jaafer Isa, March 11, 2010, Abuja.
[86] "The Renewed Clampdown," *Constitutional Rights Journal*, July–September 1995.
[87] "Abacha Digs In," *Constitutional Rights Journal*, October–December 1995; Col. Michael Ajayi, *TELL*, March 22, 1999; Major Adeyi, "Obasanjo Saved Us from the Firing Squad," *TELL*, March 22, 1999.
[88] Interview with Okwesilieze Nwodo, March 8, 2010, Abuja.

another minister contradicted him. Soft-liners in the PRC complained that the image of the military would be badly damaged by such an obvious intervention in politics.[89] Debates over the timetable of the democratic transition further exacerbated these tensions. Just as military opponents of Abacha's self-succession plan seemed to gain leverage (after meeting with the former U.S. president Jimmy Carter), Abacha then sprang another surprise by postponing the elections. At this point, Diya was still attending the PRC meetings and arguing the June 12 faction's position.[90] But in November 1997, Abacha finally dissolved the entire cabinet. He had shuffled the cabinet before, but now he attacked his rivals with new boldness.

Abacha was finally able to establish a single veto player regime in 1997 for at least three reasons. First, out of concern that Yorubas in government would back southwestern Abiola in any transition, Abacha undertook a purge of his government that made the previous dismissals of the IBB Boys look tame. In February 1997, he systematically retired every military administrator known to sympathize with the prodemocracy coalition NADECO. The press labeled it an "ethnic cleansing" of Yoruba, since the move was directed against officials in the South, where prodemocracy agitation was strongest.[91] In August, Abacha dismissed scores of Yoruba officers throughout the military. Out of sixty-three officers forced to retire, forty-nine were Yoruba and only six were from the North.[92] Three months later, the regime arrested Diya on a trumped-up conspiracy charge for planning to participate in what became known as the "phantom coup."[93] Diya and his alleged coconspirators, including two ex-ministers, were sentenced to prison for life.[94] With Diya and the other members of the June 12 faction neutralized, Abacha had a freer hand within the Provisional Ruling Council (PRC).

Second, the purges provoked little reaction from abroad, as Western democracy promotion was adrift. International sanctions had been

---

[89] Mikail Mumuni, "The Warring House of Abacha," *TELL*, May 12, 1997; Anselm Okolo, "Now, Abacha's Constituency Decides," *TELL*, June 30, 1997.

[90] John Okafor, "Aso Rock's Power Play," *TELL*, July 21, 1997; Ade Olorunfewa, "Coup Scare," *TELL*, February 16, 1998.

[91] Osa Director, "Umar on Trial," *TELL*, February 10, 1997.

[92] John Okafor, "Panic Grips the Military, *TELL*, September 8, 1997.

[93] Abdullhai Sule, "Much Ado about General Oladipo Diya," *Vanguard*, May 30, 2004; "10 Minutes in the Toilet Saved Me," *The Guardian*, April 3, 2004; Louisa Ayonote and Adegbenro Adebanjo, "God Overruled Abacha," *TELL*, March 22, 1999.

[94] John Okafor, "New Postings for Diya's Men," *TELL*, June 15, 1998; "Diya Arrested," *Africa Research Bulletin*, December 1997.

imposed against Abacha's government two years earlier, as punishment for hanging playwright Ken Saro-Wiwa and eight other human rights activists in 1995. But the sanctions were relatively limited, since Western countries and companies remained keenly interested in Nigeria's oil. The United States could have had a huge impact, since it bought 48 percent of Nigeria's oil exports. But Nigerian oil also amounted to 8 percent of total American oil consumption, and an increase in gas prices in the United States might have hurt President Bill Clinton's reelection chances the following year. In addition, Chevron, Mobil, and Shell had recently launched a venture with the Nigerian National Petroleum Company to develop liquid natural gas assets in order to preempt China or Russia. Western economic interests prevailed over demands for democratization (Sklar 2001; Lewis, Robinson, and Rubin 1998).

Then Abacha received an unexpected boost of support when on a visit to Africa in 1998, President Clinton announced, "My policy is to do all that we can to persuade General Abacha to move toward general democracy and respect for human rights." Clinton added, "If he stands for election, we hope he will stand as a civilian. There are many military leaders who have taken over chaotic situations in African countries, but have moved toward democracy. And that can happen in Nigeria; that is, purely and simply, what we want to happen."[95] The military junta interpreted this to mean that the United States would not oppose an Abacha presidency, if he won in an open election. Instead of supporting soft-liners in the junta and prodemocracy activists who were trying to unite around the goal of preventing Abacha's self-succession, the West seemed to endorse Abacha's plans publicly (Amuwo 2001, 1–56). One party leader, who went on to chair the Nigerian Senate's Foreign Relations Committee, complained, "America and these big powers always want some kind of solution," so they "[found] a way of working with Abacha."[96]

Third, institutional decay at multiple levels of government also created an opportunity for Abacha to fill the void. According to several former ministers, the FEC had stopped meeting by late 1995 (Babatope 2000).[97] In 1996, Abacha renamed the state governors "military administrators" and started describing the position as a "military posting."[98]

[95] White House, Transcript of Press Conference, Cape Town, South Africa, March 27, 1998.

[96] Interview with Senator Jibril Aminu. March 8, 2010, Abuja.

[97] Anthony Asuquo Ani, "Abacha's Loot and I," *TELL*, January 10, 2000; Wale Akin-Aina, "Jobs for the Boys," *Newswatch*, December 20, 1993.

[98] "Nigeria: New State Administrators," *Africa Research Bulletin*, August 1996.

Abacha also issued a decree that year that permitted him to remove local government chairs or appoint provisional councils. The cumulative impact of these changes on state-level authority was devastating. According to the World Bank, state autonomy reached its lowest level in Nigerian history under Abacha (World Bank 2002). Neither collective action by cabinet ministers nor subnational coordination by the states seemed feasible any longer.

Numerous generals within Abacha's inner circle started to worry that another botched democratic transition would reflect poorly on the military's reputation for honor and professionalism.[99] But the military was experiencing organizational tension that weakened its ability to check Abacha's power through a new veto player. The navy failed in its effort to weaken Abacha's national security advisor (NSA). Then air force officers complained about selective enforcement in corruption investigations by government agencies. The NSA's escape of scrutiny in the corruption investigations stimulated additional resentment throughout the military.[100] This was on the heels of compulsory retirements that disproportionately affected the air force. These jealousies made it easier for Abacha to circumvent the military altogether and consolidate power. In the end, the national security advisor reported directly to Abacha and worked outside the PRC's chain of command. While this situation faced opposition from navy and army representatives in Abacha's inner circle, Abacha prevailed over their resistance (Alli 2001, 298).

Abacha succeeded in consolidating power to a greater extent than any previous dictator, but in the process alienated and angered powerful political actors and broad social coalitions. The military services complained of a parochialism and marginalization. When the government's innermost circle, the Abacha caucus, began backstabbing one another, he tossed them out. But this complicated governance, according to one of his generals, because it meant that as a "sole administrator" Abacha received little reliable information from the population or state officials.[101] By 1997, Hausa-Fulani elites who had once hoped that

---

[99] Muyiwa Akintunde, "Firming Up," *Newswatch*, December 6, 1993. See also Luckham (1971b) for a thoughtful sociological analysis of this culture of honor within the military.

[100] John Okafor, "Grumblings over Court Martial," *TELL*, October 27, 1997; Madu Agbo, "The Purge Begins," *TELL*, September 1, 1997; Director Mumuni, "Gwarzo Goes Home," *TELL*, November 2, 1998.

[101] Interview with General Lawal Jaafer Isa, March 11, 2010, Abuja.

scuttling the 1993 elections might help them maintain northern political hegemony felt betrayed.[102] They began turning against Abacha, rejecting an overture from former president Shagari on Abacha's behalf. When eighteen traditional rulers and a coalition of former politicians issued statements opposing his government, the junta ignored them.[103] The June 12 faction's grievances lingered on, even if its leverage had been lost.[104]

It is not known which, if any, of these disgruntled parties orchestrated Abacha's death, but barely a year after the purges and military restructuring began, Abacha mysteriously died. Adding to the intrigue, Abiola died days later. As with his political nemesis, murder was never proven, but suspicions over the cause and timing of Abiola's death abound. Abiola's death simplified the succession question in some ways, since it put to rest the claim that the presumed winner of the June 12 election should be inaugurated as part of the transition to democracy. But it created a new problem: Who could pay the "Yoruba debt," accumulated from both the 1993 annulment and the 1979 Supreme Court decision that handed power to Shagari? Northern elites understood they would need to placate the Yorubas. The chair of the political committee that reviewed potential presidential candidates recalls, "There was very little interest on the part of the north to take over the presidency in 1999; more important was to get a Yoruba man you could trust."[105] Obasanjo, the dictator who had handed over power in 1979 and then endured hard time in prison under Abacha, emerged as the consensus candidate to end more than sixteen years of dictatorship.

Obasanjo's Return: Four Veto Players for the Fourth Republic (1999–2003)

Shortly after Abacha's death, a coalition of elites joined to form the People's Democratic Party (PDP), with the immediate goal of ensuring a peaceful transition to democratic rule. According to PDP Senator J. K. N. Waku, "Conservatives and progressives all agreed to team up for the purposes of assuring the military an exit." This required a party large enough

---

[102] "I Forsee a Wind of Change," *TELL*, November 13, 2000.
[103] Ima Niboro, "No Way!" *TELL*, March 31, 1997; Danlami Nmodu, "The Battle for Kahim Ibrahim House," *TELL*, May 18, 1998; Uche Maduemesi, "A Dictator at Bay," *TELL*, June 1, 1998.
[104] John Okafor, "Rumbles in the Military," *TELL*, June 1, 1998.
[105] Interview with Senator Jibril Aminu, March 8, 2010, Abuja.

and strong enough to mute "tribalism" and to demonstrate the political "maturity" of civilians.[106] At the same time, it was also the South's "turn" to rule. Thus "when we formed the PDP," its chairman said in a 2010 interview, "we were extremely determined to address the injustice to the south in terms of the control of power."[107] To reassure other sectional interests, the PDP established elaborate internal rules to rotate power and distribute offices on a geopolitical basis. In this way, Africa's largest political party became a very large umbrella: "The PDP is actually a coalition of parties that took over from the military," explained one northern senator who helped found the PDP.[108]

The new constitution put in place a presidential system modeled after the Second Republic's, including a president and a bicameral legislature, each of which had an institutional veto. In the months leading up to its promulgation in 1999, the drafting committee reassured northerners that Obasanjo would step aside when his term was over. "It is like an unwritten law," says a member of the committee. "We felt that it was an area that nobody could afford to compromise."[109] For too many Nigerians, such promises seemed hollow, and Obasanjo's government almost immediately faced a northern regional veto.

In many ways, Obasanjo seemed to be the perfect leader for this moment in Nigeria's history. He boasted strong democratic credentials, having turned over power to civilian rule peacefully in 1979 when he was the military head of state, and he was later imprisoned by Abacha's government for defending democracy. He had acquired a reputation for integrity by working with the international NGO Transparency International. He also commanded the necessary gravitas, having built a distinguished military career going back to the Biafran Civil War. Perhaps most importantly, the choice of Obasanjo meant that Nigeria would finally pay off the Yoruba debt.

As Nigeria embarked on its third attempt at democracy, the newly elected Obasanjo told the National Assembly (NASS), "All Nigerians are expecting democracy to yield dividends."[110] This new government did not enter with the same naïve illusions that had undermined democracy

---

[106] Interview with J. K. N. Waku, March 10, 2010, Abuja; Haruna Salami, "Northern Politicians Are Greedy and Selfish," *TELL*, February 4, 2002.

[107] Interview with Okwesilieze Nwodo, March 8, 2010, Abuja.

[108] Interview with Senator Jibril Aminu, March 8, 2010, Abuja.

[109] Interview with Clement Ebri, March 16, 2010, Abuja.

[110] Patrick Smith, "Nigerian Leader Sets Out His Priorities," *The Guardian* (London), June 5, 1999.

TABLE 2.1. *Election Results by Party in the Southwest Geopolitical "Zone," 1999*

	Presidential Election, Percent of the Vote		Senate Seats in National Assembly		House Seats in National Assembly	
	APP/AD	PDP	AD	PDP	AD*	PDP
Ekiti	73.2	26.9	2	1	6	0
Lagos	88.1	11.9	3	0	23	0
Ogun	69.0	30.2	3	0	9	0
Ondo	85.4	16.6	3	0	7	1
Osun	76.5	23.5	3	0	7	1
Oyo	75.3	24.7	3	0	12	2

* *Note:* The APP won one House seat in Lagos
Source: Independent National Election Commission

in the 1960s and 1980s. The new administration put the fight against corruption at the top of its agenda, launching an inquiry into government contracts hurriedly awarded during the transition, revisiting loopholes in the privatization process, and asking the international community for help to track down hundreds of millions of dollars stashed overseas during the 1990s. It also inherited high inflation, crumbling infrastructure, stagnant economic growth, and $29 billion in foreign debt. International financial institutions put pressure on the government to impose economic austerity measures in order to receive continued support.[111]

Although Obasanjo had broad credibility and appeal across Nigeria, restiveness in both the North and the South questioned his mandate. Almost immediately after his inauguration, rebels from ethnic minority groups in the Niger Delta, angry about environmental pollution and political disenfranchisement in the South, staged violent attacks against oil installations and the government. Despite his Southwest Yoruba credentials, Obasanjo was elected president with virtually no support in Nigeria's six states in that part of the country (see Table 2.1). "We didn't see Obasanjo as serving the interests of the Yorubas," explained a senior senator from Oyo State. "Obasanjo has always been anti-Yoruba. He will say he is a nationalist but we don't see him as a nationalist. We see him as always pitching his camp where his interests will be best served." The bitterness dates back to the 1979 transition when Obasanjo, as the

[111] William Wallis, "Forty Years after Independence, an Enfeebled African Giant Stirs," *Financial Times* (London), May 28, 1999.

outgoing head of state, accepted the Supreme Court's decision to award the presidency to a northerner, Shehu Shagari, instead of the Yoruba candidate, Obafemi Awolowo. "Most Yorubas did not forgive him," says the senator. "Awolowo won that election."[112] These long-standing resentments coupled with growing unrest in the oil-producing states in the Niger Delta meant that Nigeria was ruled by a southerner who was not supported by the South (LeVan, Pitso, and Adebo 2003).

The North would present an even greater challenge than the South, as calls for Islamic law coordinated diverse interests across a dozen northern states to form a regional veto. Shortly after Obasanjo's inauguration, riots involving Muslims and Christians in the northern (predominantly Hausa) city of Kano led to the deaths of hundreds of southerners living there. As a born again Christian from the South, Obasanjo calculated that it was too politically risky for him to use unilateral federal authority to crush the movement. In the 1999 elections, the All People's Party (APP), a party with some Islamic sympathies, performed well in the Northeast and Northwest (winning six out of thirteen governorships and fifteen out of thirty-nine National Assembly Senate seats, but not doing quite as well in the North Central states). The sharia issue moved to the fore in November 1999, when the Zamfara State Assembly passed legislation making it compulsory for all Muslims in the state to follow Islamic law. "Without sharia there is no Islam," explained Governor Ahmed Sani when he signed the bill. "We are Muslims and must live and die as Muslims."[113] Within months, eleven more northern state legislatures enacted Islamic criminal codes. Christians, who were a minority in the North, panicked. Thousands of people died in riots between Christians and Muslims in the North and reprisal attacks in the South.

Although enforcement of sharia was often unsystematic and haphazard, codifying these laws at a state level presented a coordinated challenge to the supremacy of the federal constitution (Angerbrandt 2011). "The plan was to make Kaduna look like an Islamic state," wrote a weekly newsmagazine, "and then, having done that, use that as a negotiating tool and a ploy to get back to relevance at the centre."[114] Moreover, the nation had held together on the basis of a delicate compromise predating independence under which Muslims agreed to resolve only civil matters through Islamic courts; the challenge from Zamfara and other northern

---

[112] Interview with Senator Abiola Ajimobi, March 15, 2010, Abuja.
[113] Mikail Mumuni, "A Zealot's Dream Come True," *TELL*, November 8, 1999.
[114] Obiora Chukwumba, "The Middle Belt Revolt," *TELL*, March 27, 2000.

states threatened this foundational federal pact by trying to extend sharia to criminal matters.

Interestingly, the divisions over sharia in 1999 were more regional than religious. "In the South, Islam is a personal and family religion," explains Richard Sklar, an expert on Yoruba politics. In the North, however, "Islam is a civilization – a system of authority and a fount of the law" (Sklar 2002, 333–348). Calls for sharia among the millions of Yoruba Muslims in the South were largely muted, as they had always been. During the constitutional debates of the 1970s and 1990s, both Christian and Muslim elites in the Southwest advocated restraint and moderation (Suberu 1997, 401–425). This was evident again in 2000, when all seventeen southern state governors issued a statement pledging unity and temperance.[115]

Notwithstanding the numerous professions of puritanism, religious and ethnic diversity among Muslims meant that the demands for sharia were hardly universal. Citizens of the religiously and ethnically heterogeneous Middle Belt states expressed profound discomfort with sharia. Elites there openly complained that sharia was "ethnopolitical" and had nothing to do with religion.[116] Eager to avoid alienating these states, many northern states decided to take a softer line on sharia (Paden 2004, 17–37). Even in Zamfara, the governor ended up pleading with business leaders, many of whom were neither indigenous nor Muslim, to stay in the state, promising that sharia would not apply to Christians. Instead of a new legal regime, sharia became a symbol of northern solidarity during a time of southern rule (Angerbrandt 2011). It served as an "effective bargaining chip" that the North could use to maintain rather than undermine Nigeria's federal structure (Mohammed 2005, 162).

In addition to Obasanjo's presidential veto and the northern regional veto, the House and Senate each possessed veto authority. At first, "there was a bit of a struggle for supremacy," recalls a two-term member from Ebonyi State. "The legislature tried to assert itself, and the executive said no, you cannot have your way."[117] The president and the legislature engaged in a series of political fights over the next few years with regard to a broad range of issues, including the federal budget, anticorruption legislation, and underdevelopment in the Niger Delta. More than

---

[115] Ben Charles-Obi, "We Demand Fiscal Federalism," *TELL*, January 22, 2001. At this summit held by the southern governors, they signaled that sharia might be acceptable if it clearly only applied to Muslims.

[116] "The Middle Belt Revolt," *TELL*, March 27, 2000.

[117] Interview with Honorable Alex Nwofe, March 10, 2010, Abuja.

political gamesmanship, these battles were part of Nigeria's effort to achieve political balance. When President Obasanjo ignored legislative prerogatives on these policy questions, the NASS launched impeachment investigations; when he objected to amendments or modifications by vetoing bills, the legislators voted to override his "nonassent." When evidence of legislative corruption surfaced, Obasanjo launched divide and conquer strategies against the NASS leadership. There were power grabs by rookie politicians (more than 80 percent of whom had never held elected office), but these exchanges were also part of establishing equilibrium between the executive and legislative arms of government.

The discord between the two arms was surprising since the president's party, the PDP, enjoyed majorities in both the House and the Senate. But the PDP had trouble maintaining party discipline, undermining the potential for a partisan veto player. Fitting with Nigeria's earlier political history, institutional and regional loyalties outstripped party loyalty in the early years of the Fourth Republic. Before the end of 1999, the first speaker of the House, Salisu Buhari, had been forced to resign by members of his own party for falsifying his academic background. The Senate president was impeached soon after for lying about his age and credentials.[118] Within months, their replacements, Ghali Na'Abba and Senator Chuba Okadigbo, respectively, were also under attack from the president's allies in the NASS for abuses of public office (Lawan 2010, 331).

As part of a power-sharing agreement, the National Assembly "zoned" leadership posts so that representatives from each of the country's six geopolitical zones (each with six states) held key offices (Dan-Musa 2004). The Senate presidency was zoned to the Southeast states, essentially guaranteeing that an Igbo would hold the post. When Senate President Chuba Okadigbo was under attack by the president, he appealed to the pan-Igbo organization Ohaneze for support. The group organized rallies, articulated a constitutional rationale for Okadigbo's survival, and acted as mediator with the presidency.[119] Okadigbo ultimately lost the battle, and the Senate impeached him for gross abuse of public office.[120] In keeping with the zoning rules, though, the Senate picked another Igbo to succeed

[118] Anselm Okolo, "End of the Road," *TELL*, November 29, 1999.
[119] Uche Maduemesi, "The Senate Should Dissolve," *TELL*, August 21, 2000; Uche Maduemesi, "Playing the Ethnic Card," *TELL*, May 15, 2000.
[120] Obiora Chukwumba and Anselm Okolo, "End Game for Okadigbo, Abubakar," *TELL*, August 7, 2000; Obiora Chukwumba, "Gone with the Wind," *TELL*, August 21, 2000; "Senate Purge," *Africa Research Bulletin*, 1–31 August; Major Adeyi, "Na'Abba's Many Wars," *TELL*, October 2, 2000.

him, who also eventually came under attack.[121] With approximately seven impeachment plots against Senate presidents by 2003, eastern politicians complained of a conspiracy to marginalize Igbo influence.

The siege on House Speaker Ghali Na'Abba soon followed Okadigbo's removal. By September 2000, Obasanjo's allies in the assembly began quietly meeting with cabinet ministers to plot impeachment of the speaker, who was deemed too confrontational. Na'Abba's battle stretched out into the PDP primaries in 2002. Obasanjo supporters in the PDP established a parallel nomination structure, creating "link men" who reported to the president in states with uncooperative governors. The Obasanjo-backed governor appointed eighty-eight special advisers shortly before the election, who, under party rules, automatically became delegates in the primary. With the deck stacked against him, Na'Abba was expelled from the party entirely.

Despite the president's frequent and successful attacks against legislative leaders who were deemed threats, many members of the House still rallied to assert their institutional authority in a number of key policy areas, including the federal budget, anticorruption reform, and Niger Delta resource allocation. From the start of Obasanjo's term, the legislature declared and vigorously defended the power to modify the president's federal budget proposals. The chairman of the Senate Public Accounts Committee commented, "We are seriously concerned about the ability of the president to comply with whatever we approved for him, especially in view of the obvious cases of non-compliance with the contents of the 1999 budget." This included both budgetary impoundments and at least seventy-one unauthorized expenditures by the president that amounted to hundreds of millions of dollars.[122] When the president finally signed the next appropriations bill in May 2000, he made a point of saying that it had been imposed on him (Eminue 2006, 164). He retaliated by announcing new federal policies on wages, reduction of the fuel subsidy, and new capital spending projects, developed without consulting either the National Assembly or the governors. This triggered a debilitating national labor strike and a prolonged standoff with the legislature, which had not even seen a draft of the president's minimum wage bill yet (Okafor 2010).[123]

---

[121] Dele Agekameh, "A House Divided," *TELL*, December 18, 2000.
[122] Anselm Okolo, "Tackling the President," *TELL*, February 21, 2000.
[123] Luky Fiakpa, "One Wage, a Thousand Battles," *TELL*, July 17, 2000.

The budget battles continued throughout Obasanjo's first term and part of his second term. For example, when the NASS set aside funds for each legislative district in the 2001 Appropriations Act, Obasanjo resisted implementation of the projects. The legislators retaliated by delaying passage of the 2002 budget, slashing recurrent spending 20 percent, increasing capital spending by 50 percent, and eventually overriding a presidential veto. They then brought impeachment charges against Obasanjo for nonimplementation of successive budgets. He was saved by two former heads of state, who brokered a political peace (Aiyede 2006; Eminue 2006). In the 2003 budget, the NASS increased spending by nearly 16 percent, and the president and the legislators squared off again. This time neither side was able to muster a passable bill or an override for more than eight months. An ad hoc committee on the budget process concluded that no spending could be ruled constitutional unless authorized by the NASS. According to the committee's chairman, its report was "unanimously carried" to a standing ovation in the chamber, and the "president quickly signed the budget."[124] The assembly made its point with the president with regard to its budget authority, and its capacity to restrain executive excess within a system of checks and balances. But it paid for its stubbornness with a declining popularity as the public complained about what it saw as petty political squabbling.

The executive and the legislature also faced off over anticorruption reforms. Legislation was passed in 2000 that created an Independent Corrupt Practices and Other Related Offenses Commission (ICPC). Obasanjo objected to a provision that would allow federal court judges to appoint independent counsel to investigate allegations of serious wrongdoing by senior executive officials. He also objected to the prosecutorial authorities for a new Economic and Financial Crimes Commission (EFCC) proposed in 2003. Obasanjo vetoed the legislation and the Senate and House voted to override it, making the bill law. The attorney general of the federation announced that the government did not recognize the law, declaring the legislative action "to all intent and purposes, null and void and it lays it open to a charge of contempt."[125] The NASS eventually lost the fight with Obasanjo over his ability to hire and fire the head of the EFCC, a provision that a Senate president later argued "completely destroys the independence of the EFCC." The attorney general also

---

[124] Interview with Honorable Alex Nwofe, March 10, 2010, Abuja.
[125] Chuks Okocha and Lillian Okenwa, "ICPC: House Also Overrides Veto," *This Day*, May 9, 2003.

continued to claim that he had the authority to approve or veto any investigation. But on provisions related to funding and other key matters, the NASS prevailed. The EFCC went on to win praise for pursuing governors and politicians, and it helped recover millions of dollars of embezzled funds. It later reported that between 1999 and 2007, states and local officials failed to spend nearly $20 billion allocated for development.[126]

Finally, the executive and legislature clashed over how to address challenges in the "South-South" zone, the six core states in the Niger Delta. After half a century of oil extraction, the Niger Delta states[127] faced problems relating to economic development, revenue allocation, and disenfranchisement. Although the area had generated hundreds of billions of dollars in federal revenue and profits for private corporations, the local communities remained mired in poverty and pollution. Even now, barely 25 percent of the area's population is literate and life expectancy is only forty-three years (Technical Committee on the Niger Delta 2008).

The NASS and the president set out to address the developmental deficit with joint legislation to create a Niger Delta Development Commission (NDDC) tasked with improving the socioeconomic conditions in the oil producing areas and coordinating the fragmented development efforts under way. While Obasanjo called the bill one of his administration's top priorities, he parted ways with the NASS on some fundamental provisions (Obasanjo 2008). Obasanjo wanted to increase the role of the military in the region and wanted states and local governments to cover a relatively high share of the cost. The chair of the Niger Delta Senate Committee reported that southern governors unanimously opposed Obasanjo's proposed amendments and that the Senate shared their concerns.[128] The Senate also insisted on congressional confirmation of commission appointees and a 3 percent tax on oil companies to help finance the commission's work. When the president rejected the bill, the NASS voted overwhelmingly in mid-2000 to override his veto, delivering a major political setback for Obasanjo.

Just as the debate over the NDDC came to a head, the president and the legislature were beginning to wage political battle over an even

---

[126] Femi Babafemi, "Councils Wasted N3tr, says EFCC," *The Guardian*, August 26, 2008.

[127] The Niger Delta area is sometimes defined more broadly than these six states (Akwa Ibom, Cross River, Bayelsa, Delta, Rivers, and Edo) of the South-South geopolitical zone, especially by communities that stand to benefit from additional development funds.

[128] "Militarising the Niger Delta Will Fail," *TELL*, November 13, 2000; Goddy Enweremadu, "NDDC Bill: House Set to Override Obasanjo's Veto," *This Day*, May 19, 2000.

stickier southern problem: how to allocate revenue from natural resource income. While the country's wealth is derived overwhelmingly from the oil producing states in the South, virtually none of that wealth goes to the people in the oil producing communities. "Resource control is a just cause as our objective is to control our God-given resources," explained Bayelsa State Governor Diepriye Almieseigha in 2001 (Ikein 2008, 90). Under an elaborate revenue allocation system, earnings from oil exports accrue to the center and then are redistributed on the basis of elaborate formulas that have been modified repeatedly since independence (Amuwo et al. 2000; Phillips 1975).

By 2000, new oil discoveries and major advancements in exploration technology made the legal definition of who owns offshore petroleum reserves a centerpiece of the resource control debate. The Obasanjo administration filed a lawsuit in 2001, arguing that the federal government has the exclusive right to the proceeds of offshore oil. While it may have been a tactical error to have filed suit against all thirty-six states (instead of only the oil producers), since this amounted to a generalized attack on states' rights, the federal government won an important victory in the Supreme Court, which upheld the so-called onshore/offshore dichotomy. The administration also won a separate court case against five Southwest states that had demanded back payments under the revenue allocation system (Suberu 2004).

The Court's decisions infuriated politicians and activists in the littoral states. One governor in the Niger Delta accused Obasanjo of blackmail and another hinted at secession, saying that the lawsuit could threaten the peace and unity of the entire country. Numerous minority groups from the area protested that the majority ethnic groups sought to deprive them of resource control.[129] The South-South governors collectively accused President Obasanjo of reneging on a promise to resolve the legal status of offshore oil through negotiation.[130] Working with one civil society organization, the South-South People's Conference, one governor called the bill "the desire of the people of the south-south geopolitical zone."[131] The National Assembly sided with the states, unanimously passing legislation that codified the governors' position and extended states' control of oil to the continental shelf. The president vetoed the bill, warning

---

[129] W. Adeyemo, "You're Greedy," *TELL*, September 24, 2001.

[130] Adegbenro Adebanjo, "Battle Cry in the South-South," *TELL*, March 12, 2001.

[131] Austin Ogwuda and Sola Adebayo, "Oil Dichotomy Bill: Ibori Backs Clark," *Vanguard*, January 21, 2003.

legislators, "Resort may even be taken to war to resolve the claims and counter-claims" with neighboring countries.[132] In response, the country's largest unions, the South-South governors, the main opposition party, and a coalition of traditional rulers from the Niger Delta called on the National Assembly to override the veto.[133]

Even though the president had won several favorable Supreme Court rulings and the support of the northern governors, he was forced to accede on the issue of the onshore/offshore dichotomy. The presidential election was only a few months away, and Obasanjo was facing a popular challenger from the North, Muhammadu Buhari, who had come out for abolition of the onshore/offshore dichotomy. Buhari was greeted enthusiastically at packed rallies in the South-South, alarming Obasanjo's northern allies who had urged him to stand firm on the resource control issue.[134] When the opposition party's regional director for the South-South was killed, many suspected political assassination (LeVan, Pitso, and Adebo 2003).[135] Obasanjo faced a sharply divided NASS and six southern governors who were furious about his handling of the resource control issue, which could sink the PDP's prospects. Polls and press accounts showed that PDP support was precarious in the South-South (Kew 2004). Essentially, Obasanjo had no choice but to bring the PDP together, if either he or the majority of the NASS were going to survive the upcoming elections. The administration resolved the impasse by tactfully brokering a compromise with the governors to extend the territory of the littoral states. Within hours, the Senate president announced that the NASS would not override the president's veto. This mended the party rift and reversed Obasanjo's electoral fortunes in the South-South,[136] where he won between 84 and 98 percent of the vote a few weeks later. While domestic and international observers alleged that many of those Niger Delta votes were fraudulent, the international community looked

---

[132] Rotimi Ajayi, "Why I Won't Sign Oil Dichotomy Bill – Obasanjo," *Vanguard*, December 12, 2002. A separate, significant aspect of the 2002 Supreme Court decision overturned the federal government's authority to deduct various expenses from oil revenues before calculating the distribution of the money to subnational government.

[133] Sola Adebayo, "Traditional Rulers Ask Lawmakers to Override Obasanjo's Veto on Oil Bill," *Vanguard*, January 29, 2003; Bature Umar, "Labour Congress to National Assembly: Override Obasanjo's Veto on Onshore/Offshore Bill," *This Day*, January 30, 2003.

[134] Efem Nkanga, "Buhari in Akwa Ibom, Promises to Abrogate Onshore/Offshore Dichotomy," *This Day*, April 10, 2003.

[135] Dominik Umosen, "Odili Is a Dictator," *TELL*, July 9, 2001.

[136] "Obasanjo, 6 Governors Reach Agreement," *This Day*, February 6, 2003.

the other way, relieved simply that the elections had not descended into violence, precipitating a coup like the one in 1983.

Obasanjo's Second Term and Institutionalization under Three Veto Players (2003–2007)

The 2003 elections heralded two important developments in the North that contributed to a change in veto players from four to three. First, "the sharia issue faded into the background" in all twelve of the states with Islamic law (Paden 2005, 159). While support for the idea of sharia in all its various forms continued at the grassroots level (Afrobarometer 2009b), many Muslim activists shifted their focus to Islam's broader social welfare principles (Bolaji 2009, 130–131). The debate over sharia had arguably damaged Nigeria's international reputation, and citizens demonstrated much more interest in the daily performance and account-ability of state government than in its religious zeal. This was illustrated dramatically in Zamfara and Kano states, where the governors' political opponents focused their criticisms on the lack of economic development to great effect. And newspaper accounts in Niger State by 2001 were describing the governor's support for sharia as "political suicide."[137] Second, a coalition of northern elites rose to defend the National Assembly as the legitimate voice of the federation. At a time when some Igbos in the East and ethnic minorities in the Niger Delta were calling for a "Sovereign National Conference," northern organizations such as the Arewa Consultative Forum insisted that the NASS handle any constitu-tional restructuring of the federation.[138]

As a result of these important shifts, northern interests that had been expressed through a regional veto prior to the elections were channeled through institutional vetoes in the House and the Senate; the presidency retained its veto in Obasanjo's second term. Having survived the battles of the first term, the National Assembly "emerged as a fledging coun-terweight to presidential authority within the separation of powers" (Lewis 2009, 182). Clientelism and corruption notwithstanding, political institutions proved increasingly capable of interest aggregation, political recruitment, and policy debate.

---

[137] Inuwa Bwala, "Riding the Sharia Tiger," *TELL*, July 30, 2001.

[138] Shola Oshunkeye, "Sticking to Their Guns," *TELL*, July 2, 2001; Danlami Nmodu, "Bracing for a Showdown," *TELL*, November 20, 2000.

TABLE 2.2. *Distribution of Seats in National Assembly*

	Seats after 1999 Election		Seats after 2003 Election	
	House	Senate	House	Senate
People's Democratic Party	206	59	223	76
All People's Party/All Nigeria People's Party	74	29	96	27
Alliance for Democracy	68	20	34	6
Other	12	1	7	0

Source: Independent National Electoral Commission

Frustration still ran deep in the Niger Delta, and the creation of the NDDC bureaucracy in 2000 had done little actually to improve socioeconomic conditions in the oil producing states. Starting in 2004, Obasanjo increasingly had to contend with rebels who took foreigners hostage and attacked oil platforms, generating an outsized effect on the national economy (and the price of oil). Yet the Movement for the Emancipation of the Niger Delta (MEND) and other groups failed to achieve their core demand to increase the share of federal revenue returned to the oil producing states – what is known as the "derivation formula." Increasing the formula from 13 to 25 percent (or higher, as some groups demanded) would have required modifying the constitution. Building a political coalition to support their cause while using sabotage and subversion proved tricky. Though the rebels' critique of underdevelopment was grounded within legitimate political discourse about economic conditions in the area (Hazen 2009; Asuni 2009b), the constituency for such a fundamental reform never gathered sufficient momentum much beyond the six core Niger Delta states. The rebels' cause thus lacked the sort of widespread interstate coordination and institutional coherence across the South that were necessary to generate a regional veto.

Fraud in the 2003 election had been especially acute in the Niger Delta, firming up the PDP's hold in the six states (Omotola 2010). But if Obasanjo felt the new crop of PDP legislators – from there or elsewhere in the country – owed him some gratitude for his heavy-handed efforts to ensure their election (see Table 2.2), he was soon disappointed by the harsh criticism directed at him. Presidential meddling in party primaries contributed to huge electoral turnover, and literally hundreds of politicians at local, state, and national levels became embroiled in legal fights over candidate nominations and election results (Legal Defence Centre

2004). Legislators immediately set out to draw boundaries on executive overreach, craft provisions prohibiting budget impoundments, and redirect money from the onshore-offshore dichotomy (legalized by the 2002 Supreme Court decision) into special federal accounts (Eminue 2006, 170–173). As in the previous four years, budget battles were at the center of legislative-executive clashes.

One major conflict arose during 2005 budget deliberations over how to estimate future revenue. Although the Iraq War had contributed to a spike in oil prices, Obasanjo and his minister of finance wanted to use modest projected earnings of twenty-seven dollars per barrel in budgeting. He compromised with the House on a thirty-dollars-per-barrel projection, but when the Senate approved a thirty-two-dollar benchmark nearly six months later,[139] the executive accused legislators of receiving bribes from the minister of education (who wanted to inflate the ministry's budget) and claimed that the legislature's operations budget was bloated. The scandal quickly led to the resignation of the Senate president and cast doubts on the credibility of the budget overall.[140]

The president finally signed a budget in April but soon announced that his ministries would refuse to spend some of the allocated money through budget impoundments. Seventy-four senators signed a resolution declaring "no retreat, no surrender" on the issue of nonimplementation. The House launched an investigation into the president's breach of the constitution, and the Senate threatened impeachment. The PDP outside the NASS intervened to resolve the impasse (much as it had in 2000) by serving as a mediator, and the party's national chair announced that the budget act would be implemented according to law.[141]

Anticorruption proposals were contentious as well, and another Senate president was forced to resign in 2005 after accusations of graft. As the 2007 elections approached, the EFCC faced charges of bias when watchdogs revealed that a majority of the 135 candidates under investigation either belonged to the opposition party or had close ties to the vice president. Vice President Atiku Abubakar, a northern member of the PDP with

[139] Chidi Nkwopara, "House Passes 2005 Budget," *This Day*, February 17, 2005; Isa Sanusi and Hameed Bello, "Senate Passes N.1.799tr Budget," *Daily Trust*, March 9, 2005.

[140] Sufuyan Ojeifo and Emmanuel Aziken, "Nigerian Senate President Resigns," *The Guardian*, March 23, 2005.

[141] Cosmas Ekpunob, "Alleged Budget Breach, 74 Senators Move against Obasanjo," *Daily Champion*, May 6, 2005; Isa Sanusi, "Impeachment Threat: Obasanjo Backs Down on Budget Cuts," *Daily Trust*, May 10, 2005; Kola Lolgbondiyan and Ndubuisi Ugah, "Obasanjo, Lawmakers Settle Differences," *This Day*, May 10, 2005.

presidential aspirations, was engaged in an acrimonious internal battle for power against Obasanjo, who opposed his candidacy. Rather than go through established institutions, the Obasanjo government swiftly set up an ad hoc panel and, after a brief two-day investigation, indicted thirty-seven candidates on various charges in order to undermine Atiku's allies (Human Rights Watch 2007).[142]

No issue better illustrates the nature of political contestation among Nigeria's veto players during this period, however, than the battle over President Obasanjo's third term. In late 2005, Deputy Senate President Ibrahim Mantu began hinting at the possibility of amending the constitution to allow President Obasanjo a third term in office. An opposition group called the Movement for the Restoration of Democracy quickly sprang to life, with the support of Vice President Abubakar and a cross section of northern political leaders.[143] Another Obasanjo term would not only deny Abubakar a shot at the top office, it also would betray the unwritten "power shift" agreement among PDP elites that the North would have its turn to rule after Obasanjo served his two terms. The PDP leadership officially endorsed a third term and threatened Abubakar with expulsion from the party if he continued to fraternize with Obasanjo's critics. It also proposed a third term for the governors as well, hoping to build a state-level coalition for a third presidential term among northern state governors.[144]

Supporters of a third term argued that Obasanjo's record of economic reform justified his continuing in office. The president suggested that he was responding to a higher calling when he explained, "God is not a God of abandoned projects."[145] A group in the National Assembly called the "National Unity Forum" also argued that the time had come for Nigerians to do away with requisite power shift and ethnoregional balancing. "I don't really care where the president comes from," the forum's leader explained, implying that it should not matter whether a southerner ruled for another four years.[146] A shadowy group calling itself the

[142] Cosmas Ekpunobi, "Senate Faults EFCC's Graft List – VP Says It's for Witch Hunt," *Daily Champion*, February 21, 2007.
[143] Anza Philips, "Campaign against Obasanjo Begins," *Newswatch*, December 5, 2005.
[144] Rotimi Ajayi, "PDP Adopts 3rd Term for Obasanjo, Govs," *Vanguard*, April 14, 2006; Rotimi Ajayi and Emeka Mamah," PDP Queries Atiku, Northern Group Threatens Reprisal Attack," *Vanguard*, April 12, 2006.
[145] "I Leave the Third Term to God," *The Punch*, April 4, 2006.
[146] Tobs Agbaegbu and Anza Philips, "Third Term Is a People's Agenda," *Newswatch*, February, 27, 2006; Jide Ajani, "3rd Term: Attah Makes Case for Reforms," *Vanguard*, April 13, 2006.

Coalition of Lagos State Youth began taking out full-page newspaper ads that praised Obasanjo's economic agenda. Using the Yoruba word for father, the ads urged people to support Obasanjo: "Ride on Baba to a safe third term in office."[147]

Obasanjo's plea to southern regional sentiments and his effort to divide northern politicians failed. National- and state-level northern politicians gathered in Kaduna as the "Northern Legislators Forum" to discuss the issue in December, joined by civil society groups such as the Arewa Consultative Forum and new ones such as the Northern Youth Alliance for Democracy. The chair of the meeting said the group's "opposition to any amendment to the constitution that will allow anyone to contest for office beyond the constitutionally stipulated two terms of four years each[,] is a unanimous one."[148] When several governors in the Southwest entertained the idea of a third term, they were roundly condemned by the Yoruba Council of Elders and the prestigious cultural organization Afenifere, based in the Southwest. Southern support was an exaggeration, a fear generated by the Southern Leadership Forum to serve Obasanjo. The Northern Governors Forum divided on the issue, but a coalition of northern state houses responded with a unanimous statement condemning the third term. Various political alliances opposed to the third term emerged within the National Assembly as well. For example, opposition politicians in the APP (after changing the name of the party to the All Nigeria People's Party, or "ANPP") threatened to derail the credibility of a constitutional review committee by pulling out of the process entirely. A new group, the Northern Senators Forum, within the NASS also condemned the president's plans.[149]

While the international community did not want to be seen as interfering directly in the political machinations of a sovereign state, international disapproval was another major force working against Obasanjo. The U.S. Embassy gingerly cautioned that "executive term limits should be respected in the interest of institutional democracy."[150] Even the chair of the subcommittee that first advanced the idea of a third term

---

[147] Advertisement, *This Day*, March 30, 2006.
[148] Tobs Agbaegbu and Sam Adzegeh, "Obasanjo's Ambition Sure to Die," *Newswatch*, December 19, 2005.
[149] Anza Philips, "The Final Plot," *Newswatch*, February 27, 2006. Sam Adzegeh, "Third Term Agenda Sponsors Will Go to Hell," *Newswatch*, February 27, 2006.
[150] Emmanuel Aziken and Habib Yakoob, "Respect Term Limit, U.S. Tells Obasanjo," *Vanguard*, May 1, 2006; "Death of Third Term Victory for Democracy – U.S.," *Daily Trust*, May 31, 2006.

understood that there was "a general fear of African regimes perpetuating themselves"; if Obasanjo could force a third term, why not a fourth?[151]

The Senate formally ended Obasanjo's bid for a third term, exercising its veto power with a decisive vote in May 2006. Obasanjo's defeat was not just a political victory for the legislature, it was an institutional victory, as Posner and Young (2007) argue in a seminal essay. The constitution itself was at issue in the debate, and its role as a foundational contract among diverse cultural communities and political interests was ultimately upheld. The debate over the third term contributed to the consolidation of democratic institutions that transcended regional cleavages. The North arguably had the most at stake since allowing Obasanjo to remain in office would have violated the power shift pact promised the North during the 1999 transition. Senator Idris Kuta declared at a Kaduna meeting that northern leaders "stand united and firm in our desire to ensure the return of the president to the north in 2007 in fulfillment of a sacred gentlemen's agreement."[152] But while the North was more outspoken in its opposition, citizen responses during Senator Mantu's hearings in all six of the country's geopolitical zones revealed overwhelming public support for limiting the president to two terms. This sentiment was subsequently confirmed in surveys.[153] "The southwest was complacent because they did not want to rock the boat of their brother," said the House PDP whip in a 2010 interview. "But by and large, Nigerians agreed on a common position on the need for him [Obasanjo] not to have another term."[154] As the vote neared, interviews with National Assembly members from different areas of the country echoed the widespread opposition.[155] A senior Yoruba senator from Oyo State argues that the third term failed because it constituted "a road to dictatorship," and because other politicians simply wanted to run for president.[156] In the end, says former Senate President Ken Nnamani, "There was no part of the country that supported the third term."[157]

[151] Interview with Senator Omar Abubakar Hambagda, March 9, 2010, Abuja.
[152] Tobs Agbaegbu and Sam Adzegeh, "Obasanjo's Ambition Sure to Die," *Newswatch*, December 19, 2005.
[153] Alifa Daniel, "Senate Dumps Constitution Review Bill," *The Guardian*, May 17, 2006. Afrobarometer Round 4 data, available at www.afrobarometer.org.
[154] Interview with Honorable Emeka Ihedioha, March 17, 2010, Abuja.
[155] Celestine Okafor, "As PDP Okays 3rd Term: We'll Shoot It Down, Reps Vow," *Vanguard*, April 15, 2006.
[156] Interview with Senator Abiola Ajimobi, March 15, 2010, Ibadan.
[157] Interview with Senator Ken Nnamani, March 9, 2010, Abuja.

Conclusion

Counting the number of veto players in each of Nigeria's regimes over 48 years has provided information about the structure of political authority and constructed this study's independent variable. These 14 veto player regimes are summarized in Table 2.3. They were populated by different types of political actors: partisan veto players such as the NCNC in the multiparty coalition government from 1960 to 1964 and the NPP from 1980 to 1981. Factions during military regimes, such as the Langtang Mafia in the early 1990s and the June 12 faction during Abacha's first few years, operated as partisan veto players in that they emerged as a stable set of preferences within institutions. The coding also included institutional bodies such as legislative chambers in each of Nigeria's three republics (1960 to 1966, 1979 to 1983, and 1999 to present) and ruling military councils during the regimes of Gowon (1966–1975), Muhammed/Obasanjo (1975–1979), and Babangida (1985–1993). Each veto player had a motive to challenge the status quo and the organizational means to coordinate preferences and demonstrably blocked a major policy initiative.

As explained in Chapter 1, veto player theory makes an important conceptual distinction between actors who have the ability to compel a policy change and those who merely wish to do so. You cannot count actors as vetoes simply because their preferences differ, as Strøm (2000) points out. Across Nigeria's regimes between 1960 and 2007, numerous political actors complained about transition plans, constitutional reforms, or the state of federalism, but failed to exercise a veto. For example, the Supreme Military Council in 1966 failed to reverse Aguiyi-Ironsi's brash decisions on military promotions affecting the regime's balance of power. In the Buhari/Idiagbon era from 1984 to 1985, Babangida's army faction fought neoliberal reforms and nearly every major economic policy initiative and lost. In the early 1990s during Babangida's rule, southern politicians allied with civil society groups to exercise a regional veto on transition plans, but the North was unable to coordinate effectively. This happened despite concerns in the North that a democratic transition would undermine traditional rulers, whose influence suffered from a series of government reforms. Yet another example of a failed veto player arose during Abacha's tenure. Between 1993 and 1998, some military insiders tried to increase the authority of civilian governorships but failed, and the navy and air force attempted to create accountability within the Provisional Ruling Council by balancing the interests of the

TABLE 2.3. *List of Veto Players*

Veto players	Years	Description and Distribution of Veto Authority (Regional Vetoes in Shaded Boxes)	
2	1960–1964	Westminster-style parliament elected in 1959. NPC holds partisan veto with 134 seats in a coalition government, which demonstrates cohesiveness during constitutional reforms creating a new federal region. The NPC is successful on civil service reforms which have implications for North/South balance of power.	NCNC holds partisan veto with 89 seats in a coalition government. It secures key portfolios and concessions on foreign policy and the census and colludes with NPC on state creation.
1	1965	Westminster-style parliament elected in late 1964. NPC runs in a coalition but when it wins a majority, it forms a government on its own. Opposition parties enjoy only token participation and they allege that a "northern agenda" dominates politics.	
2	1966	Aguiyi-Ironsi rules briefly as head of state and pushes his military promotions through despite resistance from Supreme Military Council. Federal Executive Council confined to policy implementation.	A northern coalition of politicians, military officers, and elites coordinates a regional veto against civil service reforms and the abolition of federalism.
2	1967–1974	Head of State Gowon has veto but struggles to control the governors, despite widespread corruption and frustration with the states.	An inclusive Supreme Military Council rules collectively. "Super Perm Secs" and technocrats capture authority to make and implement policy.

(continued)

TABLE 2.3. *Continued*

Veto players	Years	Description and Distribution of Veto Authority (Regional Vetoes in Shaded Boxes)		
3	1975–1979	Mohammed, then Obasanjo, as head of state has veto. Obasanjo makes some changes to draft constitution, but loses to SMC on Islamic law and key constitutional issues.	Chief of Staff, Supreme HQ has veto. Yar 'Adua is backed by Kaduna Mafia; successfully adds Islamic judicial appeals to constitution.	SMC collectively involved in policy making and pushes transition plan. Chooses successor according to preestablished procedures when Mohammed is assassinated.
3	1980–1981	President has constitutional veto; exercises strong agenda control over budget and spending bills.	NPN with 36 seats in Senate (of 95) and 168 in House (of 450) has partisan veto in a multiparty coalition with the NPP. The parties demonstrate cohesion during appropriation votes	NPP with 16 Senate seats and 78 House seats has partisan veto in a coalition with NPN. Preferences diverge on ambassadorial nominations and details of the coalition agreement. The NPP succeeds in extracting appointments and resources from NPN.
3	1982–1983	President possesses a constitutional veto. Fights Assembly on budget, PLOs, and appointments.	House has an institutional veto; successfully challenges president's ability to extend emergency authority.	Senate has an institutional veto; rejects president's supplemental appropriations bill and prevents him from borrowing money.

2	1984–1985	Buhari is head of state. He pushes through extraconstitutional military tribunals and radical economic reforms. He attempts but fails to limit the reach of the National Security Organization. Governors are limited to consultation.		Idiagbon, chief of staff, Supreme HQ, enjoys authority and backing from coalitions outside the regime. He runs the security apparatus and one of the government's major policy initiatives.
3	1986–1989	Babangida governs with army support and key northern allies. He prevails on unpopular economic reforms, reshuffles the cabinet, and survives a coup attempt.	Armed Forces Ruling Council has collective authority. It prevails on some issues of state creation and forces changes on structural adjustment economic reforms.	Soft-liner faction advances liberalization. Political Bureau weakens senior bureaucrats by expanding its authority beyond its own terms of reference. The faction pushes creation of new states and transition plans, and many members evade the ban on politics.
4	1990–1993	Babangida's AFRC reforms demonstrate he still holds a veto.	Abacha thwarts coup and uses army to acquire factional veto. He survives purges and is promoted, even while encouraging defections from Babangida loyalists.	Soft-liner faction in AFRC composed of "Langtang Mafia" and moderates. Babangida forced to reinstate General Bali.	Prodemocracy coalition including civil society groups, politicians, and traditional leaders coordinate a southern regional veto that pushes Babangida to "step aside" when election annulment leads to a stalemate.

(continued)

TABLE 2.3. *Continued*

Veto players	Years	Description and Distribution of Veto Authority (Regional Vetoes in Shaded Boxes)
2	1994–1996	Abacha as head of state governs with Provisional Ruling Council. Weak cabinet and weak National Council of State. He purges the "Babangida boys" and some of army leadership, but technocrats and democrats in his "rainbow cabinet" and bureaucrats who had fought for influence are difficult to neutralize. — Chief of General Staff Diya and the "June 12" group is the only faction within the PRC to hold a veto. They gain cabinet seats, survive purges, influence state creation choices, and argue for transition.
1	1997–1998	Abacha holds only veto by successfully dominating the Provisional Ruling Council. He abandons transition and neutralizes PRC members opposed to his "self-succession." The Federal Executive Council stops meeting entirely.
4	1999–2003	President spends some nonappropriated money and through Senate allies pushes out Senate president. — House institutional veto overrides president on NDDC and EFCC legislation. Also wins fights on supplemental appropriations. — Senate institutional veto overrides president on NDDC and EFCC. Differs from House on presidential impeachment efforts. — Northern interests coordinate on sharia to exercise regional veto, successfully demanding ethnopolitical inclusion in government and enforcement of revenue allocation formulae.
3	2004–2007	President negotiates down foreign debts; creates ad hoc investigations to shape the party and the NASS. — House institutional veto imposes some restrictions on executive budget impoundments and other spending. — Senate institutional veto forces concessions from president on various budgets, including oil revenue estimates in 2005, and derails the president's third term bid.

different military services. All of these actors advanced a distinct set of preferences, but they failed to exert enough political leverage over the policy process to achieve their goals and were therefore not coded as veto players. In other instances, such as when the PDP secured large majorities in the National Assembly in 2003, we might have expected the party to operate as a partisan veto player. Instead, its "honorables" (as the members are known) defended the interests of the legislature, affirming the authority of the assembly as an institutional actor.

Overall, this analysis and coding process support several assertions made in previous discussions about the benefits of veto players as a tool for advancing our comparative understandings of Africa in general. First, I demonstrated how federalism and authoritarianism are not entirely incompatible. Gowon's regime between late 1966 and 1975 faced challenges not only from powerful bureaucrats but from governors who efficiently coordinated their preferences within the military council. His inability to discipline the governors, even after widespread public complaints about corruption and mismanagement, was Gowon's "most obvious failure" according to his successors.[158]

Second, the exercise of regional vetoes in order to enforce Nigeria's century-old federal bargain between the North and the South reinforces the idea that authority can be constructed through extraconstitutional means. A coalition of northern bureaucrats and military officers successfully allied to block Aguiyi-Ironsi's civil service reforms in 1966 and ultimately prevented his attempted abolition of constitutional federalism. The sharia movement during the early years of the Fourth Republic, from 1999 to 2003, generated a similar regional veto for the North. A distinct coalition of governors and Hausa-Fulani elites successfully defended northern interests on a range of policies at a time when many felt insecure about the shift of power to President Obasanjo, a Christian Yoruba from the South. This does not mean that popular support for sharia was insincere, but it does show how the effort by twelve state legislatures to extend Islamic law to criminal matters was a symptom of larger struggles over federalism expressed through a northern regional identity (Elaigwu and Galadima 2003). By comparison, the Niger Delta rebels failed to meet this threshold of interstate coordination, so no regional veto formed to change the derivation formula affecting the oil producing states.

---

[158] "Nigeria: A Transitional Regime?" *Africa Confidential*, September 26, 1975; "Nigeria's Want in the Midst of Plenty," *West Africa*, August 11, 1975.

While the unsuccessful regional vetoes help illustrate the threshold my criteria set for identifying veto players, the successful regional vetoes highlight a third contribution to the comparative literature, related to informal institutions. The North and South are an inescapable part of the nation's political consciousness and cultural distinctions. But these two regions scarcely exist in "formal" terms, as the 2006 debate over "power shift" exposed. Yet the demonstrable influence of regional veto players, like the factional veto players in the military regimes, shows how informal institutions can be integrated into a veto player framework. This speaks to a critique common among Africanists: that institutional analysis tends to overlook more subtle rules of politics embedded within culture (Hyden 2012; Chabal 2009).

Fourth, this chapter demonstrated that multiple veto players can exist within authoritarian regimes. Despite 26 years of dictatorships, I coded single veto player regimes on only two occasions, covering only 3 out of the 47 years in my sample. At different times, military factions, regional coalitions, and ruling military councils all managed to limit the head of state's ability to act unilaterally by exercising a veto over a major policy. For example, the regime in power from 1975 to 1979 emasculated the previously powerful governors, but the ruler faced other checks: Obasanjo had to contend with a collective military council and a popular deputy with an autonomous base of power. In 1984 and 1985, Idiagbon shepherded the Buhari government's most visible policy initiatives and successfully resisted efforts to limit his control of the state security apparatus. During the Babangida years, the Lagos Group and Langtang Mafia soft-liners pushed political liberalization and forced his eventual resignation in 1993. Even Abacha, probably the most ruthless of Nigeria's dictators, was checked by the June 12 faction that survived his purges roughly through 1996, and it imposed huge transaction costs on him as he vacillated about a democratic transition. Consistent with the comparative authoritarian literature mentioned in the book's Introduction, dictators in these regimes faced limits on unilateral policy behavior.

By analyzing major policy debates over nearly half a century in Nigeria, this chapter has identified fourteen different veto player regimes, each one with between one and four veto players. This generated an independent variable that counts the number of political actors, understood in the broad aggregate terms defined by veto player theory, who cannot be ignored during the policy-making process. The task of the next chapter is to show how these different regimes affected government performance – measured in terms of both national collective goods enjoyed by all and local collective goods with more excludable benefits. To operationalize these policy outcomes, I adopt variables that are empirically linked to long-term economic development in the political economy literature and that reflect recurring policy priorities of Nigeria's governments. Statistical tests across a broad range of controls show that the number of veto players affects local and national collective goods differently. The results suggest that having a small number of veto players offers advantages when it comes to delivering national collective goods. But regimes with more veto players that divide power – in the spirit of Madison – demonstrate increased accountability by limiting overall spending levels on local collective goods.

3

The Impact of Nigeria's Veto Players on Local and National Collective Goods

Sub-Saharan Africa's development record over the last half-century translates into some grim realities. Millions of Africans die from curable diseases, cyclical food shortages, and ongoing civil conflict. Compared to people in other regions in the world, Africans are less likely to have access to health care, clean water, or credit, and they are more likely to die before reaching old age. Many African economies flag under the weight of widespread corruption, high unemployment, and price volatility. The optimism of the postindependence era dissipated in the 1970s and 1980s in the face of authoritarianism, mounting foreign debt, and unpopular economic reforms. Even during the democratic revival in the 1990s, Africa as a whole averaged a -0.7 percent growth rate and experienced fresh outbreaks of civil conflict and disease.

Mounting evidence suggests that many African countries are starting to break with this past, overcoming unfavorable geography, colonial legacies, and divisive social cleavages. Over the last decade, twenty-two countries have maintained economic growth rates of at least 4 percent and shown promising signs of sustainable development. Among a more select group of seventeen countries such as Burkina Faso, Mozambique, and Uganda, citizens' incomes have increased as much as 50 percent and trade has doubled (Radelet 2010). In 2013 *The Economist* reported that since the turn of the century, foreign direct investment had tripled, life expectancy rose by a tenth, and the average growth rate across the continent hit 6 percent.[1] A variety of new approaches have emerged to explain the divergence between well performing countries and those mired in poverty.

[1] Oliver August, "Aspiring Africa," *The Economist*, March 2, 2013.

One study points to empirical links between institutional quality and the political conditions conducive to progrowth policy choices (Collier and O'Connell 2008). Another influential study attributes sustainable long-term development in wealthy countries to the "inclusiveness" of their institutions (Acemoglu and Robinson 2012).

Like this new generation of institutional explanations, this chapter demonstrates that veto players structure the opportunities for good policy in one of Africa's most important countries. I systematically link the number of veto players in Nigeria to the delivery of local and national collective goods over time. Empirical tests show that the number of veto players has differential effects on these two broad categories of public policy since 1960. Other single-country veto player studies have similarly found it useful to disaggregate policy outcomes and adopt multiple measures of performance (Conley and Bekafigo 2010). This increases the analytical leverage for testing a theory with a single case, presenting a natural experiment that enables the research design to hold constant historical, geographical, cultural, and other factors. The analysis here thus presents an innovative answer to the question posed in the book's Introduction: How does the distribution of political authority affect the Nigerian government's ability to deliver policies conducive to development?

First, I contrast local and national collective goods, describing an underlying difference based on how widely their benefits are shared by citizens. Drawing upon the public goods literature, I identify budget discipline, inflation, education, and judicial efficiency as important measures of national-level collective goods. Political economy literature associates all of these variables with long-term economic development, and Nigerian governments have repeatedly pledged to improve government performance in these areas. I operationalize local collective goods with variables measuring the government's capital spending, recurrent spending, and overall government consumption. Capital spending offers a particularly good measure of local collective goods since it relates to physical infrastructure, meaning that enjoying its benefits largely depends on proximity, and rulers are often able to target it. For this reason, it is reasonable to infer the use of patronage spending from excessive increases in overall levels.

Second, I test the hypotheses formulated in Chapter 1. Statistical tests confirm the coordination hypothesis, which states that an increase in the number of veto players will result in a decline in overall levels of national collective goods. I find that regimes with more veto players have bigger budget deficits, higher rates of inflation, larger student/teacher ratios, and slower resolution of property rights cases in the courts. The results support the idea that additional veto players generate transaction costs in a process that contributes to coordination problems that impede the delivery of nonexcludable policies. In addition, the results challenge selectorate theory and other research that suggests that an increase in the number of political actors creates incentives to bargain to an efficient allocation of resources as each actor realizes his or her declining rates of payoff.

Third, I test the logroll hypothesis, which predicts that an increase in the number of veto players will have nearly the opposite effect on local collective goods: As each player successfully demands patronage, overall spending levels of these excludable goods grow. This tests an insight by Cox and McCubbins (2001), who argue that each policy actor with the leverage to prevent a change in the status quo is also in a position to extract particularistic concessions (similar to the American idea of "pork"). I reject the logroll hypothesis, though, since statistical tests show that an increase in the number of veto players actually limits overall spending levels on local collective goods. This supports ideas from the commitment tradition in veto player literature, which suggests that the conditions conducive to policy stability also contribute to accountability. Both sets of statistical models remain robust after controlling for factors such as the level of oil revenues, foreign debt, overall economic conditions, and governance through democracy or dictatorship. This means that veto players offer a compelling alternative to the explanations characteristic of the conventional wisdom outlined in the Introduction.

Fourth, a succinct qualitative analysis summarizes the delivery of local and national collective goods in Nigeria during the years covered in my sample. This is important for a variety of reasons. It links specific veto player regimes to outcomes on my dependent variable, something that we cannot discern from the overall patterns revealed through the statistical tests. This helps identify statistical outliers and provide a check against the relatively small sample size (especially with regard to the judicial data, which do not cover the full 47 years). The narratives also show that Nigeria's governments repeatedly made commitments to improve outcomes in terms of budgetary discipline, low student/teacher ratios, and my other measures of government performance, meaning that my dependent variable reflects recurring policy priorities. Finally and most importantly, since the policies used to identify veto players in Chapter 2 (based on the leverage they exercise) are different from the policy outcomes used in the statistical tests, the qualitative analysis clarifies linkages between the independent and dependent variables. In particular, the analysis provides additional examples of monitoring among veto players, illustrating mechanisms of accountability.

The conclusion to this chapter identifies the tension between these two sets of results as a "Madisonian dilemma." On the one hand, regimes that have the most veto players systematically underprovide national collective goods, a result I attribute to increased coordination problems. On the other hand, these same regimes generate accountability that limits overspending on local collective goods. This recasts the conditions for good governance in Nigeria and beyond as a balancing act between accountability that limits patronage and efficient bargaining that generates broad nonexcludable public policies.

National and Local Collective Goods as Measures of Government Performance

National and local collective goods differ in the range of people who enjoy their benefits. According to public goods theory, collective action problems often impair the provision of policies with national-level benefits. Since individual citizens reap the benefits of these public policies whether they contribute to them or not, they generate the "free-rider" problem (Olson 1965). National defense, economic growth, and low inflation are common examples of these nonexcludable polices. Free markets theoretically underprovide such national benefits because the costs of denying them to noncontributors or any segment of the population are too high – in either practical or political terms (Przeworski 2003). Government offers a common solution to this problem by providing these goods and then implementing a combination of enforcement and incentives to make sure everyone contributes (Lake and Baum 2001). However, in theoretical terms, it is the consumption of these broadly shared policies with nonexcludable benefits – not their provision by the government – that distinguishes them as national collective goods.

In order to draw conclusions about the conditions necessary to provide these policies, I operationalize national collective goods with original variables measuring macroeconomic policy, judicial performance, and provision of education. Though these measures may appear quite different, they all share properties as nonexcludable national policies that comparative literature commonly associates with long-term economic development. In addition, they all reflect policy priorities of Nigeria's governments. I then operationalize local collective goods with three different variables measuring federal spending: Government consumption captures the overall level, recurrent spending refers to expenditures on administration and staffing, and capital spending refers to investment in infrastructure. All three of these variables are used in the literature as proxies for patronage, but since capital spending generates excludable benefits, it provides the most direct measurement of local collective goods prone to patronage. My measures of national and local collective goods only measure outcomes at an aggregate level, in terms of the federal government's performance. This sacrifices some interesting subnational variation in Nigeria's development, but it enables a clear portrait of performance over time across multiple indicators.

Macroeconomic Performance

Sound macroeconomic policies can provide collective benefits at the national level by keeping food, fuel, and other necessities affordable. Conversely, macroeconomic mismanagement can lead to sharp rises in the price of consumer goods and growing deficits. Nigeria's economic record over the last five decades shows tremendous variation on these terms. The prices of consumer goods sometimes rose suddenly after years of relative stability, and federal spending often embraced overambitious development plans without ensuring sustainable revenue streams. Inflation and federal budget discipline measure relevant aspects of this performance, and in what follows I describe these two measures of my dependent variable.

Like the dictators who preceded them, Nigeria's more recent elected politicians have struggled to keep spending in line with revenue. In 2008, one of Nigeria's leading newspapers lamented, "Our country has become a prominent member of the league of failing states, not only because the government is too weak to enforce its own laws against corruption and other crimes, but because an oversized recurrent expenditure pattern has crippled the government's capacity to render basic social services to the people."[2] Despite nearly a decade of democracy, the editorial implied that the government had locked in unsustainable commitments to spending growth. Managing federal budgets has been an ongoing challenge since independence. Neither autocracy nor revenue scarcity (for example, due to falling oil prices) is solely to blame for poor performance on this front, and numerous scholars have chronicled Nigeria's budgetary policies and their broader effects. Schatz (1977) studies how Nigeria responded to the

---

[2] Adebolu Arowolo, "2009 Budget: Dead on Arrival?" *The Punch*, December 3, 2008.

economic decline of the late 1960s with technocratic solutions to revenue management. Ake (1984) and Forrest (1995) show how revenue spikes during the oil booms of the 1970s and 1980s contributed to inefficiency and corruption. Recent work by Balogun (2009) and Ikein et al. (2008) carry on this tradition by documenting government profligacy during the Fourth Republic.

One important macroeconomic indicator that captures this dimension of government performance and is commonly used to operationalize national collective goods is budgetary discipline. In general, this refers to how well the federal government keeps spending in line with revenue (Alesina and Perotti 1996; Ariyo 1996a).[3] It is therefore a good measure of policy makers' ability to coordinate their interests and agree to realistic spending constraints. Spending that consistently exceeds revenue could therefore be a sign of bargaining failures and have broader economic consequences. The Nigerian government argues that moderate levels of deficit spending (defined as 3 to 4 percent of GDP) pose few problems, but that "huge deficit financing could also lead to spiraling inflation" and economic recession (Federal Office of Statistics 1993, 111).

The underlying assumption is that it is politically more difficult to spend less than to spend more. Politicians face a tempting impulse to spend in order to protect their interests and buy influence. In Nigeria, balancing the budget is complicated by the fact that estimating federal revenue has often amounted to educated guessing of future oil prices. Optimistic estimates of the price of crude make it easier to balance a proposed budget on paper, while conservative estimates open the possibility for windfall revenue to wind up in politicians' pockets. For the statistical tests that follow, I operationalize budget discipline with the variable *fedbudget*, which is the ratio of federal spending to revenue in a given year, expressed as a share of GDP. Its values over time are illustrated in Figure 3.1, where a negative value indicates a budget deficit. This original variable is based on data gathered at the Central Bank of Nigeria and the Federal Office of Statistics.[4]

---

[3] The use of this dependent variable is not meant to endorse balanced budgets in a narrow sense, though. Economists since John Maynard Keynes and John Kenneth Galbraith have argued that moderate levels of deficit spending can stimulate an economy when countries face temporary exigent circumstances such as a spike in unemployment (Parker 2005). Indeed a core debate in the recent global recession has centered on whether tax increases should finance economic stimulus, or whether deep budget cuts are necessary for recovery. My interest here is not an effort to test that theory.

[4] Since the Central Bank of Nigeria reports 1961–1964 in fiscal rather than calendar years, I adopt a standard adjustment technique. Following economists such as Ariyo (1996b), I

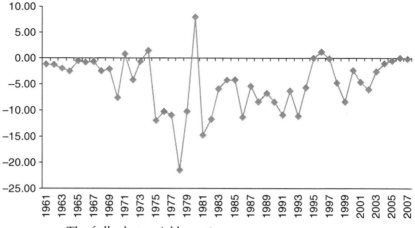

FIGURE 3.1. The *fedbudget* variable, 1961–2007.

Inflation is another important macroeconomic indicator that is commonly used in the public goods literature to operationalize national collective goods (Feng 2003; Lijphart 2012). It reflects both the cost of consumer goods and the availability of credit, broadly shared benefits that are nonexcludable and essential to long-term development. The inflation rate is important because many studies link it to long-term growth in the developing world, though a debate over the direction of the causal relationship and the significance of the effects is ongoing (Chimobi 2010). As a second measure of economic performance, the variable *inflation* here measures the annual rate of inflation reflected in the consumer price index based on data from the World Bank's World Development Indicators. The values are illustrated in Figure 3.2.

Nigeria's inflation was modest in the postindependence years, then spiked with the oil boom of the early 1970s, when the military government formed an Anti-Inflation Task Force. Its most spectacular fluctuations occurred between 1986 and 1997, when the inflation rate during any given year ranged between 5 percent and 100 percent. Government performance in this area still shows ups and downs, though they are less dramatic. Taken together, budget discipline and inflation nicely illustrate the challenge of coordinating the competing interests of political actors who

calculate *fedbudget* by converting fiscal years to calendar years using the following procedure: (previous *FY* * .25) + (current *FY* * 0.75). Similarly, the CBN only reports nine months for 1968 and nine months for 1969, so the figures I report for these years are estimates based on a twelve month calendar year.

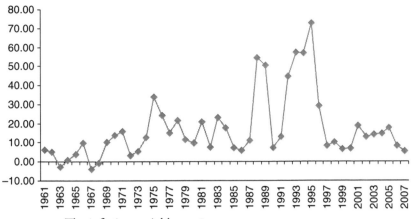

FIGURE 3.2. The *inflation* variable, 1961–2007.

often have more to gain by borrowing against the future than investing in it.

Judicial Performance

Development requires more than just sound economic policies, of course. Nigeria's late president Umaru Musa Yar'Adua understood this well, assuring the *Financial Times* of his "absolute adherence to rule of law" and promising skeptical investors that the government would enforce "all contractual agreements and covenants entered into."[5] Not long before he died in office, he said, "Restoring respect for the rule of law is honestly one thing I would want to be remembered for."[6] Scholars have also specifically linked Nigeria's inconsistent property rights protections, contract enforcement, and judicial efficiency to weak private sector activity (Malik and Teal 2008).

Like budgetary discipline or low inflation, a well-functioning judiciary promotes long- term economic growth for the reasons mentioned by Yar'Adua. By fairly and efficiently resolving disputes, courts provide a nonexcludable benefit for the greater collective public that contributes to development (North and Thomas 1973). A broad literature links judicial enforcement of property rights to long-term economic growth (Alston, Eggertsson, and North 1996; Pistor and Wellons 1999; Barzel

[5] Matthew Green, "In Pursuit of Respect for the Rule of Law," *Financial Times*, June 24, 2008.
[6] Interview, "Umaru Yar'Adua: President ... on a Mission Incredible," *The Guardian*, April 29, 2009.

1997; Manji 2005). "Where contract enforcement is efficient, businesses are more likely to engage with new borrowers or customers," reports the World Bank. "In the absence of efficient courts, firms undertake fewer investments or business transactions." Limiting the transaction costs involved in protecting property rights reduces corruption in ways that benefit all entrepreneurs, rich and poor. The bank's 2009 study concludes, "Eliminating unnecessary obstacles to registering and transferring property is therefore important for economic development" (International Bank for Reconstruction and Development 2009, 19). Like budgetary discipline or low inflation, good judicial performance is prone to coordination problems since each party in a property rights dispute would like the scales tilted in its favor. Efficient resolution of property rights therefore requires a mutual understanding that institutions that provide efficient third party arbitration serve everyone's interests.

Scholars who study Africa in particular are increasingly drawing attention to the relationship between property rights and long-term economic growth (Firmin-Sellers 2007; Onoma 2010). But unlike measuring the economy, judicial performance in the developing world is still a nascent area of empirical research (Joireman 2011). Some metrics used to gauge judicial performance include caseload, number of disposed cases, average time to resolve a case, and clearance rate (Buscaglia 1999). Other indicators measure the independence of the courts by systematically analyzing procedures for removal of judges and funding sources for the judiciary, or they gauge the perceived fairness of decisions by counting the frequency of case appeals.

Among these measures, clearance rate provides important advantages. It is calculated by taking the number of cases disposed and dividing that by the number of cases received in a given year. It therefore incorporates the cost of judicial delay, which hinders economic development where few alternative dispute resolution processes are available (Buscaglia 1999). It also provides a useful indicator of future judicial efficiency (Dakolias 1999; Buscaglia and Ulen 1997). It differs from the World Bank's well-known *Doing Business* index in that it only represents one dimension of the legal environment, of course, but the clearance rate is based on objective data (i.e., actual case counts) rather than subjective surveys of lawyers or clerks. A variety of qualitative and quantitative data are also available to assess its validity.

The clearance rate is also a good measure of judicial performance because swift resolution of cases is a stated core value in the Nigerian legal system. Section 33 in the 1979 constitution declared, "A person shall be entitled to a fair hearing within a reasonable time by a Court or other tribunal established by law." The Supreme Court later amplified this section and interpreted "reasonable time" to mean "the period of time which, in the search for justice, does not wear out the parties and their witnesses and which is required to ensure that justice is not only done but appears reasonable to persons to be done" (Craig 1988, 373). The 1989 and 1999 constitutions echo this language too (in sections 34 and 36, respectively). In a 2000 survey of state-level chief judges, half of them rated court delays as a "very high" priority. Resolving cases in a reasonable time remains a central goal of the judicial system (Langseth and Mohammed 2002).

The *clearance* variable is derived from a sample of 518 cases (449 land disputes and 69 "company" suits) that were decided in the federal high courts, appellate courts, or Supreme Court between 1960 and 1987. (I was unfortunately unable to collect more recent data during my field research since there is a very long delay between the date when an actual case is decided and the publication of that information in private law reports; some additional evidence is introduced in the qualitative analysis later.) All of the cases involve property rights, giving it an explicit link to the law and development literature exploring property rights. The land cases concern disagreements over property title, conveyance, compensation for property confiscated by the government, communal land use, and customary tenancy.[7] The company cases include actions against companies, government regulation or inspection, corporate personality or status, tax assessment, and some aspects of the bankruptcy and asset liquidation processes.[8] Published law reports reflect information starting with the court of first instance, and the courts at that level have very little discretion in deciding which cases to accept on merit. Importantly, this reduces the possibility of bias in the sample. Appendix 1 describes other possible sources of measurement error and the steps I took to mitigate them. The values of the *clearance* variable are displayed in Figure 3.3. A value of less than 1 on the *clearance* variable indicates that the court is backlogged; a value greater than 1 indicates that the court is disposing cases faster than it is receiving them.

---

[7] For a complete list of issues covered under land cases in Nigeria, see Elias (1971), Olawoye (1974), Olkany (1986), Oluyede (1989), and Aluko (1998).

[8] For a complete list of issues covered by companies cases in Nigeria, see: Orojo (1992), Tonwe (1997), or Agbadu-Fishim (1998).

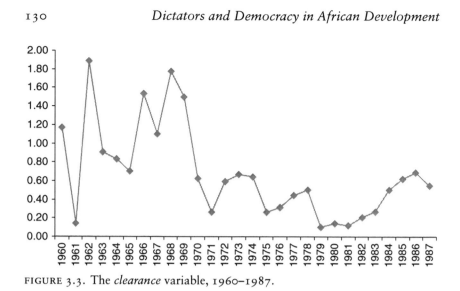

FIGURE 3.3. The *clearance* variable, 1960–1987.

It is worth clarifying that this is different from testing to see whether the judiciary itself possesses a veto through its power to hold executive branch officials accountable or repeal laws through judicial review. Also, *clearance* does not measure the perceived "fairness" of decisions. The tests here only examine whether veto players can agree that functioning courts serve their shared interest in efficient third party arbitration of property rights disputes. As with the other measures of national collective goods, good performance on the *clearance* variable therefore implicitly captures the ability of political actors to coordinate for a greater common good.

In sum, the clearance rate offers a good overall measure of judicial performance that is theoretically and empirically linked to economic development. Reducing judicial delay is necessary both as a political reform that strengthens rule of law and as an expression of the government's attitude toward entrepreneurial activity. As the attorney general of the federation explained in 2006, businesses will remain apprehensive about investing in Nigeria as long as the courts operate slowly.[9] Both legal professionals and the citizenry at large therefore value efficient resolution of property disputes in the courts. Like fiscal discipline, the efficient resolution of property rights cases constitutes a collective good that is conducive to long-term economic development. Judicial performance is also prone to coordination problems since political actors seek decisions

---

[9] Onwuka Nzeshi, "Nigeria, USAID Seek Reform of Arbitration Laws," *This Day*, June 18, 2006.

that favor their particular preferences. Policy processes reflecting this increased structural complexity should theoretically have more difficulty resolving these differences, just as collective action problems in the public goods literature do.

Education Policy Performance and Student/Teacher Ratios

Nigeria's governments also articulate a commitment to long-term development in terms of a commitment to education. Echoing a point developed by Adam Smith in *The Wealth of Nations*, these scholars argue that social policy spending constitutes an investment in "human capital" that contributes to economic performance (Galbraith 1976; Schultz 1999). There is evidence of a direct effect of education on workers' skills, which boosts productivity as they improve (Barro and Lee 2010). Investments in education and social services also contribute to growth over the long term through indirect effects (Baldacci et al. 2008; Hanushek and Woessmann 2007; Johnes 2006; Psacharopoulos 2006). The World Bank, the United Nations, and other prominent players in the international development community accept the proposition that social spending makes citizens, and the countries they live in, more productive. Evidence from Nigeria supports these findings, showing that federal investment in primary school education improves workforce quality and has indirect benefits, such as enabling women to delay marriage and have fewer children (Osili 2008).[10]

Nigeria's governments have embraced this view, rhetorically and very often through government policies, for half a century. In 1959, the federal minister of education appointed a commission to undertake education planning, and, in 1961, the federal government pledged to implement its key recommendations, including "progressive improvement in primary education throughout the Federation so that the foundation of national development may truly be laid." Realizing that Nigeria needed to train a new generation of bureaucrats, politicians, and entrepreneurs, the federal government declared that its development plans for 1962 to 1968 would "accord the highest priority to education" and were "designed to increase as rapidly and as economically as possible the high level manpower which is indispensable to accelerated development" (Federal

---

[10] Human capital investment in Nigeria also appears to have positive long run returns on productivity, wages, formal employment, and nonlabor outcomes such as infant mortality, though the effects on economic growth specifically are unclear (Kwakwa et al. 2008; Osili 2008).

Government of Nigeria 1961, 9). The federal government promised to provide substantial assistance to the states for this purpose (Federal Ministry of Economic Development 1960).

By the late 1960s, the states had taken over education through a series of reforms, and the federal government had begun exploring ways to guarantee access to primary education (Akinkugbe 1994). The result was Universal Basic Education (UBE), and in 1977 a task force on education laid out a new national policy on education and declared that "education was the most important investment Nigeria could make for its socio-economic development."[11] In 1979, the new constitution guaranteed free primary and secondary education as a basic right and codified the practice of shared responsibility for education between the federal government and the states. Two years later, invoking the discourse of human capital, the government referred to the educational system as "an instrument par excellence for effecting national development" (Federal Government of Nigeria 1981, 5). A decade later, Nigeria signed the Jomtiem Declaration of Education for All, an international agreement among nine developing nations to reduce illiteracy and promote and fund education.

When a new democratic government assumed power in 1999, constitutional provisions again enshrined the commitment to UBE.[12] The incoming speaker of the House told a group of bankers that the government "should begin to make massive investments in human capital" because education would help insulate the nation from the pain of globalization.[13] Nigeria's president embraced a similar view, explaining that "education and health determine [the] quality of human capital" and characterizing social spending as a way to turn Nigeria's large population into an advantage in the global economy.[14] In sum, access to education has been a cornerstone of developmental policy since independence, and the federal government has played a major role. In the statistical tests carried out later, I will introduce a variable to control for the federal government's varying role in implementing education.

---

[11] Editorial, "Hard Road for Education," *West Africa*, May 21, 1979.

[12] Section 18(3) of the 1999 Federal Constitution pledges the government to provide free compulsory Universal Primary Education, free secondary education, free university education, and free adult literacy programs (Federal Ministry of Education 1999–2000). See also Universal Basic Education Annual Report 2002 (Universal Basic Education Programme 2003)

[13] Ghali Umar Na'Abba, "Economic Prosperity as Foundation for Sustainable Democracy," Speech in Lagos, February 27, 2002.

[14] Interview, "Umaru Yar'Adua: President ... on a Mission Incredible," *The Guardian*, April 29, 2009.

The most widely used metrics in the comparative literature for measuring educational outcomes are enrollment rates and average years of schooling (Glewwe and Kremer 2005). While these indicators show levels of participation, they do not adequately capture the extent to which educational policies build human capital; it is these long-term effects that give education qualities as a national collective good. Student-teacher ratio (sometimes referred to as class size) is a more useful metric for understanding this dimension of education policy performance. Not only does it have demonstrable indirect effects on economic growth over the long term; it is also linked to more immediate and direct outcomes associated with better quality education (Barro and Lee 2001; Lee and Barro 2001). This is not necessarily the case with years of schooling as a measure, which has a more ambiguous relationship to student performance. Student-teacher ratios appear to impact educational outcomes in Africa specifically by improving literacy rates (Case and Deaton 1999). The education variable, *student/teacher*, is a ratio based on original data from the Federal Office of Statistics and various publications of the Federal Ministry of Education gathered during field research in Abuja, Lagos, and Ibadan.[15]

One possible source of measurement error is the fact that the federal government's role in education varies over time. In postindependence Nigeria in particular, missionaries and private institutions continued to play a large role in providing education (Abernethy 1969). To address variable government involvement, tests on the student/teacher dependent variable control for education as a percentage of overall federal spending. This variable, *ed.budget*, serves as a proxy for the federal government's varying involvement in education.[16] Further mitigating this problem is the fact that, even if the government is not a direct service provider, it regulates and has an interest in ensuring that service results "fall within politically acceptable limits" (Baum and Lake 2003, 336). Moreover, Nigeria's states overwhelmingly rely on the federal government for financial assistance

---

[15] Sources for student/teacher ratios, enrollment levels, and number of schools are as follows: years 1960–1962 from *Annual Digest of Education Statistics 1962*; years 1963–1967 from *Annual Abstract of Statistics 1968*, pp. 151–153; years 1991–2002 from *Handbook of Information on Basic Education 2003*. Other years are gathered from *Annual Abstract of Statistics* for years 1972, 1981, 1982, 1985, 1986, 1991, and 2001; *Social Statistics in Nigeria 2009*; and editions of *Statistics of Education in Nigeria* for years 1972, 1973/74, 1980–1984, and 1985–1989.

[16] The sources for education expenditures are as follows: Years 1961–1964/65 are from the *Annual Abstract of Statistics 1968*, p. 126; years 1965–1969 are from the *Annual*

to carry out their responsibilities. Subnational governments routinely refuse to implement national policies until they receive money from the federal government, either through grants-in-aid or through the federal revenue allocation system. The states "merely fold their hands and do not lift a finger till they have obtained their chunk of the so-called national cake."[17] This supports the idea that even where states have jurisdiction over implementation, central government control of the purse significantly shapes the realities of policy performance. Finally, the *ed.budget* variable is also a useful control since federal spending on education could obviously have an impact on student/teacher ratios by enabling governments to hire more teachers.

In sum, by considering education as a human capital investment, the public goods literature recasts an educated population as a public policy outcome with broad national benefits, similar to other nonexcludable goods. If coordination problems arising from additional political actors broadly impair government's ability to provide national collective goods, then each of these seemingly different policy areas should be similarly impacted by changes in the number of veto players. The tests reported later in this chapter show that the number of veto players has a systematic effect on all four of my variables measuring national collective goods. This validates my operationalizations of government performance with variables measuring macroeconomic performance, judicial efficiency, and student-teacher ratios (especially since the variables include economic and noneconomic measures of national collective goods). More importantly, the tests highlight a new explanation for why it is often so difficult for African governments to deliver on nationally beneficial polices: As the factions, leaders, and institutions described in the previous chapter gain or lose political leverage, the likelihood of government's delivering national collective goods changes. As the number of distinct political actors who have to reconcile their own interests with the broader national interest increases, it becomes more difficult to achieve policy solutions on behalf of the common good.

Abstract of Statistics 1972, pp. 124–125; years 1970–1979 are from the *Annual Abstract of Statistics 1981*, p. 145, which cites the Central Bank of Nigeria as its source; and years 1980–2002 are from the Central Bank of Nigeria, *Statistical Bulletin* Vol. 13, Part B, December 31, 2003. It should be noted that these sources report spending by function using budget estimates for some years.

[17] "Through the Eye of a Needle: States' Billion Naira Budgets Based on Expectation from the Federal Government," *The Nigerian Economist*, February 5, 1990.

Local Collective Goods and Government Consumption

Good government performance that provides local collective goods requires overcoming a different set of challenges. The divisibility of these policy outputs means they lack the nonexcludability characteristic of national collective goods. Citizens who live close to a new road, community center, or hospital benefit from these policy outputs more than citizens who must travel distances or overcome other barriers to consume these goods. This excludability means that resource distribution might follow a political logic of patronage. Research on Africa explores how patronage may be a tool for ethnic favoritism (Berman, Dickson, and Kymlicka 2004; Miguel 2004), a mechanism for unfairly preserving incumbent advantage (Tripp 2010; Gyimah-Boadi 2007), or corruption in general (Chabal and Daloz 1999; Smith 2007). Qualitative analyses often attempt to demonstrate which particular ethnic groups, individuals, or provinces benefited disproportionately from patronage, and this has been a popular line of research on Nigeria in particular (Diamond 1993; Joseph 1987; Schatz 1984). These studies provide important details about how African politics operate, but it is difficult to identify specific beneficiaries or objectively show patterns of performance reliably.

Rather than attempting to document who benefits from corruption or patronage, my approach to local collective goods follows the example of studies that utilize dramatic changes in overall levels of government consumption (meaning spending) at the national level as a sign of misallocation. When government consumption increases dramatically, it is a small inferential step to suggest that national figures demonstrate a penchant for patronage or corruption (Rose-Ackerman 1999; Lambsdorff, Taube, and Schramm 2005). In fact, the idea that downsizing government would reduce patronage and corruption motivated neoliberal reforms throughout the 1980s, when structural adjustment programs across Africa sought to reduce government consumption as a share of GDP per capita (Callaghy and Ravenhill 1993; Ake 1996; Cheru 2002). These spending cutbacks were a response to postcolonial politicians who targeted investment in industry at the expense of other economic sectors necessary for development (Chabal 2009). Such economic strategies were central to the "developmental state" model, which embraced economic planning, price controls, and lavish capital spending on infrastructure and industrialization (Bates 1981; Meredith 2011). Political reform across Africa in the 1990s had the effect of moderating both the spending excesses of the developmental state and the draconian cuts of structural adjustment (Ndulu 2008). As a dependent variable, government consumption therefore offers tremendous variation over time, which should be difficult for any single causal factor to explain. Recent political economy studies use government consumption to explain variation across countries, similarly interpreting high spending levels as a symptom of poor economic policy choices and oversized states (Bates 2008). For all of these reasons, the idea that trends in federal government consumption capture other features of government performance is well grounded in the literature.

I measure the overall federal spending in Nigeria between 1961 and 2007 with three different variables, each expressed as a share of GDP. The variable $\Delta spending$ measures changes in the overall level of government consumption, which is a common proxy for capturing patronage or misallocation of public resources at the broadest level (Arriola 2013). Next, the variable $\Delta recurrent$ measures recurrent spending, which includes salaries and administrative expenses of the federal government. High levels of recurrent spending are often considered a sign of corruption in the civil service by creating ghost employees or padding payrolls in other ways (Raadschelders and Rutgers 1996). Finally, the variable $\Delta capital$ measures capital spending by Nigeria's federal government, offering our most direct measure of local collective goods. Infrastructure spending does produce indirect benefits for people; building a hospital, for example, will probably improve the health of people who have convenient access to it. Cross-national surveys from Africa suggest that "delivering development" and "improving infrastructure" may be even more important to some citizens than the quality of representation (Young 2009). In other words, capital spending is very popular. However, large, unsustainable increases in capital spending often lead to corruption since capital-intensive projects are prone to price inflation and poor oversight (Rose-Ackerman 1999). Numerous qualitative studies of Nigeria have made similar claims about capital spendings contributing to patronage and corruption (Joseph 1987; Bates 1981). Figure 3.4 illustrates the values on the variables measuring capital and recurrent spending. (The figure leaves out government consumption overall.)

In sum, each of the three variables measuring government consumption is grounded in existing research on public finance and resource distribution that makes it an appropriate measure of local collective goods. Recurrent spending does have some qualities of excludability, since administrative spending can theoretically target jobs for certain areas, but the literature generally takes capital spending as an especially good way of operationalizing local collective goods. The next task is to see how changes in the number of veto players impact these different measures

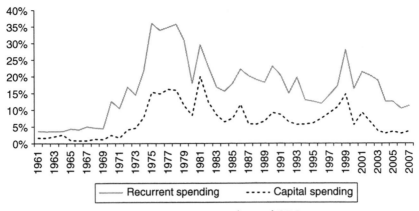

FIGURE 3.4. Government consumption as a share of GDP, 1961–2007.

of policy performance. Given the significant variation in each variable over time, and the numerous controls included in the statistical models, it should be difficult for any single variable to explain government performance systematically.

Predicting Nigeria's Policy Performance with Veto Players

Can veto players, which represent aggregated political interests and characterize the overall size of the policy-making process, account for patterns of performance in Nigeria? This section tests the hypotheses formulated in Chapter 1, using the number of veto players counted in Chapter 2 as the independent variable. If an increase in the number of veto players makes it more difficult for governments to balance budgets, resolve property rights disputes efficiently, maintain low inflation, and keep student/ teacher ratios small, then this finding would confirm the coordination hypothesis, which expects these regimes to face coordination problems that impede the delivery of national collective goods. If an increase in the number of veto players leads to growth in overall spending levels on local collective goods, then this result would confirm the logroll hypothesis. That hypothesis expects each veto player to extract payoffs through divisible policies, which should have the strongest association with capital spending levels.

To test these hypotheses, I describe factors that could interfere with the impact of veto players on these outcomes including dictatorship, foreign debt, oil revenue, or economic conditions. Drawing upon the relevant political economy literature, I explain how each of these factors could theoretically impact government performance and operationalize it as a control variable for statistical tests. An empirical analysis then demonstrates that the number of veto players in Nigeria systematically explains government performance between 1961 and 2007, confirming the coordination hypothesis and rejecting the logroll hypothesis. The results remain robust across a range of controls. The statistical significance of both sets of tests suggests that an increase in the number of veto players reduces the ability to coordinate in order to deliver national collective goods, but it also limits the ability of these self-interested actors to drive up spending on local collective goods through collusion.

Controlling for Intervening Factors

An empirical examination of my claim that the number of political actors with leverage over the policy process explains government performance needs to consider alternative explanations. A variety of mitigating conditions could influence how Nigeria's veto players affect the delivery of national and local collective goods. The statistical tests of the coordination and logroll hypotheses therefore control for a variety of other important economic and political variables characteristic of the conventional wisdom about government performance in Africa.

First, I control for the state of the economy with *GrowthGDP*, a variable from the World Bank's World Development Indicators measuring the annual gross domestic product (GDP) growth rate per capita, reported as a percentage change over the previous year. Nigeria's growth rate has varied hugely over time, ranging from double-digit lows in 1967 and 1981 to nearly 8 percent in the early 2000s. Economic growth is a common control in cross-national studies because of its potentially significant effects on other phenomena such as democratization (Bratton and Van de Walle 1997; Boix and Stokes 2003), economic reform (van de Walle 2001), or political instability (Arriola 2009). Rapid economic growth can add to the resources that politicians have available to buy support rather than invest in long-term development. The variable *GrowthGDP* accommodates these possible scenarios.

Apart from the rate of economic growth, the ability of the government to spend can also be affected by revenue levels and budgetary discipline. Such a decline in resources could shape distributional spending strategies in particular; a standard principle of free market economics is that structural budget deficits constrain spending overall (Friedman 1993). In political terms, this means that when faced with declining revenues or growing budget deficits, a government may take a more conservative approach to distributional spending, disbursing patronage only to loyal supporters. I therefore include *fedbudget* (my dependent variable measuring budgetary discipline in terms of a surplus or a deficit) as a control variable in all of the tests with local collective goods. I also include *fedbudget* as a control variable in the tests for the impact of veto players on inflation since large budget deficits could increase inflation, a point, however, that remains a subject of debate in macroeconomics (Krugman 1997; Woodford 2001).

All of the statistical tests also control for the impact of oil earnings on the federal budget. Economies that rely heavily on natural resource exploitation suffer from a variety of problems that can undermine government performance. By reducing the need to collect taxes, natural resource revenue weakens the links between citizens and politicians (Karl 1997; Ulfelder 2007), encourages government spending by incumbents seeking to hold on to political power (Robinson, Torvik, and Verdier 2006), and undermines economic growth by enabling corruption generally (Shaxson 2007a; Lewis 2007a). Controlling for the impact of oil revenues is also important because revenue levels could actually drive spending levels (Please 1967). Bad performance is arguably a consequence of revenue constraints: The state delivers fewer goods when it has less money to spend (Przeworski et al. 2000), a relationship that some scholars claim is especially strong in sub-Saharan Africa (Ekpo 1996).

Like other oil-rich countries in the developing world, Nigeria has public finances that fluctuate with oil revenue. Studies suggest that this circumstance contributes to economic instability, inflation, and lower rates of long-term economic growth (Okogu and Osafo-Kwaako 2008). By inflating revenues, oil also creates disincentives for risk taking and innovation (Utomi 2004).[18] Oil booms weaken the incentives to compromise since policy makers believe they can have it all. Controlling for oil income is therefore integral to a theory of coordination: With huge revenues from oil, policy makers should not have to make difficult budget choices about national collective goods. Oil income is also central to theoretical claims about collusion: Policy makers should be able to disburse local collective goods, rents, and patronage with little concern for the aggregate impact on deficits or revenue.

---

[18] Some research questions this relationship, suggesting that vulnerability to exogenous shocks, such as changes in oil prices, might actually stimulate the kind of risk taking conducive to growth (Gunning 2008).

The variable Δoil_{t-1} measures oil revenue as a share of overall federal revenue at time $t - 1$.[19] It is calculated from data published in the Central Bank's *Annual Reports* and other sources.[20] Expressed as a percentage, it controls for years when government revenues were unusually high or low as a result of fluctuations in oil earnings, typically caused by changes in the international price of oil. Before the late 1960s, oil earnings as a share of federal revenue never exceeded 5 percent. By 1974, oil earnings accounted for 82 percent of federal revenue. Since this first boom, oil has accounted for between 62 and 85 percent of the federal government's revenues, averaging 79 percent from 1998 to 2007. Since the data set begins in 1960, and oil revenues did not become significant until the late 1960s, it is possible to analyze the role of veto players in Nigeria before and after the country's transformation into a rentier economy.

Next I control for the level of foreign debt, an important dimension of African political economy. Foreign debt relates to domestic politics in Africa because excessive borrowing in the 1970s during the era of "big men" and personal rule contributed to subsequent debt crises (Jackson and Rosberg 1984; Hyden 2012; van de Walle 2001). Declining economies and rising debts led the 1980s to become widely known as "the lost decade" to policy makers and scholars alike (Meredith 2011). By the mid-1990s, sub-Saharan Africa's foreign debt had grown from barely US$6 billion in the postcolonial era to more than US$200 billion. At the level of domestic politics, debts, like foreign aid, amount to what Kwame Nkrumah in Ghana criticized as a "neocolonial" influence. Spending priorities and growth trends seemed to bear this out, as governments directed money to foreign debt repayment rather than social spending or investment. The chair of the joint committee on debt in Nigeria's National Assembly said in 2005, "What we have been paying yearly on external debt in the last three years represent four times the total budget for education and 15 times the budget for health. We cannot continue this way unless you want Nigerians to die."[21] Some statistical evidence supports

---

[19] Unit root tests show that the *oil* variable is not stationary, presenting serial correlation problems for a time series analysis. I therefore detrend it with first difference tests, creating Δoil_{t-1}.

[20] Significantly, few studies that report oil earnings in a time series going back to the 1960s use the Nigerian National Petroleum Company's statistics. I construct the *oil* variable using the following sources: years 1961–1969 from Central Bank of Nigeria's *Annual Report* for years 1964, 1967, and 1970; data for 1970–2001 from CBN *Statistical Bulletin*, Vol. 13, December 31, 2003; years 2002 and 2003 from the CBN *Annual Report* for 2003; years 2004–2007 from the CBN *Annual Report* for 2007.

[21] Emma Ujah and Emmanuel Aziken, "Nigeria National Assembly Committee Calls for Total Debt Cancellation," *Vanguard*, May 10, 2005.

the idea that debt servicing crowds out social spending in Nigeria (Okogu and Osafo-Kwaako 2008). At the cross-national level, there is also evidence from simulations that debt burdens reduced economic growth in sub-Saharan Africa by as much as 3 percent between 1987 and 1994 (Iyoha 1997). Foreign debt is therefore an important control not only because it has impact on domestic policy priorities, but also because it serves as a good proxy for the international influences Nkrumah warned Africa about.

In Nigeria, external debt levels have varied considerably since independence. Total external debt stood at 3.4 percent of GDP at that time and only modestly increased over the next decade. Borrowing then increased sharply, starting in the late 1970s. The global oil boom raised Nigeria's credit rating sufficiently that it was able to take out massive loans for white elephant projects that often were unfinished and were launched without much regard to their potential for generating capital to pay back the loans (Ashinze and Onwioduokit 1996; Lalude 2000; Yekini 2002). According to the Central Bank, external debt increased at an annual rate of 7.3 percent between 1983 and 1991. The end of the oil boom around 1980 made it difficult to repay and refinance the loans (Debt Management Department of the Central Bank 1992). By the 1990s, Nigeria had the largest external debt of any nation in sub-Saharan Africa. Paris Club creditors took few precautions in loaning money to a country with an expanding economy. And when Nigeria's government attempted to renegotiate loans, creditors felt the country's oil wealth made it undeserving of more favorable terms (Chevillard 2001). In 2006, the Obasanjo government succeeded in renegotiating and paying off virtually the entire foreign debt, which stood at nearly $30 billion, by committing the country's massive wave of oil earnings to loan payments. The variable $\Delta debt.ext_{t-1}$, using data from the Central Bank of Nigeria, captures changes in the debt as a share of GDP at time $t - 1$.[22]

The variable $\Delta debt.ext_{t-1}$ also takes into account the fact that multilateral creditors pushed African governments to rein in government consumption (Ake 1996; Herbst 1990). In Nigeria, such demands were particularly acute after the crash of oil prices in the early 1980s, and the government had to open itself to unpopular structural adjustment programs designed by the International Monetary Fund (IMF) and the

---

[22] The sources for this data are as follows: for years 1960–1998: "Changing Structure of the Nigerian Economy," by the Research Department of the Central Bank of Nigeria (August 2000); years 1999 through 2007 from CBN *Annual Reports* for 1999, 2001, 2002, 2005, 2006, and 2007.

World Bank (Olukoshi 1993; Biersteker and Lewis 1997). Such external pressures may impact spending outcomes by driving down government consumption.

Since Nigeria's Central Bank itself could be a factor influencing debt management, inflation, and budgetary discipline, one might specifically control for the independence or quality of that institution. When central banks are prone to political manipulation, that condition often undermines both policy credibility and policy results (Lijphart 1999). However, it is reasonable to treat central bank independence as exogenous, omitting it as a control, since research suggests that multi-veto-player regimes tend to replace central bank officials less frequently than regimes with more concentrated authority. By delegating authority over monetary policy, multi-veto-player governments offer more credible economic policy (Keefer and Stasavage 2003).

Finally, I control for the type of governance, differentiating between democracy and dictatorship. As noted in the Introduction, there are good reasons to believe that democracies offer better government performance, delivering more collective goods and providing a better quality of life for their citizens. Many of these empirical studies rely upon a minimalist definition of democracy that can ultimately be reduced to a dichotomous classification. Dummy variables indicating either democracy or authoritarianism remain common in statistical tests (Brown and Hunter 1999; Przeworski et al. 2000) and in qualitative analyses of governance (Lewis 2008). An advantage of this minimalist classification is that it "provides nonarbitrary and entirely reproducible way of distinguishing democracies from dictatorships" (Cheibub 2007, 27). In this spirit, Przeworski et al. define democracy as "a regime in which government offices are filled by contested elections" (Przeworski et al. 2000, 19). This definition also treats governments as groups of individuals who exercise power within boundaries prescribed by regime rules.

Democracies for purposes of the *democracy* variable are defined by two criteria: (1) The chief executive and the legislature must both be chosen through contested elections in which political competition guarantees the uncertainty of the winner; contestation in this sense therefore requires protection of political and civil rights; (2) the rule of law must protect the rights of citizens and impose limits on the exercise of state power.[23] Authoritarian regimes in the *democracy* variable are defined as those

---

[23] This definition differs from the coding criteria used by the preceding studies only in that I do not require an alternation of power under a stable set of rules to take place. This

that meet neither criterion. This would include, for example, "electoral authoritarian" regimes that hold elections but reduce contestation by limiting political competition.[24]

One reason for creating such a blunt dichotomy is to test whether authoritarian regimes are more than merely "nondemocracies," as suggested during the coding process in Chapter 2. One classic definition describes authoritarian regimes as "political systems with limited, not responsible, political pluralism, without elaborate and guiding ideology, but with distinctive mentalities, without extensive nor intensive political mobilization, except at some points in their development, and in which a leader or occasionally a small group exercises power within formally ill-defined limits but actually quite predictable ones" (Linz 1975, 264). Authoritarianism in this light refers to regimes that limit political rights and control the avenues for public participation. But if veto players remain statistically significant regardless of whether a regime is defined as democratic or authoritarian, this will imply that these regimes possess other institutional qualities that generate regularity in political behavior.

Some final considerations relate to interim governments, since they are short-lived structures and my variables reflect yearly values. There are two of these in my sample between 1960 and 2007. Interim governments may be set up to fail (in order to justify further authoritarian rule) or merely serve as puppets for the government that created them. There is no simple way to code such distinctions, and some of these nuances are captured in my later qualitative analysis. But interim governments by definition are meant to provide temporary leadership that facilitates a defined political transition, not to initiate broad new policies of their own. At best they are meant to continue implementation of existing policies. My default solution is to group them with their authoritarian progenitors.[25] Applying these criteria, Nigeria was governed by three democratic and six authoritarian regimes between 1961 and 2007. This includes the unsuccessful interim regime under Ernest Shonekan in 1993 as well as the successful interim regime under Abdulsalami Abubakar, which oversaw

---

is because there are only three opportunities in all the years of my sample in which this might have happened (1964, 1983, and 2003). The opportunities and probabilities for incumbents to actually be defeated have therefore not been frequent enough necessarily to code such regimes as hegemonic, uncompetitive systems.

[24] See Lindberg (2009).

[25] Grouping interim governments would probably not be necessary with more discrete measures of my dependent variable, along monthly or perhaps quarterly lines. But even then it would not be reasonable to expect a government in power for only two or three months to formulate and implement policies that affect my measures of performance.

the successful 1999 transition. Six military dictatorships account for 30 years of authoritarianism on the *democracy* variable coded as 0, and the remaining 17 years are coded as democracy. This is consistent with other dichotomous classifications of Nigeria's regimes in cross-national data sets (Cheibub 2007). The descriptive statistics for all of the independent and dependent variables are reported in Table A2.1 in Appendix 2.

Testing the Coordination Hypothesis

To test the impact of veto players on government performance, I have operationalized my dependent variable with policies that reflect recurring Nigerian government priorities and that clearly capture the conceptual distinctions between national and local collective goods. I begin by testing the coordination hypothesis, which states that an increase in the number of veto players impedes the delivery of national collective goods – policy outputs with theoretically nonexcludable benefits. The motivation for this hypothesis arises from the credible commitment tradition discussed in Chapter 1, which draws upon the literatures on bargaining and new institutional economics to suggest that regimes that have more veto players have trouble reaching agreement. Though delivering national collective goods might provide the greatest expected utility, inducing political actors with different preferences to implement such policies is difficult. Rejection of this hypothesis would imply that these regimes do in fact bargain to efficient public policy outcomes, as envisioned by selectorate theory and research that assumes low transaction costs. Support for this hypothesis would correspond with higher rates of inflation, larger budget deficits, declining values on the *clearance* variable measuring judicial efficiency, and increased student/teacher ratios. According to the public goods literature, it is theoretically difficult to exclude citizens from consuming the benefits of these policies. Where *veto* is the number of veto players, I test for correlations using ordinary least squares regressions with this basic model:

$$\bar{Y} = \beta 0 + \beta 1(veto_t) + \beta 2(democracy_t) + \beta 3(\Delta oil_{t-1}) +$$
$$\beta 4(GDPgrowth_t) + \beta 5(\Delta debt_{t-1}) + \varepsilon_t$$

To see whether regimes with more veto players are temporally associated with higher prices, I use the variable *inflation*, based on the Consumer Price Index. I lag the *vetoes* variable to time $t - 1$ under the assumption that it takes about a year for the behavior of veto players to impact inflation.[26] This model includes the *fedbudget* variable as a control, since large budget deficits might stimulate inflation (Woodford 2001). Next I use *fedbudget* as the dependent variable, to see whether the number of veto players impacts fiscal discipline by contributing to either budget deficits or surpluses. A negative coefficient on this variable indicates that revenue is less than spending as a share of GDP. Since the data are time series, an improvement from a large negative value to a small one would appear as a positive coefficient.

Support for the coordination hypothesis should also correspond with suboptimal performance on the other two measures of national collective goods. Judicial efficiency should decline in regimes with more veto players, indicated by lower values on the *clearance* variable. Policy makers appreciate the relationship between secure property rights and economic development, and they may desire the swift resolution of property disputes. But they also have much room for disagreement over whether and how to delegate such authority to a third party mechanism. The tests here attempt to determine whether veto players can cooperate and at least implicitly agree that courts serve a greater collective good by providing rule of law. Positive coefficients on the variable would signal more efficient courts. Since this variable only has $N = 26$, the model includes a separate *veto* variable lagged to time $t - 1$ in order to reduce serial correlation.

Regimes that have the most veto players should also have inferior education policy performance. As noted, virtually every government dating back to independence has proclaimed the wisdom of investing in education. This has frequently been described with the language of human capital: Spending on education is an investment in the future because it not only increases literacy in the near-term; it also contributes to national productivity in the long term. A broad literature identifies education as a human capital investment as a national collective good prone to coordination problems. Therefore, an increase in the number of veto players should correspond with larger class sizes, indicated by positive values on the *student/teacher* variable. If the test results with *clearance* and *student/teacher* are as predicted, this would also validate my operationalizations of national collective goods since these variables do not measure macroeconomic outcomes.

---

[26] A two-tailed correlation test can show whether the lag at time $t - 1$ reflects the proper relationship between the variables. The Pearson's R of .286, significant at .05 level, suggests the lag at time $t - 1$ is appropriate.

TABLE 3.1. *Impact of Veto Players on National Collective Goods,*
1961–2007

	(Model 1)** Inflation	(Model 2)*** Fedbudget	(Model 3)** Clearance	(Model 4)** Student/ teacher
Veto	–	−3.097** (−3.605)	−.306 (−1.366)	2.094** (2.486)
Veto $_{t-1}$	7.030** (2.406)	–	−.398* (−1.873)	
Democracy	−15.916*** (−3.264)	2.593* (1.661)	.056 (.292)	−1.487 (−1.004)
ΔOil $_{t-1}$	−58.277* (−1.849)	20.421** (2.083)	−1.382 (−1.350)	−6.746 (−.718)
GDP growth	.113 (.319)	.032 (.283)	.002 (.190)	.233** (2.072)
ΔDebt.ext$_{t-1}$	−.154 (−.703)	−.084 (−1.255)	.006 (.594)	.032 (.514)
Fedbudget	.023 (.960)	–	–	
Ed.budget	–	–	–	.717** (2.280)
Adj R2	.233	.279	.342	.219
N	46	46	26	46

Note: T statistics in parentheses
*Significant at the .1 level, **significant at the .05 level, ***significant at the .01 level

Tests show that veto players explain variation in each of the four dependent variables at a statistically significant level (see Table 3.1). Regimes with the most veto players are systematically correlated with inferior macroeconomic performance, less efficient courts, and larger primary school classes. Model 1, which tests inflation, demonstrates that each additional veto player is associated with a 7 percent increase in inflation the following year. The relationship is statistically significant, and the adjusted R-squared suggests that the model explains more than 23 percent of variation over time. In terms of the controls, a decline in oil revenues as a share of the federal budget is associated with lower inflation, though the results are less significant. Democracies tend to control inflation better than dictatorships, and budget deficits have no significant impact.

In Model 2, the negative coefficient on the *veto* variable shows that regimes that have more veto players tend to create budget deficits. At a statistically significant level, each additional veto player correlates with a 3 percent increase in the budget deficit as a share of GDP. (This would also mean a 3 percent decline in any budget surplus.) The large positive values on ΔOil_{t-1} indicate that oil booms correlate with budget surpluses. In addition, democracies tend to do a better job controlling deficit spending than dictatorships, though the number of veto players remains significant in both models. Interestingly, neither external debt levels nor the economic growth rate has a statistically significant relationship with these two measures of macroeconomic performance. The results on these two control variables support the idea that domestic politics, as measured by veto players, explains more variation in the delivery of national collective goods than international pressure or overall economic conditions. Even money supply, which has a well-known positive relationship with inflation in macroeconomics (Phelps 1973; Krugman 1997), is insignificant in tests (not displayed) with a variable measuring change in the Central Bank of Nigeria's supply of money and quasi-money.[27]

Veto players have similar statistical effects on the courts and education policy, the other two measures of national collective goods. Model 3 tests judicial efficiency. Because of the smaller sample size, I reduce serial correlation by using *veto* along with a variable lagged variable at time $t - 1$. The results demonstrate that the number of veto players systematically predicts the clearance rate better than any of the controls, though values on the coefficient are only significant at the .1 level ($p = .077$). The negative coefficient on the *clearance* variable means that each additional veto player corresponds with a decline in the rate at which the courts resolve property rights cases. Neither oil revenues nor the economic growth rate has any statistically significant impact on the clearance rate. This is somewhat surprising since oil booms and economic growth both are likely to stimulate consumer spending and private sector activity that inspire calls for efficient resolution of property rights cases. The coefficient on the *democracy* dummy variable is insignificant, meaning that governance through democracy or dictatorship had no systematic impact on the clearance rate. This result is consistent with the literature discussed in Chapter 2 exploring the relationship between the judiciary and different types of governance. On the one hand, Nigeria's military governments sometimes created tribunals parallel to judicial structures (Okoye 1997;

---

[27] Veto players remain significant at the .1 level (t-statistic of 1.9), the adjusted R-squared is .259, and the overall model is significant at the .01 level.

Osipitan 1987). On the other hand, the judiciary oftentimes pushed autocratic regimes for more independence, occasionally even mocking the generals in high court cases, and the military declined to suppress the courts on a surprising range of matters (Egbewole 2006). Evidence from elsewhere in the developing world similarly suggests that authoritarian rule is not inherently incompatible with a functioning judiciary (Hatchard and Ogowewo 2003). Many dictators appreciate that by providing reliable third party arbitration, courts can reassure skittish foreign investors and help the regime survive (Smith and Farrales 2010). In this regard, the results on the *clearance* variable therefore complement recent comparative research on law and development.

Model 4, looking at education, shows that each additional veto player adds two students per teacher on average. For Nigeria's teachers, more veto players bargaining at the center means larger class sizes. This is not necessarily a matter of increased enrollments, since the number of teachers also increases over time and the variable is a ratio. For example, in Nigeria's postwar period between 1970 and 1975, school enrollment levels increased on average 10 percent per year (well above what the Gowon administration planned for), yet the student/teacher ratio did not grow significantly during these years. In terms of the controls, external debt is not statistically significant, and economic growth correlates with larger, rather than smaller class sizes. The values on these two variables again support the idea that domestic politics rather than external constraints drive government performance.

The positive coefficient on the *ed.budget* variable indicates that regimes that give education spending a higher priority actually have slightly larger class sizes. As a proxy controlling for the federal government's role in education, the coefficients on *ed.budget* also suggest that education performance actually improves when states play a larger role. As noted earlier, Nigeria's states and the federal government share jurisdiction over education, but states receive almost all of their income from federal revenue allocations. The federalism literature consistently argues that this undermines the basis of local administrative control or state capacity for autonomous policy making (LeVan 2005; Lijphart 2012; Ekpo 1994). The qualitative analysis later unpacks some of this complex relationship, which is really best left for future research. But regardless of the varying federal role in education, the public goods literature argues that federal governments play a critical role in ensuring that performance in policy areas with shared jurisdiction is "politically acceptable" (Baum and Lake 2003).

Across all four models, the number of veto players predicts national collective goods outcomes at a statistically significant level, confirming the coordination hypothesis. These results hold across a range of controls. While democratic governance and the level of oil income do have an impact on macroeconomic performance, veto players systematically explain variation in the dependent variable. If we take the growth rate as an indicator of the overall conditions of the national economy, the results on *GDPgrowth* suggests that even poor countries with modest rates of economic growth can adopt policies that lead to good government performance. Perhaps most interestingly, the variable measuring debt level is not significant in any of the models. This finding suggests that domestic policy making rather than foreign pressure is central to understanding the conditions conducive to delivering national collective goods in Nigeria, and that African agency accounts for a significant amount of both good and bad policy decisions since independence.

Testing the Logroll Hypothesis

The logroll hypothesis predicts that an increase in the number of veto players will lead to higher overall spending levels on local collective goods. It tests a key insight from the distributional tradition in the veto player literature: Cox and McCubbins (2001) claim that each policy actor with the leverage to prevent a change in the status quo should theoretically also have the ability to demand local collective goods. This includes what they refer to as "fiscal pork," or targetable spending that should lead to logrolls that are expensive in the aggregate. Capital spending is a particularly good operationalization of local collective goods since it generates excludable benefits. Confirmation of this hypothesis would mean that each veto player uses its political leverage to demand excludable policies or payoffs characteristic of patronage in Africa. This would appear as overall increases in my three variables measuring government consumption. Rejection of this hypothesis would imply that veto players in these regimes live up to Madison's expectations by holding each other accountable whereby "ambition counters ambition." Rather than colluding for policy logrolls, additional veto players check one another. Generating this accountability limits excessive spending characteristic of patronage, meaning that government consumption – and capital spending in particular – should decline. Though my government consumption variables only measure spending by the federal government (and not by states), as already noted, these subnational governments are highly dependent on federal revenue allocations (Suberu 2001; Onwudiwe and

TABLE 3.2. *Impact of Veto Players on Local Collective Goods, 1961–2007*

	(Model 1)** $\Delta Spending$	(Model 2)** $\Delta Current$	(Model 3)*** $\Delta Capital$
Veto $_{t-1}$	-.033***	-.033***	-.018***
	(-3.542)	(-3.572)	(-3.116)
Democracy	-.012	-.010	-.012
	(-.760)	(-.650)	(-1.265)
ΔOil_{t-1}	-.066	-.060	-1.65**
	(0.663)	(-.592)	(-2.648)
GDP growth	.000	-6.960E-5	5.605E-5
	(-.201)	(-.061)	(.080)
$\Delta Debt.ext_{t-1}$	-.001	-.001	-.001*
	(-.788)	(-.769)	(-1.604)
Fedbudget	-.003*	-.003*	.000
	(-.1757)	(-1.819)	(-.548)
Adj R2	.185	.181	.236
N	46	46	46

Note: T statistics in parentheses
*Significant at the .1 level, **significant at the .05 level, ***significant at the .01 level

Suberu 2005). This also means that bargaining among veto players at the center is closely linked to local distributional politics.

Test results reported in Table 3.2 show that the number of veto players correlates with each type of government spending at a statistically significant level. But contrary to the predictions of the logroll hypothesis, regimes with more veto players reduce overall spending. Each additional veto player leads to a decline in all three measures of government consumption.

The independent variable is lagged at time $t - 1$ under the assumption that it takes about a year for spending decisions to be visible.[28] Government deficits shown on the *fedbudget* variable have a negative impact on the change in total government spending in Model 1 and on the change in recurrent spending in Model 2. Though the effect is not large, it does imply that government deficits curb the impulse to increase overall federal spending or recurrent spending. However, none of the other

[28] Two-tailed correlation tests between the veto player independent variable and each dependent variable show that a lag at time $t - 1$ best measures the relationship between them. For $\Delta Spending.GDP$ the Pearson's R = -.429, significant at the .01 level; for $\Delta Current.GDP$ the Pearson's R = -.432, significant at the .01 level; and for $\Delta Capital$. GDP, Pearson's R = -.359, significant at the .05 level.

controls has a statistically significant impact in these models, including *GDPgrowth* as a broad measure of national economic conditions. Even oil booms – central to explaining a broad range of policy performance in rentier regimes generally and in Nigeria specifically – have no systematic effect in Models 1 and 2, which are both statistically significant at the .05 level. Since they explain only about 18 percent of variation over time, though, we can take the results so far as persuasive but not necessarily conclusive.

The results in Model 3 show that regimes with more veto players have much lower rates of capital spending at a statistically significant level. This is especially important because this variable measuring government consumption represents the clearest operationalization of local collective goods. When the Nigerian government makes decisions to build cement plants, car factories, or hospitals, it faces choices about where to do so and therefore which communities will receive the most immediate and tangible benefits of such spending. This does not mean that good government performance eliminates local collective goods, since some citizens obviously benefit from these policy outputs. But as indicated by the comparative literature, it does strongly suggest that excessive increases are a sign of patronage or misallocations (Rose-Ackerman 1999; Joseph 1987).

Among the controls in Model 3, the variable ΔOil_{t-1} indicates that oil revenues do have an impact on capital spending. Surprisingly, though, the negative coefficient points to an inverse relationship, meaning that an increase in oil revenues actually drives down federal government capital spending. By itself, this might shock students of Nigeria familiar with the common stories about large "mobilization fees" collected in advance for construction projects that are then abandoned (Smith 2007; Osaghae 1998). Nigeria's oil booms leave plenty of room for corruption through graft, rents, and outright theft (Shaxson 2007b; Watts 2004). If corruption does indeed increase with oil income as the rentier literature implies, then the results here simply suggest that much of it simply occurs outside capital spending, arguably making the diversion of these public funds even less visible.[29] In other words, it is important not to infer a decline in corruption from this correlation.

[29] A recent investigation led by Farouk Lawan, a member of Nigeria's House of Representatives, lent support to this view when it reported in 2012 that $5 billion U.S. had gone missing over the previous decade – not because of unfinished projects but because of corruption generated through the importation of refined oil (House of Representatives Ad-Hoc Committee 2012).

Foreign debt levels indicated by the variable *Debt.ext*$_{t-1}$ have a small effect on government consumption, significant at the .1 level. This suggests either that foreign creditors discourage the Nigerian government from capital spending in favor of other investments, or that governments have to divert spending on capital projects to pay off foreign debt. The *fedbudget* variable actually loses the modest impact it had on government consumption. This indicates spending constraints due to the availability of funds from oil or other revenue do not determine whether Nigeria's governments decide to embark on capital projects. Finally, economic growth and the democracy dummy have no statistically significant impact on capital spending. This means that governments are just as likely to make good or bad decisions in periods of economic decline as in periods of prosperity, and that democratic governance explains less about spending on local collective goods than veto players. The results across all three models with local collective goods reject the logroll hypothesis.

Nigeria's Madisonian Dilemma

Though the tests with local collective goods reject the logroll hypothesis, they are in line with Madison's original ideals. He famously emphasized that for policy to be just (in addition to binding) the government must "control itself" by "supplying by opposite and rival interests." Fewer policy logrolls, manifest in lower levels of government consumption and capital spending in particular, point to an accountability effect that is missing from much of the veto player literature reviewed in Chapter 1. There, we noted how Madison in "Federalist Number 51" explains how each separate and sovereign branch checks the other. The veto player literature directly acknowledges this view of checks explicitly in research measuring for accountability (Andrews and Montinola 2004), and indirectly by suggesting that veto players provide checks (Haggard and McCubbins 2001). For whatever reason, though, veto player studies focus almost explicitly on policy stability, often neglecting this notion of accountability emphasized by Madison.

My confirmation of the coordination hypothesis means that regimes with more veto players have more trouble reaching agreement for the reasons identified by the bargaining literature and new institutional economics. It also suggests that regimes do not automatically bargain to efficient public policy outcomes, as envisioned by selectorate theory and the institutional research described in Chapter 1 that assumes low transaction costs. The test results find a clear correlation between an increase in the number of veto players and a decline in the overall levels of national collective goods. The rejection of the logroll hypothesis means that these same regimes are more likely to restrain spending on local collective goods and limit opportunities for patronage, contrary to the expectations of the distributional tradition in the literature. My empirical analysis has thus uncovered a tension: Regimes that promote good government performance in one area of public policy may undermine it in the other. I call this a "Madisonian dilemma" since good government performance, on the one hand, requires effective coordination for the delivery of national collective goods, but it also needs to curtail the collusion inherent in policy logrolls that include costly patronage spending. Nigeria's search for good governance entails the need to balance these two countervailing pressures. This also means that one cannot simply say that regimes with the most (or the fewest) veto players are better or worse; politics entails a kind of endogenous equilibrium, which for Nigeria is inescapably bound to the conditions of its creation.

One potential limitation with my variables is that they require inferences about policy outcomes from aggregate figures. With regard to capital spending, for example, we do not, for example, draw conclusions about performance based on the observed number of hospitals, schools, or factories built. Yet for that same reason, these variables offer the advantage of being directly related to federal policy decisions – the arena where veto players bargain with each other, and where coordination efforts either succeed or fail. Statistical results helpfully reveal patterns of performance. Another potential limitation of the variables concerns the interpretation of time series data with a limited number of years as observations.[30] (This is especially true for the *clearance* test results, since the law reports that provide information about companies and land cases are published very slowly.) I mitigate this problem through the inclusion of appropriate statistical controls as well as the qualitative analysis that follows. This analysis also clarifies the causal mechanism at work in the correlations reported in the statistical tests, illustrating how Nigeria's veto players effectively structure the policy process and linking particular regimes to observable outcomes.

---

[30] Only in Model 2 does the Durbin Watson statistic of 1.630 clearly indicate the absence of autocorrelation in the residuals. Results for the three other models are indeterminate.

A Qualitative Examination of Policy Performance, 1961–2007

Thus far, statistical tests have demonstrated that delivery of national collective goods, including inflation, budget deficits, education policy, and judicial efficiency, was more difficult in regimes with more veto players. This confirms the coordination hypothesis, since delivering these nonexclusionary goods entails bargaining with additional political actors. Tests of the logroll hypothesis offered some surprising results with regard to local collective goods. Rather than increasing government consumption as predicted, increases in the number of veto players systematically contributed to *declines* in capital and recurrent spending. This offers support for the theoretical claim that veto players have indirect impacts on accountability, much as Madison argued. This relationship was especially strong with the variable measuring capital spending – our clearest measure of local collective goods. These results remained robust across a broad set of controls including external debt, democratic regimes, economic growth, and oil revenues.

The tests convincingly estimate overall trends, but by themselves they tell us little about performance during particular periods or under specific regimes. In addition, the policies used to identify veto players in Chapter 2 are different from the policy outcomes we tested for here. The brief qualitative analysis that follows joins these worlds: It associates the measures of government performance used in the quantitative tests with particular veto player regimes identified through the coding process. It also demonstrates when coordination was difficult, and when accountability was facilitated, as a result of the number of veto players. Readers more interested in the big picture with regard to Nigeria's performance, or the broader implications of veto player theory, should feel free to skip to the chapter's Conclusion. Readers interested in (or perhaps skeptical of) the epistemology here are urged to read on, since what follows is meant to complement, rather than substitute for, the quantitative analysis.

Specifically, this section serves five useful functions. First, it permits identification of statistical outliers. Though the regressions establish a systematic relationship between the number of veto players and the dependent variable at a statistically significant level, the adjusted-R squared values also mean that some regimes did not behave as predicted. For example, regimes with three or four veto players sometimes delivered national collective goods or indulged in logrolls of local collective goods. Second, this section offers a check against a relatively small sample size, since none of the variables has more than forty-seven years of data. Mixed-method approaches can also address the problem of equifinality – a situation in which different historical processes lead to similar outcomes (George and Bennett 2004; Rueschemeyer, Stephens, and Stephens 1992). Here I note that different regimes with the same number of veto players also display some variation in their relationship to government performance, since the policy actors in each regime are shaped in part by the conditions they inherit from their predecessors. Third, this section disaggregates the government consumption data, highlighting specific policy areas that contributed to capital spending or drove up deficits. Fourth, since the measures of my dependent variable only capture annual data in calendar years, the analysis here often describes more discrete differences. Fifth, by relating distinct veto player regimes to performance trends, the narrative provides additional justifications for the operationalizations of my dependent variable as policies reflecting recurring government priorities. Low inflation, budget discipline, small student/teacher ratios, efficient courts, and modest levels of capital and recurrent spending all reflect common government objectives in Nigeria. As measures of government performance, my variables thus reflect insights from comparative political economy as well as recurring government priorities.

Postcolonial and Postwar Government Performance

Nigeria's independence was the climax of a political transition initiated during the 1950s and advanced through national elections in 1959. In many ways the performance of the coalition government, with the NPC and the NCNC operating as two partisan veto players, seemed to validate the euphoric national response to political freedom. An economic growth rate of 4 percent more than doubled between 1962 and 1963, and agricultural productivity enjoyed large gains. Up until 1965, 70 percent of the export revenue was from agricultural exports, including cocoa, groundnuts, rubber, cotton, and palm oil.[31] Unlike in most of Nigeria's neighbors, this economic diversity provided some insulation from economic shocks. The juxtaposition of developmental progress and imperial withdrawal seemed noncoincidental. Only months before independence in 1960 Britain's prime minister had poetically described a "wind of change" sweeping Africa as the imperial powers either prepared to leave or faced rising demands for them to do so.

In Nigeria's early postindependence years, the government ran modest deficits (averaging only 1.4 percent of GDP) and generally maintained

---

[31] "Nigeria on the Move," *West Africa*, March 5, 1966.

inflation of less than 4 percent. With education, there were large regional disparities to overcome as a result of colonial policies, since the British had cut a deal with Muslim elites in the North to limit missionary activities – including English language education – to the South (Abernethy 1969; Coleman 1958). Even with enrollment increases in the North as these same elites realized that this had put the region at a tremendous disadvantage in competing for jobs, classrooms averaged 31 pupils for each teacher. The judiciary acted efficiently throughout much of the 1960s, with the average clearance rate of 1.16 indicating that the courts disposed of property rights cases as quickly as new ones were being filed. This remained so even with an increase in the total number of cases filed between 1960 and 1965, and an 11 percent increase in population that could contribute to a corresponding increase in new cases.

In the run-up to the December 1964 elections, the NPC-NCNC government approved increases in wages and salaries that raised recurrent expenditures; capital spending also grew more than expected, especially with additions to the military's accounts. A report on the state of implementation of the National Six Year Development Plan added that "democracy has turned out to be more expensive than envisaged," especially since census results had to be rerun and the elections turned out to be fabulously expensive.[32] With the shift to a single veto player following the December 1964 elections due to the NPC's outright majority, there was a decline in economic optimism. In early 1966, the finance minister went to Paris to borrow money from the World Bank and other institutions in order to finance millions of pounds (Nigeria had not yet converted to *naira*) of capital spending anticipated by the development plan.[33] Overall, the improved delivery of national collective goods supports the coordination hypothesis, while the increased capital and recurrent outlays in regimes with only one or two veto players point to spending logrolls.

With southerners feeling marginalized and angry, ethnic riots in 1965 were followed by military coups in 1966, and then the Biafran civil war, which lasted two and a half long years. (Since no federal money went to capital or recurrent spending in the East while the region was attempting secession, the numbers are unusually low during those years.) In this second half of the decade, following the collapse of the First Republic, the clearance rate for property rights cases stayed above 1.0, and the federal

---

[32] "Chief Festus' Eighth Budget," *West Africa*, April 10, 1965; "Two Years of Nigeria's Plan," *West Africa*, May 1, 1965.
[33] "Backing Nigeria's Future," *West Africa*, February 19, 1966.

government maintained budget deficits of less than 2.5 percent of GDP. Oil began providing new revenue as its share of federal receipts leaped from 1 percent in 1966 to more than 25 percent in 1970. Nigeria also began a break with the colonial economy based in agricultural commodities controlled by marketing boards (Bates 1981).

Though the deficit hit 7.5 percent of GDP after the war ended in January 1970, this was followed by four optimistic years of budget surpluses that redirected government spending to much-needed reconstruction. "After the civil war we thought we should bring everybody together," said Gowon in a recent interview.[34] The government set out to train more teachers, increase primary enrollments, and repair schools damaged during the war. Even before Gowon left office in 1975, most of these goals had been met. School enrollment levels increased well above the targets, growing by about 10 percent per year starting in 1970, yet classroom size did not grow significantly during these years. The student/teacher ratio averaged 33.4 during Gowon's tenure from 1966 to 1975.

The postwar situation was far from rosy, though. The war devastated the infrastructure in the East, where the Igbos had fought for secession, and throughout much of the South. Hospitals were badly in need of repair, for example, so the government increased capital expenditures. Noting the "acute" shortage of health personnel, the administration set out to build dozens of new medical schools and teaching hospitals (Federal Government of Nigeria 1970). Despite the revenue boost from the oil boom, the government squandered most of its export earnings on import-substitution industrialization, a policy that neglected agriculture – the bedrock of the economy in the First Republic (Forrest 1995). Consumers used cash and an overvalued currency to import food items and luxury goods instead of generating savings or making investments (Iwayemi 1979). By 1971, the cost of food had already increased 50 percent over seven years, with the biggest increase in costs occurring in 1970.[35]

Gowon and the "superbureaucrats" responded to the problems posed by rising prices and growing government consumption by forming an Anti-Inflation Task Force. In addition to blaming reckless consumer spending habits, the task force attributed inflation to wage increases and unsustainable current and capital spending levels, which unrealistically anticipated consistently high oil revenues. Increases in current and capital expenditures averaged 23 percent from 1966 to 1969 but rose to

---

[34] Interview with General Yakubu Gowon, March 16, 2010, Abuja.
[35] Editorial, "Who Pays for the War?" *West Africa*, January 9–15, 1971.

more than 108 percent between 1970 and 1973 (Federal Government of Nigeria 1975). A 1971 commission on wages pushed up recurrent spending through large public sector wage increases. Ironically, the commission hoped that establishing parity between public and private wages would prevent upward inflationary spirals, expecting that pay levels in one sector would simply be pressured upward by the other.[36] Civil service wages were increased again in 1974 with yet another commission on public sector spending (Bienen 1983). Between 1971 and 1975, recurrent spending increased from 918 million naira to 4.7 billion, amounting to a third of the spending as a share of GDP by the time Gowon left office. Overall, for a regime with only two veto players, this exponential increase in government consumption exemplifies a policy logroll in the midst of limited accountability across the government. The government's delivery of national level collective goods during the Gowon years generally supports the coordination hypothesis, though the high rates of inflation are outlying results (attributable in part to the monetary effects of the oil boom).

When the Mohammed/Obasanjo regime took over with the 1975 coup, and the number of veto players increased from two to three, the government faced the task of bringing this sagging economy under control. Instead, the inflation rate tripled to 34 percent in barely a year and budget deficits resumed. Between 1976 and 1979 the federal government budget deficits ran above 10 percent as a share of GDP. The sharp decline in fiscal discipline can be blamed in part on the government's unrealistic projections of generous oil revenues for the indefinite future. In addition, new federal government commitments, including large education grants, drove up spending. For example, the Third National Development Plan projected an increase in primary enrollment from 4.7 million naira in 1973 to 11.5 million students at the end of the 1975–1980 period (Federal Ministry of Economic Development 1975). The government committed a greater share of its budget to education than at any other time in the country's history – then or since. Yet the recurrent spending still missed the mark and the government failed to hire enough teachers to compensate for growing enrollments, leading to an increase in class size (Abolade 2000; Bienen 1983). In 1979 the student/teacher ratio hit a peak of more than 40 pupils per teacher.

The increase in the number of veto players had two other important effects: First, the clearance rate of property rights cases plummeted from

---

[36] "Fixing Fair Shares for All," *West Africa*, December 3, 1971.

an average of .9 between 1970 and 1975, to .3 during the Mohammed/
Obasanjo years from 1975 to 1979. Second, the level of capital spending showed some evidence of restraint as it declined from 15 percent to
11 percent of GDP. In sum, the suboptimal delivery of national collective
goods is largely consistent with the coordination hypothesis's expectations for a three veto player regime, and the decline in government consumption suggests fewer policy logrolls.

The government's last budget before the 1979 democratic transition
called for many of the reforms necessary to establish fiscal discipline. In
his outgoing budget speech, Obasanjo called for "tightening our belts."
The budget reduced recurrent expenditures by 10 percent and nearly
halved capital expenditures. It also imposed new custom duties and
import restrictions, hoping to reduce the flood of imports and increase
government revenues.[37] The administration's calls for fiscal restraint
earned praise. "The 1979–1980 import and foreign exchange measures
may not make this military government immensely popular in the short
run," wrote a prominent economist, "but they should prove to be an
extremely important legacy to its civilian successor."[38] Other macroeconomic policies showed signs of shortsightedness, though. Inflation was
already above 11 percent and food prices had risen sharply through the
1970s (Iwayemi 1979). This passed on a huge political burden to the
incoming democratic regime, led by a president whose party lacked a
majority in the National Assembly and whose election was immediately
challenged in the Supreme Court.

The Second Republic and Nigeria's Second Attempt at Democracy
Though Shehu Shagari prevailed in court, he still faced a legitimacy deficit,
rising inflation, declining revenues, and a budget full of unpopular spending cuts put in place by the outgoing military administration. The shift to
a presidential system was meant to unify the country, but Shagari instead
spent the next two years embroiled in disputes with the National Party
of Nigeria (NPN) and the Nigeria People's Party (NPP), the two partisan
veto players in coalition in the newly elected National Assembly.

The regime struggled to deliver national collective goods for the dura-
tion of its existence through 1983. Judicial performance remained a serious
problem, with a clearance rate of property rights cases averaging .17

---

[37] "Still a Need for Tightened Belts," *West Africa*, April 9, 1979.
[38] Lawrence A. Rupley, "Why Nigerian Spending Has Grown and Grown," *West Africa*,
June 4, 1979.

during the regime's four years. The student/teacher ratio improved modestly from 42:1 in 1979 to 36:1 the following year as a result of the hiring of forty-two thousand new teachers recruited for the Universal Basic Education (UBE) Programme. But as enrollments increased, the new administration could not keep up, and the ratio steadily worsened, the regime averaged 38 students per teacher over its four year tenure. More to the point, the ambitious plans for UBE and other social spending worked at odds with the fiscal discipline guidelines inherited from the previous regime. The government appeared on track in July 1980 when it reported a surplus exceeding 2 billion naira (up from a deficit of 1.4 billion). However, despite some new tax revenue, budget deficits soon resumed, reaching nearly 15 percent of GDP in 1981. Government consumption went from 18 percent of GDP in 1980 to nearly 30 percent in 1981. An overvalued currency contributed to this excess, and as in the 1970s wealthy consumers again took advantage of exchange rates to purchase luxury imports rather than investing in economic productivity (Lewis 1997). President Shagari blamed consumers for the economic decline, pointing to their "insatiable appetite for imported goods."[39]

The states also bore some of the blame since they launched ambitious projects that they expected the federal government to finance. The federal government had planned to guarantee on-loans to the states, and it announced new macroeconomic controls to maintain the country's creditworthiness abroad so that it could do so.[40] The government instead adopted the worst of both worlds: a 46 percent increase in money supply in 1980 and a huge increase in external borrowing (on unfavorable terms) the following year. In 1981 inflation hit 20 percent, and in August a prominent opposition governor accused the president of lying about the economy and further complained about cutbacks in his state's share of grants from the federal government. President Shagari's economic adviser accused him of playing politics and again shifted blame, pointing a finger at the states' reckless spending. He also played down the significance of external factors such as declining oil revenues.[41] Barely a month later, the administration reversed itself and the budget director made clear the severity of the situation. He announced hiring and travel freezes and

[39] "Nigerian Turning Point," *West Africa*, May 3, 1982.
[40] "Rules for Borrowing by States," *West Africa*, July 7, 1980.
[41] "Shagari Accused of Lying" and "Austerity Measure Out," *Nigerian Tribune*, August 10, 1981; E. C. Edozien, "Shagari's Letter Only a Warning Signal," *Nigerian Tribune*, August 18, 1981.

a 30 percent "reservation" on all capital projects until the end of the year.[42]

By the end of 1981 the multiparty coalition collapsed and the regime reverted to institutional veto players rooted in the House, the Senate, and the presidency. The student/teacher ratio increased slightly from 36 to 38 pupils per teacher, and the government reported a deficit of 14.8 percent of GDP. By the following year there was a general "loss of financial control and discipline in the public economy" (Forrest 1995, 165). Short on revenue, the government borrowed more money. All nineteen state governments accumulated huge external debts, totaling $8 billion (U.S.), and pushed the country toward a desperate search for foreign exchange. Strikes by the country's largest union further set the economy back, as workers protested government corruption and cuts in wages (Falola and Ihonvbere 1985). By December 1983, inflation climbed to nearly 23 percent as the government signaled that it would adopt a more conservative fiscal policy.

Authoritarian Rule: The Long Stretch, 1983–1999

When General Muhammadu Buhari staged a coup on New Year's Eve 1983, he immediately blamed his predecessors for failing to "cultivate financial discipline and prudent management of the economy," relying too much on external borrowing and heavy deficit spending (Akinnola 2000, 66). The Buhari-Idiagbon regime, operating through two veto players, then embarked on strategies to increase foreign exchange earnings, reduce inflation, cut spending, and refinance the debt. The federal government's debt-to-service ratio at the time was approaching 35 percent (Osaghae 1998). The government declared its intention to hold the rate of inflation in 1985 to 30 percent, with a 1 percent GDP growth rate.[43] Over the regime's short tenure – less than two years – revenues inched upward and inflation moved down from 18 percent in 1984 to approximately 7 percent in 1985.

Capitalizing on complaints about the Second Republic's shortcomings, the government set its sights on corruption. It began with administrative reforms of the judiciary, including the abolition of the Federal Judicial Service, which handled staffing. In its stead the government created a judicial committee to advise the Supreme Military Council on appointments, anticipating that it would insulate judicial appointments from

---

[42] "Austerity Measures to Save N1 billion," *West Africa*, September 1981.
[43] "Government Hopes to Keep Inflation Rate Down," *The Guardian*, January 3, 1985.

local politics (Aguda 1988). Most notably, the government set up four military tribunals, explaining that these special courts would be a central tool in the War on Indiscipline (WAI). Among his accomplishments in 1984, Buhari proudly listed "greater security (enhanced by public executions)" and "exemplary punishment for persons responsible for the rot of the nation."[44] In an improvement over the Shagari regime during the Second Republic, the clearance rate of property rights cases increased from an average of .17 to .56.

Education, the other national collective good analyzed here, stood out among the government's weak indicators. Contrary to what the coordination hypothesis expects for a two veto player regime, the student/teacher ratio reached the all-time peak of more than 44 pupils per teacher. During the government's final months in office, an independent newspaper observed that education "has received a literal drubbing in the past year." It editorialized that "federal policy is still actuated by the false presumption that genuine industrialization, social harmony and political stability are possible without mass education."[45]

The government's austerity measures were also felt in dramatic cuts to local collective goods. Capital spending had been 23 and 17 percent of GDP in 1982 and 1983, respectively – the final two years of the Second Republic. The Buhari-Idiagbon regime's cuts took their toll on infrastructure. According to the Ministry of Education figures, there were nearly three thousand *fewer* primary schools in operation in 1985 compared to 1984 (Federal Office of Statistics 1985). The capital spending cuts were felt in other sectors too. Regarding the 1985 budget proposal, the president of the Nigerian Medical Association complained that "the allocation to health is ridiculously low," adding that "the average Nigerian now is a lot worse off than a year ago."[46] The health ministry actually spent only about half of the money the federal government budgeted for health care in 1984 (Okafor, Abumere, Egunjobi, and Ekpenyong 1998). Doctors went on strike twice within a six month period to protest the federal government's inadequate spending.[47] Capital spending was 6.5 percent of GDP in 1984 and 7.5 percent in 1985, the lowest levels since the early 1970s. In sum, the performance of national collective goods was largely what the coordination hypothesis expects from the regime with only two

[44] "Nigeria on the Road to Recovery," *The Guardian*, January 1, 1985.
[45] "1985 Budget: The Beginning of Recovery (3)," *The Guardian*, January 9, 1985.
[46] "Doctors Frown at Budget Allocation to Health," *The Guardian*, January 15, 1985.
[47] Orojomo, "Health Gets Biggest Vote Ever," *The Guardian*, January 3, 1986.

veto players, but its reductions in local collective goods are outliers in the statistical findings. This is arguably due to the government's staking its legitimacy on anticorruption policies and the priority given WAI.

Babangida's coup in late 1985 capitalized in no small part on the unpopularity of this retrenchment and WAI's harsh tactics (Olanrewaju 1992). In his maiden speech, Babangida abrogated repressive decrees and began releasing prisoners detained under WAI's broad sweeps. Property rights cases wound their way through the courts quickly and the clearance rate reached .69 in 1986. This was the courts' best performance since 1973. (As explained earlier, the data used to construct this variable unfortunately drop off after 1987.) To confront the abysmal education policy performance under Buhari-Idiagbon, the 1986 budget plan unveiled huge increases in education spending. In the administration's budget speech, Babangida declared, "Education has been so relegated to the background that it is in danger of imminent collapse."[48] The budget provided relief to cash-strapped states by increasing recurrent spending for teachers' salaries and administration.[49] The teachers' union still complained later that they received their salaries irregularly from the states and urged the federal government to take over education completely (Obidi 1998).

That same year the country suffered negative economic growth and the deficit amounted to more than 11 percent of GDP. But the government held inflation to 5.7 percent, and it successfully reined in an overvalued naira.[50] Taking heat from unions and civil society groups for structural adjustment, the government offered a "reflationary budget" in 1988, lifting the freeze on wages, anticipating "modest" deficits, and acknowledging that spending ran the risk of stimulating inflation.[51] This macroeconomic approach failed. Inflation reached 50 percent and roughly stayed there through 1989.

Around the time the regime's fourth veto player began taking shape in 1990, the government decentralized some authority over education to the states (Akinkugbe 1994). Proponents of free primary education initially called the combination of reforms "tragic and unfortunate." But

---

[48] Transcript of Babangida's Speech, "1986 Budget: The Beginning of a New Path," *The Guardian*, January 6, 1986.

[49] Goddy Nnadi, "Education Vote to Aid Implementation of 6-3-3-4 System," *The Guardian*, January 4, 1986.

[50] Transcript of Babangida's speech, "1986 Budget: The Beginning of a New Path," *The Guardian*, January 1, 1986; Nkem Ossau, "Naira Will Continue on Path of Adjustment," *The Guardian*, January 1, 1986.

[51] Cover story, "It's Spending Ease in '88," *The Nigerian Economist*, January 6–19, 1988; "Budget (1988)," *Africa Research Bulletin*, January 31, 1988.

even with large increases in student enrollments between 1990 and 1993, the government reported improvements in the student/teacher ratio from 41:1 to 37:1 over that period. However, the regime struggled a great deal more over other national collective goods. The administration announced a rigid new budget plan for high growth, balanced budgets, and low inflation.[52] As in 1988 and 1989, budget deficits were never improved beyond 6 percent of GDP for the regime's remaining years in office.

Promising to move the country toward a democratic transition on a positive note, Babangida said in 1992 the budget would "enforce financial discipline at all levels." To accomplish this, the government froze capital spending.[53] Instead of praising the budget for discipline, in contrast to earlier years, economists openly mocked the promise to balance budgets and said the Central Bank of Nigeria must be able to "say no to Federal Government finance excesses."[54] When federal revenues declined, the government devalued the currency, borrowed on credit, and printed more money. The Federal Office of Statistics reported that the 1992 budget anticipated a 2.1 billion naira surplus, but in a stark reversal the following year it forecast a 44 billion naira deficit. It warned that servicing deficits by printing money would contribute to price escalation and "runaway inflation" (Federal Office of Statistics 1993, 112). The warning was unheeded. The following year a fragile interim government under Ernest Shonekan inherited a 100 percent inflation rate[55] and a budget deficit exceeding 11 percent of GDP. With the exception of the education sector, where the student/teacher ratio improved slightly, the government otherwise left behind a weak record on the other measures of national collective goods: large deficits and historically high inflation. And though the regime's four veto players decreased government consumption to 15 percent of GDP in 1992, it hit 20 percent in 1993 – precisely where the government had left it after its ambitious budget plans in the early 1990s. Logrolls, rather than intragovernmental accountability, prevailed in the regime's final year, presenting an outlier to the regression results.

When Sani Abacha took over from the short-lived interim government, he formed an Economic and Finance Committee to chart a new

---

[52] "Ministerial Breakdown of the 1992 Budget," *The Guardian*, January 4, 1992.

[53] Transcript of Babangida Speech. "Watershed of Our National Evolution," *The Guardian*, January 2, 1992.

[54] Alex Ogundadegbe, "Who Will Keep the Federal Government in Check?" *The Guardian*, January 10, 1992.

[55] Bolla Olowo, "Fiscal Reflections," *West Africa*, January 24–30, 1994. The inflation rate for all of 1993 was 57 percent.

economic course. He faced only a single veto, from the "June 12" faction, which insisted on honoring the annulled 1993 elections. The government reported a 57 percent inflation rate in 1994 and ran a budget deficit of slightly above 5 percent of GDP. The cabinet abruptly stopped meeting in mid-1994 and Abacha dissolved the Finance Committee. Budgets for the next two years benefited from increased revenues supposedly from stricter enforcement of taxes and duties (Okunrounmu 1996); both oil and nonoil revenue more than doubled from 1994 to 1995. The government actually ran a small surplus in 1995 and 1996 in line with the expectations of the coordination hypothesis. Although inflation was still high, it dropped down to 29 percent. By 1997 federal deficit spending and inflation appeared to be under control, and the average classroom size was reportedly 36 pupils per teacher. In sum, the delivery of these various national collective goods improved with the reduction in the number of veto players from the previous regime.

However, this performance also corresponded with an increase in graft, as mechanisms of horizontal and vertical accountability were dismantled and undermined after the elimination of the June 12 faction's veto in 1996. During Abacha's two final years in office, social services, economic conditions, and education all declined. Corruption was so rampant that the equivalent of $305 million U.S. was reported missing from various ministries and parastatals, and the finance minister refused to disburse money for capital spending.[56] For example, only 35 billion of the 61 billion naira budgeted for such projects from a special trust fund for petroleum earnings was actually spent. Eventually the government ceased publishing audits of most accounts (Olaniyan 1996). The final figures for capital and recurrent spending both show large increases as government consumption rose from 11 percent in 1996 to 28 percent in 1999 just before the transition. These spending habits conform to the statistical tests of the logroll hypothesis.

In the education sector, the student/teacher ratio had been down to 33:1 in 1996, but by the time Abacha died in 1998, it was nearly 40:1. The National Primary Education Commission and the World Bank found that it was common for two classes to be housed in one classroom, "rooms which are, generally, in poor states of repair" (National Primary Education Commission 1999, x). A study of more than a thousand schools in thirteen states carried out by Nigerian political scientists further documented the poor conditions of schools under Abacha

---

[56] Chris Ogbonna, "One Step Forward, Two Backward," *TELL*, July 14, 1997.

(Gboyega, Ogunsanya, and Okunade 1998). Under conditions of a single veto player during Abacha's final two years, the government seemed to deliver neither national nor local collective goods with any reliability.

The Return of Democracy, the Return of Obasanjo

The swift transition to democracy in 1999 restored the former dictator Olusegun Obasanjo to office – this time as an elected president facing institutional vetoes in the House and Senate, and the regional veto rooted in the North. The new administration began by documenting widespread corruption and the grim state of the country. A government study reported that of 332,408 classrooms in 44,292 primary schools, only 42 percent were in good condition while the remainder required significant rehabilitation (Tahir 2001). The economy was also in rough shape. In 2000 inflation climbed to 14.5 percent and the deficit hit 60 billion naira ($578 million) in the first half of the year alone. Economists at first complained that despite a transition to democracy, there was no major change in economic policy or the government's spending priorities, and they listed macroeconomic instability and low growth as serious problems (Taiwo 2001, 28; Akpakpan 2000). Obasanjo's administration shot back when his chief economic adviser said, "Most of the problems of budget implementation could be attributed largely to the military dictatorship under which the planning and budgeting process operated for over a decade" (Asiodu 2000, 9). The new administration declared its intention to maintain single-digit inflation and to keep the budget deficit within the Central Bank of Nigeria's (CBN's) benchmark of less than 3 percent of GDP. An economic strategy document, *Obasanjo's Economic Direction, 1999–2003*, established as goals foreign debt cancellation, job creation, and infrastructure upgrades to improve industrial capacity (Fadahunsi 2005).

The economic challenge became clear when a minimum wage increase and the elimination of a national fuel subsidy infuriated the governors, the National Assembly, and unions alike (Okafor 2010). The governors considered it an unfunded mandate, and the legislators noted that neither the wage increase nor the subsidy elimination had been authorized by legislation.[57] Cuts from the subsidy would have done little good alongside the huge increases in capital spending anyway, including a 40 percent increase in 2001 alone, and civil service wage increases. Contrary to the

---

[57] Luky Fiakpa, "One Wage, a Thousand Battles," *TELL*, July 17, 2000.

statistical findings for the logroll hypothesis, spending by all three tiers of government (federal, state, and local) grew during these first few years of democracy under four veto players. In the face of rising inflation and looming foreign debt payments, the CBN printed more money (Iyoha 2002). Money supply increased 38 percent in 2000, and 20 percent in 2001. The National Assembly increased the president's proposed capital spending by an additional 63 percent (Nnanna 2002; Sanusi 2002), the equivalent of a $1.5 billion increase. The chairman of the Senate Appropriations Committee expressed his alarm about the increased spending commitments for 2002 in the face of declining revenue estimates, bluntly commenting, "We cannot allow this trend to continue."[58] At the end of Obasanjo's first term in 2003, the country faced double-digit inflation and signs of broad fiscal indiscipline.

In sum, Obasanjo's first term seemed surprisingly disappointing in terms of national collective goods, with increases in class size and rising inflation looming. The 8.5 percent budget deficit in 1999 dropped to 2.4 percent of GDP in 2000, well within the government's traditional Keynesian-inspired target, but it was back above 6 percent in 2003. The reinvented Universal Basic Education program similarly let down denizens with high hopes for democracy's return: Classrooms remained in poor condition and with more than 41 pupils per teacher. In terms of local collective goods, the resumption of legislative politics offered a ray of hope once the excesses of 2000 and 2001 were under control. Capital spending declined from nearly 15 percent of GDP at the time of the transition, to less than 4 percent at the end of his term. Rather than a logroll, anticipated from the rhetorical flourish of the new generation of politicians demanding local collective goods, the dispersion of authority across four veto players limited some of the patronage-style spending.

After his reelection in 2003, Obasanjo jettisoned the earlier generation of advisers who had come of age during military-era oil booms. He recruited in their place a new economic team that comprised reform-minded technocrats (Lewis 2007a). Following on several years during which the Finance Ministry, the Central Bank, and the National Assembly showed little restraint, the economy started to show signs of improvement. Real GDP continued to grow, as did the manufacturing sector and domestic savings. The National Economic Empowerment and Development Strategy (NEEDS) formed a cornerstone of the president's economic reforms. Recapitalization and financial consolidation

[58] Ibim Semenitari, "Nigeria Is Broke," *TELL*, October 20, 2003.

increased foreign deposits in banks, and the government moved forward on privatization (Mailafia 2008). This controversially included monetarization of various civil service benefits. "The regime made serious efforts to enforce budget discipline," notes one recent study. The International Monetary Fund in fact approved its first Policy Support Instrument for Nigeria in 2005, demonstrating confidence in the government's economic policies. Foreign reserves grew from $8 billion in 1999 to more than $28 billion in 2005 (Balogun 2009, 119). The new finance minister, Ngozi Okonjo-Iweala, started publishing data about fiscal transfers to the states in order to increase local oversight and private sector confidence in the economy.

With the shift of Southwest electoral support to Obasanjo and the reduced political saliency of sharia in the North, bargaining over national collective goods meant fewer veto players to contend with, even if their differences on issues such as budget authority remained intense. For example, the chair of a budget reform committee complained that each budget contained scores of new capital spending proposals even if the previous years' projects remained unfinished or abandoned. Recurrent spending amounted to "a kind of conspiracy," with expenses for unproductive seminars, travel, or fictitious maintenance.[59] On other issues such as debt rescheduling, the National Assembly shared much of the executive's agenda. The chair of a joint legislative committee on debt incredulously documented in 2005 how previous administrations had cumulatively borrowed $17 billion, paid back $22 billion, and Nigeria still owed foreign creditors $36 billion.[60] The National Assembly expressed a commitment (at least formally) to controlled spending and borrowing through a Fiscal Responsibility Bill. It also went along with increased transparency of oil revenues through implementing legislation for an Extractive Industries Transparency Initiative. The reforms proved timely. The international price of sweet light crude oil doubled during President Obasanjo's first administration, which ended as the Iraq War began in 2003 –driving the price of oil upward even further.

The Ministry of Finance managed to direct some windfall savings into foreign reserves as hoped, but enhanced oil earnings introduced new problems. Nigeria typically produces about 2.5 million barrels of sweet light crude oil per day. The administration set a target of 3 million barrels,

[59] Interview with Alex Nwofe, March 10, 2010. Abuja.
[60] Emma Ujah and Emmanuel Aziken, "Nigeria National Assembly Calls for Total Debt Cancellation," *Vanguard*, May 10, 2005.

which it failed to meet because of persistent input and infrastructure problems. Oil spills had always interfered with full capacity, for example, with government statistics recording 2,159 spills between 1991 and 1996 (Azaiki and Ikein 2008). In addition to this recurring challenge, the government now had to contend with sabotage by militant groups and theft of oil through "bunkering," directly and illegally siphoning it out of pipelines. An independent commission formed by the government, the Technical Committee on the Niger Delta, estimated losses at 700,000 barrels per month and $17 billion for 2006 alone (Technical Committee on the Niger Delta 2008). Despite these losses, revenue increased as oil prices doubled during Obasanjo's second term. Overall, during his first seven years in office, the government's total gross revenue increased 140 percent.

Delivery of national collective goods measured by education policy was inconsistent under Obasanjo's administration. Over his eight years in office as president, the primary student/teacher fluctuated wildly, ranging from 36 to 46 pupils per teacher. His final years seemed to bring this under control, averaging 39.6 (which is still high, considering targets). Assessing the eight years of education performance under President Obasanjo's watch, the World Bank reported, "Despite significant efforts during the past eight years, much remains to be done in the education sector," including the need to increase enrollments, especially in the North. It concluded, "The overall quality of education remains poor at all levels and varies considerably within and across states" (Nigeria: A Review of the Costs and Financing of Public Education 2008, 1).

The macroeconomic picture in many ways tells a more consistent story of improving performance with the three veto players operating after 2003, limiting the coordination problems that had plagued Obasanjo's first administration. Early in his second term, the IMF noted that money supply was more than twice the CBN target and inflation had more than doubled from the previous year.[61] Yet by the end of 2004, the budget deficit was barely 1 percent of GDP and remained below 1 percent for the remainder of his term. Inflation did hit nearly 18 percent in 2005, but Obasanjo's finance team managed to halve that in 2006 to 8 percent. That year the government put windfall oil revenue to good use when it refinanced Nigeria's Paris Club loans, paying off most of its foreign debts. Finance Minister Okonjo-Iweala called the debt payoff "our biggest

---

[61] Samuel Famakinwa, "Economy Records 10.75 Percent Growth, Says IMF," *This Day*, March 15, 2004.

achievement," and it facilitated some collaboration on other public finance issues too.[62]

Throughout Obasanjo's second term, in the regime under three veto players, capital spending never went above 3.5 percent as a share of GDP, and overall government consumption stayed within the range of 10 to 11 percent of GDP. When Nigeria inaugurated Umaru Musa Yar'Adua as president in 2007, his first budget speech noted that poverty was still widespread, but that the country had recently made impressive macroeconomic gains that laid the groundwork for more sustainable development. To grow the country into one of the world's twenty largest economies, he pledged to achieve single digit inflation and to push the economic growth rate above 11 percent.[63] He passed away in office in 2010 without achieving either one of those goals, leaving his successor (Goodluck Jonathan) with new challenges, including a violent new Islamic rebellion in the Northeast.

Summary: Trends and Outliers

The goal of this brief qualitative analysis was neither to link specific veto players to explicitly stated policy preferences nor to apologize for authoritarianism by showing how dictators sometimes facilitated good governance. Instead, one purpose was to complement the statistical tests by identifying outliers and some inconsistencies within each cluster of variables measuring local and national collective goods. For example, in some regimes the four variables measuring national collective goods did not all perform the same way, even though the evidence otherwise points to a statistical pattern. Another objective was to link specific regimes, which represent distinct configurations of veto players, to the policy outputs measuring my dependent variable. Doing so provided additional evidence of the causal mechanism theorized in Chapter 1 and revealed through the struggles over political power analyzed in Chapter 2.

In which regimes did additional veto players impair delivery of national collective goods, lending support to the coordination hypothesis? And did these regimes also limit policy logrolls, attesting to a Madisonian dilemma? Babangida's prolonged tenure of eight years provides a natural experiment to answer these questions since the regime underwent change in veto players midstream, in 1990, and quickly experienced a

---

[62] Paul Vallely, "Interview with Mrs. Ngozi Okonjo-Iweala," *The Independent* (London) May 16, 2006.

[63] Boniface Chizea, "The Economy in 2007," *This Day*, January 1, 2008.

macroeconomic decline. The budget that year included promises about balanced budgets and low inflation. But when federal revenues declined, the government devalued the currency, borrowed on credit, and printed more money. The results were a ballooning deficit, and inflation levels approaching triple digits at times. Aside from the slight improvements in student/teacher ratios in the regime's final years, the steep decline in macroeconomic management corresponds with the coordination hypothesis's predictions. The additional veto player also corresponded with the decline in government consumption to 15 percent of GDP in 1992, down from 20 percent two years earlier. This is consistent with the test results for the logroll hypothesis, but then spending climbed back up to 20 percent in 1993. On the basis of the qualitative discussion, we know that 1993 stands out as an unusual moment in Nigeria's history, when the government essentially lost control after the catastrophic annulment of the presidential elections. The policy logroll manifest in this spending spike in annual data is a consequence of the ensuing profligacy of the Abacha regime that took over in August 1993, following two months of postelection political chaos.

The differences between Obasanjo's first and second terms as president provided a similar natural experiment, offering stronger support for the statistical findings for the logroll and the coordination hypotheses. During his first term between 1999 and 2003, Nigeria faced double digit inflation and large budget deficits. Then came a reduction in veto players from four to three. By the end of 2004, the budget deficit was barely 1 percent of GDP and it remained at similarly low levels for the remainder of Obasanjo's second term. When he left office in 2007, revenue was up, inflation was down, and virtually all of Nigeria's foreign debts had been paid off (or significantly refinanced). Though the schools experienced a huge surge in enrollments, the average student/teacher ratio improved slightly from 41.6 in his first term to 39.6 in his second term. In terms of local collective goods, capital expenditures (our most direct measure) never went above 3.6 percent of GDP even though the legislature often demanded new spending on capital expenditures during Obasanjo's second term. In other words, the regime seemed to confront the Madisonian dilemma head on by coordinating for national collective goods and constructing new restraints on patronage spending that would appear as policy logrolls.

The three veto players in the Mohammed/Obasanjo regime (1975–1979) led to the "belt tightening" on government consumption and local collective goods, and delivery of national collective goods generally declined. That slide continued during the Second Republic (1979–1983) that followed, as the new democracy struggled with high inflation, large budget deficits, slow clearance rates, and various fiscal crises characteristic of coordination problems. The apparent checks and balances did little to limit spending on local collective goods (though the anomaly with the statistical results would be sharper if the regime had four veto players instead of three).

By comparison, did regimes with only one or two veto players fare any better in terms of national collective goods, and did efforts to limit excesses with local collective goods suffer as the statistical results suggested? During Abacha's initial years in office, there was some improvement in national collective goods, as evidenced in the budget surpluses, reductions in inflation, and smaller student/teacher ratios. But government consumption rose dramatically, as did corruption, complementing the statistical findings on the logroll hypothesis. Can this experience be compared to other two veto player regimes in the sample? This is an important question because an affirmative answer would reinforce the validity of veto players as a tool for comparing Nigeria's different military governments with each other. The results for the Buhari-Idiagbon regime are mixed: Education performance declined but judicial efficiency improved, inflation went down, and the budget deficit shrank. Since the regime lasted less than two years (1984–1985), Gowon's eight year tenure offers a better test. Delivery of national collective goods supports the statistical results for the coordination hypothesis with the exception of inflation, which increased dramatically. The qualitative analysis, however, pinpointed money supply and poor management of the exchange rate as contributing factors to this outlying result. In terms of policy logrolls, it is clear that the regime indulged in a large increase in government consumption, far beyond its vision of postwar reconstruction. The widespread corruption among the regime's governors (previously discussed in Chapter 2) generally fits with our expectations of a regime lacking the sort of broad checks and balances with a larger number of veto players.

Conclusion

This chapter began by establishing distinctions between national and local collective goods, and then operationalizing these public policies using variables drawn from the political economy literature that reflect recurring priorities of Nigeria's governments since independence. After identifying appropriate controls, I tested the two hypotheses formulated in Chapter 1, using the veto players identified in Chapter 2 as an independent variable. Statistical tests confirmed the coordination hypothesis by demonstrating an inverse and statistically significant correlation between the number of veto players and national collective goods. Specifically, an increase in veto players corresponded with higher rates of inflation, larger budget deficits, bigger student/teacher ratios, and lower court clearance rates. Additional veto players stimulate coordination problems that broadly impact the government's ability to make classrooms less crowded, to reassure investors about private property rights enforcement, to keep consumer prices modest, and to formulate budgets that reflect fiscal responsibility.

However, contrary to the expectations of the logroll hypothesis, an increase in veto players *reduced* delivery of local collective goods, manifest in declines in overall levels of government consumption. The significant effect on capital spending, the clearest measure of local collective goods, is especially important because it is targetable and excludable spending. Spikes in these outlays are a good proxy for such maldistribution, while more modest levels of spending imply that the government is building schools, roads, or hospitals. The results suggest that an increase in the number of veto players reduces the latitude that any single political actor has to engage in clientelism or patronage spending. This differs from the distributional tradition exemplified by Cox and McCubbins (2001), who theorized that each political actor with a veto should be able to extract concessions in the form of particularistic payoffs that resemble local collective goods. But it conforms to the expectations described in Chapter 1 that the number of veto players affects transaction costs.

The contradictory effects of veto players present Nigeria with a Madisonian dilemma – how to balance the need for coordinating preferences in order to deliver broad national policy benefits with the need for accountability when it comes to targetable policies that are the focus of the distributional tradition in the literature. Madison envisioned a system of checks and balances that would prevent government abuse of authority and channel citizen "passions" into competing institutional interests. Even though policy stability was not his principal concern, this has become the primary focus of most veto player studies. The results here indicate that supporting good government performance requires incentives for both coordination and accountability. With too few veto players, Nigeria ends up with corruption and patronage; with too many veto players it experiences fiscal indiscipline, clogged courts, and crowded classrooms.

The results remain robust across a variety of controls characteristic of the conventional wisdom for government performance in Africa. The statistically weak impact of external debt supports the notion that domestic political institutions can overcome external policy constraints. This is an especially important point with respect to Africa, where numerous studies argue that most countries have not escaped colonialism's harmful economic legacies (Lange 2009; Young 1994), while others highlight the potential for policy choice to break from path dependent histories (Radelet 2010; Ndulu et al. 2008). The limited impact of economic growth and oil revenue similarly suggests that politics are primary when explaining Nigeria's policy performance, and the mere presence of electoral democracy inadequately captures important characteristics of politics. The number of veto players captures the structural features of these politics, and the independent variable's relationship with the multiple measures of government performance remains robust across these various controls. All of this amounts to compelling evidence that seemingly different collective goods respond to this structuring of the policy process in similar ways.

This chapter demonstrates that veto players are a useful tool for capturing complex political structures, and that the broad institutional characteristics of the policy process have meaningful effects on everyday life. Veto players systematically impact policy outcomes that matter for Nigeria's long-term economic and social development. High inflation increases the costs of food, housing, and other essentials. Large budget deficits borrow from the future to finance the promises of present-day rulers. An ineffective education policy undermines human capital formation. Inefficient courts jeopardize long-term economic investment by prolonging the resolution of property rights disputes and generating uncertainty about the legal environment.

But none of the results is meant to suggest that life in Nigeria was rosy. The United Nations Development Programme recently found that inequality in Nigeria increased dramatically between 1985 and 2004 (United Nations Development Programme 2009). And in 2012, the Nigerian government reported that 63 percent of the population lived on a dollar a day (Nigerian Bureau of Statistics 2012). The evidence here suggests that over the long term, achieving just and sustainable development in Nigeria involves facing the Madisonian dilemma. Traditional chiefs, inspiring democratic activists, ordinary citizens, and probably some unsavory political actors will all have roles to play. Before exploring Nigeria's current trajectory, to see whether it is moving in a positive developmental direction, the next chapter explores Zimbabwe and Ghana as cases illustrating how the veto player model can constructively be applied elsewhere.

4

Analytic Equivalents in Ghana and Zimbabwe

There has been no shortage of praise for Ghana over the last several years. The British newspaper *The Telegraph* called the defeat of Ghana's ruling party in peaceful elections in 2009 "a rare example of democracy in action in Africa."[1] A major report on Africa's transitional economies by the McKinsey Global Institute highlighted Ghana's economic growth, increased export of processed goods, and 14 percent net gain in primary school enrollment (McKinsey Global Institute 2010). Zimbabwe, on the other hand, has a stalled educational system and an electoral process that often descends into violence and a few years ago recorded the world's highest inflation rate. UNICEF's 2011 Country Program Action Plan described "a mirage of social and economic obstacles" that have resulted in negative economic growth and alarming rates of infant mortality.[2]

In this chapter, I develop historical narratives about these two very different countries: Ghana stands out as one of the best candidates for an African success story, enjoying high rates of economic growth and peaceful but vigorous democratic competition. Zimbabwe, a former white settler colony in the grip of one of Africa's most stubborn dictators, endures ongoing political violence and hunger. I use these divergent paths to explore the comparative potential of veto players as analyzed in this study. I do not attempt to identify veto players with the operational rigor applied in Chapter 2, to carry out statistical tests similar to those applied to Nigeria, or to assess the state of democratization. My goals here are

---

[1] Sebastien Berger, "Ghana Elections Provide Rare Democratic Success in Africa," *The Telegraph* (London), January 4, 2009.
[2] UNICEF, "Zimbabwe: Country Overview." www.unicef.org/zimbabwe/overview.html

more modest. I aim to probe the conceptual validity of my causal variable by analyzing interactions among different types of political actors whose efforts to advance their preferences influence the expansion and contraction of the policy process. The individual, institutional, collective, and partisan actors here are not identified explicitly as veto players, but are treated as "analytic equivalents." Borrowing on this idea emergent in qualitative research methods, I take the political actors in the following discussion as representations of political leverage that estimate the underlying distribution of political authority.

Another goal here is to explore the nature of formal and informal power structures further through state-society interactions. In Ghana, labor unions, military factions, rural pressure groups, and other social forces shaped the policy process even amid repression, and the government's ability to co-opt them decayed. In Zimbabwe, it was the degeneration of institutions (not their absence) that led Robert Mugabe to turn to uncertain allies, and then to enter into a coalition with a political rival that effectively limited one of his major patronage mechanisms. As in Nigeria, institutions were neither paper tigers nor mere proxies for elites, and rulers sometimes became beholden to actors capable of coordinating interests and imposing high transaction costs on policy-making processes. These shifting centers of power in broad terms impacted the government's ability to deliver local and national collective goods.

First, I briefly discuss the uses of case studies in comparative politics, exploring how new "postparadigmatic" research offers a path to theories that link microlevel processes to historical junctures and structural conditions. Case studies often emulate quantitative reasoning to establish an empirical relationship, explain outliers in results, or are otherwise chosen on the basis of statistical outcomes in "nested" research designs. By contrast, innovative qualitative techniques now often use case studies in "explanation sketches" or "analytic narratives" in order to elaborate on causal mechanisms tested elsewhere or to generate new hypotheses. I describe how searching for analytic equivalents of veto players in this chapter's two cases helps explore the application and potential limits of this comparative concept.

Second, a brief narrative of Ghana's postindependence political history draws connections between the emergence of new policy constraints and changing economic conditions. Competing military factions, economic coalitions, and rival political parties generated constantly shifting policy processes roughly from the time of Ghana's first military coup in 1966 to its last coup in 1981. Not until institutional consolidation took place in the 1980s as a result of political decentralization, a rising middle class, and increased bureaucratic autonomy did Ghana begin to break with postindependence habits of political instability and economic mismanagement. Unlike analyses that often attribute this shift to enlightened (if authoritarian) leadership, I emphasize the ability of different policy visions to compete without precipitating state crises. By the time of the democratic transition in 1993, policy change no longer required regime change because institutions already embedded this equilibrium. At least three critical junctures emerge in the narrative, including a policy reversal in 1969 that led to the formation of new interest groups opposed to austerity, the coup led by Jerry Rawlings in 1979 that unleashed populist anger against corruption and economic collapse, and a debate over economic policy in the mid-1980s that dispersed authority through rising social forces. Each one shifted the distribution of veto authority in some significant way.

Third, another short narrative follows Zimbabwe's path to the 2008 power-sharing agreement among rival political parties. I discuss tensions among the parties and the importance of a party merger in 1987. I trace the rise of an opposition movement through economic liberalization, coalition building, and electoral challenges. I describe opposition gains in the 1990 elections, the defeat of the ruling party's constitutional referendum in 2000, and a 2008 power-sharing agreement as three critical junctures that shaped veto authority. Unlike the institutional consolidation that preceded Ghana's transition to democracy, Zimbabwe's incumbent regime arrived at that critical historical juncture in 2008 ill equipped to arbitrate among competing factions. When a dispute arose over election results, the president's political options were shaped and constrained by stubborn allies as well as powerful new critics. This distribution of political authority, which included an opposition with some veto powers, limited the president's ability to reallocate local collective goods on political terms. It also coincided with some macroeconomic gains.

This examination of Ghana and Zimbabwe allows us to study further competing institutional actors, interest articulation, and the exercise of collective political leverage through social bases of authority. Each narrative identifies historical pivot points, competing interests, and key political actors who analytically resemble veto players. Thinking comparatively about this study's independent variable permits us to explore in general terms how well the individual, collective, and institutional qualities we have associated with veto players reasonably estimate the expansion or contraction of the policy process. Like Babangida and some of Nigeria's dictators, the case of Zimbabwe provides another tough test of whether multiple veto players really operate in authoritarian regimes, while the examination of Ghana encourages us to relocate the origins of its encouraging trajectory in earlier structural political shifts.

A Few Notes on the Uses of Case Studies

Focusing on government performance in Nigeria over time has offered a number of advantages for this study. A research design utilizing a single case study makes it possible to hold factors such as colonial history, the number of ethnic groups, and various national or historical conditions constant. This reduces the number of variables that present plausible alternative explanations. It also enables "thick description" of complex political and social phenomena that is largely lost in large-N studies. This is especially true with regard to veto player research, which, as noted in Chapter 1, tends to focus on quantitative cross-national analysis (and is typically limited to developed countries). But testing a theory with a single country also has limitations in terms of generalizability because it is difficult to assess the contributions of the empirical findings or to determine the broader utility of concepts. These are enduring issues with particular salience in African studies, where the case for exceptionalism – the notion that the continent and its particular polities defy meaningful comparison – remains strong (Mamdani 1999; Chabal 2009). In what follows I do not rehash the various trade-offs inherent in different research designs and methodologies. Instead, I describe recent ideas such as "analytic equivalents" that orthogonally approach these familiar debates in comparative politics. This sets up the subsequent narratives of Ghana and Zimbabwe as explorations of actors resembling veto players, and the structural conditions that generate them.

In the classic version of the comparative method developed by Lijphart, supplemental cases are typically used to overcome the problem of "many variables, few cases." The method, based partly on John Stuart Mill's philosophy, can be used to interpret existing results, explore outliers, confirm the validity of results, or generate new hypotheses (Lijphart 1971). The utility of case studies in this view depends on the number and range of observations (Eckstein 1975). A leading text on qualitative research treats summarized historical detail as statistical in the sense that it is "an expression of data in abbreviated form," and the authors argue that single-observation research design presents the risk that findings will be extended through analogy rather than rigorous analysis. "As with comparative studies in general," they write, "we always do better (or in the extreme, no worse) with more observations" (King, Keohane, and Verba 1994, 212). Even for studies that deliberately focus on a single country, Lees argues that "thick description" must still emulate the comparative method to the greatest extent possible (Lees 2006). This leads to strong presumptions that qualitative research designs need to increase the number of cases. Examples of common techniques for doing so include making subnational comparisons (across regions within a country, for example) or conducting time series analysis, as this study does by treating each one of Nigeria's fourteen veto player regimes as a distinct case.

A different view suggests that given a different set of goals, cases need not strive to emulate statistical inference. George and Bennett argue that a great strength of case studies resides in their ability to explore causal mechanisms in detail (George and Bennett 2004).[3] For example, Weinstein (2007) uses what he calls "explanation sketches" to situate rebel choices within institutional frameworks. Summaries of supplemental cases provide just enough information to fill in the causal mechanism's details using logic and some basic research on the cases. This approach to case studies can help uncover intervening variables or conditions that activate the causal process. Lange (2009) uses two tiers of qualitative analysis to supplement statistical findings with thirty-nine countries over four decades: Four detailed case studies examine the causal mechanisms and the statistical outliers, and then a dozen "abbreviated" case studies examine the generalizability of his claims. I see such approaches as creative responses to the era that has been called the "paradigm wars," in the early 2000s, when qualitative and area studies specialists rebelled against rational theories' ambitions as well as the perceived hegemony of positivist empiricism (Lichbach 2009). More than simply new methodologies, the use of narrative techniques thus represents a creative response to some of these ontological debates, drawing together area studies, comparative theory, and different empirical orientations.

This chapter uses case studies of Ghana and Zimbabwe in two ways. First, I use them as a tool for concept validation. Rather than attempting to code new sets of veto players, the narratives here simply strive to identify "analytically equivalent phenomena" that are manifest in different

---

[3] Drezner's (2006) review of their book, *Case Studies and Theory Development*, disputes this advantage of qualitative research by arguing that formal and quantitative studies are just as well equipped for hypothesis generation or exploration of causal mechanisms.

terms in different contexts (George and Bennett 2004, 19–20). I do not therefore aim to apply the coding criteria established in Chapter 1 to additional cases, but my analysis is meant to imply that doing so is feasible in a variety of new contexts. This requires a conscientious effort to avoid "conceptual stretching," a problem in qualitative studies in which a researcher treats substantially different cases as similar in order to increase the sample size (Sartori 1970). Loosening definitional criteria and multiplying descriptors are symptoms of conceptual stretching. The concept of neopatrimonialism presents one obvious example, as several recent studies suggest that has been applied so broadly that it provides diminishing analytical leverage as a descriptor of state patronage structures (Pitcher, Moran, and Johnston 2009; Bach 2011). In sum, case studies can refine, clarify, and delimit concepts. Even without explicit testing, they can guide us through data and find connections to additional literatures (Lichbach 2009).

Second, the case studies here explore shifting state-society relations that shape veto player regimes. (Recall that in this study each regime constitutes a particular configuration of veto players.) In Chapter 2, I identified veto players by working backward from attempts to challenge policy, and then in Chapter 3 I linked those political actors to government performance. Here I abridge those steps by focusing on historical junctures that formed the basis for institutional change in Ghana and Zimbabwe. These pivot points represent moments when shifts among political actors with veto authority should lead to visible changes in policy performance. Institutional change during such historical junctures is significantly constrained by what Cheeseman and Tendi (2010) call the "politics of continuity." This derives not only from self-interest in the status quo, but from the high costs of institutional change; reform is time-consuming and existing implementation infrastructures – organizations and bureaucracies – may be greater than the sum of their parts. Historical processes are self-reinforcing, and this characteristic makes the "critical junctures" where change occurs important for broader analytical purposes (Pierson 2000). For example, African countries followed different democratization trajectories depending on whether they had French or British colonial histories (Widner 1994a). Similarly, many African economies remain dependent on the same export crops they were dependent on half a century ago (African Development Bank 2011). Case studies can clarify complex interaction effects that contribute to such path dependency (George and Bennett 2004). The use of critical junctures helps identify the moments that depart from self-reinforcing paths. Shifts to new veto player regimes have qualities of visibility that punctuate social histories, even though their precise causes may be complex or indeterminate.

The case studies here follow analytic narratives, which trace "the behavior of particular actors, clarify sequences, describe structures, and explore patterns of interaction" (Bates et al. 1998, 10). This qualitative technique builds a theoretically relevant succession of events, bounded by theoretical and historical parameters (Lichbach 2009). In Ghana, the narrative focuses on the period from the fall of Kwame Nkrumah in 1966 to the democratic elections of 1992. During this period struggles over economic liberalization were about much more than simply the content of policy or attitudes toward free markets. They dealt with tensions between autonomous state action and populist strategies of leader legitimation, as well as challenges to government power from emergent economic classes. Zimbabwe's narrative covers a period of roughly twenty years leading up to the power-sharing agreement in 2008. Since Robert Mugabe is often regarded as an all-powerful strongman, it should be difficult to demonstrate that countervailing centers of power exist. Zimbabwe therefore presents a "least likely" case (Eckstein 1975): For our purposes, it is a good case precisely because it should be difficult to identify veto players with the capacity to defy such domination and unilateralism. Broad social coalitions and new political parties contributed to setbacks for Mugabe, leading to limits on his distributive strategies.

As in Chapter 2, efforts by military factions, political parties, and military ruling councils to exercise veto power in these cases shaped both the distribution of authority, as well as the ability of policy makers to coordinate for national interest or collude for self-interest. "Theory must be complemented by contextual knowledge," argues Bates. "Embedding narrative accounts in theories" improves our ability to judge an explanation (Bates 1997, 168). The brief analysis uncovers some analytic equivalents of veto players, sketching out the mechanisms and the conditions that empower some political actors but not others.

Ghana's Transformation from Institutional Uncertainty to Regime Formation

When the first American president of African descent traveled to Africa in 2009, he chose to visit Ghana rather than some of the continent's major powers. Many Nigerian elites took President Barack Obama's trip as a snub to their country's emerging status as an economic and diplomatic leader.[4] But Nigeria's 2007 elections had been so corrupt that the largest domestic civil society coalition called for the results to be cancelled.[5] Kenya, the homeland of President Obama's father, had just held national elections that had descended into violence (Kiai 2008). By contrast, Ghana had just held its fifth national election since its transition to democracy in 1993, and it had led to the country's second peaceful alternation of power between political parties.[6] This coincided with democratic reforms in the judiciary, security sector, and other government services (Gyimah-Boadi 2009). In 2012, Ghana experienced a smooth succession to the vice president when President John Atta Mills passed away in office; peaceful – and competitive – presidential elections followed a few months later. Impressive economic gains have accompanied these improvements in political freedom. Though inflation remained high and federal budget deficits lingered in the double digits, Ghana sustained a growth rate of 4 percent of GDP per capita between 2004 and 2007. In 2010, the World Bank reported that the percentage of Ghanaians living in poverty had dropped 11 points (from 39.5 to 28.5 percent) over the previous seven years. Judged by a variety of standards, Ghana's Fourth Republic offers a largely positive example of African political development.

Political and economic stability seemed unlikely on the basis of Ghana's early independence years. Indeed, the country struggled through seven transitions of power and five military regimes between 1957 and 1993 (see Table 4.1). The political and social institutions that had stabilized imperial rule destabilized attempts at democratic governance, a cycle that would not be effectively broken for three decades. Before the 1980s, interest aggregation bottlenecks meant that policy change required regime change, and political elites faced few checks on patronage and corruption. During the 1980s, it was not merely a leader who transformed the country, in the form of Jerry Rawlings; his choice of policies was in fact shaped and constrained by new constituencies and coalitions that restructured the policy-making process. The narrative thus

---

[4] Karin Brulliard, "Obama's Trip to Ghana Inspires Envy in Nigeria," *Washington Post*, July 11, 2009.

[5] Billionaire philanthropist Bill Gates similarly opted for Ghana after Nigeria's President Goodluck Jonathan in 2013 pardoned politicians convicted of corruption and other crimes. See Ogala Emmanuel, "Alamieyeseigha's Pardon – Nigeria Alienated – Bill Gates Arrives Ghana," *Premium Times*, March 26, 2013.

[6] The first alternation occurred in 2000 when the New Patriotic Party defeated the National Democratic Congress led by Jerry Rawlings; the second one restored power to the NDC. Such alternations are still relatively rare in Africa (Bratton 2008; Rakner and Van de Walle 2009).

TABLE 4.1. *Ghana's Governments, 1956–Present*

Chief Executive	Name of Party/Form of Government	Years
Kwame Nkrumah	First Republic: Convention People's Party (CPP)	1957–1966
Party government	National Liberation Council (NLC) – military	1966–1969
Kofi A. Busia (prime minister)	Second Republic: Progress Party (PP)	1969–1972
Edward Akufo-Addo (president)	PP	1970–1972
Col. I. K. Acheampong	National Redemption Council (NRC) – military	1972–1978
Lt. Gen. Frederick Akuffo	NRC-AMC – military	1978–1979
Dr. Hilla Limann	Third Republic: People's National Party (PNP)	1979–1981
Flt. Lt. Jerry John Rawlings	Provisional National Defense Council (PNDC) – military	1982–1992
Flt. Lt. Jerry John Rawlings	Fourth Republic: National Democratic Congress (NDC)	1992–2000
John A. Kufuor	New Patriotic Party (NPP)	2000–2008
John Atta Mills	National Democratic Congress (NDC)	2008–2012
John Dramani Mahama	National Democratic Congress (NDC)	2012–present

shows how official mobilization that began as co-optation often ended up empowering new actors. It also shows how policy deadlocks within governments were symptoms of competing vetoes, and how structural factors such as a rising middle class cohered at critical moments and eventually successfully made policy demands through labor, students, or civil servants.

Background: Imperial Imprints on Society and Economy

When Britain withdrew in 1957 from what was then called the Gold Coast, Ghana's economy was experiencing a boom. In the years leading up to independence, incoming president Kwame Nkrumah had successfully orchestrated a national development plan (1951–1956) that focused on developing a skilled labor force. That investment initially paid off. Between 1955 and 1962, GDP increased in real terms by 40 percent. Government consumption also increased, but adverse macroeconomic effects were mitigated by the high levels of foreign investment. Like many newly decolonizing countries, Ghana unfortunately soon realized it still had to import most of its capital goods (Szereszewski 1966a). The level of imports gradually increased at the same time that export prices fell, introducing some stress into the economy.

Colonialism left behind enduring images in the form of uneven regional development, interethnic mistrust, and an undiversified economy (Szereszewski 1960). Most of the service economy was concentrated in Accra, while agriculture dominated the middle zone and the North. The regions in Western, Eastern, and Ashanti areas were mostly associated with forestry, cocoa, and mining. The most development occurred in regions with economies utilizing a larger share of the labor pool (Szereszewski 1966b). At the turn of the century, political leaders attempted to diversify exports with new mining enterprises. Exports such as palm kernels, rubber, and timber also seemed encouraging, but often proved unsustainable. Britain's total control over the economic surplus created a lasting distortion on terms of trade and set the stage for the postindependence policies of state intervention to undo the damage (Howard 1978).

Under Nkrumah, monetary and fiscal policy became important tools for insulating the economy from price fluctuations of cocoa and other exports, a task made urgent by a 75 percent increase in the value of imports between 1952 and 1959 (Killick 1966). A second national development plan (1957–1959) set out to encourage economic diversification through state-led industrialization, as did the third development plan, launched in 1964. But a steep drop in the price of cocoa and depletion of exchange reserves drove up the price of imports (Anunobi 1994). With lower agricultural export earnings, Ghana lacked the revenues necessary to finance ambitious plans to industrialize, reduce agricultural dependence, redistribute economic wealth, and usher the country into economic and cultural modernity.[7]

Nkrumah also attempted to confront one of colonialism's many harmful legacies in the distinct social cleavages politicized around ethnic identity. His party, the Convention People's Party (CPP), served as a voice of strident nationalism, casting external actors in neocolonial terms in order to unify the country's disparate voices. His administration pursued an ambitious nation-building project to cultivate a strong sense of national identity that he hoped would promote labor force integration,

---

[7] See Bates (1981) for a more general discussion of this phenomenon in postcolonial Africa.

productivity, and economic development (Gyimah-Boadi and Asante 2006). Attempting to indoctrinate the next generation, he formed the "Ghana Young Pioneers" to preach the ideology of Nkrumaism, including his populist brand of Pan-Africanism, to children. But ethnic rivalries continued to play out among the major political parties (Adjibolosoo 2003), and Nkrumah's dreams of development and national integration were frozen when the military seized control in 1966.

Post-Nkrumah Politics: Regime Change as Policy Reversal, 1966–1981

For the next fifteen years, ethnic parochialism, regionalism, and new economic interests informed the policy debates among military factions, competing political parties in failed democratic experiments, and popular coalitions seeking power. Ethnic tensions accented regional developmental differences – legacies of colonial development strategies. The 1970s entailed what Chazan describes as a period of group consolidation, deepening social linkages based on class and ethnicity (Chazan 1983). Major economic interests formed along divergent urban and rural policy preferences, especially as cities such as Accra grew. Rural producers were essential to the economy, but urban constituencies rooted in labor and industry were dominant political players, and the disharmony among these groups grew as competing visions for national development began playing out in the streets. From the time of the first coup through the early 1980s, government after government struggled to balance the economic and political interests of these different sectors.

Philosophical differences over economic policy in Ghana resembled debates taking place across the continent. On one side stood those who favored a developmental state that protected prices, incentivized indigenous investments, and remained friendly with labor; on the other side stood political elites and an emerging bourgeoisie sympathetic to free markets (Ake 1996). Neither military regimes with repression and centralized authority nor democratic regimes with big tent political parties could successfully sustain policy commitments on these contentious issues. Governments had to contend with agitation by labor and urban civil society groups. These competing demands from emergent vetoes led to policy coordination problems, with resulting macroeconomic manipulation such as price controls, subsidies, and excessive increases in money supply.

Ghana's first military regime, affiliated with the National Liberation Council (NLC), abandoned Nkrumah's development plan and sold state enterprises to private investors (Killick 1978). Economic problems worsened, and the government devalued Ghana's currency by 44 percent (Anunobi 1994). The NLC accomplished this complete reversal from the developmental state through a tight knit junta, having dissolved parliament, banned the CPP, and "practically joined forces with Nkrumah's civilian opponents" (Kandeh 2004, 67). These civilians dominated the electoral commission, a consultative Political Committee, and its successor organization that advised the junta. The NLC also built technocratic alliances with bureaucrats.

Elections in 1969 paved the way for a democratic transition of power to a parliamentary regime with Kofi Busia as prime minister.[8] A civilian from the Akan ethnic group, Busia set out to stabilize the rapidly deteriorating economy with a second wave of policy reversals. "There is no evidence that the Progress Party Government under Busia pursued a continuity of any economic program introduced by the NLC," maintains one authoritative study (Anunobi 1994, 202). The price of cocoa exports declined over the next several years, hurting the basic standard of living across the country. Then when Busia devalued the currency again, reserves fell to historically low levels. To cope, the government introduced IMF-sponsored reforms and liberalized the external sector. Inflation fell to 3 percent by 1970 (Fosu and Aryeetey 2008).

This was an important historical juncture for the new nation because labor unions, students, and other middle-class actors formed a cohesive pressure group and staged massive protests in opposition to the austerity measures. The civil service, angered by reductions in allowances and government perks, formed a second pressure group. The military formed a third, powerful interest group. After overwhelmingly casting their votes for Busia in the election, the military had grown furious with budget cuts and a swift decline in their quality of life (Boahen 1997, 108–109). Alleging ethnic bias, soldiers also complained about the "Akanization" of the officer corps.

Anger against Busia peaked in 1972, and Colonel Ignatius Kutu Acheampong overthrew the prime minister in a successful coup. There was already ethnic anti-Akan resentment within the military, and Acheampong's assumption of power only exacerbated the problem (Kandeh 2004; Gyimah-Boadi and Asante 2006). He reordered the regime structure, shifting the composition of the ruling coalition. He also created a broad-based National Redemption Council (NRC), which

---

[8] Busia returned again through the Second Republic's elections.

included a range of powerful military officials, the head of the police, and the attorney general. The new government suspended Busia's development program initiatives and revalued the currency at about two-thirds of its original value. Inflation due to food shortages and high prices of commodities increased from 18.7 percent to 50.5 percent. The NRC also imposed strict import controls and tried to mobilize the rural sector to increase agricultural production with Operation Feed Yourself. The program initially enjoyed widespread support and some measure of success (Anunobi 1994). But economic health remained largely dependent on high global cocoa prices, and Operation Feed Yourself grew unpopular because the population interpreted it as organizing imposed from above. Together, these factors contributed to political decay and economic deterioration. As the broad-based government bickered, poverty increased and inflation grew. The black market and commercial profiteering thrived. Reversing his earlier strategy, Acheampong refused to devalue Ghana's currency again. Instead, the government reintroduced comprehensive import licensing and continued to print more money through the central bank (Jeffries 1989).

The regime reorganized itself under a Supreme Military Council (SMC) in 1975, and the NRC took on an advisory role. Dominated entirely by military officials, the SMC concentrated authority and drastically reduced the influence over policy making previously enjoyed by top bureaucrats. This reorganization effectively reduced the number of potential veto players. Insulated from bourgeois pressures that challenged the government from within, the regime became "a highly personalist (or neopatrimonial) machine, seeking to benefit individual favourites or networks of clients with varying degrees of concern for larger social aggregates" (Jeffries 1989, 75). The regime used corrupt networks known as *kalabule* to reward loyalty, and the checks on such patronage strategies declined. To mobilize popular support, the regime adopted a policy of *yentua*, meaning "we will not pay," thus repudiating foreign debts (Boahen 1997).

Powerful constituencies soon realized that not everyone was benefiting equally from *kalabule* patronage, and the exclusion inspired resentment and mobilized new regional political forces. For example, in 1977, in the Volta region in the Southeast, ethnic Ewes and Akan began organizing against the military government (Chazan 1983). In the North, tensions escalated between the Konkomba and Dagomba: A National House of Chiefs created by Busia had empowered Dagomba but alienated Konkomba communities, who felt that their political influence did not match their growing economic success as commercial farmers. Despite an

SMC ban on ethnic-based associations, such parochial politics continued throughout the Acheampong years (Talton 2010). Perhaps even more significantly, labor organized against policies that forced workers and a rising middle class to endure much of the pain of economic liberalization. Labor had an organizational advantage because of its concentration in the cities, and it formed alliances with other urban actors, including students and middle-class professionals. Unions effectively challenged liberalization policies through strikes and mass actions that caused significant social unrest (Herbst 1991, 176).

The government organized a referendum on sharing power with civilians, perhaps with the intention of letting off some of the steam and diverting popular frustrations. But the vote created a political opening for even more widespread opposition to the regime, culminating in General Akuffo's coup in 1978. His government lasted less than a year. Currency devaluation, government spending cuts, abolition of price controls, and other economic shock measures endorsed by the International Monetary Fund drew unions, civil servants, and students back into the streets. Adding to popular anger was the government's refusal to punish the military officers profiting from *kalabule* (Kandeh 2004, 69–70). The popular pressures rooted in common complaints from regions, and the growing labor power, were coalescing into coherent veto authority on economic reforms. Unable to advance its policy preferences in this short-lived regime, labor soon had a chance to flex its muscle.

Flight Lieutenant Jerry Rawlings led a coup attempt in 1979. He initially failed, and Akuffo loyalists threw him into prison. Rawlings was then liberated by a popular uprising that was propelled in part by anger over government corruption largely by the same social forces that had rebelled against Akuffo. Rawlings formed an Armed Forces Revolutionary Council (AFRC) that ruthlessly prosecuted corruption at the highest levels of government. Senior military officials were executed under the so-called House Cleaning exercise, and the AFRC undertook important economic decisions such as the abolition of cocoa marketing boards, but it also instituted price controls and fuel rationing. AFRC decision making was saddled by competing factions, a condition that contributed to the accountability generated by the house cleaning. But political reform rather than economic policy dominated policy debates, and it put back in motion the transition plan initiated by the SMC under Acheampong (Kandeh 2004).

The civilian People's National Party (PNP) rose to power through national elections in 1979 organized by the military government. The

PNP, led by Hilla Limann, faced a country divided over economic policy and simmering with ethnic resentments. The economy was collapsing under its heavy debt repayment burden and lack of confidence in central government authority. The government encouraged agriculture by giving loans to peasants and commercial farmers. Like the Akuffo government, though, Limann failed to stem the economic decline (Anunobi 1994; Chazan 1983). The regime turned to unpopular economic austerity measures prescribed by the International Monetary Fund and the World Bank, again devaluing the currency and scaling back spending (Hutchful 2002). Further signs of the regime's deterioration included a dysfunctional judiciary unable to deal with *kalabule*, as well as the failure of political parties to channel economic and political grievances – manifest in the regional and labor organizing that had propelled Rawlings out of prison and into power – through political institutions. Added to this, clashes between the Konkomba and Nunumba in the North caused the most severe ethnic fighting since independence, linking the sense of political disenfranchisement to serious social instability (Hansen 1987).

Predemocratic Institutional Consolidation

Rawlings staged a second successful coup in 1981, in what became known as the December 31st Revolution. The new regime under a Provisional National Defence Council (PNDC) enjoyed support from progressive social forces, including students and a range of urban workers, and encountered little outright opposition from rural producers. Significantly, it included northern military elites, whose participation undermined accusations of the coup's being motivated by regional bias (Hansen 1987). The new government's "revolutionary" or popular credentials should not be overstated, though. "This time, the public's reaction to the coup was mixed," recalls the current president, John Dramani Mahama, in his recent memoir. "The revolving door of leadership was making Ghanaians restive, uncertain about their future" (Mahama 2012, 211). Chazan (1983) suggests that they did set in motion a permanent change in the outdated model of state-society relations that had impeded institutional consolidation and economic recovery under previous regimes. The Rawlings government tried to advance its policy preferences by increasing bureaucratic autonomy, mobilizing citizens through new government organs, and adopting a political strategy that sought to balance urban and rural interests. What the regime created was new avenues for interest aggregation; different policy visions could compete and prevailing ideas acquired the legitimacy needed for implementation. By the time of the democratic transition in 1993, policy change no longer required regime change. This shift was as much due to the diverse interests represented on the PNDC as it was to the civil society interests that constructed hard fought veto powers from below.

A number of scholars describe the state's political autonomy as one important feature of this era (Jeffries 1991; MacLean 2010). The government faced tremendous political pressure from the urban middle class, particularly during its first year in office, when the PNDC adopted structural adjustment policies to reduce inflation and government expenditures. But the "military-led populist regime provided Rawlings with considerable room to maneuver," writes Rothchild, "enabling him to impose a variety of harsh measures intended to rehabilitate the economy" (Rothchild 1991, 6). This structure effectively insulated the Ghanaian state from society, "allowing it considerable autonomy from domestic pressures" and facilitating "the implementation of programs that lack[ed] wide popular support" (Rothchild 1991, 14). Unlike many African countries suffering from "partial reform syndromes," or incomplete implementation of structural adjustment (van de Walle 2001), the PNDC effectively advanced a comprehensive economic reform program. The social and economic consequences were harsh. But the International Monetary Fund and the World Bank viewed them favorably, and this helped the regime acquire symbolic political support and aid from abroad in 1983.

Official mobilization was a second feature of the Rawlings years. At first glance, the PNDC resembles many other authoritarian governance institutions designed for co-optation, including representation of the regime's critics from labor, civil society, and student activist groups. It provided an umbrella of legitimacy for the regime, but it failed to live up to its formal designation as the highest policy-making body. Beside it sat a Committee of Secretaries, composed of cabinet ministers drawn from across the country's ethnic constituencies. When it attempted to formulate a fixed policy process it deadlocked (Hansen 1987, 177–178). Though official mobilization co-opted potentially independent voices in civil society and took a top-down view of political organizing, it also enabled other coalition building. Diverse constituencies created linkages between the government and civil society; one should not assume that in the early years of the regime the government sympathizers in civil society were simply dupes.

A shadowy group, the Dzulekofe Mafia, supposedly funded Rawlings's second coup on behalf of business leaders, soldiers, and intellectuals from the Volta region sympathetic with progressive political reform. It was largely allied with the June Fourth Movement (JFM), a radical social movement made up of workers, students, and political activists named in honor of the date of Rawlings's 1979 coup (Kandeh 2004). Loosely associated with socialism and Marxism, JFM attributed Ghana's economic crisis to underdevelopment rooted in the colonial regime's exploitation and extraction of resources. It sought an immediate move toward socialism. Its rival, the Marxist-Leninist New Democratic Movement (NDM), argued that a swift – and possibly forced – transition to socialism was not possible in Ghana (Ray 1986). A network of so-called workers' and people's defense committees created channels for popular participation, coordinated overall by a National Defence Committee (NDC). Buttressed by a myth cultivated by the regime of spontaneous formation, these organizations attacked elite corruption in the name of popular democracy. Once in operation, they had two divergent tasks. They supported the regime by providing intelligence about grassroots activism and tried to guard working-class interests against state-led attacks (Hansen 1987; Hutchful 2002). On the whole, Rawlings's regime famously embraced populism. But one distinct faction formed around the moderate NDM philosophy and another formed around the JFM and more radical elements.

The debate over the economic recovery plan marked a critical historical juncture for Ghana's constantly shifting regimes because it contributed to institutional consolidation in three ways. First, PNDC attacks on wealth as a sign of corruption quickly became unpopular. These PNDC-led investigations by quasi-judicial organizations looking for impropriety were discredited as instruments of repression rather than as anticorruption tools. The informal courts were quickly merged with the formal judiciary (Kandeh 2004, 82–83). But the failure of these institutions and their successful integration into the government changed the way populist groups perceived policy failure.

Second, technocrats in the economic ministries allied with independent elite organizations such as lawyers' groups and churches who shared bourgeois interests. With that political cover, and the NDC's influence over policy minimized, Rawlings launched his economic recovery plan in 1983 and began criticizing the defense committees (Ninsin 1991; Chazan 1991). When some JFM members were implicated in a coup attempt in 1984, the government used it as an excuse to dismantle the people's defense committees and create an "authoritarian administrative regime" (Jeffries 1991). Rawlings subsequently suppressed the workers' defense committees' hard-line activists, replacing many union leaders with political allies. This contributed to a decline in labor strikes and allowed the government to enact economic liberalization reforms that would prove painful to the working class.

Finally, a new geography of state-society relations informed the self-interest of policy makers at the center. Ethnic communities such as the Kumasi and the Ashanti, who felt slighted by previous regimes, became part of a new economic coalition (Herbst 1991, 1993). By the time of the PNDC's withdrawal from power, policies predicated on urban bias were no longer politically viable. The government had secured a rural support base by raising prices of export crops to benefit agricultural producers (Rothchild 1991). It was increasingly difficult for Rawlings to expect compliance from allies or swift co-optation of his critics; the policy process was changing despite his best efforts. One sign of this was the 1992 elections, when the government received support from rural constituencies for the first time. By the beginning of the 1990s, says Chazan, "there was too great a gap between the authoritarian practices of the government and the pluralist distribution of power in society" (Chazan 1991, 39).

Summary

The narrative here investigated Ghana's unstable economic policy making and institutional uncertainty between 1966 and 1993. This long period culminating in institutional consolidation was consumed by debates over economic policy and underlying questions about how to resolve competing demands, including some inflamed by a sense of ethnic exclusion. Through shifting centers of power, the analysis found the basis for veto authority in institutions, military factions, political parties, and broad but cohesive coalitions that united labor with other pressure groups. From this perspective, macroeconomic manipulation during the governments of Busia, Acheampong, and Nkrumah was a symptom of policy making shaped by processes that included broader economic and social interests. Busia faced demands from organized labor, the civil service, and military pressure groups who shared common grievances about the government's ability to deliver on macroeconomic promises. The Rawlings regime eventually faced new constituencies that dispersed political authority. The military government's autonomy in the early 1980s limited potential veto authority from below, demonstrated by the government's snubbing of social movements that had helped restore Rawlings to power and with economic policies that broke with urban bias. But it was not long before pressure groups including technocrats, churches, and the emerging middle class articulated a shared set of demands that pressured the government outside corporatist or co-opted channels of interest articulation. Labor, for example, had many of its demands met in the 1980s, including rent reductions and cost controls, notwithstanding economic liberalizations (Rothchild and Gyimah-Boadi 1989). An important visible effect of this restructuring was the decline of corrupt *kalabule* practices (Ahiakpor 1991; Jeffries 1982). Overall, these new avenues of participation amounted to a new postcolonial bargain between the state and society – a bargain that has endured for more than two decades now. Governance reflects a balance of authority that facilitates delivery of national collective goods while keeping the country's past with *kalabule* in check.

The results of Ghana's democratic rebirth in the 1990s are perhaps more mixed than is often acknowledged in glowing accounts of Rawlings's supposed noble willingness to bear the political costs of neoliberal reforms. Rawlings's vision, says one scholar in retrospect, "resulted in the drafting of the Constitution, formation of many political parties, and holding of the 1992 elections, all based on good planning to guarantee the restoration of electoral and political systems in Ghana" (Adedeji 2001, 19). Rawlings may have planted the seeds of economic growth and democratization, but four decades after Nkrumah, poverty remains widespread and economic diversity remains limited. On the political front, even the 2008 elections, which influenced Obama's choice of Ghana for a presidential visit, have been questioned (Jockers, Kohnert, and Nugent 2010). It also remains unclear whether new oil exports, which came online in late 2011, will exacerbate these problems by engineering a resource curse or whether the revenue windfall will restore the promises of independence. But today the political institutions accommodate a range of preferences, and they create a level of certainty about the process by which political leaders are chosen and economic decisions are made. Compared to the struggles for institutional consolidation, and the often-brutal years that preceded them, Ghanaians see this as progress.

Veterans, Voters, and Emergent Vetoes in Zimbabwe

The first round of Zimbabwe's presidential election in March 2008 failed to produce a winner, prompting a runoff in June. Facing the threat of losing power for the first time since independence in 1980, President Robert Mugabe resorted to a familiar repertoire of repressive tactics. Thugs aligned with Mugabe's ruling Zimbabwe African National Union–Patriotic Front (ZANU-PF) engaged in a campaign of intimidation and terror across the countryside (Godwin 2010; Human Rights Watch 2011). The opposition's lead presidential candidate, Morgan Tsvangirai, from the Movement for Democratic Change (MDC), withdrew from the runoff out of concern that the violence would spread and the elections would lack credibility. Mugabe retained control, but political and social unrest was pervasive. Only a few months later the MDC reached a power-sharing agreement with the ZANU-PF and formed a unity government in which Mugabe remained president and Tsvangirai became prime minister. The move disappointed some of MDC's supporters, since it meant joining forces with the very officials culpable in human rights abuses against the party. But it was also the culmination of years of organizing, strategizing, and sacrifice by opposition forces to loosen Mugabe's hold on power. In effect, analytic equivalents of veto players, operating as "pressure points" across different levels of state and society, made this unexpected deal possible. It was an exercise in regime construction in the sense that it redistributed political authority, even if it has not necessarily facilitated political liberalization, as scholars have noted (Cheeseman and Tendi 2010).

The following narrative does not aim to predict whether the 2008 deal will contribute to democratization in Zimbabwe. Instead, I describe the road to the power-sharing regime and examine how the MDC acquired its share of authority, despite its withdrawal from the elections. The MDC succeeded in claiming some power from a repressive government discredited by a failed economy and unable to maintain internal cohesion by leveraging its own grassroots coalition. The narrative also suggests a causal link comparable to Nigeria's experience, since these economic failures were a symptom of challenges the ruling party faced even from its own ruling coalition. An expanding policy process with new actors posed coordination problems among Mugabe's allies who blocked democracy, and it presented new opportunities for endogenously generated accountability.

Elections and Protests as Paths to Power Sharing

Zimbabwe was one of the last African countries to win its independence, and liberation occurred only after a protracted armed struggle against white European settlers. After achieving military victory in 1980, Mugabe emerged as head of the new government. In those early years, his regime showed promising inclinations toward reconciliation and democratization. Mugabe extended an olive branch by including white ministers in his government, thereby reassuring white farmers who controlled a vast majority of the productive land and who feared violent acts of revenge. The Zimbabwe African National Union (ZANU) government also kept communication open with its former rival, the Zimbabwe African People's Union (ZAPU). His government created ethnic balance within the cabinet in order to ensure the representation of interests from the country's eight provinces (Laakso 2003b).

While positive, these institutional innovations did not address the deeper ideological and factional conflicts that had roots in the liberation struggle.[9] A violent crackdown in ZAPU strongholds in Matabeleland, attacks on white farmers, and a purge of former allies soon scarred the postindependence years; the reasons for Mugabe's change of heart remain a subject of intense historical debate (Holland 2008; Kriger 2003a; Chikuhwa 2004). A 1987 merger between ZANU and ZAPU, creating the ZANU-PF, briefly restored a sense of optimism but only superficially resolved their differences (Moore 2008).

Zimbabwe held elections in 1990, just as a global wave of democratization was reaching Africa's shores. Civil society coalitions in Benin and Togo demonstrated the strength of nascent democratic movements when they declared national conferences "sovereign," granting themselves the authority to draft new constitutions (Robinson 1994; Nwajiaku 1994). At the time, opposition parties were outright illegal in thirty-two African countries; during the previous three decades, incumbent parties had been victorious in 150 electoral contests, with only a handful of exceptions such as Senegal resulting in party turnover (Meredith 2011). Between 1989 and 1992, the tide swiftly shifted, bearing competitive elections to more than half of the countries in Sub-Saharan Africa (Widner 1994b). Zimbabwe had formally practiced multiparty democracy since independence, but the elections in 1990 were perhaps the first real sign that electoral competition could seriously challenge the regime, amounting to an important historical juncture.

ZANU-PF entered the 1990 political cycle severely weakened by the "Willowgate" corruption scandal. Five cabinet ministers had been prosecuted for acquiring and selling government vehicles for huge profits, exploiting a shortage of cars in the country (Dorman 2003). When Mugabe pardoned some of those convicted and dropped charges against others, public anger boiled over. ZANU-PF's former secretary general,

---

[9] Moore (2008) and Holland (2008) both argue that these ideological tensions date back to the colonial era itself. Beech (2008) attributes Mugabe's violent tactics to the repressive institutions he inherited.

Edgar Tekere, who had been expelled from the party after criticizing party members for corruption in 1988, seized the opportunity to form the Zimbabwe Unity Movement (ZUM). The new party railed against economic deterioration and the imperial executive, which had been recently strengthened by a reduction in the number of parliamentary seats open for competition (Meredith 2007, 86–90). In the elections, ZUM attracted former ZANU supporters dissatisfied with the 1987 merger. In 1990, Mugabe was shocked by ZUM's strong showing at the polls, particularly in urban areas. While he continued to profess a commitment to multiparty competition for several more years, factionalism within the ZANU-PF and abysmally low electoral turnout in the presidential elections embarrassed the government.

The opposition was not immune to internal bickering. ZUM and its allies boycotted 1995 parliamentary elections, while various new parties made few electoral inroads (Laakso 2003a). However, for the remainder of the decade, Mugabe's unpopular economic structural adjustment program promoted opposition unity and defections by incumbent politicians. For Mugabe's ZANU-PF supporters in government, the economic reforms threatened their traditional avenues for accumulation. By 2000, even Mugabe's supporters in government began to worry that they had a weak footing in the private sector and, with a shrinking public sector, fewer resources for delivering local collective goods as patronage (Carmody and Taylor 2003). As in other African countries undergoing structural adjustment, liberalization led to civil service layoffs and pressures to limit capital spending that imposed new limits on patronage as a political strategy for survival (van de Walle 2001).

Political parties and civil society groups – including some opposed to political liberalization – emerged as pressure points organizing to exercise vetolike influence over economic distribution and policy. Veterans of the war for liberation constituted one such important pressure point. In the regime's early years, veterans worked to establish ZANU's rural base and deepen its support among civil servants, army soldiers, and urban workers. Far from unwitting dupes of Mugabe, veterans collaborated with Mugabe's government when it protected their interests, but they guarded their autonomy when it did not (Kriger 2003b). In 1991, they formed the Zimbabwe National Liberation War Veterans Association (ZNLWVA). Later angered by Mugabe's growing sympathy for neoliberalism and the discovery in 1997 that veterans' benefit funds had been looted, veterans marched on the presidential palace. The active army's hands-off attitude toward the protesters implied a level of sympathy with their cause

(Carmody and Taylor 2003). This put Mugabe in a politically difficult position. He was often forced to placate veterans in order to shore up his ruling coalition.

Labor, led by the Zimbabwe Congress of Trade Unions (ZCTU), emerged as a second essential pressure point. "Over time," according to a new book detailing the rise of Zimbabwe's opposition parties, "unionists built a stronger and more professional labor movement that could serve as an effective watchdog and, eventually, check on government" (Lebas 2011, 68). The economic structural adjustment program left Zimbabwe with high budget deficits, depreciating exchange rates, rising consumer costs due to subsidy cuts, and increased inflation. The first half of the decade saw barely a hundred strikes, but 232 strikes were held in 1997 alone, and more than 250 took place over the next two years. The government established new channels for negotiating with labor, which reduced the number of strikes. But a revised economic strategy fell flat, and national collective goods continued to suffer, including rising federal budget deficits and declining economic growth. Accelerated currency depreciation undermined the agricultural sectors as well (Kanyenze 2004). Food riots broke out in 1997, ushering in a period of mass mobilization and protest. ZCTU partnered with civil society organizations to demand democracy and workers' rights. In 1997, they organized the largest labor strike since 1948 (Saunders 2007). The success led union organizers to circulate pamphlets explicitly arguing that "nonparticipation gives unchecked power," while participation in strikes redistributes power (Lebas 2011, 74). The government did not resort to violence, as it had during the Matabeleland crackdown in the 1980s. This apparent restraint by the government inspired more independent political organizing.

With electoral avenues limited, opposition groups built a grassroots coalition among Catholic organizations, lawyers' groups, and labor around demands for a new constitution. Formed in 1997, the National Constitutional Assembly (NCA) constituted a third critical pressure point. The government beat and detained the charismatic ZCTU leader, Morgan Tsvangirai, but realized that it could not ignore the NCA as a national political force (Laakso 2003a). Mugabe understood that the constitutional referendum amounted to a new strategy to unseat him, but calculated that he had to embrace it since so many forces had aligned in support (Holland 2008, 179). An unpopular military deployment to the Congo added to anger against the regime (Meredith 2007, 142). Proposed tax hikes and a weak economy had stripped ZANU-PF of its political capital and patronage resources, as did new social forces. Mugabe tried to discourage civil society protest through legislation limiting the role of churches and NGOs in civic education, but unintentionally "politicized" numerous associations that had previously avoided direct political agitation (Dorman 2003). Labor unions that had previously emphasized wages and working conditions increased their calls for political reform now too (Lebas 2011).

The defeat of the government referendum on the draft constitution in 2000 effectively vetoed a core component of the regime's political survival strategy, marking a second historic juncture. The NCA and Tsvangirai's newly formed MDC argued convincingly throughout the constitutional debate that the country needed radical institutional reforms to rein in the executive. This setback for ZANU-PF signaled that grassroots organizing combined with splits within the regime might actually lead to political turnover. In other words, voting might do more than simply let government opponents let off steam: It legitimized the opposition's growing leverage.

Sharpening the sense of crisis within the ZANU-PF, the MDC nearly emerged victorious in the 2000 parliamentary elections, throwing the ruling party's machinery into defense mode. Taking notice of its electoral losses in Manicaland, North Matabeleland, and South Matabeleland, provinces that had previously registered opposition but never presented a unified front (Laakso 2003a), ZANU-PF began a violent campaign to intimidate MDC candidates and supporters in those regions. The ruling party also spearheaded a rival labor federation, the Zimbabwe Federation of Trade Unions (ZFTU), in an effort to neutralize the MDC's growing base of support in urban areas. The MDC had received only 10 percent of the vote in the capital of Harare in 1995, but swept the city in 2000, winning 76 percent of the vote.

"Fast Track Land Reforms" formed an important element of ZANU-PF's political strategy after 2000. Landownership invoked deep nationalist sentiments since white settlers had owned huge shares of land, including some of the most fertile farmland. The Fast Track reforms were more than merely patronage, since they followed from an ongoing historical realignment of urban and rural classes and a reorganization of the agricultural sector to remedy past injustices (Cliffe et al. 2011). But land, as a local collective good, did provide ZANU-PF with a tool for rewarding loyal supporters (Zamchiya 2011). And since the NCA had put land reform squarely at the center of its agenda, the independent political reform movement congealing around the opposition put Mugabe's rural support at risk. The ZANU-PF responded by promising land to veterans and rural supporters, and the government looked the other way when farms were forcibly seized from white farmers. Despite describing the land seizures as spontaneous mass actions, Mugabe later admitted, "We were in control" (Holland 2008, 231). "The farm invasions formed an essential part of a political strategy to combat the growing influence of the MDC and to win back rural support by using the promise of land resettlement" (Feltoe 2004, 199). A controversial analysis by Mamdani argues that the seizures symbolized justice for historical inequities rooted in Rhodesia's racist colonialism.[10] Mugabe's "land reform measures, however harsh, have won him considerable popularity," thus illustrating how he survived "not only by coercion but by consent" (Mamdani 2008, 17). Adopting populist discourse intentionally appealing to the veterans, Mugabe referred to the Fast Track reforms as a "Third Chimurenga," or war of liberation.

Getting to the 2008 Global Political Agreement to Share Power

After 2000, electoral outcomes became increasingly uncertain, despite the corruption and violence meant to preordain victory for Mugabe's party. Human rights organizations documented murders, kidnappings, rapes, and other horrific forms of intimidation during "Operation Murambatsvina" (Moore 2008). Voters in Manicaland and Matabeleland stood their ground against Mugabe in the 2002 presidential elections. By 2005, public opinion surveys showed that three-quarters of Zimbabweans favored replacing their political leaders through elections (Masunungure 2009). The MDC won a slim majority of the seats in the National House of Assembly that year, but a splinter faction broke off when Tsvangirai supported a boycott of the Senate elections due to ongoing intimidation. Changes to the electoral act that year stipulated that a runoff would take place if the winner of the 2008 presidential election did not secure a majority of votes (Ndapwadze and Muchena 2009).

The economy was a huge factor in the 2008 elections. After a cumulative 44 percent economic decline in GDP over the previous decade, economists estimated that Zimbabwe's hyperinflation rate was one of the highest ever recorded – second only to Hungary's in July 1946. Unemployment and poverty plagued 80 percent of the population. The nation suffered chronic shortages of fuel, electricity, water, and food. Farm seizures by Mugabe supporters hurt domestic food production

[10] See the letter from Timothy Scarnecchia et al., "Re: Lessons of Zimbabwe," *London Review of Books*, December 1, 2009.

(Tarisayi 2009), and the agricultural sector declined 12 percent in 2001 alone. In urban areas, harassment and extortion by the government-sponsored ZFTU undermined productivity (Saunders 2007). There is evidence that the land reforms benefited the rural poor, and not simply Mugabe's supporters, thus promoting a redistributive economic purpose (Moyo 2011). But the farm seizures and the Fast Track Land Reforms clearly inspired foreign investors to pull out: The World Bank halted development aid, and the International Monetary Fund suspended Zimbabwe's voting rights and access to financial support. Isolated from the West, the Mugabe government secured alternative financial backing from Russia and China and mobilized some political support from its African neighbors (Badza 2009). That strategy produced some limited successes, such as the South African Development Community's calling for an end to sanctions.

In this polarized context, neither Mugabe nor Tsvangirai received a majority of the votes in the March 2008 presidential contest, and a run-off was scheduled for June (Booysen 2009). Even in pro-Mugabe strongholds in ethnic Shona areas, the MDC appealed to rural voters who were frustrated with the government, demonstrating that the opposition was now more than just an urban phenomenon. ZANU-PF mounted a militarized response. A new organization, the Joint Operations Command (JOC), anchored a military-security network recruited from the military ranks to harass the opposition violently (Bratton and Masunungure 2008; Thornycroft 2008). JOC cadres used published electoral results in rural areas to target villages where ZANU-PF support showed slippage (Kriger 2008). Dozens of MDC supporters were killed, and violent farm seizures escalated when Mugabe spoke of a "final solution" to white colonialism (Ansell 2008). A vacillating MDC, fearful of escalating the violence, decided to boycott the runoff election.

How, then, did Tsvangirai become prime minister through a power-sharing agreement that effectively marks a third historic juncture? This question is particularly interesting since most electoral boycotts typically fail to win concessions from incumbent parties, and the international community was not exactly unified in its opposition to Mugabe. Even the incoming Obama administration expressed doubts about whether a power-sharing agreement could advance political reform (Guma 2009). In addition, many civil society groups who had backed the MDC objected to sharing power with Mugabe on the grounds that doing so would grant impunity for human rights violations and delegitimize the domestic basis of the "sovereign moment," the historical juncture when citizens collectively express their consent to be governed and establish how to allocate power (LeVan 2011).

In the end, at least three factors contributed to the establishment of the 2008 power-sharing agreement, which symbolized the emergence of viable vetoes. First, the constitutional requirement of a runoff ultimately worked in the opposition's favor. Runoffs are designed to stimulate political moderation, since the two largest vote getters must make appeals to other minor parties dropped from the ballot (Shugart and Carey 1992). ZANU-PF appears to have anticipated that elections would not likely advance to a second round with the MDC split into several factions and a handful of minor candidates running. From the perspective of Mugabe's supporters, "harmonization" of the presidential and legislative elections constituted risk insurance, since for the first time it could calculate on a "coattails" effect (i.e., expecting that its legislative candidates would benefit from voters' choosing a presidential candidate on the same ballot). All of the legislative gains by the opposition for the previous two decades had occurred with a staggered election calendar, with presidential and legislative elections occurring during different years. In other words, Mugabe's party properly predicted a plausible gain based on an institutional advantage through the electoral system. But it was not big enough to secure a majority in the first round, throwing the party and its allies into a state of crisis. ZANU-PF underestimated the MDC's rural support.

Second, Mugabe's party was suffering under the strains of elite fragmentation, forcing Mugabe to reach out to less reliable allies lying largely beyond reach of the state. By 2008 ZANU-PF was rapidly losing what internal cohesion it had.[11] Following patterns established in the postindependence era, Mugabe approached veterans' groups in order to reinforce his crumbling political coalition. Yet far from being mere tools of Mugabe, as often implied by the Western media, ZNLWVA demonstrated a strident independence streak: allying with the government when it served their interests and protesting when it did not, similar to veterans' activism in the 1980s (Kriger 2003b). The veterans' groups were "both independent of Mugabe and ZANU-PF, and could claim national support" (Mamdani 2008, 17). After the power-sharing agreement was in place, Tsvangirai told the U.S. ambassador that Mugabe was "being managed by hardliners," and giving this faction a concession might help

---

[11] Some Mugabe critics argue that the sanctions actually undermined the leverage of moderate voices within the regime (Bomba and Minter 2010).

advance political reform.[12] Mugabe also lost political leverage as a result of his attempts to dominate the bureaucracy responsible for implementing the land policy by insulating it from the usual ministerial means of control (Alexander 2006). While such maneuvers represent a desire for dominance, they can also paradoxically contribute to political isolation. This proved hazardous for a regime increasingly dependent on coalition members with a capacity to act as veto players and hold national policy hostage.

A third factor contributing to the power-sharing arrangement was the progressive degeneration of institutions capable of moderating the regime's internal disputes and channeling the interests of allies. Since 1990, the ZANU-PF government had repeatedly subverted the authority of the courts and the parliament, institutions that could have arbitrated elite conflict. The regime failed to channel public frustrations into responsive policies not only because politicians lacked the will, but also because the institutions had been destroyed. Land reform took place on a large scale, but in many ways it fragmented efforts to transform the regime. Because of deep ideological and factional conflicts still unresolved from the liberation struggle, the ruling party had stood in a weak position vis-à-vis both the state bureaucracy and rural chiefs, and it began consolidating its reach by maintaining a state of emergency instead of investing in institutions that could resolve or at least defuse the conflicts (Beech 2008). By the 2000 elections, Mugabe faced both popular frustration and elite fragmentation (Laakso 2003a). Even the violence employed on ZAPU in the early 1980s and the 1987 merger had not fully alleviated the ideological and factional conflicts left unresolved from the liberation struggle. By the end of 2008, faced with a powerful opposition party, a collapsed economy, and international isolation, Mugabe's government found itself without hegemony over its own internal rivals and institutions weakened by ZANU-PF's own political tactics. Left with few options, it had a practical solution in the power-sharing agreement.

Viewing the regime in terms of such countervailing sociopolitical forces is important because it implies that Mugabe's motivations run deeper than simply a lust for power. Bratton and Masunungure note how important it is to "resist reducing the future of Zimbabwe to the fate of one man." Mugabe's alliance with hard-liners in the years leading up to the power-sharing agreement led to an "institutionalized system of authority with

[12] "Zimbabwe: Tsvangirai Asks the West for Help on Changing the Status Quo," AllAfrica. com, December 9, 2010.

clear rules, structures, and incentives," which they conclude will outlast Mugabe himself (Bratton and Masunungure 2008, 42). The opposition was aided by ZANU-PF's abysmal response to Zimbabwe's deteriorating economy and inability to reassure key allies. To cut out possible opponents, regime hard-liners had impulsively sabotaged political institutions that had actually served to moderate elite factionalism, aggregate political demands from different social sectors, and relieve popular pressures for reform.

Tsvangirai ultimately became prime minister through bargaining rather than the ballot box because, like a partisan veto player, the MDC had the organizational capacity to make political demands on a stubborn regime. Labor and civil society mobilization had been on the rise for two decades, and the discredited elections drew the attention of transnational civil society actors and foreign governments. International sanctions discredited the regime, and South African diplomatic intervention put pressure on Mugabe (Masunungure and Badza 2010). The 2008 power-sharing agreement was due to the MDC's slow accretion of strength. It built its grassroots political force over more than two decades, slowly chipping away at the ruling party's electoral support and constructing alternative centers of power through labor and broad segments of society.

Summary

This narrative describes an expansion and contraction of Zimbabwe's countervailing powers that suggest analytical equivalents to veto players in the form of hard-line regime factions, parties, and civil society coalitions. Sometimes regime shifts were a function of democratization pressures, as when the NCA defeated the government's constitutional referendum, or when the MDC successfully negotiated a share of power. But they also entailed the rising or waning influence of groups such as the war veterans and rural partisans loyal to ZANU-PF and the nationalist struggle it symbolizes. This ideology retains a powerful unifying effect for the ruling party, apart from the party's ability to distribute patronage or function for interest aggregation and conflict resolution (Levitsky and Way 2012). This also means, as Terrance Ranger explains, "Mugabe is not just a crazed dictator or a corrupt thug" (Ranger 2009, 14). Mugabe did not ultimately enter into the 2008 power-sharing deal out of goodwill. The agreement was a product of popular mobilization, as well as ZANU-PF policy concessions to conservative political organizations and coalition building with military factions benefiting from the status quo. For the opposition MDC and for Mugabe's illiberal allies alike, the electoral standoff represented a historical juncture long in the making.

Another important observation concerns the consequences for government performance. On the one hand, ZANU-PF adopted policies to redistribute patronage through radical land reforms intended to mobilize its core supporters. These policies bear a clear resemblance to my formulation of local collective goods. Unlike the proxies I relied on in Chapter 3, though, these deliverables were clearly politically directed patronage. Though land seizures have not completely disappeared, they declined after 2008; with the power-sharing agreement it was more difficult to allocate resources on an exclusionary basis.[13] On the other hand, political pressures and regime reconstruction in the years leading up to the agreement plunged macroeconomic performance to new lows. This pairing of outcomes with local and national collective goods bears some similarities with Nigeria.

This analysis validates some of the broad claims about veto players as an important institutional distinction among regimes. In Zimbabwe, as in Ghana, changes in the distribution of public authority, often through alliances bridging state and society, impacted public policies similar to the national and local collective goods examined previously. The expansion and contraction of this policy space can occur independently of democratization, as suggested by the divergent preferences of the MDC and hard-liner war veterans regarding political liberalization. Finally, since Mugabe's harsh rule makes Zimbabwe a "least likely" case for finding veto player–style checks on the ruler's authority, the presence of such countervailing powers highlights the importance of understanding institutions and their social bases of support even under strong dictators.

Conclusion

Building on qualitative techniques that complement the classic comparative method, this chapter used two brief narratives to analyze how interactions among institutions, military factions, powerful elites, and political parties shape the structure of the policy process. Rather than identifying veto players as I did with Nigeria in Chapter 2, here

---

[13] It is worth repeating that the Fast Track Land Reforms were more than just political patronage, and their economic impact remains a subject of considerable debate. For an overview, see the special issue of *The Journal of Peasant Studies* published in 2011 (vol. 35, no. 5).

I attempted to locate their analytic equivalents by describing historical junctures in Ghana between 1966 and 1993, and in Zimbabwe during the two decades leading up to the 2008 power-sharing agreement. These junctures represent pivot points that signal the redistribution of political authority, with some visible consequences for the delivery of collective goods. The chapter's primary purpose was concept validation of veto players, this study's independent variable.

In both cases we saw how formal authority often depended on political bargains with civil (and sometimes uncivil) society. As in many African countries, opposition to economic liberalization inspired reactions from labor and social forces that brought their influence to bear not just on specific issues but on the underlying conditions for formulating and legitimating national policy (Widner 1994b; Callaghy and Ravenhill 1993; Olukoshi 1993). Since that era, we have seen Ghana move toward democratic consolidation with alternations of power among political parties, while Zimbabwe's democratization trajectory remains highly uncertain. When both countries prepared for elections in 2008, Ghana's economy held steady with a 4 percent annual GDP growth per capita, while Zimbabwe's economy contracted and millions of people were without food. Yet, as in Nigeria, the analytic narratives suggest that the addition or the loss of political actors with the ability to exercise leverage over the policy process is more than just a function of democracy. I did not carry out quantitative tests like those in Chapter 3, but this expansion or contraction of the policy process, as political actors either gained or lost their leverage, corresponded with some visible changes in collective goods.

In Zimbabwe, the militarization of politics by ZANU-PF during the 2008 elections followed the regime's reaction to the escalating political uncertainty in the 1990s. The electoral reforms that required a runoff in the 2008 presidential elections worked in the opposition's favor. But rules by themselves did not win the MDC its morsel of political authority. Like northern elites in Nigeria worried about a southern Christian president taking over in 1999, or the democratic social movement opposed to Babangida in the early 1990s, Zimbabwe's opposition had to construct the basis for its power. In much the same way, recontracting over Zimbabwe's regime through an extraconstitutional power-sharing agreement was not a foregone conclusion, attributable simply to electoral results or international pressure to compromise. It was links with labor, civil society, and increasingly rural producers that contributed to the MDC's political leverage.

One should not treat Zimbabwe's opposition in unitary terms, and the party faced defections that potentially threatened its influence. From this perspective, the ruling party's merger with a rival group in 1987 perhaps meant to deter the rise of this opposition. So when Mugabe's opponents made unexpected gains in the 1990 elections, this situation constituted an important critical juncture. Coalition building through the NCA during that decade, culminating in further electoral setbacks for the government and the defeat of its referendum on the constitution in 2000, signaled a second pivot point for the regime. By then, elite fragmentation within ZANU-PF led Mugabe to rekindle alliances with hard-liners whose flair for autonomy undermined his ability to act unilaterally. With declining electoral support and questionable external legitimacy, the ruling party could offer few firm guarantees to them. By 2008, the time of the third critical juncture in the narrative, ZANU-PF increasingly drew upon a military-security apparatus to repress its enemies.[14] This policy has contributed to portrayals of Mugabe as an all-powerful unitary actor. But the party is central to his power, and it in turn has depended upon allies with a history of independent collective action. At the time of the power-sharing agreement, political institutions that could have moderated the regime's internal tensions (or persuasively co-opted its critics) had been decimated, generating structural weaknesses for the MDC to exploit. If the 2013 presidential election is our indicator, Mugabe's victory suggests this controversial agreement to share power contributed little to democratization.

In terms of the previous chapter's measurements of government performance, Zimbabwe's Fast Track Land Reforms constitute a large-scale attempt to redistribute highly particularistic benefits. The costs of these exclusionary goods added up quickly as ZANU-PF found itself scrambling to appease not only its traditional partners, but also potential threats from its rising democratic opponents. Much as the framework in Chapter 1 expects from this expanded policy space, the power-sharing agreement drew a partisan veto player into the government, limiting ZANU-PF's discretion. Land seizures were not reversed under the terms of the power-sharing agreement, but they did largely cease. However, there is little question that macroeconomic performance improved, though

---

[14] The recently deceased U.S. Congressman Donald Payne, a longtime member and former chair of the House of Representative's Foreign Affairs Subcommittee on Africa, met with Mugabe for nearly four hours around this time. Officials present told me that he left believing that Mugabe considered himself a hostage to the hard-liners and that he saw no viable options for stepping down.

reliable data are especially sparse for Zimbabwe during these years. This result departs from the statistical findings in Chapter 3 and could perhaps be explained by emergent vetoes stimulating scrutiny of macroeconomic controls. As noted in Chapter 1, such economic policy authority is often taken as exogenous in veto player studies, and future research could focus on this critical juncture to clarify those conditions further.

Ghana's narrative examines postindependence authoritarianism and concludes with the 1993 transition to democracy, though the purpose is not necessarily to explain democratization. The narrative identifies key elite factions and their multifaceted relationships with social coalitions and the economy. The divide over economic policy displays some historical continuity between Nkrumah and his critics, with exclusion from the process linked to ethnic alienation and subaltern demands. In the 1970s, ethnic organizing flourished despite a formal ban and labor unrest perpetually threatened economic policy. The widespread state mobilization of the 1980s that preceded the 1993 democratic transition, and the conditions for a new coalition of urban-rural interests, contributed to institutional consolidation by allowing the state to follow through on policy choices without exacerbating political exclusion. This is not to apologize for the PNDC's human rights record or to ignore ethnic tensions under Rawlings, but rather to suggest that the regime succeeded in internalizing competing policy positions.

Ghana experienced its own harmful economic inefficiencies through *kalabule*, a local collective good that explicitly implies a corrupt or clientelistic exchange, which we could only indirectly infer from the local collective goods variables analyzing Nigeria's government performance in Chapter 3. Ghana's narrative is not necessarily meant to offer a contrasting rosy picture in the form of some kind of economic miracle. Instead, it more generally points to a different set of social cleavages and economic coalitions that balanced a need for popular inclusion with elite politics, creating the structural conditions for coordinating in the national interest. Even prior to Ghana's transition in 1993, collective and institutional vetoes rooted in state and society were limiting the opportunities for patronage through local collective goods.

In the end, the concept of a veto player provides a simplified representation of political authority. As with any variable, measurement entails the risks of reducing unique histories and intricate social process to a mere symbol or number. The brief narrative analyses in this chapter, probing for pressure points and historical junctures that shaped the emergence of veto power, have reinforced the possibilities of identifying competing policy preferences and the political actors who act upon them. What we see here overall is that concepts such as veto players need not embrace exceptionalism or universalism. They can contribute to what Laitin describes as "a comparative politics that is sensitive to the particularities of each society, yet asks broad and general questions about all societies" (Laitin 1986, xii). Which political actors have the capacity to act upon their interests? When do socially constructed centers of authority limit the more formally vested manifestations of power? How does the distribution of political authority impact the distribution of policy benefits?

In this spirit, this chapter has also identified some potential limits of my formulation of veto players. Compared to the analysis in previous chapters, international factors probably played an even bigger role in Zimbabwe. In Nigeria, the junta was largely able to evade sanctions in the 1990s; by the mid-2000s its debt rescheduling significantly reduced foreign leverage, and the quantitative test results pointed to surprisingly weak impact of foreign debt on policy outputs over time. By contrast, Zimbabwe faced significant international isolation in the 2000s. Future applications and adaptations of veto players could further specify these domestic-international interactions, and some research on power-sharing agreements with vetoes appears to be moving in that direction (Ram and Strøm 2013). The extensive literature on structural adjustment in Africa offers one entry point for doing so, but new kinds of international ties, including Africa's numerous booming economies, suggest the relationships will now be quite different. Economic stabilization with institutional consolidation since the 1990s has improved the quality of life for millions of Africans, but it is also arguably increasing their governments' influence in global politics (LeVan 2010). In addition, the urban/rural balance in both Ghana and Zimbabwe bears some resemblance to Nigeria's bargain between North and South, explored in Chapter 2. But a more complete analysis of Ghana and Zimbabwe would clearly want to develop the subnational coordination mechanisms in greater detail, drawing upon comparative federalism and other research.

In the book's next and final chapter, I claim that the field of comparative politics can benefit from a return to Madison's foundational insights, which constitute an underappreciated inspiration for veto player theory. I also return to a discussion of Nigeria to argue that the succession problems it confronted in 2006 and again in 2010 promoted institutional consolidation. The resolution of these challenges offers signs of an encouraging shift in the social cleavages that have long handicapped efforts at national integration and government performance. The articulation of competing preferences through a more inclusive policy process has the potential for both restraint and cooperation.

5

Madison's Model Unbound

In the one hundred years since its creation by imperial fiat in 2014, Nigeria has grown to become the most populous country in Africa, home to the largest political party on the continent, and one of the world's chief oil exporters. It overcame the injustices of colonialism only to endure civil war, violent rebellions, and recurring cycles of military rule. This study built a holistic picture of the postindependence period's complex social and historical landscape by explaining how different institutions, individuals, and organized interests competed as veto players to advance their policy preferences. On the basis of a multimethod analysis covering half a century, I then demonstrated that the number of veto players affects government performance in Nigeria over time. To measure government performance, I distinguished between two broad categories of public policy: national collective goods, which are broadly enjoyed by the population on the whole because it is theoretically too costly to deny their benefits to some segment of the population, and local collective goods, whose benefits are more excludable, meaning that they can often be targeted to some citizens. I constructed variables for each set of public policies using data gathered during extensive field research and based on operationalizations of concepts in the public goods literature.

Quantitative and qualitative analysis demonstrated that the number of veto players impacted these two categories of public policy quite differently. A "coordination" hypothesis predicted that an increase in the number of veto players would impede the delivery of national collective goods because it is more difficult for political actors in these regimes to coordinate their interests for the broader common good. Statistical tests confirmed this hypothesis by demonstrating that an increase of veto players in Nigeria contributed to bigger budget deficits, higher rates of inflation, larger student/teacher ratios, and more inefficient resolution of property rights court cases. A "logroll" hypothesis then predicted that an increase in veto players would lead to visible excesses in local collective goods, anticipating that each political actor with the ability to extract policy concessions will drive up government spending on policies with excludable benefits. Using three different measures of government spending as a share of GDP per capita as proxies for local collective goods, statistical tests rejected this hypothesis: The number of veto players was inversely related to capital spending, recurrent spending, and the overall level of government expenditures. The impact on capital spending is especially significant since it is the clearest measure of local collective goods, and excessive expenditure levels can be interpreted as a sign of targetable patronage. For empirical tests within an African country this is an important finding since it implies that the structure of the policy process, which can expand or contract over time, affects the overall levels of patronage spending. It further suggests that rather than simply using their leverage to extract particularistic policies, veto players appear to improve accountability by monitoring each other's behavior. The results for both sets of tests hold across a broad set of controls that represent common explanations for African government performance failures, including debt, dictatorship, poverty, and petroleum.

The results of tests of these twin hypotheses suggest that the conditions conducive for the delivery of national collective goods are different from the conditions necessary to limit excess spending on local collective goods. I characterize this as a "Madisonian dilemma" because African development requires good government performance in both policy areas. Economic growth requires delivery of national collective goods in the form of fiscal discipline, human capital investment in education, and efficient resolution of property rights disputes. Madison himself took a long-term view of development, writing of "industry from which property results, and that enjoyment which consists not merely in its immediate use, but in its posthumous destination to objects of choice and kindered affection" (Hamilton et al. 2008, 350). Development also requires local collective goods, including capital spending that builds infrastructure such as schools or hospitals and recurrent spending that pays the salaries of civil servants who implement government policy. But such excludable policy outputs can be susceptible to targeting for political gain, and excessive spending levels are a sign of such manipulation. Madison knew that the institutional separation of interests could check wastefulness or maldistribution, yet existing veto player analyses tend to emphasize policy stability rather than accountability.

In this final chapter, I examine how veto player theory and my findings on Nigeria contribute to emerging areas of research. By disaggregating government performance into two broad categories, my results with variables measuring local collective goods provided new insights about the conditions conducive to patronage in Africa. In addition, veto players present an alternative way of conceptualizing authority in nondemocratic regimes, and they provide a conceptual framework for integrating informal institutions into political analysis. My analysis suggests that the greatest risk to Nigeria's emerging democracy lies in threats to the underlying federal bargain between North and South. This adds to new constructivist thinking about grassroots sources of authority in federal systems, and the 1914 unification of these two disparate regions remains at the core of urgent questions involving participation, representation, and stability. This chapter then explores how signs of institutional consolidation in Nigeria since 2007 inform our understanding of democratization. Finally, returning to Madison, I argue that a proper division of power can help advance policy accountability, citizen empowerment, and institutional consolidation. There is reason for cautious hope that Nigeria is slowly moving toward political integration through competitive representation.

Advancing Comparative Analysis in Africa

In this book's Introduction, I surveyed the development literature on government performance in Africa, which generally attributes success or failure to the quality of leadership, the level of ethnic diversity, the relative wealth of the state, and the extent of democracy. These explanations do contribute to our understanding of African politics, but recent research reveals some of their limits: Citizens are increasingly voting for performance and not just parochialism or ethnicity; illiberal governments sometimes sustain high rates of economic growth; and neither resource scarcity nor resource wealth seems to doom African progress. Numerous countries have even overcome the burdens of foreign debt, which accumulated during the harsh years of structural adjustment in the 1980s, by rescheduling it and redirecting the benefits of economic growth to investment.

In Chapter 1, I showed how veto player theory offers an alternative explanation for government performance by liberating the "veto" from its association with presidentialism and American politics. It proposes a causal relationship between political actors whose agreement is necessary to change existing policy and government performance. These actors can be individual or collective, and they can exercise leverage through institutions or "partisan" actors that originate within them. While cohesive political parties are the most common example of partisan veto players, I described the characteristics of military factions that can be treated similarly. I also outlined "regional" veto players as a special type that can form under rare conditions in Nigeria when either the North or the South, the country's broadest sociocultural cleavages, coordinates its shared regional interests. Such geopolitical balancing is not so unusual in federal systems, and the unification of these two regions lies at the core of Nigeria's existence as a country.

I also identify two different streams in the veto player literature. The "distributional" tradition either expects improved provision of nonexcludable public policies, as veto players realize the declining returns of payoffs, or anticipates policy logrolls, as each veto player demands side payments. The "commitment" tradition in the literature suggests that transaction costs increase with the number of veto players. This undermines the coordination necessary for the delivery of national collective goods, but it leads to monitoring that limits excessive spending characteristic of patronage. Thus the two different traditions generate conflicting expectations for how an increase in the number of veto players should impact the delivery of local and national collective goods. I state a coordination hypothesis that predicts that an increase in veto players will undermine the delivery of national collective goods, and a logroll hypothesis that predicts that these same regimes will engage in logrolls of excessive government spending in order to pay off each veto player.

To count as veto players in Nigeria, I said political actors must (1) have a motive for challenging policy based on distinct preferences; (2) have a mechanism for coordinating common interests and reducing information costs if the actor is collective; and (3) prevail on at least one major policy issue. In Chapter 2, I applied these criteria to identify fourteen veto player regimes over 47 years in Nigeria by focusing largely on debates over budgetary policy, transition plans, and constitutional questions relating to federalism. My purpose in counting the number of veto players was to estimate the overall distribution of political authority and therefore create my independent variable. Consistent with the veto players literature, most vetoes were institutional. Partisan vetoes, originating as stable sets of preferences within institutions, operated during the early years of the

First Republic (1960–1964) and the first two years of the Second Republic (1980–1981). Regional vetoes operated on only three occasions: in 1966, from 1990 to 1993, and from 1999 to 2003. Each head of state between 1960 and 2007 held an individual veto. To demonstrate the nonarbitrary nature of my coding criteria, I pointed to examples of vetoes that failed to emerge, including a military faction centered on Ibrahim Babangida during the dictatorship of Muhammadu Buhari (1984–1985) and moderates on the ruling council during Sani Abacha's regime who attempted to enhance the power of the governors in the mid-1990s. Overall, this chapter provided a portrait of Nigeria's politics since independence, and the disagreements among veto players revealed the costs of coordinating interests as well as the self-interest that often drives patronage politics in Africa.

In Chapter 3, I statistically tested two hypotheses to determine how an increase in the number of veto players affects government performance across a range of different public policies. Tests of the coordination hypothesis demonstrated that an increase in the number of veto players undermines delivery of national collective goods, leading to larger budget deficits, higher rates of inflation, higher student/teacher ratios, and inefficient resolution of property rights cases. I chose these variables because the political economy literature associates good outcomes with long-term development, and since these policies theoretically have nonexcludable benefits, it is more difficult for policy makers to coordinate their interests for a broader common good. The findings are contrary to selectorate theory and models that presume the absence of transaction costs since the relationship indicates that multiple veto players do not automatically bargain to an efficient allocation of resources in order to avoid particularistic payoffs.

Tests of the logroll hypothesis then found that an increase in veto players actually restrains overall levels of recurrent and capital spending. The unexpected rejection of the logroll hypothesis means that rather than using their political leverage to extract policy concessions that drive up overall spending levels, veto players form checks against each other, much as Madison theorized. To amplify this point, a succinct qualitative analysis at the end of Chapter 3 provided numerous examples of this accountability. For example, with the rise of a new regional veto from the South in the early 1990s, massive capital spending by the Babangida regime declined. It resumed with the Abacha regime, especially in the mid-1990s, after the reduction in the number of veto players with the neutralization of the June 12 faction within the ruling military council.

It is no accident that the outgoing military regime (with its three veto players) in 1979 successfully imposed cuts to capital spending, and that Obasanjo's first term as president in 1999–2003 generated tough new anticorruption institutions. The narratives also provided evidence of the relationship between the number of veto players and the ability to coordinate, as anticipated by the bargaining literature. For example, the reduction in the number of veto players between Obasanjo's first term as president (1999–2003) and his second (2003–2007) enabled a new economic team to bring inflation and deficit spending under control and virtually eliminate the country's foreign debt. The qualitative analysis served important methodological purposes too by identifying statistical outliers, linking specific regimes to particular outcomes on the dependent variable, and compensating for the sample's modest size.

Both sets of results remain robust across a broad range of controls including democratic governance, foreign debt levels, overall economic conditions, and oil as a share of federal revenue. These variables stand in for the standard explanations for government performance, as outlined in the book's Introduction. Democratic governments tend to have lower levels of inflation and are slightly more likely to reduce budget deficits. But democracy has no statistically significant impact on student/teacher ratios, the efficient resolution of property rights cases, or overall levels of local collective goods. While democracy in and of itself is a worthy goal for many reasons, these results suggest that we need to think not only about the extent of political freedom but also about the distribution of authority in the policy process. Veto players provide a helpful conceptual tool for this task. External debt was not correlated with any of my measures of national collective goods, and it had only a weak correlation with one of my measures for local collective goods: capital spending. These results imply that domestic politics, as captured through veto players, have been more important than international pressures on policy makers in Nigeria. Ultimately this finding restores a sense of agency to politicians and bureaucrats today, and it should give Nigeria's people a sense of control over their nation's destiny.

The economic growth rate per capita had no statistically significant relationship with local collective goods, or with macroeconomic outcomes. (Economic growth did correlate with larger student/teacher ratios, suggesting perhaps that families send their children to school as soon as the economy picks up.) This presents a challenge to classic modernization theories mentioned in the book's Introduction. It implies that even the country's poverty, with tens of millions of people living on a dollar a day, does not present an insurmountable barrier to sound economic planning for long-term development. As for oil revenues, they had an impact on the two macroeconomic measures but were not statistically significant in the tests with education and judicial performance (the other two measures of national collective goods). The strong statistical relationship between oil revenues and capital spending implies that oil booms do stimulate patronage; in terms of my broader analysis, this is especially hazardous under conditions with only a few veto players since these regimes have fewer opportunities for monitoring. For the tests relating to education performance, I also control for the federal government's varying role in education, and for the tests relating to inflation, I control for budget deficits and broad money supply by the central bank. Still, the bottom line after accounting for all these potentially intervening factors is that the explanatory power of veto players remains systematic and strong.

To probe the comparative potential of veto players, Chapter 4 searches for their "analytical equivalents" in Ghana between 1966 and 1993, and in Zimbabwe between 1987 and 2008. Rather than attempting to identify veto players with the rigor applied to Nigeria in Chapter 2, analytic narratives of these two cases probe the validity of veto players as a comparative concept. Veto players prove useful for specifying some of the shifting state-society relations in Ghana's period leading up to institutional consolidation, and they identify some constraints on an autocrat in Zimbabwe. But the analysis also reveals some limits of my model, including significant international factors that affected the distribution of authority in Zimbabwe. In the end, this study makes at least four broad contributions to our comparative understanding of Africa, outlined in what follows.

Patronage and Government Performance in Africa

First, patronage is an enduring theme in the study of African politics, and as noted in the Introduction and Chapter 1, research in the area studies tradition often attempts to demonstrate which particular communities were excluded or benefited disproportionately. Recent studies have produced advances that encourage broader generalizations and analytical comparisons based on microlevel data. For example, behavioral experiments and cross-national surveys debate whether citizens want local collective goods benefiting their particular communities or broad policy platforms promised to the nation on the whole (Wantchekon 2003; Gyimah-Boadi 2007; van de Walle 2003; Young 2009). In Ghana, for example, only one of ten voters claims to be "decisively influenced" by clientelism, ethnicity, or family ties, factors that encourage resource distribution on an excludable basis. Voters focus on "issues of incumbent performance or the general stance of the candidate/party on future policy," rather than exclusionary, particularistic benefits (Lindberg and Morrison 2008, 114). Where citizens are evaluating policy makers on the basis of performance, this research therefore also challenges long-standing findings (or assumptions) about ethnically motivated voting (Ferree 2011). These studies speak to changing citizen demands, and some explore how political institutions influence the supply of patronage as well (Posner 2005).

My study contributes to our understanding of patronage in Africa in a different way. After disaggregating government performance into non-excludable national goods and excludable local goods, I show how the underlying structure of the policy process, as characterized by veto players, differentially impacts these two broad categories of public policy. This recasts good governance as a quest for a balance between institutional incentives for accountability, which help limit patronage, and the conditions conducive to coordination that enable governments to provide broad policy benefits at the national level. This means there are no easy institutional answers, and the results in Chapter 3 suggest that democracy is only part of the solution. It also means that the pressures to make the policy process broadly inclusive of additional preferences, which are a common feature of struggles for representation in Africa, may exacerbate coordination problems that impede delivery of national collective goods. Clarifying citizen attitudes about political inclusion, and the representative institutions meant to achieve it, would constitute one important line of future research, which has only been examined by major surveys such as the Afrobarometer in limited ways.

We can only infer information about patronage from my operationalizations of local collective goods, with exorbitant levels of federal spending implying patronage or clientelism. But this allows us to provide a broad snapshot of the policy process over half a century, and it facilitates generalizations about government performance trends in Nigerian, which are difficult to identify simply through stories of ghost employees (distorting recurrent spending) or abandoned infrastructure projects (pointing to wasteful capital spending). I hope that the reader will thus value the benefits inherent in different approaches to understanding Nigeria, from research in the area studies tradition that tells us about the motivations and the mind-sets of Nigeria's political personalities, to the conceptual approaches such as the one here that enable new modes of comparative analysis.

Veto Player Analysis in Developing Countries, with Developing Institutions

Second, this study contributes to the development and broadening of veto player theory. Through the logroll hypothesis, I tested a longstanding assumption about the relationship between veto players and excludable policies (Cox and McCubbins 2001; Lyne 2008). The results were different than anticipated. In Nigeria, an increase in the number of veto players at the national level corresponded with a decrease in the delivery of local collective goods, as measured by capital and recurrent spending. But these results are very much in line with a view of veto players as agents of accountability, and close to Madison's original arguments regarding the impact of divided power.

Departing from numerous quantitative studies, this study also grounds veto players in relevant social processes and historical conditions. As noted in Chapter 1, some scholars acknowledge the importance of context in identifying these individual, collective, and institutional political actors (Cheeseman and Tendi 2010; Alence 2004), but few tackle the task. Doing so in less developed countries presents special challenges, as institutional consolidation is incomplete and social transformations are still under way. In fact, veto player analysis had previously been applied almost exclusively to wealthy democracies.

Chapter 2 took on the challenge of identifying veto players in these more difficult contexts using memoirs, interviews, and other primary sources gathered during field research in Nigeria. By acknowledging the veto power of informal institutions such as military factions and regional coalitions, as well as of formal institutions such as legislatures, parties, and presidents, this coding process invokes Madisonian principles that find social forces at the root of political power. This study is thus not a top-down analysis of hollow constitutions, disconnected elites, or institutional formalities. It acknowledges that the exercise of authority is a collective and public process, even when political actors strive to conceal their behavior or intentions. Through careful consideration of historical context, my model accommodates the possibility that bottom-up pressures can influence the distribution of political authority and blur the boundaries between state and society. For example, during the Babangida era (1985–1993), we saw how political soft-liners in the regime generated political cover for a civil society prodemocracy movement, and how the advancement of sharia law during Obasanjo's first term (1999–2003) shifted authority away from the federal government and into a northern regional coalition. But the conditions under which these informal institutions can truly exercise veto authority over national policy are rare. By establishing strict criteria for coding veto players, I not only identified conditions for when these political actors succeed or fail, I also tackled a recurring question in comparative studies of Africa, concerning how to incorporate the informal basis of authority rooted in society.

Subnational Coordination, Identities, and Federalism

Third, this book also contributes to a comparative understanding of federalism. Nigeria currently has thirty-six states and is broken into six geopolitical zones that consist of six states each. The two distinct regions, North and South, which joined to form Nigeria one hundred years ago, still represent the broadest subnational cleavages, even though the constitution only recognizes local, state, and federal units. The National Assembly rotates its leadership positions by zone and the major political parties have zonal coordinators. One implication is that two of the political units essential to identity, discourse, and coordination only exist informally in the civic imagination. This informality sometimes poses problems, an argument I develop in my concluding thoughts about the Fourth Republic that follow.

Another implication is that these tiered political units create a repertoire of identities and open various paths to constructed authority. As we saw in Chapter 2, Nigeria's states sometimes coordinate to make demands on the center, even when federalism has been formally weak. Under a military regime in 1966, for example, states effectively mobilized around issues of states' rights. But subnational actors also often articulate grievances in zonal or regional terms. Resource control is essentially a demand from the six South-South states of the Niger Delta that has been adopted by political entrepreneurs in that part of the country. The discourse is less salient elsewhere in the South; that is why the Delta activists tends to emphasize zonal (or local) rather than regional rhetoric.

Rational choice theory developed the idea of repertoires to see how individuals navigate among many social identities in a given situation (Laitin 1992). Subsequent research has emphasized how constructivist principles help explain the sources of these repertoires and why some identities rather than others become salient (Posner 2005; Chandra 2012). The study of federalism in Africa might similarly benefit from revisiting sociological traditions (Livingston 1956). Joining these approaches with veto player principles would give us a picture of the social processes that give identities meaning as well as the strategic contexts that make them useful. Some international relations research is experimenting with this sort of constructivist thinking, exploring, for example, how political actors build sovereignty from the ground up in the international system (Lake 2003; Englebert 2009). In future research, I plan to explore why some states are more powerful than others – even in symmetrical federal systems that go to great lengths to level the political playing field across these subnational units.

Advancing the Study of Comparative Authoritarianism

Finally, the model used here to analyze performance across different types of regimes contributes to an emerging literature on comparative authoritarianism. The Arab Spring has raised hopes for democratization across North Africa, and more than a dozen African countries are showing signs of sustainable good governance and economic development. At the same time, dictatorships remain in a surprising range of countries, and recent coups in five Sub-Saharan African nations since 2008 have interrupted what otherwise seemed to be a collective continental march toward democracy.[1] In its 2012 edition of *Countries at the Crossroads*, the nongovernmental organization Freedom House, documented an overall decline in government performance across thirty-five countries. In terms of government accountability and public voice, civil liberties, rule of law, and anticorruption measures, declines consistently exceeded progress (Freedom House 2012).

Until recently, the dominant approach to understanding authoritarianism involved creating elaborate taxonomies of regime types. This became prevalent over the last decade, when many governments simultaneously possessed democratic characteristics and rulers who often behaved as dictators. To understand these governments stuck in the middle between democracy and authoritarianism, concepts such as "electoral authoritarianism" (Schedler 2006; Lindberg 2009) or "semi-authoritarianism" (Ottaway 2003) now populate political science terminology. Significantly, this generation of scholars aims to understand these illiberal regimes as a distinct form of ruling that can endure over time, rather than as regimes on their way to liberalization and democracy (Levitsky and Way 2010; Tripp 2010). This latter point is especially important with regard to Africa,

---

[1] The coups were in Mauritania (2008), Guinea (2008), Niger (2010), Mali (2012), and the Central African Republic (2013).

where democratization scholars have criticized modernization theory's most simplistic assumptions that economic and political development move in a unilinear direction (Mamdani 1995; Edozie 2009). Veto player analysis contributes to these efforts by demonstrating how seemingly different regimes face similar pressures to represent societal interests. Veto player models conceptualize regimes in terms of the distribution of policy leverage, rather than the overall level of freedom or distance from the presumed goal of democratization. The number of political actors with the ability to impose transaction costs on the policy process tells us a lot about the general structure of political authority.

In his groundbreaking study, Tsebelis (2002) noted that veto players typically exist in authoritarian regimes, but identifying them requires detailed knowledge of these cases. This study took on that task and in doing so also contributed to a wave of research that challenges the characterization of dictators as omniscient rulers. These scholars strive to situate power within institutional and historical contexts by clarifying linkages between social forces and elite interests (Gandhi 2008; Brownlee 2007; Slovik 2012). The ability of a ruler to act unilaterally is informed by a number of conditions emanating from some of the inherent flaws of authoritarianism.

For example, because dictators typically gain power through force or extraconstitutional means, their governments are immediately susceptible to charges of illegitimacy. On the eve of the third wave of democratization, one classic study concluded, "Without exception, from the Bolsheviks to the autocratic praetorians of Uganda and Libya, from the Nazis to Franco, Salazar, Nasser and Perón, modern autocracies and authoritarian regimes seek popular legitimacy and support" (Perlmutter 1981, 10). Speaking directly to the situation in Nigeria, the architect of the 1975 coup said, "While there are several problems that confront a military government on coming to power, the first critical issue is that of legitimizing itself" (Garba 1995, 163). Ghana's numerous dictatorships (examined in Chapter 4) have shown that "the problem of legitimacy is a more serious problem for military governments because they lack the necessary constitutional and legal conditions that form the usual basis for modern government" (Ninsin 1991, 50). Babangida made such overtures when he seized power in Nigeria's 1985 coup, declaring, "Government, be it civilian or military, needs the consent of the people to govern."[2]

---

[2] Maj. Gen. Babangida, speech transcript, *West Africa*, September 2, 1985.

To cope with this legitimacy problem, dictators often recruit experts. In Chile, Augusto Pinochet mustered help from technocratic and legal experts (Remmer 1989; Sanders 1978). Alliances built with technocrats and academic specialists were a defining feature of Pinochet's and other Latin American authoritarian regimes in the 1960s and 1970s (O'Donnell 1999). Jerry Rawlings in Ghana similarly turned to a cadre of "patriotic professionals" who guided the government to economic stability by identifying a popular basis for increasing rural agricultural production (Jeffries 1991). In Nigeria, Yakubu Gowon's regime exemplifies this approach with the so-called superbureaucrats who operated with high levels of autonomy, sometimes formulating the very policies they would implement.

Another weakness of authoritarianism is that dictators face a high degree of identifiability. This makes it easy for them to claim credit for policy successes, but this also binds them to policy failures. This dilemma creates incentives for dictators to distribute risk. When economic reforms implemented by Babangida led to huge price increases, he blamed the cabinet.[3] Rulers take extra care to placate the private sector, military elites, and others in their ruling coalition, especially during troubled economic times (Haggard and Kaufman 1998). In Ghana in the 1980s, for example, the ruling coalition around Jerry Rawlings sought affirmation from the people. "When intervention came, a large constituency was in place," write Rothchild and Gyimah-Boadi, that "contributed substantially to regime legitimacy" (Rothchild and Gyimah-Boadi 1989, 221).

Distributing the blame for policy failures or unpopular reforms generates some uncertainty and potential risks for autocratic rulers, since doing so can alienate former loyalists or give skeptics who were co-opted into the government a reason to reconsider. Even in Zimbabwe, Chapter 4 illustrated how Mugabe strategically adopted policies to court loyalists. Mugabe is clearly a dictator who is willing to encourage or tolerate violence, writes Mamdani, but Mugabe has survived because he built a ruling coalition through policies (Mamdani 2008). Over the long term, official efforts to enhance legitimacy and distribute risk can invite new challenges to the government, as we saw in the case of Ghana. They can also generate alternative centers of power with veto authority, as occurred during the Gowon regime (1966–1975), or create new political openings that contribute to unanticipated reforms, as under the later years of the Babangida regime (1985–1993).

[3] "Nigeria: New Ruling Council Announced," *Africa Research Bulletin*, March 15, 1989.

For a number of reasons, dictators therefore have incentives to make their behavior predictable, even when they have tools for repression at their disposal (Holmes 2003). The moments of good government performance in this study during Nigeria's dark years of dictatorship thus do not compensate for the suffering endured by so many citizens. But veto player analysis suggests that we can better understand the conditions that led to the delivery of national collective goods or rational levels of spending on local collective goods by attempting to understand the distribution of policy-making authority. The obstacles to good government performance in Nigeria originate in structural conditions of politics and society, and institutions have some ability to shape outcomes. We should take this demonstrated capacity to overcome development barriers as an encouraging finding for a country scarred by colonialism, with millions of people who are still waiting for democracy's dividends.

Hope Springs Eternal? Nigeria's Fourth Republic

Throughout this study, I have left aside the question of whether Nigeria is moving toward democracy or whether political changes mask an illiberal hybrid regime. Instead, I have focused on identifying veto players in detail, and then demonstrating how they affect two broad categories of public policy over half a century. But if the results of my empirical tests point to a Madisonian dilemma, what are the chances that Africa's troubled giant might actually resolve this performance dilemma? To answer this question, the following analysis picks up where my quantitative data set ends. I point to signs of institutional consolidation and civic engagement that just might help Nigeria resolve its Madisonian dilemma. I describe the profoundly corrupt and flawed elections that tainted the transfer of power as President Obasanjo left office in 2007. This created a legitimacy deficit for the new president that was exacerbated when he soon completely disappeared from public view for more than five months. Nigeria peacefully navigated its way through this constitutional crisis over presidential succession in 2010 and averted another one a few months later when the president challenged a pact binding the ruling party by announcing that he would run in 2011. Nigeria survived this challenge, too, and this constitutes progress toward democratization. But given the nation's enduring struggles over identity, participation, and representation, perhaps the best source of hope is evidence of institutional consolidation and interest aggregation.

The Tainted Transfer of Power

The peaceful transfer of power from one civilian administration to another in 2007 closed the book on Obasanjo's tenure detailed in Chapter 2. The historic handover was tainted not only by Obasanjo's unsuccessful maneuvering to get a third term, but also by massive fraud and violence during the elections. The Transition Monitoring Group, a civil society coalition with fifty thousand trained observers on the ground, called the elections a "charade" and demanded new ones immediately. The process had "fallen far short of basic international and regional standards for democratic elections," a European Union team concluded and, therefore, "cannot be considered to have been credible."[4] The large gains posted by the ruling party cast doubt on the competitiveness of the still-young democracy. The PDP's hold on the National Assembly increased to 87 of 109 Senate seats. Opposition in the Senate fragmented among the All Nigeria People's Party with 13 seats, the Action Congress with 6, and the remainder distributed among minor parties. The PDP took 247 of 360 seats in the House of Representatives and picked up an additional governorship, giving it control of twenty-eight of the thirty-six state executives (LeVan and Ukata 2010).

Nigeria's new president, Umaru Musa Yar'Adua, tried to counter the cynicism with hopeful messages about his commitment to public integrity and public goods. In his inaugural address, Yar'Adua declared, "We will concentrate on rebuilding our physical infrastructure and human capital in order to take our country forward. We will focus on accelerating economic and other reforms in a way that makes a concrete and visible difference to ordinary people." In a discreet nod to supporters of a third term for Obasanjo, who had campaigned on the need for continued economic reform, Yar'Adua said, "Our economy already has been set on the path of growth. Now we must continue to do the necessary work to create more jobs, lower interest rates, reduce inflation and maintain a stable exchange rate.... All this will increase our chances for rapid growth and development."[5] In his budget speech the following January, Yar'Adua conceded that despite the impressive macroeconomic gains set in motion by his predecessor, more than half the country lived in poverty. To grow the country into one of the world's twenty largest economies, he pledged

---

4 "What Election Observers Say," BBC, April 23, 2007.
5 Josephine Lohor, Chuks Okocha, and Juliana Taiwo, "Yar'Adua – It's Time for Restoration," *This Day*, May 30, 2007.

to achieve single-digit inflation and to push the economic growth rate above 11 percent.[6]

To make good on his pledge regarding public integrity, Yar'Adua quickly filed allegations of corruption against Obasanjo administration officials. The Obasanjo team had rushed through contracts worth approximately 2 trillion naira (U.S.$13.5 billion) during its final weeks.[7] The new attorney general also revoked contracts for health care centers worth 37 billion naira (U.S.$245 million), accusing Obasanjo of trying to arrange for a direct deduction from the federation account to circumvent the National Assembly.[8] Since governors' constitutionally protected immunity expired with their terms of office in May 2007 as well, the Economic and Financial Crimes Commission (EFCC) launched new investigations and issued indictments for money laundering, theft, and other corruption charges.[9] Because of the cloud hanging over the governors, Yar'Adua omitted them from his ministerial nominees. (He also wanted to prevent political challenges from within his cabinet.)[10] The National Assembly played its part in the anticorruption fight when the House of Representatives impeached its first female speaker, Patricia Etteh, after an investigation uncovered evidence that she diverted government money to pay for home renovations.[11] Her criminal prosecution stalled when the Independent Corrupt Practices and Other Related Offences Commission (ICPC) staff could not agree on how to proceed. But the impeachment established a small measure of confidence in the assembly's ability to enforce its own ethics rules.

By 2008, a familiar malaise had set in. Of the ten EFCC indictments against former governors, none produced convictions. "When Obasanjo was around the EFCC did very well," recalled the House minority whip, who drafted some of the legislation creating the commission. But hinting at a bias in its prosecutions, he noted that "there were people who were not touched," and by 2010 the president wanted to dominate all aspects of the EFCC.[12] The attorney general said the political prosecutions could not proceed because he had not approved them. On top of

---

[6] Boniface Chizea, "The Economy in 2007," *This Day*, January 1, 2008.

[7] Francis Ottah Agbo, "Disengagement Deals," *The News*, June 18, 2007.

[8] George Agba, "Govt Indicts Obasanjo over N37 Billion Health Project," *Leadership*, July 22, 2008.

[9] Oluokun Ayorinde and Tony Orilade, "Facing Justice," *The News*, July 30, 2007.

[10] Desmond Utomwen, "Yar'Adua's Team," *The News*, July 16, 2007.

[11] Tony Orilade, "Madam Speaker under Fire," *The News*, September 3, 2007.

[12] Interview with Honourable Farouk Adamu Aliyu, March 18, 2010, Abuja.

that, the administration removed a popular EFCC prosecutor pursuing the governors, demoted him, and then publicly humiliated him at a law enforcement graduation ceremony. Civil society groups across the board, from the Christian Association of Nigeria to the Nigerian Bar Association, accused Yar'Adua of abandoning his pledge to public integrity.[13] Taking the president to task for EFCC failings, the Senate set out to insulate the anticorruption agency from political interference by removing any presumed authority the attorney general had to approve investigations.[14]

Yar'Adua's administration argued with the legislature over many of the same issues his predecessor had, despite the PDP's large majorities in the House and Senate. Nonimplementation of the federal budget remained a serious problem. In July 2009, some legislators threatened to impeach Yar'Adua when he protested changes to the budget made by the National Assembly.[15] Significantly, though, the public showed more tolerance for the messy operation of checks and balances, unlike in the early years of the Fourth Republic, when citizens expressed impatience with the National Assembly. Afrobarometer recorded a solid majority either agreeing or strongly agreeing (54 percent) that "the National Assembly should ensure that the President explains to it on a regular basis how his government spends taxpayers' money." A follow-up question revealed that less than a quarter of the population (24 percent) thought "the president should pass laws without worrying what the National Assembly thinks" (Afrobarometer 2009c).

Militant unrest in the Niger Delta continued. Violence peaked in 2006, when more than 150 hostages were taken over the course of the year, including American, European, and Asian foreign workers, and then abated during the April 2007 elections. After Yar'Adua entered office, militant activity had resumed in full force.[16] One difference was that an ethnic minority figure from the southern state of Bayelsa, Goodluck Jonathan, now served as vice president. Some militant groups claimed that nothing had changed with his election, since little had been done to

---

[13] "Outrage over Ribadu," *This Day*, November 24, 2008; Nick Tattersall, "Top Nigerian Anti-Graft Official Quits," *Reuters*, November 20, 2008.

[14] Emmanuel Aziken, "Senate to Remove EFCC from AGF Influence," *Vanguard*, December 30, 2008.

[15] Davidson Iriekpen, "Eradicating Corruption – Hope on the Horizon?" *This Day*, May 18, 2009; Iyobosa Uwugiaren, "Impeachment Threat: AC, CNPP, Aturu Dare Reps," *Leadership*, July 21, 2009.

[16] These figures are my own calculations, based on searches using Lexus/Nexus and AllAfrica.com.

address their underlying grievances relating to environmental cleanup, development, and resource control. But the government acknowledged those issues directly and, in 2008, created a technical committee with an inclusive membership from civil society and politics. Its final report concluded that solutions to the problems in the Niger Delta had already been identified in seventeen previous commissions and that action on those recommendations was what was needed (Technical Committee on the Niger Delta 2008). The government launched an amnesty plan in 2009 that drew nearly twenty thousand militants out of the swamps. The minister of defense expressed concern about ongoing militant attacks and explained that the military needed to show restraint with its response.[17]

To some extent, basic economics drove the amnesty. Nigeria typically produces about 2.5 million barrels of sweet light crude oil per day. The administration set a target of 3 million barrels, which it failed to meet. In addition to the usual problem of oil spills, the oil sector now had to deal with sabotage and theft by militant groups. Local militants had become adept at "bunkering," directly and illegally siphoning oil out of pipelines. The Technical Committee on the Niger Delta estimated losses at 700,000 barrels per month or U.S.$17 billion in 2006 alone (Technical Committee on the Niger Delta 2008). In other words, political economy accounted in part for the amnesty. The amnesty was designed, in part, to shore up the security of the oil industry and reassure international companies that Nigeria was a safe place to do business. Several companies working in the oil sector, including one that had operated in the Delta since the 1960s, had already pulled out because of the uncertainty and violence.[18] Shell Petroleum disclosed that the federal government was losing $1.5 billion per year from the theft of crude oil, and Vice President Jonathan openly attempted to reassure investors about the state of security.[19]

The amnesty produced only limited success, as some state governments neglected their implementation role in the rehabilitation and reintegration process and the weapons buyback program was so profitable that it was unclear whether the participants turning in guns were actually militants (Asuni 2009a). Perhaps even more significant, the amnesty process lacked

---

[17] Segun James and Juliana Taiwo, "Rising Violence in Niger Delta Worries Yar'Adua," *This Day*, March 4, 2009.
[18] Olukun Ayorinde and Okafor Ofiebor, "Quick Descent to Anarchy," *The News*, August 27, 2007.
[19] Hector Igbikiowubo, "Nigeria: Country Loses $1.5 Billion Yearly to Oil Theft – Shell," *Vanguard*, March 3, 2009; Leon Usigbe, "VP Jonathan Decries N-Delta Kidnapping," *Vanguard*, March 4, 2009.

a corresponding political process to address the underlying failures of representation that inspired the rebellion in the first place.

An Acting President Acts Presidential

This was the state of the country when President Yar'Adua became so ill, in November 2009, that he disappeared from public view. His prolonged absence, lasting nearly six months, precipitated the most acute constitutional crisis since the 1999 transition. The cabinet declined to assess his condition, dodging its constitutional authority (and some argued obligation) to do so. The Supreme Court ordered the cabinet to act, giving it fourteen days. When that deadline lapsed, the Senate passed a resolution in February declaring Goodluck Jonathan acting president. The Nigerian Governors Forum chair, a prominent northerner, declared, "The period of ambiguity is over." He urged Nigerians to distinguish between the Senate action and Yar'Adua's ongoing formal status as the president.[20] This endorsement of Jonathan as a temporary executive also implied that Yar'Adua would eventually recover – a view that sounded increasingly unrealistic as his public absence inexplicably dragged on.

As the crisis unfolded, at least three conditions that might have fueled state collapse instead nudged Nigeria closer to institutional consolidation. First, fraud and violence had marred the 2007 elections and raised doubts about whether the president had a mandate to govern at all. A scholarly study argued that the elections, "which normally should be the epitome expression of popular sovereignty," instead subverted it (Ibrahim and Ibeanu 2009, 1). But aside from electoral appeals winding their way through the courts, frustration over the elections faded with surprising swiftness and there was little sustained outrage. "Protests were remarkably few," notes the U.S. ambassador, especially compared to the popular anger after the failed elections in Kenya later that year (Campbell 2011, 108). "There was a relative lull," said the president of the Campaign for Democracy, the civil society coalition that fought for democracy throughout the 1990s.[21]

In 2010, by contrast, civil society took to the streets, defying a police ban on protests reminiscent of Babangida's final years. Unlike during those tumultuous times, though, when activists demanded a new government, the 2010 protests aimed to *defend* existing political institutions. Human

---

[20] Adekunle Jimoh, "Jonathan Is in Charge, Says Governors' Forum," *The Nation* (Nigeria), March 2, 2010.
[21] Stella Sawyerr, "Now, the People Power," *TELL*, March 22, 2010.

rights activists, citizens, and even Nollywood actors formed coalitions to demand an end to the impasse over the presidency. Thousands of citizens organized by the Save Nigeria Group (SNG) marched through the streets of the capital with placards and a petition listing three straightforward demands: (1) Dissolve the cabinet because it had failed to act on the presidential crisis; (2) fire the electoral commissioner, who was impeding electoral reform; and (3) "end the invisible presidency" by constitutionally transferring power to the vice president.[22] The extent of popular mobilization was remarkable, since the constitution itself had been decreed without much public input. The people reclaimed a small measure of popular sovereignty.

A few members of the House of Representatives responded by moving for impeachment of Yar'Adua, noting constitutional language on extended absences. Some politicians backing the SNG argued that the coalition should instead pressure the cabinet to make a decision about Yar'Adua's health. This would be more consistent with the constitution, and it seemed all the more reasonable since the Senate passed a nonbinding resolution rather than a bill.[23] However, opposition leaders allied with the SNG coalition countered "that the National Assembly owes direct allegiance to the Nigerian people." Governors, including many from the North, supported this position along with a coalition of activists and elites.[24]

Second, frustration with the elections and government performance created the possibility (however remote) that the military might capitalize on citizens' disappointments and attempt to seize power. Previous military coups, including those in 1966 and 1983, had occurred when support for democracy was at a low point and military takeover had actually been welcomed. Over the course of Obasanjo's two terms, the percentage of Nigerians who were either "not very" or "not at all" satisfied with democracy had quadrupled, from 14 to 56 percent. In a nationwide survey following the 2007 elections, 30 percent of Nigerians agreed with the statement "Since elections sometimes produce bad results, we should adopt other methods for choosing this country's leaders" (Afrobarometer 2009a, 5). Though there was less civil unrest than in 1983, the uncertainty surrounding Yar'Adua's extended absence started to appear to be

---

[22] Sebastine Obasi, "Back on the Streets," *Newswatch*, March 22, 2010.
[23] Interview with Farouk Adamu Aliyu, March 18, 2010, Abuja.
[24] Lawrence Njoku and John Ogiji, "Anxiety as N'Assembly Decides on Yar'Adua," *The Guardian*, January 11, 2010.

a worthy pretext for military rule. The State Security Service ransacked Goodluck Jonathan's office and psychically blocked access to Yar'Adua's chair ("First Take Nigeria: More Presidential Turmoil" 2010). A military conspiracy sounded even more credible when a brigadier general from the North led three hundred troops to meet Yar'Adua's plane when he returned from medical treatment abroad without the knowledge of Goodluck Jonathan or the chief of defense staff.[25] But when opposition parties alleged that the military answered only to the president (and therefore not the "acting" president), the top army official said, "The Army would like to reassure Nigerians that it has not shifted from its commitment to the tenets of democracy and absolute loyalty to constituted civil authorities."[26] Top military officials repeatedly offered such assurances, while diligent journalists ultimately exposed members of Yar'Adua's inner circle who had been planting untrue news stories designed to stoke fears of a coup.[27] International pressure played a role, too, as the United States and numerous countries urged a peaceful civilian resolution to the crisis.

Third, the presidential crisis forced politicians and civil society to confront "power shift," the elite pact within the People's Democratic Party that stipulated that the presidency would alternate between North and South. After eight years of Obasanjo, a Christian southerner, the political debt owed to the Yorubas from the annulled election of 1993 and the controversial Supreme Court decision of 1979 was deemed to have been paid. Under this agreement, it was the North's "turn" to rule, and formally swearing in Jonathan, a southerner, would therefore violate this agreement. It would also give him an obvious advantage as a candidate in subsequent presidential elections. Northern elites defended the pact, sometimes referring to it as a zoning arrangement. In February, the Northern Governors Forum, representing nineteen of the thirty-six states, issued a statement defending the status quo, saying it was unnecessary for Yar'Adua to issue a communiqué about the vice president's status as acting president.[28] This indicated confidence in both Jonathan's

[25] Kingsley Omonobi, "Yar'Adua – Presidency Investigates Deployment of Troops without Jonathan, Dike's Knowledge," *Vanguard*, March 1, 2010. Pius Mordi, "Unusual Military Deployment Raises Poser in Aso Rock Power Play," *Business Day*, February 25, 2010.

[26] "Yar'Adua: We'll Never Contemplate Coup or Carry Out Security Breach – Army," *Vanguard*, February 26, 2010.

[27] Anayochukwu Agbo, "The New Plot against Jonathan," *TELL*, March 15, 2010.

[28] John Shiklam, "Northern Governors Reject Jonathan," *Daily Champion*, February 5, 2010.

team and the legal basis for their authority. When the minister for information presented her colleagues in the cabinet with a memo asking that President Yar'Adua "officially hand over to the Vice-President to function as Acting President," the Northern Caucus in the National Assembly reacted by demanding her resignation.[29] They thought it was unfair and disloyal for her in effect to call her boss's bluff. An editorial that week in a leading newsmagazine criticized the northern representatives for engaging in parochial politics as the 50th Anniversary of Independence neared: "At the country's golden age, we expect our leaders to have thrown overboard their primordial agenda of sectionalism and ethnicism in for those of mature nationalism, unity and an engaging, robust brotherly plurality."[30]

When Yar'Adua passed away in May 2010, power shift was debated explicitly in the context of the upcoming national elections. If the PDP allowed Jonathan to run for president, it would throw the party's founding pact into doubt. Key party members spoke out against this, including the national chairman, who said unequivocally that the North would hold the presidency until 2015.[31] The former military ruler Babangida ominously warned the PDP that power must stay with the North in 2011.[32]

Why did not power shift hold? In the end, the pact was set aside because the conditions that necessitated it had passed. When it was first imposed during the transition to democracy in 1999, elites from different regions converged on power shift as a principle for building consensus around the goal of ending military rule. "Conservatives and progressives all agreed to team up for the purposes of assuring the military exit from governance," explained a party founder, who is now vice chair of a prominent group of northern elites. During his tenure as a senator, the National Assembly members actually backed down from some of the early impeachment charges against the president out of fear that power would shift to the North if Obasanjo was impeached – and therefore throw the transition's pact into doubt.[33] The architects of this pact within the ruling party had in fact hoped that the power shift principle would someday become irrelevant. They argued it should be left out of the constitution because it would trivialize leadership, replacing it with "ethnic sentiment."[34] A northern senator

[29] Editorial, "The Cabal and Akunyiyi's Home Truth," *The Punch*, March 11, 2010.
[30] Editorial, "Time to End This Rigmarole," *TELL*, March 15, 2010.
[31] "PDP Govs Choose Yar'Adua's Successor," *The Nation*, March 14, 2010.
[32] John Nwanliogu, "Babangida's Plan B," *Insider Weekly*, March 14, 2011.
[33] Interview with JKN Waku, March 10 2010, Abuja.
[34] Interview with Clement Ebri, March 16, 2010, Abuja.

explained that power shift was a necessary but temporary compromise: "After 2015 or even from 2011, it could be decided by the whole country that we will not be zoning anymore."[35] The popular pan-Yoruba organization, Oodu'a People's Congress (OPC), questioned the pact from the start, saying that any informal agreement between the North and South would not address the underlying problems of federalism. "It is not a matter of power shift," said the organization's national coordinator in 1999. "OPC would accord respect to good leadership, to good governance, and to good government."[36]

Though the expiration date for the pact was unclear, it seemed to be at hand. The informality of the pact began to work against those who defended it. A mere two months after the national chair insisted on power staying with a northern president, the party backtracked as a top official emerged from party deliberations to declare, "Zoning is not a rigid arrangement," and adding, "Jonathan is free to contest" the presidential election.[37] "Zoning is not above the constitution," explained the first PDP chairman in defense of Jonathan's 2011 candidacy.[38] Seeking support from northern elders, Jonathan met with the Northern Political Leaders Forum and secured a compromise and some measure of support.[39] The elite nature of the pact started to seem antiquated after a decade of political participation through democratic mechanisms.

Throughout the contentious debate over whether he should succeed the president, in accordance with the constitution, or whether the PDP's power shift precluded a southerner's ruling, Jonathan dodged the issue and simply started acting as president. While newspapers lampooned Yar'Adu's inner circle (and particularly his wife) in daily cartoons and commentaries, Jonathan remained above the fray, portraying himself as a competent and capable leader. He reshuffled the cabinet as SNG demanded and fired the national security advisor, who had allegedly kept him in the dark about Yar'Adua's return.[40] In his place, Jonathan appointed a prominent northerner and likely 2011 presidential candidate who had opposed Obasanjo's earlier third term bid (a move that therefore purchased some protection against the former president's

---

35 Interview with Jibril Aminu, March 8, 2010, Abuja.
36 "Oodu'a Congress Is the Most Vibrant Yoruba Organization," *The Guardian*, January 10, 1999.
37 Henry Umoru, "PDP Set to Dump Zoning," *Vanguard*, May 22, 2010.
38 Onyeka Ajumobi-Onochie, "Jonathan Has Right to Contest," *Insider Weekly*, March 14, 2011.
39 Chris Ajaero, "Pact of Controversy," *Newswatch*, March 14, 2011.
40 Anayochukwu Agbo, "Red Card for Mr. President," *TELL*, March 22, 2010.

meddling, too).[41] Jonathan skillfully dodged questions about whether he would run for president.[42] Making clear that he did not fear a coup, he left the country to visit the United States. In Washington, he succinctly outlined his policy priorities as electoral reform, Niger Delta development, fighting corruption, and improving electricity – providing a layer of detail that demonstrated a reassuring measure of technical engagement. In sum, the nation began to see Jonathan as the president simply because he was acting presidential.

In April 2011, Jonathan prevailed in an election widely praised as one of the freest and fairest in Nigeria's history, even if it was far from peaceful (National Democratic Institute for International Affairs 2012). As much as a process to choose a president, the election amounted to a referendum on power shift. The opposition candidate, the former dictator Muhammadu Buahri, outperformed Jonathan across the North. But 9.4 million eligible voters from the region's nineteen northern states cast their lot for Jonathan. Performance and policy showed some promise of replacing regionalism and parochialism as the basis of political preferences in Nigeria.

Madison's Model Unbound

It took years for African nations to recognize and deconstruct colonialism's lasting legacies. In Africa, imperial influences lingered on in state-society dynamics that created artificial chiefs and bureaucracies rife with corruption. One study observed that at independence Nigeria's courts swallowed English laws of real property "hook, line and sinker" (Oluyede 1985, 94). African economies that struggled to reduce dependence on one or a few exports in the postcolonial era have only recently begun to show their potential for multisector performance and sustained development. During the first decade of the new millennium, economic growth in many nations started to show a new ability to overcome adversity, whether understood in terms of geographic disadvantages, resource constraints, or colonial legacies (Ndulu and O'Connell 2008; Radelet 2010).

If economies took decades to transform, constitutions by contrast were more malleable. The newly independent countries swiftly discarded their institutional inheritance, for the better and sometimes for

[41] Femi Macaulay, "Gusau, Protector of Power Who May Yet Wear the Crown," *The Nation*, March 14, 2010.

[42] Christine Amanpour, "I Won't Force Myself to Meet Yar'Adua, Says Jonathan," CNN, April 14, 2010.

the worse (Deng et al. 2008). Like other African countries enchanted by nationalist promises, Nigeria opted for a clean break with its past, severing its constitutional links to Britain and becoming a full republic only three years after independence. In 1979, Nigeria adopted a presidential system modeled after the United States'. During the debate and drafting, the embassy in Lagos was pleasantly surprised by the flood of requests for *The Federalist Papers* (Horowitz 1979). Members of the U.S. House of Representative's Judiciary Committee provided direct input into the process. This mirrored the widespread appeal of Madisonian principles elsewhere in the developing world: At one point every country in Latin America governed through a presidential system (Przeworski 2010, 63). Of course, the failure of Nigeria's Second Republic plunged the country into its longest and darkest stretch of dictatorships. The Nigerian poet Chinweizu in "The Epidemic" describes how a political system built on fear and repression will eventually backfire:

> The wraith of distrust, rolling his eyes
> and waving a gun, sent shot after shot
> into the ranks of the barricaded trembling;
> while terror in terror found a friend. (Chinweizu 1978)

It took more than sixteen long years for Nigerians to arrive at the 1999 transition, when the nation found itself again poised before the kind of bright tomorrow described half a century earlier by Langston Hughes and Nnamdi Azikiwe. Once again, Nigeria turned to comparative constitutional principles to build its constitution. "Our democracy is based on the presidential system. It is almost mirrored from the United States," former Senate President Ken Nnamani told me. "We start our constitution by saying, 'We the people,' just exactly like the Americans." However, "Democracy is not working exactly in Nigeria as it is in the US, although the principles are the same."[43]

In the end, a variety of ideas from around the world inspired Nigeria's institutional architects. Numerous constitutional conventions, electoral reform commissions, and even Babangida's Political Bureau took a global perspective. My own experience with Nigerian politics began in 1999, when a small group of reformers in the National Assembly asked me for analysis of anticorruption procedures in six different countries. They debated the pros and cons of each, met with a coalition of a dozen civil society organizations to hear what citizen activists wanted, and then

---

[43] Interview with Senator Ken Nnamani, March 9, 2010, Abuja.

passed legislation (though that part took a few years!). To manage its incredible social heterogeneity, Nigeria has adopted its own particular mix of democratic principles, including the zoned rotation of offices within almost every political unit, even in Local Government Areas.

Like Indonesia and other nations transitioning from authoritarian rule at the turn of the century, Nigeria adopted principles to divide power in the Madisonian tradition. "States emerging from long bouts of authoritarianism," writes Horowitz, "certainly do see advantages to both the separation of powers and the entrenchment of rights" (Hamilton et al. 2009, 520). To this end, Nigeria's use of first-past-the-post (FPTP) for its elections strives for integration rather than inclusion based on some type of segmentation (ideological, ethnic, or otherwise). While FPTP has been less popular in recent constitutional drafting than proportional representation methods that more directly embrace principles of inclusiveness (Norris 2008, 115–116), in Nigeria, it has served to mute parochialism and encourage coalition building across ethnic and regional divides. The cross-regional defeat of Obasanjo's bid for a third term, a series of confessional self-doubting dialogues convened by the Federal Character Commission in 2009, and the dubious future of power shift in the wake of the 2011 elections won by Jonathan suggest that Nigeria is closer to balancing Madisonian ideals: accountability through divided interests and representation through public contestation.

"On a candid examination of history," Madison told the Virginia Convention, "turbulence, violence and the abuse of power, by the majority trampling on the rights of the minority, have produced factions and commotions, which, in republics, have more frequently than any other cause produced despotism" (Madison 2006a, 144). He feared that rule by the people could either strengthen republican democracy or legitimize dictatorship and, therefore, expressed a cautious view of mass participation. He is therefore often associated with a more elitist view of democracy, in which the people need rulers to determine what is in their best interests (Przeworski 2010, 22–24). However, Madison also appreciated that popular passions inspire civic thinking. He put no small measure of trust in the judgment of citizens in a poor, newly independent country, divided over race and economic differences but drawn together by distaste for British colonialism. He argued for a free "commerce of ideas" in order to identify the common good and to direct government efforts toward it (Sheehan 2009, 98–99). Thousands of Africans have embraced a similar view in surveys over the last decade, by defining democracy in terms of the protection of the freedoms necessary to disagree (Bratton 2008).

Amid such disagreements, institutions can increase the likelihood that elites and the public alike will balance passion with reason. There are always surprises and unintended consequences, and therefore some part of politics always operates more as art than as science. Veto player analysis can nevertheless help us understand the processes through which various types of political actors attempt to advance divergent goals, and the theory outlined in this book has, it is hoped, done justice to the contexts that inspire and enable them.

Appendix 1

Possible Measurement Error in the *Clearance* Variable

There are at least five possible sources of measurement error in this construction of the *clearance* variable. First, the actual number of cases filed in a given year is likely higher than represented here because the official law reports only include cases after they are decided; they do not necessarily list all of the new cases filed in a given year. For this reason, I calculate clearance rate only through 1987, when the published information about new cases drops steeply.[1] Second, population growth over time might increase the number of cases filed. However, since *clearance* is a ratio variable, any increase in the number of new cases is measured in relation to the number of resolved cases. Third, if one of the two types of cases in my sample takes longer to resolve than the other on average, then this would bias my variable by improperly combining different kinds of cases in a single variable. Indeed, a number of legal scholars at the University of Ibadan raised this concern during my field research. However, the two types of cases are highly correlated (Pearson's $R > 0.9$), meaning that they offer similar overall information about property rights cases with the benefit of increasing the sample size. Fourth, although law reports offer the most reliable information about court decisions in Nigeria, they are usually privately published and do not contain the total universe of cases. This could lead to an unrepresentative sample. To address this concern, I cross-checked my list of 550 cases with a more comprehensive index of cases dating back to 1880 (Olaitan 1998).[2]

[1] For example, the clearance rate for 1960 is based on cases whose decisions were actually reported in 1966, 1968, and 1975. More land cases were almost certainly filed in 1960, but the only information available about 1960 is from the law reports, which announce when cases are decided and are published later.
[2] One-third of all Supreme Court cases decided between 1963 and 1997 involved land disputes (Alabi 2002).

I found only very minor differences in the distribution of cases reported compared to the cases indexed.

Finally, major changes to the legal system could weaken the sample's representativeness. For example, Nigeria's 1978 Land Use Act vested control of all land in trust with the military governors of the states. Critics described this as state seizure of property, especially after the decree was entrenched in the constitution in 1979 (Awogu 1984). This singularly important transformation of Nigerian land law, which granted states such broad authority, might have stimulated new complaints, since it theoretically made property owners more vulnerable to government action. However, the number of new cases in my sample does not significantly change after 1979. Supreme Court data further attest to the representativeness of my sample, since its caseload reveals a *decline* in land disputes between 1979 and 1983, both in absolute terms and as a share of cases (Alabi 2002). Since the numbers for the years immediately after the decree resemble those preceding the decree, it is likely any change in the clearance rate after 1979 cannot be attributed to an increase in cases. In most areas pertaining to private sector activity, a recent study laments, Nigerian laws have hardly changed at all since independence (Kwakwa et al. 2008). This condition supports the notion that drastic changes in the legal system do not undermine the sample's representativeness over time.

Similarly, it is possible that the civil war led to changes in law that created economic uncertainty and discouraged capital formation (Bates 2004). But the courts operated sufficiently during this tumultuous period that the data for these two and a half years are still usable. "Generally speaking," writes the former chief justice of Ondo State, "the Courts were permitted to continue to perform their traditional role of adjudication between citizen and citizen, and between the citizen and the State" (Aguda 1988, 122). Even though the government took steps to limit the scope of their jurisdiction, judges kept their jobs and the situation was "comparatively favourable for the operation of the judiciary" (Ezejiofor 1977).

Appendix 2

Descriptive Statistics for Variables

TABLE A2.1. *Descriptive Statistics*

	N	Minimum	Maximum	Mean	Standard Deviation
Vetoes	47	1	4	2.83	.94
ΔOil_{t-1}	46	−.17	.25	.02	.09
Democracy	47	0	1	.40	.50
GDPgrowth	47	−17.75	21.97	1.20	7.20
Ed.budget	47	.55	13.59	6.21	2.66
$\Delta Debt.ext_{t-1}$	46	−23.80	35.90	−.08	11.37
Inflation	17	9 79	70.81	17.06	17.19
Fedbudget	47	−21.39	7.89	−4.17	5.71
Clearance	27	.11	1.89	.66	.50
Student/teacher	47	28.5	57.8	37.4	5.24
$\Delta Spending$	46	−.1295	.1426	.001295	.0532
$\Delta Recurrent$	46	−.1295	.1426	.001659	.0536
$\Delta Capital$	46	−.0917	.1164	.000428	.0342

References

Abernethy, David B. 1969. *The Political Dilemma of Popular Education: An African Case*. Stanford, CA: Stanford University Press.

Abolade, J. O. 2000. *Quality Control in Basic Education*. Edited by Federal Ministry of Education, *Universal Basic Education for Nigeria: Proceedings of the Education Mini Summit, 1999–2000*. Abuja: Federal Ministry of Education.

Abubakar, Dauda. 2004. "Leadership and the Challenges of Rebuilding a Nation." In *Nigeria's Struggle for Democracy and Good Governance: A Festscrift for Oyeleye Oyediran*, edited by Adigun Agbaje, Larry Diamond and Ebere Onwudiwe, 153–166. Ibadan: University of Ibadan Press.

Acemoglu, Daron, and James A. Robinson. 2012. *Why Nations Fail: The Origins of Power, Prosperity, and Poverty, Crown Business*. New York: Random House.

Achebe, Chinua. 1983. *The Trouble with Nigeria*, reprint. Portsmouth, NH, and Oxford: Heinemann Educational.

Achike, Okay. 1980. *Groundwork of Military Law and Military Rule in Nigeria*, original ed., 1978. Enugu, Nigeria: Fourth Dimension Publishers.

Adamolekun, Lapido. 1997. "Transforming the Civil Service." In *Transition without End: Nigerian Politics and Civil Society under Babangida*, edited by Larry Jay Diamond, Oyeleye Oyediran and A. H. M Kirk-Greene, 363–375. Boulder, CO: Lynne Rienner.

Adebayo, A. G. 1993. *Embattled Federalism: History of Revenue Allocation in Nigeria, 1946–1990*. New York: Peter Lang.

Adedeji, J. 2001. "The Legacy of Jerry Rawlings in Ghanaian Politics, 1979–2000." *African Studies Quarterly* no. 5 (2):2–12.

Adekanye, J. 'Bayo. 1997. "The Military." In *Transition without End: Nigerian Politics and Civil Society under Babangida*, edited by Larry Jay Diamond, Oyeleye Oyediran and A. H. M Kirk-Greene, 55–80. Boulder, CO: Lynne Rienner.

——— 1999. *The Retired Military as Emergent Power Factor in Nigeria*. Ibadan: Heinemann.

Ademoyega, Adewale. 1981. *Why We Struck: The Story of the First Nigerian Coup*. Ibadan: Evans.

Adichie, Chimamanda Ngozi. 2006. *Half of a Yellow Sun*. New York: Random House.

Adjibolosoo, Senyo. 2003. "Ethnicity and the Development of National Consciousness: A Human Factor Analysis." In *Critical Perspective on Politics and Socio-Economic Development in Ghana*, edited by Wisdom J. Tetty, Korbla Puplampu and Bruce Berman, 107–132. Leiden: Koninklijke Brill.

African Development Bank. 2011. African Economic Outlook 2011. United Nations.

Afrobarometer. 2002. Key Findings about Public Opinion in Africa. Afrobarometer Briefing Paper No. 1, http://www.afrobarometer.org/files/documents/briefing_papers/AfrobriefNo1.pdf.

2006. Performance and Legitimacy in Nigeria's New Democracy. Afrobarometer Briefing Paper No. 46, http://afrobarometer.org/files/documents/briefing_papers/AfrobriefNo46.pdf.

2009a. Popular Attitudes toward Democracy in Nigeria: A Summary of Afrobarometer Indicators, 2000–2008, Afrobarometer Briefing Paper, http://afrobarometer.org/files/documents/democracy_indicators/nig_r4_di.pdf.

2009b. Popular Perceptions of Shari'a Law in Nigeria, Afrobarometer Briefing Paper No. 58, http://afrobarometer.org/files/documents/briefing_papers/AfrobriefNo58.pdf.

2009c. Summary of Results: Round 4 Survey in Nigeria, http://afrobarometer.org/files/documents/summary_results/nig_r4_sor.pdf.

Agbadu-Fishim, J. T. 1998. *Principles of Nigerian Company Law*. Ogun State, Nigeria: IPS Educational Press.

Aguda, T. Akinola. 1988. "The Judiciary and the System of Laws." In *Nigeria since Independence: The First 25 Years*, edited by Tekena N. Tamuno and J. A. Atanda, 112–138. Ibadan: Heinemann.

Ahiakpor, J. C. 1991. "Rawlings, Economic Policy Reform, and the Poor: Consistency or Betrayal?" *Journal of Modern African Studies* no. 29 (4):583–600.

Ahmad Khan, Sarah. 1994. *Nigeria: The Political Economy of Oil*. Oxford: Oxford University Press.

Aiyede, Emmanuel Remi. 2006. "Legislature-Executive Relations in Nigeria's Democracy." In *Challenges of Sustainable Democracy in Nigeria*, edited by Emmanuel O. Ojo, 140–154. Ibadan: John Archers.

Ake, Claude. 1984. *Political Economy of Nigeria*. London: Longman.

1996. *Democracy and Development in Africa*. Washington, DC: Brookings Institution Press.

Akinkugbe, O. O. 1994. *Nigeria and Education: The Challenges Ahead, Proceedings and Policy Recommendations of the Second Obafemi Awolowo Foundation Dialogue*. Ibadan and Lagos: Spectrum Books.

Akinnola, Richard. 2000. *Fellow Countrymen: The Story of Coup d'Etats in Nigeria*. Lagos: Rich Konsult.

Akpakpan, Edet B. 2000. "An Appraisal of the Performance of the 1999 Federal Budget." *NCEMA Policy Analysis Series* no. 6 (1):11–21.

Alabi, Mojeed Olujinmi A. 2002. *The Supreme Court in the Nigerian Political System, 1963–1997*. Ibadan: Demyaxs Press.

Alence, Rod. 2004. "Political Institutions and Developmental Governance in Africa." *Journal of Modern African Studies* no. 42 (2):163–187.

Alesina, Alberto, and Roberto Perotti. 1996. "Fiscal Discipline and the Budget Process." *The American Economic Review* no. 86 (2):401–407.

Alexander, Jocelyn. 2006. *The Unsettled Land: State-Making and the Politics of Land in Zimbabwe*. Oxford: James Currey.

Alli, M. Chris. 2001. *The Federal Republic of Nigerian Army: The Siege of a Nation*. Lagos: Malthouse Press.

Alston, Lee J, Thráinn Eggertsson, and Douglass Cecil North. 1996. *Empirical Studies in Institutional Change, Political Economy of Institutions and Decisions*. Cambridge and New York: Cambridge University Press.

Aluko, Oluwole. 1998. *The Law of Real Property and Procedure*. Ibadan: Spectrum Law.

Aluko, Yetunde. 2009. "Corruption in Nigeria: Concept and Dimensions." In *Anti-Corruption Reforms in Nigeria since 1999*, edited by David U. Enweremadu and Emeka E. Okafor, 1–10. Ibadan: IFRA.

Ames, Barry. 1987. *Political Survival: Politicians and Public Policy in Latin America, California Series on Social Choice and Political Economy*. Berkeley: University of California Press.

Amnesty International. 1974. Chile, www.amnesty.org.

Amuwo, 'Kunle. 2001. "Transition as Democratic Regression." In *Nigeria during the Abacha Years, 1993–1998*, edited by Kunle Amuwo, Daniel C. Bach and Yann Lebeau, 1–56. Ibadan, Nigeria: Institut Francais de Recherche en Afrique.

Amuwo, 'Kunle, Adigun Agbaje, Rotimi Suberu, and Georges Herault. 2000. *Federalism and Political Restructuring in Nigeria*, original ed., 1998. Ibadan: Spectrum.

Andrews, Josephine T., and Gabriella Montinola, R. 2004. "Veto Players and the Rule of Law in Emerging Democracies." *Comparative Political Studies* no. 37 (1):55–87.

Angerbrandt, Henrik. 2011. "Political Decentralisation and Conflict: The Sharia Crisis in Kaduna, Nigeria." *Journal of Contemporary African Studies* no. 29 (1):15–31.

Ansell, Amy E. 2008. "Operation 'Final Solution': Intimidation and Violence against White Farmers in Post-Election Zimbabwe." *Association of Concerned Africa Scholars Bulletin* no. 79:42–46.

Anunobi, Fredoline. 1994. "The Political Economy of Instability in Ghana." In *International Dimensions of African Political Economy*, 185–213. Lanham, MD: University Press of America.

Arendt, Hannah. 1969. *On Violence*. New York: Harcourt, Brace & World.

Ariyo, Ademola. 1996a. "Budget Deficit in Nigeria, 1974–1993: A Behavioral Perspective." In *Economic Reform and Macroeconomic Management in*

Nigeria, edited by Ademola Ariyo, 263–278. Ibadan: Centre for Public-Private Cooperation.

1996b. *Economic Reform and Macroeconomic Management in Nigeria*. Ibadan: Centre for Public-Private Cooperation.

Arriola, Leonardo. 2009. "Patronage and Political Stability in Africa." *Comparative Political Studies* no. 42 (10):1339–1362.

Arriola, Leonardo R. 2013. *Multi-Ethnic Coalitions in Africa: Business Financing of Opposition Election Campaigns*. New York: Cambridge University Press.

Art, David. 2012. "What Do We Know about Authoritarianism after Ten Years?" *Comparative Politics* no. 44 (3):351–373.

Ashinze, J. O., and E. A. Onwioduokit. 1996. "Economic Growth and Foreign Debt: A Case Study of Nigeria." *Central Bank of Nigeria Economic and Financial Review* no. 34 (1):523–540.

Asiodu, Philip. 2000. "Budget Implementation." *NCEMA Policy Analysis Series* no. 6 (1):7–10.

Asiodu, P. Chiedo. 1979. "The Civil Service: An Insider's View." In *Nigerian Government and Politics under Military Rule, 1966–1979*, edited by Oyeleye Oyediran, 73–95. New York: St. Martin's Press.

Asuni, Judy. 2009a. *Understanding the Armed Groups of the Niger Delta*. New York: Council on Foreign Relations.

Asuni, Judy Burdin. 2009b. *Blood Oil in the Niger Delta*. Washington, DC: U.S. Institute of Peace.

Awogu, F. Olisa. 1984. *The Judiciary in the Second Republic of Nigeria, 1979–1983*. Onitsha: Pacific College Press.

Awolowo, Obafemi. 1966. *Path to Nigerian Freedom*, 1st ed. London: Faber.

Ayadi, Folorunso, and Felix Ayadi. 2008. "The Impact of External Debt on Economic Growth: A Comparative Study of Nigeria and South Africa." *Journal of Sustainable Development in Africa* no. 10 (3):235–264.

Ayee, Joseph R. A. 2007. "A Decade of Political Leadership in Ghana, 1993–2004." In *Ghana – One Decade of the Liberal State*, edited by Kwame Boafo-Arthur, 165–187. New York: Zed Books.

Azaiki, Steve, and Augustine A. Ikein. 2008. "Oil and Gas Politics in the Niger Delta." In *Oil, Democracy, and the Promise of True Federalism in Nigeria*, edited by Augustine A. Ikein, D. S. P. Alamieyeseigha and Steve Azaiki, 73–84. Lanham, MD: University Press of America.

Babatope, Abiola. 2000. *The Abacha Years: What Went Wrong?* Lagos: CSS Press.

2001. *The House in Session: Glimpses from the Second Republic*. Ibadan: AiKE Books.

Bach, Daniel C. 2011. "Patrimonialism and Neopatrimonialism: Comparative Trajectories and Readings." *Commonwealth & Comparative Politics* no. 49 (3):275–294.

Badza, Simon. 2009. "Zimbabwe's 2008 Harmonized Elections: Regional and International Reaction." In *Defying the Winds of Change: Zimbabwe's 2008 Elections*, edited by Eldred Masunungure, 149–175. Harare: Weaver Press.

Baldacci, Emanuele, Benedict Clements, Sanjeev Gupta, and Qiang Cui. 2008. "Social Spending, Human Capital, and Growth in Developing Countries." *World Development* no. 36 (8):1317–1341.

Balogun, M. J. 2009. *The Route to Power in Nigeria: A Dynamic Engagement Option for Current and Aspiring Leaders.* New York: Palgrave Macmillan.

Barkan, Joel D. 2009. *Legislative Power in Emerging African Democracies.* Boulder, CO, and London: Lynne Rienner.

Barro, Robert J., and Jong-Wha Lee. 2001. "International Data on Educational Attainment: Updates and Implications." *Oxford Economic Papers* no. 53 (3):541–563.

2010. "A New Data Set of Educational Attainment in the World, 1950–2010." National Bureau of Economic Research Working Paper no. 15902.

Barros, Robert. 2003. "Dictatorship and the Rule of Law: Rules and Military Power in Pinochet's Chile." In *Democracy and the Rule of Law*, edited by Jose Maria Maravall and Adam Przeworski, 188–222. Cambridge: Cambridge University Press.

Barzel, Yoram. 1997. *Economic Analysis of Property Rights.* Cambridge: Cambridge University Press.

Basedau, Matthias, Gero Erdmann, Jann Lay, and Alexander Stroh. 2011. "Ethnicity and Party Preference in Sub-Saharan Africa." *Democratization* no. 18 (2):462–489.

Basedau, Matthias, Gero Erdmann, and Andreas Mehler. 2007. *Votes, Money and Violence: Political Parties and Elections in Sub-Saharan Africa.* Sweden: Nordiska Afrikainstitutet.

Bates, Robert H. 1997. "Area Studies and the Discipline: A Useful Controversy?" *PS: Political Science and Politics* no. 30 (2):166–169.

2004. "On The Politics of Property Rights by Haber, Razo, and Maurer." *Journal of Economic Literature* no. 42:494–500.

2008. "Domestic Interests and Control Regimes." In *The Political Economy of Economic Growth in Africa, 1960–2000*, edited by Benno Ndulu, Stephen O'Connell, Robert Bates, Paul Collier and Chukwuma Soludo, 176–201. Cambridge: Cambridge University Press.

Bates, Robert H., Avner Greif, Margaret Levi, Jean-Laurent Rosenthal, and Barry Weingast. 1998. *Analytic Narratives.* Princeton, NJ: Princeton University Press.

1981. *Markets and States in Tropical Africa: The Political Basis of Agricultural Policies.* Berkeley: University of California Press.

Baum, Matthew A., and David Lake. 2003. "The Political Economy of Growth: Democracy and Human Capital." *American Journal of Political Science* no. 47 (2):333–347.

Beech, Kaspar. 2008. "Subverted Institutions and Democratisation: Zimbabwe and the Struggle for Democracy." *Africana* no. 2 (2):88–137.

Berman, Bruce. 1998. "Ethnicity, Patronage, and the African State." *African Affairs* no. 97:305–41.

Berman, Bruce, Eyoh Dickson, and Will Kymlicka. 2004. *Ethnicity and Democracy in Africa.* Oxford and Athens, OH: James Currey and Ohio University Press.

Bienen, Henry. 1983. *Oil Revenues and Policy Choice in Nigeria.* Staff Working Paper #592 ed. Washington, DC: World Bank.

Biersteker, Thomas, and Peter M. Lewis. 1997. "The Rise and Fall of Structural Adjustment in Nigeria." In *Transition without End: Nigerian Politics and*

Civil Society under Babangida, edited by Larry Diamond, Anthony Kirk-Greene and Oyeleye Oyediran 303–332. Boulder, CO, and London: Lynne Rienner.

Bleck, Jaimie, and Nicolas van de Walle. 2011. "Parties and Issues in Francophone West Africa: Towards a Theory of Non-Mobilization." *Democratization* no. 18 (5):1125–1145.

Boafo-Arthur, Kwame. 2007. *Ghana – One Decade of the Liberal State*. New York: Zed Books.

Boahen, A. Adu. 1997. "Ghana: Conflict Reoriented." In *Governance as Conflict Management: Politics and Violence in West Africa*, edited by I. William Zartman, 95–148. Washington, DC: Brookings Institution Press.

Boix, Carles. 2003. *Democracy and Redistribution*. Cambridge and New York: Cambridge University Press.

Boix, Carles, and Susan Stokes. 2003. "Endogenous Democratization." *World Politics* no. 55:517–549.

Bolaji, M. H. A. 2009. "Shari'ah in Northern Nigeria in Light of Asymmetrical Federalism." *Publius: The Journal of Federalism* no. 40 (1):114–135.

Bomba, Briggs, and William Minter. 2010. Zimbabwe: Demystifying Sanctions and Strengthening Solidarity. *Pambazuka News*, April 15, 2010.

Booysen, Susan. 2009. "The Presidential and Parliamentary Elections in Zimbabwe, March and June 2008." *Electoral Studies* no. 28:150–155.

Brambor, Thomas, William Roberts Clark, and Matt Golder. 2007. "Are African Party Systems Different?" *Electoral Studies* no. 26 (2):315–323.

Bratton, Michael. 2008. "The 'Alternation Effect' in Africa." In *How People View Democracy*, edited by Larry Diamond and Marc F. Plattner, 117–128. Baltimore: Johns Hopkins University Press.

Bratton, Michael, Ravi Bhavnani, and Tse-Hsin Chen. 2011. Voting Intentions in Africa: Ethnic, Economic, or Partisan? *Afrobarometer Working Paper* No. 127.

Bratton, Michael, and Mwangi Kimenyi. 2008. Voting in Kenya: Putting Ethnicity in Perspective. Afrobarometer Briefing Paper No. 95, http://www.afrobarometer.org/files/documents/working_papers/AfropaperNo95.pdf.

Bratton, Michael, and Eldred Masunungure. 2008. "Zimbabwe's Long Agony." *Journal of Democracy* no. 19 (4):41–55.

Bratton, Michael, and Robert Mattes. 2009. Neither Consolidating nor Fully Democratic: The Evolution of African Political Regimes, 1999–2008. Afrobarometer Briefing Paper No. 67, http://www.afrobarometer.org/files/documents/briefing_papers/AfrobriefNo67.pdf.

Bratton, Michael, and Nicolas Van de Walle. 1997. *Democratic Experiments in Africa: Regime Transitions in Comparative Perspective*. Cambridge and New York: Cambridge University Press.

Brown, David S., and Wendy Hunter. 1999. "Democracy and Social Spending in Latin America, 1980–1992." *American Political Science Review* no. 93 (4):779–790.

Brown, David, and Wendy Hunter. 2004. "Democracy and Human Capital Formation: Education Spending in Latin America, 1980–1997." *Comparative Political Studies* no. 37 (7):842–864.

Brownlee, Jason M. 2002. "Low Tide after the Third Wave: Exploring Politics under Authoritarianism." *Comparative Politics* no. 34 (4):477–498.

Brownlee, Jason. 2007. *Authoritarianism in an Age of Democratization*. Cambridge and New York: Cambridge University Press.

Bueno de Mesquita, Bruce, James D. Morrow, Randolph Siverson, and Alastair Smith. 2001. "Political Competition and Economic Growth." *Journal of Democracy* no. 12 (1):57–72.

Bueno de Mesquita, Bruce, Alastair Smith, Randolph M. Siverson, and James D. Morrow. 2003. *The Logic of Political Survival*. Cambridge, MA and London: MIT Press.

Bunce, Valerie, and Sharon Wolchik. 2010. "Defeating Dictators: Electoral Change and Stability in Competitive Authoritarian Regimes." *World Politics* no. 62 (1):43–86.

Buscaglia, Edgardo. 1999. *Comparative International Study of Court Performance Indicators: A Descriptive and Analytical Account*. Washington, DC: World Bank.

Buscaglia, Edgardo, and Thomas Ulen. 1997. "A Quantitative Assessment of the Efficiency of the Judicial Sector in Latin America." *International Review of Law and Economics* no. 17:275–291.

Callaghy, Thomas M, and John Ravenhill. 1993. *Hemmed In Responses to Africa's Economic Decline*. New York: Columbia University Press.

Cameron, Charles. 2000. *Veto Bargaining: Presidents and the Politics of Negative Power*. Cambridge: Cambridge University Press.

Campbell, John. 2011. *Nigeria: Dancing on the Brink*. Lanham, MD: Rowman & Littlefield.

Carmody, Pdraig, and Scott Taylor. 2003. "Industry and the Urban Sector in Zimbabwe's Political Economy." *African Studies Quarterly* no. 7 (2&3):53–80.

Casar, Amparo. 2002. "Executive-Legislative Relations in Mexico." In *Legislative Politics in Latin America*, edited by Scott Morgenstern and Benito Nacif, 114–145. Cambridge: Cambridge University Press.

Case, Anne, and Angus Deaton. 1999. "School Inputs and Educational Outcomes in South Africa." *Quarterly Journal of Economics*: 1047–1088.

Chabal, Patrick. 2009. *Africa: The Politics of Suffering and Smiling, World Political Theories*. London: Zed Books.

Chabal, Patrick, and Jean-Pascal Daloz. 1999. *Africa Works: Disorder as Political Instrument, African Issues*. London and Bloomington: International African Institute in association with James Currey, Oxford and Indiana University Press.

Chandra, Kanchan. 2009. "Making Causal Claims about the Effects of Ethnicity." In *Comparative Politics: Rationality, Culture, and Structure*, edited by Mark Lichbach and Alan Zukerman. Cambridge and New York: Cambridge University Press.

2012. *Constructivist Theories of Ethnic Politics*. New York: Oxford University Press.

Chazan, Naomi. 1983. *An Anatomy of Ghanaian Politics: Managing Political Recession, 1969–1982*. Boulder, CO: Westview Press.

1991. "The Political Transformation of Ghana under the PNDC." In *Ghana: The Political Economy of Recovery*, edited by Donald Rothchild, 21–47. Boulder, CO: Lynne Rienner.

Cheeseman, Nic, and Blessing-Miles Tendi. 2010. "Power-Sharing in Comparative Perspective: The Dynamics of 'Unity Government' in Kenya and Zimbabwe." *Journal of Modern African Studies* no. 48 (2):203–229.

Chehabi, H. E., and Juan J. Linz. 1998. "A Theory of Sultanism 2: Genesis and Demise of Sultanistic Regimes." In *Sultanistic Regimes*, edited by H. E. Chehabi and Juan J. Linz, 26–48. Baltimore and London: Johns Hopkins University Press.

Cheibub, Jose Antonio. 2007. *Presidentialism, Parliamentarism, and Democracy*. Cambridge and New York: Cambridge University Press.

Cheru, Fantu. 2002. *African Renaissance: Roadmaps to the Challenge of Globalization*. London: Zed Books.

Chevillard, Nicole. 2001. "Nigeria's External Debt: Evolution, Mix and Current Issues." In *Nigeria during the Abacha Years, 1993–1998*, edited by Daniel C. Bach, Yann Lebeau and 'Kunle Amuwo, 219–234. Ibadan, Nigeria: Institut Francais de Recherche en Afrique.

Chikuhwa, Jacob. 2004. *A Crisis of Governance: Zimbabwe*. New York: Algora Publishing.

Chimobi, Omoke Philip. 2010. "Inflation and Economic Growth in Nigeria." *Journal of Sustainable Development* no. 3 (2):159–166.

Chinweizu. 1978. *Energy Crisis and Other Poems*. Lagos: NOK.

Clague, Christopher, Philip Keefer, Stephen Knack, and Mancur Olson. 1997. "Democracy, Autocracy, and the Institutions Supportive of Economic Growth." In *Institutions and Economic Development: Growth and Governance in Less-Developed and Post-Socialist Countries*, edited by Christopher Clague, 91–120. Baltimore and London: Johns Hopkins University Press.

Clark-Bekederemo, J. P. 1981. *A Decade of Tongues: Selected Poems 1958–1968, Drumbeat*. London: Longman.

Cliffe, Lionel, Jocelyn Alexander, Ben Cousins, and Rudo Gaidzanwa. 2011. "An Overview of Fast Track Land Reform in Zimbabwe: Editorial Introduction." *Journal of Peasant Studies* no. 38 (5):907–938.

Coase, Ronald H. 1960. "The Problem of Social Cost." *The Journal of Law and Economics* no. 3:1–44.

Coleman, James S. 1958. *Nigeria: Background to Nationalism*. Berkeley and Los Angeles: University of California Press.

Collier, Paul. 2003. "Implications of Ethnic Diversity." In *African Economic Development* edited by Emmanuel Nnadozie, 149–177. Amsterdam, Boston, London, and New York: Academic Press.

Collier, Paul, and Jan Willem Gunning. 2008. "Sacrificing the Future: Intertemporal Strategies and Their Implications for Growth." In *The Political Economy of Econoimc Growth in Africa, 1960–2000*, edited by Benno Ndulu, Stephen O'Connell, Robert Bates, Paul Collier and Chukwuma Soludo, 202–224. Cambridge: Cambridge University Press.

Collier, Paul, and Stephen O'Connell. 2008. "Opportunities and Choices." In *The Political Economy of Economic Growth in Africa, 1960–2000*, edited by

Benno Ndulu, Stephen O'Connell and Robert Bates, 76–137. Cambridge: Cambridge University press.

Conley, Richard S., and Marija A. Bekafigo. 2010. "'No Irish Need Apply'? Veto Players and Legislative Productivity in the Republic of Ireland, 1949–2000." *Comparative Political Studies* no. 43 (1):91–118.

Constituency Delimitation Commission. 1964. *Report of the Constituency Delimitation Commission, 1964*. Lagos: Federal Republic of Nigeria.

Cooter, Robert. 2000. *The Strategic Constitution*. Princeton, NJ: Princeton University Press.

Cox, Gary, and Mathew McCubbins. 2001. "The Institutional Determinants of Economic Policy Outcomes." In *Presidents, Parliaments, and Policy*, edited by Stephan Haggard and Mathew McCubbins, 21–63. New York: Cambridge University Press.

Craig, Justice E. B. 1988. Administration of Criminal Justice: Speedy Disposal of Criminal Cases in the Lower Courts. Paper read at All-Nigeria Judges' Conference Papers 1988, September 4–11, 1988, at Abuja.

Crepaz, Markus, and Ann W. Moser. 2004. "The Impact of Collective and Competitive Veto Points." *Comparative Political Studies* no. 37 (3):259–285.

Dakolias, Maria. 1999. "Court Performance around the World: A Comparative Perspective." World Bank Technical Paper no. 430.

Dan-Musa, Iro Abubakar. 2004. *Party Politics and Power Struggle in Nigeria*. Edited by Anthony Ubani. Abuja: Regent.

Debt Management Department of the Central Bank. 1992. "Management of External Debt: Nigeria's Experience." *Central Bank of Nigeria Economic and Financial Review* no. 30 (1):70–81.

DeLancey, Virginia. 2001. "The Economies of Africa." In *Understanding Contemporary Africa*, edited by April A. Gordon and Donald L. Gordon, 101–42. Boulder, CO: Lynne Rienner.

Deng, Francis Mading, Daniel J. Deng, David K. Deng, and Vanessa Jiménez. 2008. *Identity, Diversity, and Constitutionalism in Africa*, 1st ed. Washington, DC: United States Institute of Peace.

Dent, M. J. 1971. "The Military and the Politicians." In *Nigerian Politics and Military Rule: Prelude to the Civil War*, edited by S. K. Panter-Brick, 78–93. London: Athlone Press University of London.

Deutsch, Karl W. 1961. "Social Mobilization and Political Development." *American Political Science Review* no. 55 (3):493–514.

Diamond, Larry. 1988. *Class, Ethnicity and Democracy in Nigeria: The Failure of the First Republic*. Houndmills, UK: Macmillan Press.

———. 1993. "Nigeria's Perennial Struggle against Corruption: Prospects for the Third Republic." *Corruption and Reform* no. 7:215–225.

Diamond, Larry Jay, Oyeleye Oyediran, and A. H. M Kirk-Greene. 1997. *Transition without End: Nigerian Politics and Civil Society under Babangida*. Boulder, CO: Lynne Rienner Publishers.

Diamond, Larry Jay, and Marc F. Plattner. 2010. *Democratization in Africa: Progress and Retreat*, 2nd ed., A Journal of Democracy Book. Baltimore: Johns Hopkins University Press.

Dike, Victor E. 2003. *Nigeria and the Politics of Unreason: A Study of the Obasanjo Regime*. London: Adonis & Abbey.

Dorman, Sara Rich. 2003. "NGOs and the Constitutional Debate in Zimbabwe: From Inclusion to Exclusion." *Journal of Southern African Studies* no. 29 (4):845–863. doi: 10.2307/3557390.

Doucouliagos, Hristos, and Mehmet Ali Ulubasoglu. 2008. "Democracy and Economic Growth: A Meta-Analysis." *American Journal of Political Science* no. 52 (1):61–83.

Downs, Anthony. 1957. *An Economic Theory of Democracy*. New York: Harper.

Drezner, Daniel W. 2006. "Notes from a Generalist." *Qualitative Methods* no. 4 (1):34–37.

Dudley, Billy J. 1971. "Western Nigeria and the Nigerian Crisis." In *Nigerian Politics and Military Rule: Prelude to the Civil War*, edited by S. K. Panter-Brick, 94–110. London: Athlone Press University of London.

   1973. *Instability and Political Order: Politics and Crisis in Nigeria*. Ibadan: University of Ibadan Press.

Eckstein, Harry. 1975. "Case Study and Theory in Political Science." In *Handbook of Political Science*, edited by Fred I. Greenstein and Nelson W. Polsby, 79–135. Reading, MA: Addison-Wesley.

Economist Intelligence Unit. 2010. Democracy Index 2010: Democracy in Retreat. London.

Edozie, Rita Kiki. 2009. "Electoral Authoritarians and Delegative Democrats: Reconstructing African Democratic Consolidation in Africa." In *Reconstructing the Third Wave of Democracy: Comparative African Democratic Politics*, 128–154. Lanham, MD: University Press of America.

Egbewole, Wahab. 2006. "Independent Judiciary and Sustainable Democracy." In *Challenges of Sustainable Democracy in Nigeria*, 209–234. Ibadan: John Archers.

Ekpo, Akpan H. 1994. "Fiscal Federalism: Nigeria's Post-Independence Experience, 1960–90." *World Development* no. 22 (8):1129–1146.

   1996. "Pattern of Public Expenditure in Nigeria: 1960–92." In *Economic Reform and Macroeconomic Management in Nigeria*, edited by Ademola Ariyo, 219–242. Ibadan: Centre for Public-Private Cooperation.

Elaigwu, J. Isawa, and Habu Galadima. 2003. "The Shadow of Sharia over Nigerian Federalism." *Publius* no. 33 (3):123–144.

Elias, Teslim O. 1971. *Nigerian Land Law*, 4th ed. London: Sweet and Maxwell.

Emelifeonwu, David. 1997. "1993: Crisis and Breakdown of Nigeria's Transition to Democracy." In *Dilemmas of Democracy in Nigeria*, edited by Paul Beckett and Crawford Young, 193–216. Rochester, NY: University of Rochester Press.

Eminue, Okon. 2006. "Executive-Legislative Relations: Some Preliminary Observations on the Budget Process." In *Challenges of Sustainable Democracy in Nigeria*, edited by Emmanuel O. Ojo, 154–182. Ibadan: John Archers Press.

Englebert, Pierre. 2009. *Africa: Unity, Sovereignty, and Sorrow*. Boulder, CO: Lynne Rienner.

Ezejiofor, G. 1977. "A Judicial Interpretation of the Constitution: The Nigerian Experience during the First Republic." In *The Supreme Court of Nigeria*, edited by A. B. Kasunmu, 67–89. Ibadan: Heinemann.

Fadahunsi, Akin. 2005. "The Obasanjo Administration, 1999–2003: An Appraisal of the Economy and the Proposed Redirection." In *Democratic Rebirth in Nigeria*, edited by Aaron T. Gana and Yakubu B. C. Omelle, 91–114. Plainsboro, NJ: African Centre for Democratic Governance.

Falola, Toyin, and Matthew Heaton. 2008. *A History of Nigeria*. Cambridge and New York: Cambridge University Press.

Falola, Toyin, and Julius Omozuanvbo Ihonvbere. 1985. *The Rise and Fall of Nigeria's Second Republic, 1979–84*. Third World Books. London: Zed Books.

Farris, Jacqueline, and Mohammed Bomoi. 2004. *Shehu Musa Yar'Adua: A Life of Service*. Abuja: Shehu Musa Yar'Adua Foundation.

Federal Government of Nigeria. 1960. *Report on the Nigeria Federal Elections, December 1959*. Lagos.

    1961. *Educational Development, 1961–1970*. Lagos: Federal Government Printer.

    1970. *Second National Development Plan, 1970–74*. Lagos: Federal Government Printer.

    1975. *First Report of the Anti-Inflation Task Force*. Lagos: Federal Ministry of Information Press.

    1981. *National Policy on Education, 1981*, rev. ed. Lagos: Federal Government Printer.

Federal Military Government. 1986. *Report and Recommendations of Justice Uwaifo Special Panel*. Lagos: Federal Military Government.

Federal Ministry of Economic Development. 1960. *National Development Plan, 1962–1968*. Lagos: Federal Ministry of Economic Development.

    1975. *Third National Development Plan, 1975–1980*, Vol. 1. Lagos. Federal Ministry of Economic Development.

Federal Ministry of Education. 1999–2000. Universal Basic Education for Nigeria: Proceedings of the Education Mini Summit, November 29, 1999, 2000, at Abuja.

Federal Office of Statistics. 1985. *Annual Abstract of Statistics 1985*, 1985 ed. Lagos: Federal Office of Statistics.

    1993. *Review of the Nigerian Economy 1992*. Lagos: Federal Office of Statistics.

Feltoe, Geoffrey. 2004. "The Onslaught against Democracy and Rule of Law in Zimbabwe in 2000." In *Zimbabwe: The Past Is the Future*, edited by David Harold-Barry, 193–223. Harare: Weaver Press.

Feng, Yi. 2003. *Democracy, Governance, and Economic Performance: Theory and Evidence*. Cambridge, MA, and London: MIT Press.

Ferree, Karen. 2011. *Framing the Race in South Africa: The Political Origins of Racial-Census Elections*. Cambridge and New York: Cambridge University Press.

Firmin-Sellers, Kathryn. 2007. *The Transformation of Property Rights in the Gold Coast: An Empirical Study Applying Rational Choice Theory*. Cambridge: Cambridge University Press.

"First Take Nigeria: More Presidential Turmoil." 2010. *Council on Foreign Relations*, February 24.

Fish, M. Steven, and Robin S. Brooks. 2004. "Does Diversity Hurt Democracy?" *Journal of Democracy* no. 15 (1):154–166.

Forrest, Tom. 1995. *Politics and Economic Development in Nigeria*, updated ed., *African Modernization and Development Series*. Boulder, CO: Westview Press.

Fosu, Augustin Kwasi. 1999. "The External Debt Burden and Economic Growth in the 1980s: Evidence from Sub-Saharan Africa." *Canadian Journal of Development Studies* no. 20 (2):307–318.

2007. "Fiscal Allocation for Education in Sub-Saharan Africa: Implications of the External Debt Service Constraint." *World Development* no. 35 (4):702–713.

Fosu, Augustin, and Ernest Aryeetey. 2008. "Ghana's Post-Independence Economic Growth, 1960–2000." In *The Economy of Ghana: Analytical Perspectives on Stability, Growth, and Poverty*, edited by Ernest Aryeetey Isser and Ravi Kanbur, 36–77. Accra: Woeli.

Frantz, Erica, and Natasha Ezrow. 2011. *The Politics of Dictatorship: Institutions and Outcomes in Authoritarian Regimes*. Boulder, CO: Lynne Rienner.

Freedom House. 2012. *Countries at the Crossroads*. New York: Freedom House.

Friedman, Milton. 1993. *Why Government Is the Problem, Essays in Public Policy*. Stanford, CA: Hoover Institution on War, Revolution, and Peace, Stanford University.

Galbraith, John Kenneth. 1976. *The Affluent Society*, 3rd rev. ed. Boston: Houghton Mifflin, original ed., 1958.

Gana, Aaron T., and Samuel G. Egwu. 2003. *Federalism in Africa: Framing the National Question*, Vol. 1. Trenton, NJ, and Eritrea: Africa World Press.

Gandhi, Jennifer. 2008. *Political Institutions under Dictatorship*. Cambridge and New York: Cambridge University Press.

Garba, Joseph Nanven. 1995. *Fractured History: Elite Shifts and Policy Changes in Nigeria*. Princeton, NJ, and Owerri: Sungai.

Gboyega, Alex. 1979. "The Making of the Nigerian Constitution." In *Nigerian Government and Politics under Military Rule, 1966–1979*, edited by Oyeleye Oyediran, 235–258. New York: St. Martin's Press.

1989. "The Public Service and Federal Character." In *Federal Character and Federalism in Nigeria*, edited by Peter P. Ekeh and Eghosa Osaghae, 164–187. Ibadan: Heinemann Educational Books.

Gboyega, Alex, Mobolaji Ogunsanya, and Bayo Okunade. 1998. *An Evaluation of the Liberalization of Funding and Administration of Primary Education in Nigeria as a Result of SAP, National Research Network on Liberalization Policies in Nigeria*. Ibadan: Nigerian Institute of Social and Economic Research.

Geddes, Barbara. 2003. *Paradigms and Sandcastles: Theory Building and Research Design in Comparative Politics*. Ann Arbor: University of Michigan Press.

Gelbach, Scott, and Edmund Malesky. 2010. "The Contribution of Veto Players to Economic Reform." *Journal of Politics* no. 72 (4):957–975.

George, Alexander L., and Andrew Bennett. 2004. *Case Studies and Theory Development in the Social Sciences*. *BCSIA Studies in International Security*, Cambridge, MA, and London: MIT Press.

Gibson, Clark C., and James D. Long. 2009. "The Presidential and Parliamentary Elections in Kenya, December 2007." *Electoral Studies* no. 28:497–502.

Glaeser, Edward L., Rafael La Porta, Florencio Lopez-de-Silanes, and Andrei Shleifer. 2004. "Do Institutions Cause Growth?" *Journal of Economic Growth* no. 9 (3):271–303.

Glewwe, Paul, and Michael Kremer. 2006. "Schools, Teachers, and Education Outcomes in Developing Countries." In *Handbook on the Economics of Education*, edited by E. A. Hanushek and F. Welch, 945–1011. Amsterdam: North Holland.

Godwin, Peter. 2010. *The Fear: Robert Mugabe and the Martyrdom of Zimbabwe*. New York: Little, Brown.

Gorodinichenko, Yuriy, and Yegor Grygorenko. 2008. "Are Oligarchs Productive? Theory and Evidence." *Journal of Comparative Economics* no. 36 (1):17–42.

Guma, Lance. 2009. "Zimbabwe: Barack Obama Plans Increased Pressure on Mugabe." January 28. Radio broadcast.

Gunning, Jan Willem. 2008. "Shocks, Risk, and African Growth." In *The Political Economy of Economic Growth in Africa, 1960–2000*, edited by Benno Ndulu, Stephen O'Connell, Robert Bates, Paul Collier and Chukwuma Soludo, 297–314. New York: Cambridge.

Gyimah-Boadi, E. 2007. "Political Parties, Elections, and Patronage." In *Votes, Money and Violence: Political Parties and Elections in Sub-Saharan Africa*, edited by Matthais Basedau, Gero Erdmann and Andreas Mehler. Uppsala: Sweden: Nordiska Afrikainstitutet.

2009. "Another Step Forward for Ghana." *Journal of Democracy* no. 20 (2):138–52.

Gyimah-Boadi, E., and Richard Asante. 2006. "Ethnic Structure, Inequality, and Public Sector Governance." In *Ethnic Inequalities and Public Sector Governance*, edited by Yusuf Bangura, 241–260. New York: Palgrave Macmillan and United Nations Research Institute for Social Development.

Habyarimana, James, Macartan Humphreys, Daniel Posner, and Jeremy M. Weinstein. 2007. "Why Does Ethnic Diversity Undermine Public Goods Provision?" *American Political Science Review* no. 101 (4):709–725.

2009. *Coethnicity: Diversity and the Dilemmas of Collective Action*. New York: Russell Sage Foundation.

Haggard, Stephan, and Mathew McCubbins. 2001. *Presidents, Parliaments, and Policy, Political Economy of Institutions and Decisions*. Cambridge and New York: Cambridge University Press.

Haggard, Stephen, and Robert Kaufman. 1998. "The Political Economy of Authoritarian Withdrawals." In *Origins of Liberty: Political and Economic Liberalization in the Modern World*, edited by Paul Drake and Mathew McCubbins, 92–114. Princeton, NJ: Princeton University Press.

Hallerberg, Mark. 2010. "Empirical Applications of Veto Player Analysis and Institutional Effectiveness." In *Reform Processes and Policy Change: Veto*

Players and Decision-Making in Modern Democracies, edited by Thomas Konig, George Tsebelis and Marc Debus, 21–43. New York: Springer.

Halperin, Morton H., Joseph T. Siegle, and Michael M. Weinstein. 2010. *The Democracy Advantage: How Democracies Promote Prosperity and Peace*, rev. ed. New York: Routledge.

Hamilton, Alexander, James Madison, John Jay, and Lawrence Goldman. 2008. *The Federalist Papers, Oxford World's Classics*. Oxford and New York: Oxford University Press.

Hamilton, Alexander, James Madison, John Jay, and Ian Shapiro. 2009. *The Federalist Papers: Alexander Hamilton, James Madison, John Jay. Rethinking the Western Tradition*. New Haven, CT: Yale University Press.

Hansen, Emmanuel. 1987. "The State and Popular Struggles in Ghana, 1982–86." In *Popular Struggles for Democracy in Africa*, edited by Peter Anyang Nyong'o, 170–208. London: Zed Books.

Hanushek, Eric A., and Ludger Woessmann. 2007. "The Role of Education Quality for Economic Growth." *SSRN eLibrary*.

Hatchard, John, and Tunde Ogowewo. 2003. *Tackling the Unconstitutional Overthrow of Democracies: Emerging Trends in the Commonwealth*. London: Commonwealth Secretariat.

Hazen, Jennifer M. 2009. "From Social Movement to Armed Group: A Case Study from Nigeria." *Contemporary Security Policy* no. 30 (2):281–300.

Heger, Lindsay, and Idean Salehyan. 2007. "Ruthless Rulers: Coalition Size and the Severity of Civil Conflict." *International Studies Quarterly* no. 51:385–403.

Henisz, Witold J. 2000. "The Institutional Environment for Economic Growth." *Economics and Politics* no. 12 (1):1–31.

Henisz, Witold, and Bennet Zelner. 2006. "Interest Groups, Veto Points, and Electricity Infrastructure Deployment." *International Organization* no. 60 (Winter):263–286.

Herbst, Jeffrey. 1990. "The Structural Adjustment of Politics in Africa." *World Development* no. 18 (7):949–958.

    1991. "Labor in Ghana under Structural Adjustment: The Politics of Acquiescence." In *Ghana: The Political Economy of Recovery*, edited by Donald Rothchild, 173–192. Boulder, CO: Lynne Rienner.

    1993. *The Politics of Reform in Ghana, 1982–1991*. Berkeley: University of California Press.

Hirschman, Albert O. 1970. *Exit, Voice, and Loyalty Responses to Decline in Firms, Organizations, and States*. Cambridge, MA: Harvard University Press.

Holland, Heidi. 2008. *Dinner with Mugabe*. New York: Penguin Books.

Holmes, Stephen. 2003. "Lineages of the Rule of Law." In *Democracy and the Rule of Law*, edited by Jose Maria Maravall and Adam Przeworski, 19–61. Cambridge: Cambridge University Press.

Horowitz, Donald. 1979. "About-Face in Africa: The Return to Civilian Rule in Nigeria." *Yale Review* no. 68 (2):192–206.

House of Representatives Ad-Hoc Committee. 2012. Report to Verify and Determine the Actual Subsidy Requirements and Monitor the Implementation of the Subsidy Regime in Nigeria. Abuja: National Assembly.

Howard, Rhoda. 1978. *Colonialism and Underdevelopment in Ghana*. New York: Africana.

Human Rights Watch. 2007. *Election or Selection?* New York: Human Rights Watch.

2011. *Perpetual Fear: Impunity and Cycles of Violence in Zimbabwe*. New York: Human Rights Watch.

Hutchful, Eboe. 2002. *Ghana's Adjustment Experience: The Paradox of Reform*. Geneva and Oxford: United Nations Research Institute for Social Development and James Currey.

Hyden, Goran. 2012. *African Politics in Comparative Perspective*, 2nd ed. Cambridge and New York: Cambridge University Press.

Ibrahim, Jibrin, and Okechukwu Ibeanu. 2009. "The 2007 Elections and the Subversion of Popular Mandate in Nigeria." In *Direct Capture: The 2007 Nigerian Elections and the Subversion of Popular Sovereignty*, edited by Jibrin Ibrahim and Okechukwu Ibeanu, 1–8. Abuja: Centre for Democracy and Development.

Ibrahim, Omar Farouk. 1997. "Religion and Politics: A View from the North." In *Transition without End Nigerian Politics and Civil Society under Babangida*, edited by Larry Jay Diamond, Oyeleye Oyediran and A. H. M Kirk-Greene, 427–447. Boulder, CO: Lynne Rienner.

Ikein, Augustine. 2008. "Oil and Federalism." In *Oil, Democracy, and the Promise of True Federalism in Nigeria*, edited by Augustine Ikein, D. S. P. Alamieyeseigha and Steve Azaiki, 85–93. Lanham, MD: University Press of America.

Ikein, Augustine A., D. S. P. Alamieyeseigha, and Steve Azaiki. 2008. *Oil, Democracy, and the Promise of True Federalism in Nigeria*. Lanham, MD: University Press of America.

Ikoku, S. G. 1985. *Nigeria's Fourth Coup d'Etat: Options for Modern Statehood*. Enugu, Nigeria: Fourth Dimension.

International Bank for Reconstruction and Development. 2009. *Doing Business in Nigeria 2010*. Washington, DC: World Bank.

Iwayemi, Akin. 1979. "The Military and the Economy." In *Nigerian Government and Politics under Military Rule, 1966–1979*, edited by Oyeleye Oyediran, 47–72. New York: St. Martin's Press.

Iyoha, Milton. 1997. "Policy Simulations with a Model of External Debt and Economic Growth in Sub-Saharan African Countries." *Nigerian Economic and Financial Review* no. 2:21–49.

2002. "Review of the 2001 Federal Budget Performance." *NCEMA Policy Analysis Series* no. 8 (1):27–43.

Jackson, Robert H., and Carl G. Rosberg. 1984. "Personal Rule: Theory and Practice in Africa." *Comparative Politics* no. 16 (4):421–42.

Jeffries, Richard. 1982. "Rawlings and the Political Economy of Underdevelopment in Ghana." *African Affairs* no. 81 (324):307–317.

1989. "Ghana: The Political Economy of Personal Rule." In *Contemporary West African States*, edited by Donald B. Cruise, John Dunn O'Brien and Richard Rathbone, 79–98. Cambridge: Cambridge University Press.

1991. "Leadership Commitment and Political Opposition to Structural Adjustment in Ghana." In *Ghana: The Political Economy of Recovery*, edited by Donald Rothchild, 157–171. Boulder, CO: Lynne Rienner.

Jega, Attahiru M. 2007. *Democracy, Good Governance and Development in Nigeria*. Ibadan: Spectrum.

Jensen, Nathan, and Leonard Wantchekon. 2004. "Resource Wealth and Political Regimes in Africa." *Comparative Political Studies* no. 37 (7):816–841.

Jockers, Heinz, Dirk Kohnert, and Paul Nugent. 2010. "The Successful Ghana Elections of 2008: A Convenient Myth?" *Journal of Modern African Studies* no. 481 (1):95–115.

Johnes, Geraint. 2006. "Education and Economic Growth." *SSRN eLibrary*.

Joireman, Sandra Fullerton. 2011. *Where There Is No Government: Enforcing Property Rights in Common Law Africa*. Oxford and New York: Oxford University Press.

Joseph, Richard A. 1987. *Democracy and Prebendal Politics in Nigeria the Rise and Fall of the Second Republic, African Studies Series*. Cambridge: Cambridge University Press.

Kandeh, Jimmy D. 2004. *Coups from Below: Armed Subalterns and State Power in West Africa*. New York and Houndmills, Palgrave Macmillan.

Kanyenze, Godfrey. 2004. "The Zimbabwe Economy 1980–2003: A ZCTU Perspective." In *Zimbabwe: The Past Is Future*, edited by David Harold-Barry, 107–146. Harare: Weaver Press.

Kapuscinski, Ryszard. 2001. *The Shadow of the Sun*. Translated by Klara Glowczewska. New York: Vintage International and Random House.

Karl, Terry Lynn. 1997. *The Paradox of Plenty: Oil Booms and Petro-states, Studies in International Political Economy*. Berkeley: University of California Press.

Keefer, Philip, and David Stasavage. 2003. "The Limits of Delegation: Veto Players, Central Bank Independence, and the Credibility of Monetary Policy." *American Political Science Review* no. 97 (3):407–420.

Kew, Darren. 2004. "The 2003 Elections: Hardly Credible but Acceptable." In *Crafting the New Nigeria: Confronting the Challenges*, edited by Robert I. Rotberg, 139–173. Boulder, CO: Lynne Rienner.

Kiai, Maina. 2008. "The Crisis in Kenya." *Journal of Democracy* no. 19 (3):162–168.

Killick, Tony. 1966. "The Possibilities of Economic Control." In *A Study of Contemporary Ghana: The Economy of Ghana*, edited by Walter Birmingham, I. Neustadt and E. N. Omaboe, 411–438. Evanston, IL: Northwestern University Press.

1978. *Development Economics in Action: A Study of Economic Policies in Ghana*. New York: St. Martin's Press.

King, Gary, Robert O. Keohane, and Sidney Verba. 1994. *Designing Social Inquiry: Scientific Inference in Qualitative Research*. Princeton, NJ: Princeton University Press.

Kirk-Greene, Anthony H. M. 1971. *Crisis and Conflict in Nigeria: A Documentary Sourcebook, 1966–1969*. Vol. 1: *January 1966–July 1967*. London: Oxford University Press.

Konig, Thomas, George Tsebelis, and Marc Debus. 2010. *Reform Processes and Policy Change: Veto Players and Decision-Making in Modern Democracies.* New York: Springer.

Kriger, Norma. 2003a. *Guerrilla Veterans in Post-War Zimbabwe: Symbolic and Violence Politics, 1980–87.* Cambridge: Cambridge University Press.

2003b. "War Veterans: Continuities between the Past and the Present." *African Studies Quarterly* no. 7 (2 & 3):139–152.

2008. "Can Elections End Mugabe's Dictatorship?" *Association of Concerned Africa Scholars Bulletin* no. 79:2–6.

Krugman, Paul R. 1997. *The Age of Diminished Expectations: U.S. Economic Policy in the 1990s,* 3rd ed. Cambridge, MA: MIT Press.

Kukah, Matthew H. 1999. *Democracy and Civil Society in Nigeria.* Ibadan: Spectrum Books.

Kukah, Matthew Hassan. 2003. *Religion, Politics and Power in Northern Nigeria.* Ibadan: Spectrum Books and Safari Books.

Kurtz, Marcus, and Sarah M. Brooks. 2011. "Conditioning the 'Resource Curse': Globalization, Human Capital, and Growth in Oil-Rich Nations." *Comparative Political Studies* no. 44 (6):747–770.

Kwakwa, Victoria, Adeola Adenikinju, Peter Mousley, and Mavis Oswusu-Gyamfi. 2008. "Binding Constraints to Growth in Nigeria." In *Economic Policy Options for a Prosperous Nigeria,* edited by Paul Collier, Chukwuma Soludo and Catherine Pattillo, 13–44. New York: Palgrave Macmillan.

Laakso, Liisa. 2003a. "Opposition Politics in Independent Zimbabwe." *African Studies Quarterly* no. 7 (2 & 3):113–137.

2003b. "Regional Voting and Cabinet Formation." In *Twenty Years of Independence in Zimbabwe: From Liberation to Authoritarianism,* edited by Staffan Darnolf and Liisa Laakso, 122–139. New York: Palgrave Macmillan.

Laitin, David. 1982. "The Sharia Debate and the Origins of Nigeria's Second Republic." *Journal of Modern African Studies* no. 20 (3):411–430.

1992. *Language Repertoires and State Construction in Africa.* Cambridge and New York: Cambridge University Press.

Laitin, David D. 1986. *Hegemony and Culture: Politics and Religious Change among the Yoruba.* Chicago: University of Chicago Press.

Lake, David. 2003. "The New Sovereignty in International Relations." *International Studies Review* no. 5 (3):303–323.

Lake, David, and Matthew Baum. 2001. "The Invisible Hand of Democracy: Political Control and the Provision of Public Services." *Comparative Political Studies* no. 34 (6):587–621.

Lalude, Goke. 2000. "The Consequences of Nigeria's Debt Burden on a New International Economic Order." *Nigerian Journal of Economic History* (3):74–83.

Lambsdorff, Johann Graf, Markus Taube, and Mattias Schramm. 2005. *The New Institutional Economics of Corruption.* London and New York: Routledge.

Lange, Matthew. 2009. *Lineages of Despotism and Development: British Colonialism and State Power.* Chicago: University of Chicago Press.

Langseth, Petter, and Abba Mohammed. 2002. *Strengthening Judicial Integrity and Capacity in Nigeria*. Abuja: Nigerian Institute for Advanced Legal Studies and the UN Office for Drug Control and Crime Prevention.

Lawan, Mamman. 2010. "Abuse of Impeachment Powers in Nigeria." *Journal of Modern African Studies* no. 48 (2):311–338.

Lebas, Adrienne. 2011. *From Protest to Parties: Party-Building and Democratization in Africa*. Oxford: Oxford University Press.

Lee, Jong-Wha, and Robert J. Barro. 2001. "Schooling Quality in a Cross-Section of Countries." *Economica* no. 68:465–488.

Lees, Charles. 2006. "We Are All Comparativists Now: Why and How Single-Country Scholarship Must Adapt and Incorporate the Comparative Politics Approach." *Comparative Political Studies* no. 39 (9):1084–1108.

Legal Defence Centre. 2004. *Nigeria: Tribunals and the 2003 Elections*. Translated by Basil Ugochukwu, International Foundation for Election Systems (Under contract with USAID). Lagos: Legal Defence Centre.

Leon, Tony. 2010. "The State of Liberal Democracy in Africa." In *Development Policy Analysis*, edited by Center for Global Liberty and Prosperity. Washington, DC: CATO Institute.

LeVan, A. Carl. 2005. "Federal Structure, Decentralization and Government Performance." In *Nigerian Federalism in Crisis: Critical Perspectives and Political Options*, edited by Ebere Onwudiwe and Rotimi T. Suberu, 207–219. Ibadan: Program on Ethnic and Federal Studies.

——— 2010. "The Political Economy of African Responses to the U.S. Africa Command." *Africa Today* no. 57 (1):2–23.

——— 2011. "Power Sharing and Inclusive Politics in Africa's Uncertain Democracies." *Governance: A Journal of Policy, Administration, and Institutions* no. 24 (1):31–53.

——— 2014. "Analytic Authoritarianism and Nigeria." *Commonwealth and Comparative Politics* no. 52 (2):1–20.

LeVan, A. Carl, Titi Pitso, and Bodunrin Adebo. 2003. "Elections in Nigeria: Is the Third Time a Charm?" *Journal of African Elections* no. 2 (2):30–47.

LeVan, A. Carl, and Patrick Ukata. 2010. "Nigeria." In *Countries at the Crossroads: A Survey of Democratic Governance 2010*, edited by Sanja Kelly, Christopher Walker and Jake Dizard. New York: Freedom House.

Levitsky, Steven R., and Lucan Way. 2012. "Beyond Patronage: Violent Struggle, Ruling Party Cohesion, and Authoritarian Durability." *Perspectives on Politics* no. 10 (4):869–889.

Levitsky, Steven, and Lucan Way. 2010. *Competitive Authoritarianism: Hybrid Regimes after the Cold War. Problems of international politics*. Cambridge and New York: Cambridge University Press.

Lewis, Peter M. 1994. "Endgame in Nigeria? The Politics of a Failed Democratic Transition." *African Affairs* 93 (372):323–340.

——— 1997. "Politics and the Economy: A Downward Spiral." In *Dilemmas of Democracy in Nigeria*, edited by Paul Beckett and Crawford Young, 303–28. Rochester, NY: University of Rochester Press.

——— 2007a. *Growing Apart: Oil, Politics, and Economic Change in Indonesia and Nigeria*. Ann Arbor: University of Michigan Press.

2007b. Identity, Institutions and Democracy in Nigeria. Afrobarometer Briefing Paper No. 68, http://www.afrobarometer.org/files/documents/working_papers/AfropaperNo68.pdf.

2008. "Growth without Prosperity in Africa." *Journal of Democracy* no. 19 (4):95–109.

2009. "Rules and Rents in Nigeria's National Assembly." In *Legislative Power in Emerging African Democracies*, edited by Joel D. Barkan, 166–204. Boulder, CO: Lynne Rienner.

Lewis, Peter M., Pearl T. Robinson, and Barnett Rubin. 1998. *Stabilizing Nigeria: Sanctions, Incentives, and Support for Civil Society*. New York: Century Foundation Press.

Lichbach, Mark. 2009. "Thinking and Working in the Midst of Things." In *Comparative Politics: Rationality, Culture, and Structure*, edited by Mark Lichbach and Alan Zukerman, 18–71. Cambridge: Cambridge University Press.

Lijphart, Arend. 1971. "Comparative Politics and the Comparative Method." *American Political Science Review* no. 65:682–693.

1999. *Patterns of Democracy: Government Forms and Performance in Thirty-Six Countries*. New Haven, CT: Yale University Press.

2012. *Patterns of Democracy: Government Forms and Performance in Thirty-Six Countries*, 2nd ed. New Haven, CT: Yale University Press.

Lindberg, Staffan I. 2006. *Democracy and Elections in Africa*. Baltimore: Johns Hopkins University Press.

2009. *Democratization by Elections: A New Mode of Transition*. Baltimore: Johns Hopkins University Press.

Lindberg, Staffan I., and M. K. C. Morrison. 2008. "Are African Voters Really Ethnic or Clientelistic? Survey Evidence from Ghana." *Political Science Quarterly* no. 123 (1):95–122.

Lindberg, Staffan, and Youngmei Zhou. 2009. "Co-Optation Despite Democratization in Ghana." In *Legislative Power in Emerging African Democracies*, edited by Joel Barkan, 147–175. Boulder, CO: Lynne Rienner.

Linz, Juan J. 1975. "Totalitarian and Authoritarian Regimes." In *Handbook of Political Science*, edited by Fred Greenstein and Nelson Polsby, 175–411. Reading, MA: Addison-Wesley.

Lipset, Seymour Martin. 1959. "Some Social Requisites of Democracy: Economic Development and Political Legitimacy." *American Political Science Review* no. 53 (1):69–105.

1998. "George Washington and the Founding of Democracy." *Journal of Democracy* no. 9 (4):24–38.

Livingston, William S. 1956. *Federalism and Constitutional Change*. Oxford: Clarendon Press.

Logan, Carolyn, and Robert Mattes. 2010. Democratizing the Measurement of Democratic Quality: Public Attitude Data and the Evaluation of African Political Regimes. Afrobarometer Working Paper No. 123, http://www.afrobarometer.org/files/documents/working_papers/AfropaperNo123.pdf.

Looney, Robert E., and P. C. Frederiksen. 1987. "Consequences of Military and Civilian Rule in Argentina: An Analysis of Central Government Budgetary Tradeoffs, 1961–1982." no. 20 (1):34–46.

Luckham, Robin. 1971a. *The Nigerian Military: A Sociological Analysis of Authority and Revolt, 1960–67*. Cambridge: Cambridge University Press.

1971b. "Officers and Gentlemen of the Nigerian Army." *Transition* no. 39:38–55.

Lupia, Arthur, and Kaare Strøm. 2008. "Bargaining, Transaction Costs, and Coalition Governance." In *Cabinets and Coalition Bargaining: The Democratic Life Cycle in Western Europe*, edited by Kaare Strøm, Wolfgang Muller and Torbjorn Bergman, 85–122. Oxford: Oxford University Press.

Lyne, Mona. 2008. *The Voter's Dilemma and Democratic Accountability: Latin America and Beyond*. University Park: Penn State University Press.

MacIntyre, Andrew. 2001. "Institutions and Institutions and Investors: The Politics of the Financial Crisis in Southeast Asia." *International Organization* no. 55 (1):81–122.

MacLean, Lauren M. 2010. *Informal Institutions and Citizenship in Rural Africa: Risk and Reciprocity in Ghana and Cote d'Ivoire*. Cambridge and New York: Cambridge University Press.

Madison, James. 2006a. "Defense of the Constitution." In *Selected Writings of James Madison*, edited by Ralph Ketcham, 142–53. Indianapolis and Cambridge: Hackett, original ed., 1788.

2006b. "Judicial Power." In *Selected Writings of James Madison*, edited by Ralph Ketcham, 155–58. Indianapolis and Cambridge: Hackett Publishing, original ed., 1788.

2006c. "Political Essays: Government and Government in the United States." In *Selected Writings of James Madison*, edited by Ralph Ketcham, 210–213. Indianapolis and Cambridge: Hackett Publishing, original ed., 1792.

Magaloni, Beatriz. 2008. "Credible Power-Sharing and the Longevity of Authoritarian Rule." *Comparative Political Studies* no. 41 (4/5):715–741.

Mahama, John Dramani. 2012. *My First Coup d'Etat and Other True Stories from the Lost Decades of Africa*, 1st U.S. ed. New York: Bloomsbury.

Mailafia, Obadiah. 2008. "Economic Growth and Policy Choice in Nigeria: Lessons from the Asia Pacific." In *Economic Policy Options for a Prosperous Nigeria*, edited by Paul Collier, Chukwuma Soludo and Catherine Pattillo, 167–184. New York: Palgrave Macmillan.

Mainwaring, Scott, and Anibal Perez-Linan. 2003. "Level of Development and Democracy: Latin American Exceptionalism, 1945–1996." *Comparative Political Studies* no. 36 (9):1031–1067.

Malesky, Edmund, and Paul Schuler. 2010. "Nodding or Needling: Analyzing Delegate Responsiveness in an Authoritarian Parliament." *American Political Science Review* no. 104 (3):482–502.

Malik, Adeel, and Francis Teal. 2008. "Towards a More Competitive Manufacturing Sector." In *Economic Policy Options for a Prosperous Nigeria*, edited by Paul Collier, Chukwuma Soludo and Catherine Pattillo, 247–274. New York: Palgrave Macmillan.

Mamdani, Mahmood. 1995. "A Critique of the State and Civil Society Paradigm in Africanist Studies." In *African Studies in Social Movements and Democracy*, edited by Mahmood Mamdani and Ernest Wamba-dia-Wamba, 602–616.

Dakkar, Senegal: Council for the Development of Social Science Research in Africa.

1996. *Citizen and Subject: Contemporary Africa and the Legacy of Late Colonialism. Princeton Studies in Culture/Power/History.* Princeton, NJ: Princeton University Press.

1999. "Historicizing Power and Responses to Power: Indirect Rule and Its Reform." *Social Research* no. 66 (3):859–886.

2008. "Lessons of Zimbabwe: Mugabe in Context." *London Review of Books* no. 30 (23).

Manji, Ambreena. 2005. "Cause and Consequence in Law and Development." *Journal of Modern African Studies* no. 41 (1):119–138.

Masunungure, Eldred. 2009. "Introduction." In *Defying the Winds of Change: Zimbabwe's 2008 Elections*, edited by Eldred Masunungure, 1–10. Harare: Weaver Press.

Masunungure, Eldred V., and Simon Badza. 2010. "The Internationalization of the Zimbabwe Crisis: Multiple Actors, Competing Interests." *Journal of Developing Societies* no. 26 (2):207–231.

McKinsey Global Institute. 2010. *Lions on the Move: The Progress and Potential of African Economies.*

Meredith, Martin. 2007. *Mugabe: Power, Plunder, and the Struggle for Zimbabwe's Future.* New York: Public Affairs.

2011. *The Fate of Africa: A History of Fifty Years of Independence*, rev. and updated ed., original ed., 2006. New York: Public Affairs.

Miguel, Edward. 2004. "Tribe or Nation? Nation Building and Public Goods in Kenya versus Tanzania." *World Politics* no. 56:327–62.

Moghalu, Kingsley Chiedu. 2013. *Emerging Africa: How the Global Economy's "Last Frontier" Can Prosper and Matter.* Ibadan: Bookcraft.

Mohamed, Mutasim Ahmed Abdelmawla. 2005. "The Impact of External Debts on Economic Growth: An Empirical Assessment of the Sudan, 1978–2001." *Eastern Africa Social Science Research Review* no. 21 (2):53–66.

Mohammed, Kyari. 2005. "Religion, Federalism and the Shari'a Project in Northern Nigeria." In *Nigerian Federalism in Crisis: Critical Perspectives and Political Options*, edited by Ebere Onwudiwe and Rotimi T. Suberu, 147–164. Ibadan: Program on Ethnic and Federal Studies.

Montesquieu, Charles de Secondat, Anne M. Cohler, Basia Carolyn Miller, and Harold Samuel Stone. 1989. *The Spirit of the Laws. Cambridge Texts in the History of Political Thought.* Cambridge and New York: Cambridge University Press.

Moore, David. 2008. "Coercion, Consent, Context: Operation Murambatsvina and ZANU(PF)'s Illusory Quest for Hegemony." In *The Hidden Dimensions of Operation Murambatsvina*, edited by Maurice Vambe, 25–39. Harare: Weaver Press.

Moore, Winston, and Chrystol Thomas. 2010. "A Meta-Analysis of the Relationship between Debt and Growth." *International Journal of Development Issues* no. 9 (3):214–225.

Morlino, Leonardo. 2009. "Are There Hybrid Regimes? Or Are They Just an Optical Illusion?" *European Political Science Review* no. 1 (2):273–296.

Moyo, Sam. 2011. "Three Decades of Agrarian Reform in Zimbabwe." *Journal of Peasant Studies* no. 38 (3):493–531.

Muhammadu, Turi, and Mohammed Haruna. 1979. "The Civil War." In *Nigerian Government and Politics under Military Rule, 1966–1979*, edited by Oyeleye Oyediran, 25–46. New York: St. Martin's Press.

Mulligan, Casey B., Ricard Gil, and Xavier Sala-i-Martin. 2004. "Do Democracies Have Different Public Policies than Nondemocracies?" *Journal of Economic Perspectives* no. 18 (1):51–74.

National Democratic Institute for International Affairs. 2012. Final Report on the 2011 Nigerian General Elections. Washington, DC: National Democratic Institute.

National Primary Education Commission. 1999. *Social Sector Client Consultations: The Case of Public Primary Education in Nigeria*. Abuja.

Ndapwadze, Anyway Chingwete, and Ethel Muchena. 2009. "The Quest for Change: Public Opinion and the Harmonized March Elections." In *Defying the Winds of Change: Zimbabwe's 2008 Elections*, edited by Eldred Masunungure. Harare: Weaver Press.

Ndulu, Benno. 2008. "The Evolution of Global Development Paradigms and Their Influence on African Economic Growth." In *The Political Economy of Economic Growth, 1960–2000*, edited by Benno Ndulu, Stephen O'Connell, Robert Bates, Paul Collier and Chukwuma Soludo, 315–347. Cambridge: Cambridge University Press.

Ndulu, Benno J., and Stephen O'Connell. 2008. "Policy Plus: African Growth Performance, 1960–2000." In *The Political Economy of Economic Growth in Africa, 1960–2000*, edited by Benno Ndulu, O'Connell, Robert Bates, Paul Collier and Chukwuma Soludo, 3–75. Cambridge and New York: Cambridge University Press.

Ndulu, Benno J., Stephen A. O'Connell, Robert H. Bates, Paul Collier, and Chukwuma Soludo. 2008. *The Political Economy of Economic Growth in Africa, 1960–2000*, Vol. 1. Cambridge and New York: Cambridge University Press.

Nigerian Bureau of Statistics. 2012. *Nigeria Poverty Profile 2011*.

Ninsin, Kwame. 1991. "The PNDC and the Problem of Legitimacy." In *Ghana: The Political Economy of Recovery*, edited by Donald Rothchild, 49–68. Boulder, CO: Lynne Rienner.

Nnanna, O. J. 2002. "Monetary and Financial Sector Policy Measures in the 2002 Budget." *NCEMA Policy Analysis Series* no. 8 (1):45–61.

Norris, Pippa. 2008. *Driving Democracy: Do Power-Sharing Institutions Work?* Cambridge and New York: Cambridge University Press.

North, Douglass. 1990. *Institutions, Institutional Change and Economic Performance*. Cambridge and New York: Cambridge University Press.

North, Douglass, and Robert P. Thomas. 1973. *The Rise of the Western World: A New Economic History*. Cambridge: Cambridge University Press.

North, Douglass, and Barry Weingast. 1989. "Constitutions and Commitment: The Evolution of Institutions Governing Public Choice in 17th Century England." *Journal of Economic History* no. 49 (4).

Nwajiaku, Kathryn. 1994. "The National Conferences of Benin and Togo Revisited." *Journal of Modern African Studies* no. 32 (3):429–447.

Nyerere, Julius. 1973. "Freedom and Development." In *Freedom and Development: A Selection from Writings and Speeches, 1968–1973*, edited by Julius Nyerere. London: Oxford University Press.

Obasanjo, Olusegun. 2004. *Nzeogwu*. Ibadan: Spectrum Books, original ed., 1987.

2008. "Niger Delta Development Commission: A Federal Government Perspective." In *Oil, Democracy, and the Promise of True Federalism in Nigeria*, edited by Augustine Ikein, D. S. P. Alamieyeseigha and Steve Azaiki, 103–108. Lanham, MD: University Press of America.

Obidi, S. S. 1998. "Institutional Arrangements for the Management of Primary Education in Nigeria, 1988–1993." *Quarterly Journal of Administration* no. 29 (1 and 2):274–280.

O'Donnell, Guillermo. 1999. *Counterpoints: Selected Essays on Authoritarianism and Democratization*. Notre Dame, IN: University of Notre Dame Press.

2003. "Horizontal Accountability: The Legal Institutionalization of Mistrust." In *Democratic Accountability in Latin America*, edited by Scott Mainwaring and Christopher Welna, 34–54. New York: Oxford University Press.

Ojo, Abiola. 1987. *Constitutional Law and Military Rule in Nigeria*. Ibadan: Evans Brothers.

Okafor, Obiora Chinedu. 2010. "The Nigerian Courts and Labour-Led Anti–Fuel Price Hike Struggles, 1999–2007." *Journal of African Law* no. 54:95–118.

Okafor, Stanley, S. I. Abumere, Layi Egunjobi, and D. B. Ekpenyong. 1998. *Structural Adjustment and Access to Essential Social Services: A Case Study of Health Care Services in Selected States*. Ibadan: Nigerian Institute of Social and Economic Research.

Okediji, Tade. 2011. "Social Fragmentation and Economic Growth: Evidence from Developing Countries." *Journal of Institutional Economics* no. 7 (1):77–104.

Okogu, Bright, and Philip Osafo-Kwaako. 2008. "Issues in Fiscal Policy Management under the Economic Reforms, 2003–07." In *Economic Policy Options for a Prosperous Nigeria*, edited by Paul Collier, Chukwuma Soludo and Catherine Pattillo, 187–203. New York: Palgrave Macmillan.

Okoye, Festus. 1997. *Special and Military Tribunals and the Administration of Justice in Nigeria*. Kaduna: Human Rights Monitor.

Okunrounmu, T. O. 1996. "The 1995 Budget Performance: A Review." *NCEMA Policy Analysis Series* no. 2 (1):11–21.

Olaniyan, I. F. 1996. "Fiscal Policy Issues and Expenditure Programmes in the 1996 Budget." *NCEMA Policy Analysis Series* no. 2 (1):55–69.

Olanrewaju, Ayo. 1992. *The Bar and the Bench in Defence of Rule of Law in Nigeria*. Lagos: Nigerian Law.

Olawoye, C. 1974. *Title to Land in Nigeria*. Lagos: University of Lagos Press.

Olivier de Sardan, J. P. 1999. "A Moral Economy of Corruption in Africa?" *Journal of Modern African Studies* no. 37:25–52.

Olkany, M. C. 1986. *The Nigerian Law of Property*. Enugu, Nigeria: Fourth Dimension.

Olson, Mancur. 1965. *The Logic of Collective Action: Public Goods and the Theory of Groups*. Cambridge, MA, and London: Harvard University Press.

2000. *Power and Prosperity: Outgrowing Communist and Capitalist Dictatorships*. New York: Basic Books.

Olugbemi, Stephen O. 1979. "The Civil Service: An Outsider's View." In *Nigerian Government and Politics under Military Rule, 1966–1979,* edited by Oyeleye Oyediran, 96–109. New York: St. Martin's Press.

Olukoshi, Adebayo O. 1993. *The Politics of Structural Adjustment in Nigeria.* London, Ibadan, and Portsmouth, NH: James Currey, Heinemann Educational Books, and Heinemann.

1995. "Bourgeois Social Movements and the Struggle for Democracy in Nigeria: An Inquiry into the 'Kaduna Mafia.'" In *African Studies in Social Movements and Democracy,* edited by Mahmood Mamdani and Ernest Wamba-dia-Wamba, 245–278. Dakkar, Senegal: Council for the Development of Social Science Research in Africa.

Oluyede, P. A. 1985. "Development in Land Law and Law of Conveyancing." In *The Challenge of the Nigerian Nation: An Examination of Its Legal Development, 1960–1985,* edited by T. Akinola Aguda, 94–123. Ibadan: Heinemann Educational Books.

Oluyede, Peter. 1989. *Modern Nigerian Land Law.* Ibadan: University of Ibadan Press.

Omoruyi, Omo. 1989. "Federal Character and the Party System in the Second Republic." In *Federal Character and Federalism in Nigeria,* edited by Peter Ekeh and Eghoasa Osaghae, 188–229. Ibadan: Heinemann.

1999. *The Tale of June 12: The Betrayal of the Democratic Rights of Nigerians.* London: Press Alliance Network.

Omotola, J. Shola. 2010. "Elections and Democratic Transition in Nigeria under the Fourth Republic." *African Affairs* no. 109 (437):535–553.

Onoma, Ato Kwamena. 2010. *The Politics of Property Rights Institutions in Africa.* Cambridge and New York: Cambridge University Press.

Onwudiwe, Ebere, and Rotimi T. Suberu. 2005. *Nigerian Federalism in Crisis: Critical Perspectives and Political Options.* Ibadan: Program on Ethnic and Federal Studies.

Orojo, Olakunle J. 1992. *Company Law and Practice in Nigeria.* Lagos: Mbeji and Associates.

Osaghae, Eghosa E. 1989. "The Federal Cabinet, 1951–1984." In *Federal Character and Federalism in Nigeria,* edited by Peter Ekeh and Eghosa Osaghae. Ibadan: Heinemann Educational Books.

1998. *Crippled Giant: Nigeria since Independence.* Bloomington: Indiana University Press.

Osaghae, Eghosa. 2010. "The Limits of Charismatic Authority and the Challenges of Leadership in Nigeria." *Journal of Contemporary African Studies* no. 28 (4):407–422.

Osili, Una Okonkwo. 2008. "The Impact of Universal Primary Education on Socio-Economic Outcomes: A Nigerian Experiment." In *Economic Policy Options for a Prosperous Nigeria,* edited by Paul Collier, Chukwuma Soludo and Catherine Pattillo, 373–396. New York: Palgrave Macmillan.

Osipitan, T. 1987. "Administration of Criminal Justice: Fair Trial, Presumption of Innocence and the Special Military Tribunals." In *Law and Development*, edited by J. A. Omotola and A. A. Adeogun. Lagos: Lagos University Press.

Othman, Shehu. 1989. "Nigeria: Power for Profit – Class, Corporatism, and Factionalism in the Military." In *Contemporary West African States*, edited by Donal B. O'Brien, John Dunn and Richard Rathbone, 113–144. Cambridge and New York: Cambridge University Press.

Ottaway, Marina. 2003. *Democracy Challenged: The Rise of Semi-Authoritarianism*. Boulder, CO: Lynne Rienner.

Otubanjo, Femi. 1989. "National Security." In *Nigeria since Independence: The First 25 Years*, edited by Tekena Tamuno and J. A. Atanda, 44–64. Ibadan: Heinemann.

Oyediran, Oyeleye. 1979. *Nigerian Government and Politics under Military Rule, 1966–1979*. New York: St. Martin's Press.

    1997. "The Political Bureau." In *Transition without End: Nigerian Politics and Civil Society under Babangida*, edited by Larry Diamond, Anthony Kirk-Greene and Oyeleye Oyediran, 81–103. Boulder, CO, and London: Lynne Rienner.

Oyediran, Oyeleye, and Alex Gboyega. 1979. "Local Government and Administration." In *Nigerian Government and Politics under Military Rule, 1966–1979*, edited by Oyeleye Oyediran, 169–191. New York: St. Martin's Press.

Oyugi, Walter. 2006. "Coalition Politics and Governments in Africa." *Journal of Contemporary African Studies* no. 24 (1):53–79.

Paden, John. 2004. "Unity with Diversity: Toward Democratic Federalism." In *Crafting the New Nigeria: Confronting the Challenges*, edited by Robert I. Rotberg, 17–37. Boulder, CO: Lynne Rienner.

    2005. *Muslim Civic Cultures and Conflict Resolution: The Challenge of Democratic Federalism in Nigeria*. Washington, DC: Brookings Institution Press.

Parker, Richard. 2005. *John Kenneth Galbraith: His Life, His Politics, His Economics*. New York: HarperCollins.

Pattillo, Catherine, Helene Poirson, and Luca Ricci. 2004. "What Are the Channels through Which External Debt Affects Growth?" *IMF Working Paper* no. 4 (15).

Pavão, Nara. 2010. "Review: Counting Veto Players." *American Political Science Association Comparative Politics* no. 21 (1):25–27.

Perlmutter, Amos. 1981. *Modern Authoritarianism: A Comparative Institutional Analysis*. New Haven, CT, and London: Yale University Press.

Phelps, Edmund. 1973. "Inflation in the Theory of Public Finance." *Swedish Journal of Economics* no. 75 (1):67–82.

Phillips, Adedotun O. 1975. "Revenue Allocation in Nigeria, 1970–1980." *Nigerian Journal of Economic and Social Sciences* no. 17 (2):1–28.

Pierson, Paul. 2000. "Increasing Returns, Path Dependence, and the Study of Politics." *The American Political Science Review* no. 94 (2):251–267.

Pistor, Katharina, and Philip A. Wellons. 1999. *The Role of Law and Legal Institutions in Asian Economic Development, 1960–1995*. Oxford and New York: Oxford University Press.

Pitcher, Anne, Mary H. Moran, and Michael Johnston. 2009. "Rethinking Patrimonialism and Neopatrimonialism in Africa." *African Studies Review* no. 52 (1):125–56.

Please, Stanley. 1967. "Saving through Taxation–Reality or Mirage." *Finance and Development* no. 4 (1):24–32.

Posner, Daniel. 2004. "The Political Salience of Cultural Difference: Why Chewas and Tumbukas are Allies in Zambia and Adversaries in Malawi." *American Political Science Review* no. 98:529–545.

2005. *Institutions and Ethnic Politics in Africa*. Cambridge and New York: Cambridge University Press.

Posner, Daniel, and Daniel Young. 2007. "The Institutionalization of Political Power in Africa." *Journal of Democracy* no. 18 (3):126–140.

Prempeh, Kwasi. 2010. "President's Untamed." In *Democratization in Africa: Progress and Retreat*, edited by Larry Jay Diamond and Marc F. Plattner, 18–32. Baltimore: Johns Hopkins University Press.

Programme, Universal Basic Education. 2003. *UBE Annual Report 2002*. Abuja: Universal Basic Education Programme.

Przeworski, Adam. 2003. *States and Markets: A Primer in Political Economy*. Cambridge and New York: Cambridge University Press.

2010. *Democracy and the Limits of Self-Government*. Cambridge: Cambridge University Press.

Przeworski, Adam, Michael E. Alvarez, Jose Antonio Cheibub, and Fernando Limongi. 2000. *Democracy and Development: Political Institutions and Material Well-Being in the World, 1950–1990*. Cambridge Studies in the Theory of Democracy. Cambridge and New York: Cambridge University Press.

Psacharopoulos, George. 2006. "The Value of Investment in Education: Theory, Evidence, and Policy." *Journal of Education Finance* no. 32 (2):113–136.

Raadschelders, Jos, and Mark R. Rutgers. 1996. "The Evolution of Civil Service Systems." In *Civil Service Systems in Comparative Perspective*, edited by Hans A. G. M. Bekke, James L. Perry and Theo A. J. Toonen, 67–99. Bloomington, IN: Indiana University Press.

Radelet, Steven. 2010. *Emerging Africa: How 17 Countries Are Leading the Way*. Washington, DC: Center for Global Development.

Rakner, Lise, and Nicolas Van de Walle. 2009. "Democratization by Elections? Opposition Weakness in Africa." *Journal of Democracy* no. 20 (3):108–121.

Ram, Megha, and Kaare Strøm. 2013. Mutual Veto and Power-Sharing. *Midwest Political Science Association*. Chicago.

Ranger, Terrence. 2009. "Re: Lessons of Zimbabwe." *Association of Concerned Africa Scholars Bulletin* no. 82:14.

Ray, Donald I. 1986. *Ghana: Politics, Economics and Society*. London: Frances Pinter.

Remmer, Karen L. 1989. "Neopatrimonialism: The Politics of Military Rule in Chile, 1973–1987." *Comparative Politics* no. 21 (2):149–170.

Riker, William H. 1962. *The Theory of Political Coalitions*. Westport, CT: Greenwood Press.

Robinson, James A., Ragnar Torvik, and Thierry Verdier. 2006. "Political Foundations of the Resource Curse." *Journal of Development Economics* no. 79 (2):447–468.

Robinson, Pearl T. 1994. "The National Conference Phenomenon in Francophone Africa." *Comparative Studies in Society and History* no. 36 (3):575–610.

Roeder, Philip. 1994. "Varieties of Post-Soviet Authoritarian Regimes." *Post-Soviet Affairs* no. 10 (1):61–101.

Rose-Ackerman, Susan. 1999. *Corruption and Government*. Cambridge: Cambridge University Press.

Rothchild, Donald. 1991. "Ghana and Structural Adjustment: An Overview." In *Ghana: The Political Economy of Recovery*, edited by Donald Rothchild, 3–17. Boulder, CO: Lynne Rienner.

Rothchild, Donald, and E. Gyimah-Boadi. 1989. "Populism in Ghana and Burkina-Faso." *Current History*:221–244.

Rueschemeyer, Dietrich, Evelyne Huber Stephens, and John D. Stephens. 1992. *Capitalist Development and Democracy*. Chicago: University of Chicago Press.

Rustow, Dankwart A. 1970. "Transitions to Democracy: Toward a Dynamic Model." *Comparative Politics* no. 2 (3):337–363.

Sachs, Jeffrey D. 2012. "Government, Geography, and Growth." *Foreign Affairs*.

Sakyi, E. Kojo. 2010. "Overview of Article 78(1) and Executive-Legislative Relations under the 1992 Constitution." *African Journal of Political Science and International Relations* no. 4 (7):263–271.

Salih, Mohamed Abdel Rahim M. 2003. *African Political Parties: Evolution, Institutionalism and Governance*. London and Sterling, VA: Pluto Press.

Samuels, David J., and Matthew S. Shugart. 2010. *Presidents, Parties, and Prime Ministers: How the Separation of Powers Affects Party Organization and Behavior*. Cambridge: Cambridge University Press.

Sanders, Thomas G. 1978. "Military Government in Chile." In *The Politics of Antipolitics*, edited by Brian Loveman and Thomas M. Davies, 270–287. Lincoln and London: University of Nebraska Press.

Sanusi, H. U. 2002. "Fiscal Policy Focus of the 2002 Budget." *NCEMA Policy Analysis Series* no. 8 (1):79–89.

Sartori, Giovanni. 1970. "Concept Misformation in Comparative Politics." *American Political Science Review* no. 64 (4):1033–1053.

Saunders, Richard. 2007. "Trade Union Struggles for Autonomy and Democracy in Zimbabwe." In *Trade Unions and the Coming of Democracy in Africa*, edited by Jon Kraus, 123–156. New York: Palgrave.

Schatz, Sayre P. 1977. *Nigerian Capitalism*. Berkeley: University of California Press.

Schatz, Sayre. 1984. "Pirate Capitalism and the Inert Economy of Nigeria." *Journal of Modern African Studies* no. 22 (1).

Schedler, Andreas. 2006. *Electoral Authoritarianism: The Dynamics of Unfree Competition*. Boulder, CO, and London: Lynne Rienner.

Schiavon, Jorge A. 2000. "Structural Reforms in Latin America: International and Domestic Constraints in the Initiation, Implementation, and Consolidation of the Structural Reform Process." *Latin American Studies Association* and *Centro de Investigacion y Docencia Economicas*. Paper presented at the Latin American Studies Association Annual Meeting in Miami, March 16–18, 2000.

Schneider, Cathy Lisa. 1995. *Shantytown Protest in Pinochet's Chile*. Philadelphia: Temple University Press.

Schultz, T. Paul. 1999. "Health and Schooling Investments in Africa." *Journal of Economic Perspectives* no. 13 (3):67–88.

Shaxson, Nicholas. 2007a. "Oil, Corruption, and the Resource Curse." *International Affairs* no. 83:1123–40.

2007b. *Poisoned Wells: The Dirty Politics of African Oil*. New York: Palgrave Macmillan.

Sheehan, Colleen A. 2009. *James Madison and the Spirit of Republican Self-Government*. New York: Cambridge University Press.

Shevtsova, Lilia. 2001. "Russia's Hybrid Regime." *Journal of Democracy* no. 12 (4):65–70.

Shugart, Matthew S., and John Carey. 1992. *Presidents and Assemblies*. Cambridge: Cambridge University Press.

Sklar, Richard. 2001. "An Elusive Target: Nigeria Fends Off Sanctions." In *Nigeria during the Abacha Years, 1993–1998*, edited by 'Kunle Amuwo, Daniel C. Bach and Yann Lebeau, 259–288. Ibadan, Nigeria: Institut Francais de Recherche en Afrique.

2002. "Nigerian Politics in Perspective, 1967; Postscript 1969." In *African Politics in Postimperial Times: The Essays of Richard L. Sklar*, edited by Toyin Falola, 333–348. Trenton, NJ: Africa World Press.

Sklar, Richard L. 2004. *Nigerian Political Parties: Power in an Emergent African Nation*. Trenton, NJ, and Eritrea: Africa World Press and Princeton University Press, original ed., 1963.

Slovik, Milan W. 2012. *The Politics of Authoritarian Rule*. New York: Cambridge University Press.

Smith, Charles Anthony, and Mark Jorgensen Farrales. 2010. "Court Reform in Transitional States: Chile and the Philippines." *Journal of International Relations and Development* no. 13 (2):163–193.

Smith, Daniel Jordan. 2007. *A Culture of Corruption: Everyday Deception and Popular Discontent in Nigeria*. Princeton, NJ: Princeton University Press.

Stasavage, David. 2005a. "Democracy and Education Spending in Africa." *American Journal of Political Science* no. 49 (2):343–358.

2005b. "The Role of Democracy in Uganda's Move to Universal Primary Education." *Journal of Modern African Studies* no. 43 (1):53–73.

Stepan, Alfred. 1999. "Federalism and Democracy: Beyond the U.S. Model." *Journal of Democracy* no. 10 (4):19.

Strøm, Kaare. 2000. "Delegation and Accountability in Parliamentary Democracies." *European Journal of Political Research* no. 37 (3):261–89.

Strøm, Kaare, Wolfgang C. Müller, and Torbjörn Bergman. 2003. *Delegation and Accountability in Parliamentary Democracies*. Oxford: Oxford University Press.

Suberu, Rotimi. 2000. "States' Creation and the Political Economy of Nigerian Federalism." In *Federalism and Political Restructuring in Nigeria*, edited by

'Kunle Amuwo, Adigun Agbaje, Rotimi Suberu and Georges Herault, 276–296. Ibadan: Spectrum.

2004. "Democratizing Nigeria's Federal Experiment." In *Crafting the New Nigeria: Confronting the Challenges*, edited by Robert I. Rotberg, 61–83. Boulder, CO: Lynne Rienner.

Suberu, Rotimi T. 1997. "Religion and Politics: A View from the South." In *Transition without End: Nigerian Politics and Civil Society Under Babangida*, edited by Larry Diamond, Anthony Kirk-Greene and Oyeleye Oyediran, 401–425. Boulder and London: Lynne Rienner Publishers.

2001. *Federalism and Ethnic Conflict in Nigeria*. Washington, DC: United States Institute of Peace Press.

Szereszewski, Robert. 1960. "The Sectoral Structure of the Economy, 1960." In *A Study of Contemporary Ghana: The Economy of Ghana*, edited by Walter Birmingham, I. Neustadt and E. N. Omaboe, 62–88. Evanston, IL: Northwestern University Press.

1966a. "The Performance of the Economy, 1955–62." In *A Study of Contemporary Ghana*, edited by Walter Birmingham, I. Neustadt and E. N. Omaboe, 39–61. Evanston, IL: Northwestern University Press.

1966b. "Regional Aspects of the Structure of the Economy." In *A Study of Contemporary Ghana: The Economy of Ghana*, edited by Walter Birmingham, I. Neustadt and E. N. Omoboe, 89–105. Evanston, IL: Northwestern University Press.

Tahir, Gidado. 2001. "Federal Government Intervention in Universal Basic Education." *UBE Forum* no. 1 (1):1–12.

Taiwo, I. O. 2001. "Performance Appraisal of the Year 2000 Federal Budget." *NCEMA Policy Analysis Series* no. 7 (1):19–34.

Talton, Benjamin. 2010. *Politics of Social Change in Ghana: The Konkomba Struggle for Political Equality*. New York: Palgrave MacMillan.

Tarisayi, Eustinah. 2009. "Voting in Despair: The Economic and Social Context." In *Defying the Winds of Change: Zimbabwe's 2008 Elections*, edited by Eldred Masunungure, 11–24. Harare: Weaver Press.

Technical Committee on the Niger Delta. 2008. *Report of the Technical Committee*. Abuja.

Thornycroft, Peta. 2008. "Zimbabwe: Ndira Body Found." *Association of Concerned Africa Scholars Bulletin* no. 79:46–48.

Tonwe, S. O. 1997. *Company Law in Nigeria*. Lagos: Amfitop Books.

Tordoff, William. 2002. *Government and Politics in Africa*. Bloomington: Indiana University Press.

Treisman, Daniel. 2000. "Decentralization and Inflation: Commitment, Collective Action or Continuity." *American Political Science Review* no. 94 (4):837–856.

Tripp, Aili Mari. 2010. *Museveni's Uganda: Paradoxes of Power in a Hybrid Regime. Challenge and Change in African Politics*. Boulder, CO: Lynne Rienner.

Tsebelis, George. 1995. "Decision Making in Political Systems: Veto Players in Presidentialism, Parliamentarism, Multicameralism, and Multipartyism." *British Journal of Political Science* no. 25 (3):289–325.

2002. *Veto Players: How Political Institutions Work*. New York and Princeton, NJ: Russell Sage Foundation with Princeton University Press.

2010. "Veto Player Theory and Policy Change: An Introduction." In *Reform Processes and Policy Change: Veto Players and Decision-Making in Modern Democracies*, edited by Thomas Konig, George Tsebelis and Marc Debus, 1–20. New York: Springer.

Tsikata, G. Kwaku. 2007. "Challenges of Economic Growth in a Liberal Economy." In *Ghana: One Decade of the Liberal State*, edited by Kwame Boafo-Arthur, 49–85. Dakar: CODESRIA Books.

Tukur, Mahumd M. 2004. "Needed: Better Leadership." In *Crafting the New Nigeria: Confronting the Challenges*, edited by Robert I. Rotberg, 239–250. Boulder, CO, and London: Lynne Rienner.

Uchendu, Victor Chikezie. 1965. *The Igbo of Southeast Nigeria. Case Studies in Cultural Anthropology*. Fort Worth, TX: Harcourt Brace Jovanovich College.

Ugalde, Luis Carlos. 2000. *The Mexican Congress: Old Player, New Power, Significant Issues Series*. Washington, DC: CSIS Press.

Ulfelder, Jay. 2007. " Natural-Resource Wealth and the Survival of Autocracy." *Comparative Political Studies* no. 40 (8):995–1018.

United Nations Development Programme. 2009. *Human Development Report, Nigeria 2008–2009: Achieving Growth with Equity*. Abuja: UNDP.

Utomi, Patrick. 2004. "Nigeria as an Economic Powerhouse: Can It Be Achieved?" In *Crafting the New Nigeria: Confronting the Challenges*, edited by Robert I. Rotberg, 125–137. Boulder, CO: Lynne Rienner.

Valenzuela, Arturo. 1991. "The Military in Power: The Consolidation of One-Man Rule." In *The Struggle for Democracy in Chile, 1982–1990*, edited by Paul W. Drake, Ivan Jaksic, San Diego University of California, Center for Iberian and Latin American Studies, Berkeley University of California, Center for Latin American Studies and Institute of the Americas, 21–71. Lincoln: University of Nebraska Press.

van Cranenburgh, Oda. 2009. "Restraining Executive Power in Africa: Horizontal Accountability in Africa's Hybrid Regimes." *South African Journal of International Affairs* no. 16 (1):49–68.

van de Walle, Nicolas. 2001. *African Economies and the Politics of Permanent Crisis, 1979–1999. Political Economy of Institutions and Decisions*. Cambridge and New York: Cambridge University Press.

2003. "Presidentialism and Clientelism in Africa's Emerging Party Systems." *Journal of Modern African Studies* no. 41 (2):297–321.

Vaughan, Olufemi. 1997. "Traditional Rulers and the Dilemma of Democratic Transitions in Nigeria." In *Dilemmas of Democracy in Nigeria*, edited by Paul Beckett and Crawford Young, 413–34. Rochester, NY: University of Rochester Press.

2000. *Nigerian Chiefs: Traditional Power in Modern Politics 1890s–1990s*. Rochester, NY: University of Rochester Press.

Wantchekon, Leonard. 2003. "Clientelism and Voting Behavior: A Field Experiment in Benin." *World Politics* no. 55:399–422.

Watts, Michael. 2004. "Resource Curse? Governability, Oil and Power in the Niger Delta, Nigeria." *Geopolitics* no. 9 (1):50–80.

Watts, Ronald L. 1999. *Comparing Federal Systems*. Montreal and Kingston: McGill-Queen's University Press.

Weeks, Jessica L. 2008. "Autocratic Audience Costs: Regime Type and Signaling Resolve." *International Organization* no. 62 (1):35–64.

Weghorst, Keith R., and Staffan I. Lindberg. 2011. "Effective Opposition Strategies: Collective Goods or Clientelism?" *Democratization* no. 18 (5):1193–1214.

Weinstein, Jeremy M. 2007. *Inside Rebellion: The Politics of Insurgent Violence*. Cambridge and New York: Cambridge University Press.

Weldon, Jeffrey. 2002. "The Legal and Partisan Framework of the Legislative Delegation of the Budget in Mexico." In *Legislative Politics in Latin America*, edited by Scott Morgenstern and Benito Nacif, 377–410. Cambridge and New York: Cambridge University Press.

Widner, Jennifer. 1994a. "Political Reform in Anglophone and Francophone African Countries." In *Economic Change and Political Liberalization in Sub-Saharan Africa*, edited by Jennifer Widner, 49–79. Baltimore: Johns Hopkins University Press.

　　1994b. *Economic Change and Political Liberalization in Sub-Saharan Africa*. Baltimore: Johns Hopkins University Press.

Wills, Garry. 1981. *Explaining America: The Federalist*. Garden City, NY: Doubleday.

Wood, Elisabeth Jean. 2000. *Forging Democracy from Below: Insurgent Transitions in South Africa and El Salvador*. Cambridge Studies in Comparative Politics. Cambridge and New York: Cambridge University Press.

Woodford, Michael. 2001. "Fiscal Requirements for Price Stability." *Journal of Money, Credit, and Banking* no. 33 (3):669–728.

World Bank. 2002. *Nigeria: State and Local Government in Nigeria*. Washington, DC: World Bank.

　　2008. *Nigeria: A Review of the Costs and Financing of Public Education*. Washington, DC: World Bank.

Wright, Joseph. 2008. "Do Authoritarian Institutions Constrain? How Legislatures Affect Economic Growth and Investment." *American Journal of Political Science* no. 52 (2):322–343.

Yekini, T. K. 2002. *External Debt Burden and Macroeconomic Performance in Nigeria, 1970–1999*, NISER Monograph Series. Ibadan: Nigerian Institute of Social and Economic Research.

Young, Crawford. 1994. *The African Colonial State in Comparative Perspective*. New Haven, CT: Yale University Press.

Young, Daniel. 2009. Is Clientelism at Work in African Elections? A Study of Voting Behavior in Kenya and Zambia. AfroBarometer Working Paper No. 106, http://www.afrobarometer.org/files/documents/working_papers/AfropaperNo106.pdf.

Zamchiya, Phillan. 2011. "A Synopsis of Land and Agrarian Change in Chipinge District, Zimbabwe." *Journal of Peasant Studies* no. 38 (5):1093–1122.

Zinecker, Heidrun. 2009. "Regime-Hybridity in Developing Countries: Achievements and Limitations of New Research on Transitions." *International Studies Review* no. 11:302–331.

Index

Abacha, Sani, 18, 77, 84, 87, 88, 89, 90,
    91, 92, 93, 94, 95, 96, 112, 118, 164,
    165, 166, 171, 172, 215
Abiola, Moshood Kashimawo Olawale, 86,
    87, 88, 89, 90, 91, 92, 95
Abubakar, Abdulsalami, 143
Abubakar, Atiku, 108
Accra, 185, 186
Acheampong, Ignatius Kutu, 187, 188,
    189, 193
Achebe, Chinua, 18, 19
Action Congress, 225
Action Group, 58, 60, 61, 62, 63, 69
Afenifere, 91, 110
AFRC, See Armed Forces Ruling Council
AG, See Action Group
Aguiyi-Ironsi, Johnson Thomas
    Umunnakwe, 63, 64, 65, 66, 112, 117
Akan, 187
Ake, Claude, 125
Akintola, Samuel, 60, 61
Akuffo, Frederick, 189, 190
Alence, Rod, 40
All Nigeria People's Party, 110, 225
All People's Party, 98
Amnesty International, 37
Anglo-Nigerian Defense Pact, 59
Angola, 11
ANPP, See All Nigeria People's Party
Anti-Inflation Task Force, 126
APP, See All People's Party
Arab Spring, 221
Arab-Israeli War, 69

Arendt, Hannah, 38
Arewa Consultative Forum, 106, 110
Aristotle, 8
Armed Forces Ruling Council
    (Ghana), 189
Armed Forces Ruling Council (Nigeria),
    81, 82, 83, 84, 85, 87, 89
Ashanti, 193
Atta Mills, John, 183
authoritarianism
    dictatorship, 3, 4, 7, 8, 9, 10, 11, 23,
        25, 26, 33, 37, 38, 39, 46, 53, 56, 95,
        111, 118, 122, 137, 142, 144, 146,
        147, 166, 212, 215, 221, 222, 224,
        235, 236
Authoritarianism, 5, 6, 8, 23, 24, 26, 124,
    205, 213, 221, 224
Autocracy, See Authoritarianism
Awolowo, Obafemi, 43, 57, 59, 61, 62, 69,
    72, 76, 98
Azikiwe, Nnamdi, 1, 58, 63, 75, 235

Babangida, Ibrahim, 7, 77, 79, 80, 81,
    82, 83, 84, 85, 86, 87, 88, 89, 90,
    112, 118, 163, 164, 170, 178, 206,
    215, 219, 222, 223, 229, 232,
    235, 249
Balewa, Abubakar Tafawa, 58
Balewa, Tafawa, 63
Bali, Domkat, 84
Balogun, M. J., 125
Bates, Robert, 182
Baum, Matthew, 28

Bayelsa State, 227
Benin, 10, 11, 196
Bennett, Andrew, 180
Benue State, 79
Biafra, 82, 96, 156
Blair, Tony, 16
Boafo-Arthur, Kwame, 16
Boko Haram, 31
Bolsheviks, 222
Bratton, Michael, 203
Britain, 1, 42, 53, 155, 184, 185, 235
British, 14, 16, 43, 52, 57, 59, 156, 176
Browlee, Jason, 40
Buhari, Muhammadu, 77, 78, 79, 80, 81,
    82, 84, 100, 105, 112, 118, 161, 162,
    163, 172, 215, 234
Burkina Faso, 23, 120
Bush, George, 75
Busia, Kofi, 187, 188, 193

Cameron, Charles, 48
Cameroon, 10
Campaign for Democracy, 229
Carter, Jimmy, 92
CATO Institute, 39
census 1973, 68
Central Bank of Nigeria, 125, 141, 142,
    147, 164, 166, 167, 169
Chabal, Patrick, 16
Chandra, Kanchan, 13, 220
Chazan, Naomi, 186, 188, 190,
    192, 193
Cheeseman, Nicolas, 181
Chevron, 93
Chile, 7, 32, 37, 223
China, 6, 17, 32, 93, 201
Chinweizu, Ibekwe, 235
Christian Association of Nigeria, 227
Civil Liberties Organization, 91
civil service, 60, 61, 65, 66, 67, 69, 78,
    117, 136, 166, 168, 187, 193, 197
civil war, 68, *See also* Biafra
clientelism, 5, 11, 15, 48, 106, 173,
    208, 218
Clinton, Bill, 93
Coalition of Lagos State Youth, 110
colonialism, 3, 4, 6, 10, 14, 15, 19, 25, 31,
    33, 42, 43, 52, 79, 120, 156, 157, 174,
    179, 181, 185, 186, 192, 200, 201,
    211, 224, 234, 236
Committee of Secretaries, 191
conceptual stretching, 181

constructivism, 213, 221
Convention People's Party, 185, 187
corruption, 2, 6, 8, 10, 11, 12, 17, 18, 30,
    62, 63, 68, 77, 78, 79, 94, 97, 99, 100,
    101, 102, 106, 108, 117, 120, 124,
    125, 128, 135, 136, 139, 151, 161,
    163, 165, 166, 172, 174, 178, 183,
    189, 192, 196, 197, 200, 216, 226,
    227, 234, 235
Council of Ministers, 64
Council of State, 77
coups
    African, generally, 6, 24, 221
    Ghana 1966, 177, 186
    Ghana 1972, 187
    Ghana 1978, 189
    Ghana 1979, 30, 178, 189, 192
    Ghana 1981, 177, 191
    Nigeria, 2
    Nigeria 1966, 17, 63, 64, 65, 66, 82,
        156, 230
    Nigeria 1975, 69, 71, 158, 222
    Nigeria 1983, 25, 77, 79, 106,
        161, 230
    Nigeria 1985, 25, 80, 163, 222
    Nigeria 1993, 89
    Nigeria's "phantom" coup, 92
Cox, Gary, 48, 122, 149, 173
CPP, *See* Convention People's Party
Cross Rivers State, 76

Dagomba, 188
Danjuma, T. Y., 70
Dasuki, Ibrahim, 88
debt (foreign), 2, 3, 4, 12, 13, 25, 26, 30,
    51, 77, 97, 120, 122, 137, 140, 141,
    142, 147, 148, 149, 152, 154, 161,
    166, 168, 169, 171, 174, 188, 190,
    209, 212, 213, 216
December 31st Revolution, 190
Decree Number 1, 64, 65, 77
Democratic Republic of the Congo,
    11, 198
democratization, 4, 5, 6, 8, 12, 16, 19, 23,
    24, 26, 30, 83, 93, 138, 176, 181, 194,
    195, 196, 204, 205, 206, 207, 208,
    213, 221, 222, 224
    Third Wave, 6, 12, 23, 222
derivation formula, 107, 117
Diya, Oladipo, 90, 91, 92
Dramani Mahama, John, 190
Dzulekofe Mafia, 191

Ebonyi State, 99
Economic and Finance Committee, 164
Economic and Financial Crimes
    Commission, 102, 103, 108, 226, 227
EFCC, *See* Economic and Financial Crimes
    Commission
Egypt, 40
Elections
    Ghana, 183
    Ghana 1969, 187
    Ghana 1979, 189
    Ghana 1992, 182, 193, 194
    Ghana 2008, 194, 206
    Ghana 2009, 176
    Literature on, 8, 24, 39, 74, 142,
        143, 236
    Nigeria, 71
    Nigeria 1959, 58, 155
    Nigeria 1964, 61
    Nigeria 1964–65, 59, 62, 63, 156
    Nigeria 1979, 72, 74, 76, 159, 231
    Nigeria 1983, 76
    Nigeria 1993, 86, 87, 88, 89, 90, 95, 98,
        165, 171, 231
    Nigeria 1998, 91, 93
    Nigeria 1998–99, 98
    Nigeria 2003, 101, 106, 107, 167
    Nigeria 2007, 24, 26, 105, 108, 183,
        224, 225, 227, 229, 230
    Nigeria 2011, 16, 224, 232, 233,
        234, 236
    United States 1996, 93
    Zimbabwe, 202, 206
    Zimbabwe 1990, 178, 196, 197
    Zimbabwe 1995, 197
    Zimbabwe 2000, 199, 203
    Zimbabwe 2002, 200
    Zimbabwe 2008, 178, 194, 195, 200,
        201, 202, 206
    Zimbabwe 2013, 207
Enahoro, Anthony, 59
Etteh, Patricia, 226
European Union, 225
Extractive Industries Transparency
    Initiative, 168
Ezonbodor, N. A., 59

Fast Track Land Reforms, 199, 201, 207
Federal Character Commission, 236
Federal Electoral Commission, 63
Federal Executive Committee, 93
Federal Executive Council, 66, 67, *See* FEC

Federal Judicial Service, 161
Federal Office of Statistics, 125, 133
federalism, 5, 26, 30, 31, 42, 43, 52, 57,
    61, 66, 68, 112, 117, 148, 209, 213,
    214, 220, 221, 233
First Republic, Nigeria, 57, 58, 65, 68, 72,
    75, 76, 156, 157, 215
Forrest, Tom, 125
Fourth Republic, Ghana, 183
Fourth Republic, Nigeria, 109, 125
Franco, Francisco, 222
Freedom House, 6, 8, 24, 221
Fulani, 14, 57, 58, 60, 65, 78, 87, 88,
    94, 117

Gandhi, Jennifer, 39
George, Alexander, 180
Ghana, 6, 10, 11, 16, 29, 30, 31, 35, 37,
    46, 59, 140, 175, 176, 177, 178, 179,
    180, 181, 182, 183, 184, 185, 186,
    188, 192, 193, 194, 205, 206, 208,
    209, 217, 222, 223
Gold Coast, *See* Ghana
Gowon, Yakubu, 17, 53, 66, 67, 68, 69, 70,
    71, 82, 85, 112, 117, 148, 157, 158,
    172, 223
Gyimah-Boadi, E., 223

Hausa, 14, 57, 58, 60, 65, 74, 87, 88, 94,
    98, 117
Horowitz, Donald, 236
Houphouët-Boigny, Felix, 23
House of Assembly, Zimbabwe, 200
House of Representatives, Nigeria, 58, 59,
    62, 72, 73, 74, 75, 76, 99, 100, 101,
    102, 106, 108, 111, 132, 161, 166,
    225, 226, 227, 230
House of Representatives, United
    States, 235
Hughes, Langston, 1, 235
Human capital, 9, 11, 12, 131, 132, 133,
    134, 145, 174, 212, 225
Huntington, Samuel, 6

IBB Boys, 89, 92
ICPC, *See* Corrupt Practices and Other
    Related Offences Commission
Idiagbon, Tunde, 77, 79, 82, 112, 118, 161,
    162, 163, 172
Igbo, 57, 58, 61, 63, 64, 65, 66, 67, 72, 73,
    75, 76, 100
Ikein, Augustine, 125

Independent Corrupt Practices and Other
Related Offenses Commission,
102, 226
Indonesia, 41, 236
informal institutions, 3, 5, 26, 27, 30, 31,
33, 34, 40, 42, 43, 53, 55, 118, 177,
192, 213, 219, 220, 233
International Monetary Fund, 141, 168,
187, 189, 190, 191, 201
Iran, 40
Iraq War, 108, 168
Islamic law, 26, 28, 71, 78, 98, 106, 117,
See also Sharia
Israel, 59, 80
Ivory Coast, 23

Jega, Attahiru, 17
JFM, *See* June Fourth Movement
JOC, *See* Joint Operations Command
Johnson Sirleaf, Ellen, 19
Joint Operations Command, 201
Jomtiem Declaration, 132
Jonathan, Goodluck, 1, 2, 16, 31, 170,
227, 229, 231, 232
Joseph, Richard, 18
June Fourth Movement, 192

Kaduna Mafia, 71, 76, 78, 87
Kaduna State, 74, 90, 91, 98, 111
Kagame, Paul, 6
Kano
Emir of, 64
Kano State, 87, 106
Kenya, 6, 16, 46, 183, 229
Kenyatta, Jomo, 16
Kingibe, Baba Gana, 90
Konkomba, 188, 190
Kumasi, 193
Kuta, Idris, 111

Labor, *See* Unions
Lagos, 42, 67, 85, 87, 118, 133, 235
Lagos Group, 84
Laitin, David, 209
Lake, David, 28
Land Use Act, 239
Lange, Matthew, 180
Langtang Mafia, 84, 112, 118
Lees, Charles, 180
Limann, Hilla, 190
Lipset, Seymour Martin, 19

Madison, James, 4, 19, 20, 22, 26, 29, 30,
32, 33, 40, 41, 44, 50, 51, 52, 119,
149, 152, 154, 173, 209, 212, 213,
215, 236
Madisonian dilemma, 4, 29, 31, 44, 51,
54, 123, 153, 170, 171, 173, 174,
212, 224
Madueke, Allison, 90
Malaysia, 17, 40
Mamdani, Mahmood, 223
Mandela, Nelson, 19
Manicaland, 199, 200
Mantu, Ibrahim, 109, 111
Masunungure, Eldred, 203
Matabeleland, 196, 198, 199, 200
Mauritania, 2
McCubbins, Mathew, 46, 48, 50, 122, 149,
152, 173, 219
McKinsey Global Institute, 176
MDC, 199, *See* Movement for Democratic
Change
MEND, *See* Movement for the
Emancipation of the Niger Delta
Mexico, 34, 35, 37
Middle Belt, 72, 85, 88, 99
Mill, John Stuart, 179
Ministry of Education, 133, 162
Mobil, 93
modernization theory, 5, 6, 8, 9, 25, 31,
216, 222
Mohammed, Murtala, 68, 69, 70, 71, 78,
158, 171
Montesquieu, 32
Movement for Democratic
Change, 195, 199, 200, 201, 202, 204,
205, 206
Movement for the Emancipation of the
Niger Delta, 107
Movement for the Restoration of
Democracy, 109
Movement for Unity and Progress, 90
Mozambique, 120
Mubarak, Hosni, 9
Mugabe, Robert, 9, 177, 182, 194, 195,
196, 197, 198, 199, 200, 201, 202,
203, 204, 205, 207, 223
Musa, Balarable, 74
Museveni, Yoweri, 6

Na'Abba, Ghali, 100, 101
Nasser, Gamal Abdel, 222

National Assembly, Nigeria, 26, 35, 71, 72,
  73, 74, 75, 76, 83, 96, 98, 100, 101,
  102, 104, 106, 108, 109, 110, 111,
  117, 140, 159, 166, 167, 168, 220,
  225, 226, 227, 230, 232, 235
National Association of Nigerian
  Students, 81
National Constitutional Assembly, 198,
  204, 207
National Council of States, 70
National Defence Committee, 192
National Democratic Coalition, 91, 92
National Liberation Council, 186, 187
National Medical Association, 81
National Party of Nigeria, 72, 73, 74, 75,
  76, 79, 159
National Primary Education
  Commission, 165
National Redemption Council, 187
National Republican Party, 86
National Security Organization, 79
National Unity Forum, 109
National War College, 88
Natural resource exploitation,
  See Resource curse
NCA, *See* National Constitutional
  Assembly
NCNC, National Council of Nigeria and
  the Cameroons, 58, 59, 60, 61, 62, 63,
  112, 133, 155, 156
NDC, *See* National Democratic
  Coalition
NDDC, *See* Niger Delta Development
  Commission
NDM, *See* New Democratic Movement
neo-colonialism, 140, 185
neopatrimonialism, 39, 181, 188
New Democratic Movement, 192
New institutional economics, 49, 51, 53,
  144, 152
New Partnership for Africa's
  Development, 16
Niger Delta, 31, 42, 85, 97, 98, 99, 101,
  103, 104, 105, 106, 107, 117, 169,
  220, 227, 234
  amnesty, 228
  Technical Committee on, 169
Niger Delta Development Commission,
  103, 107
Niger State, 80, 106
Nigeria People's Party, 159

Nigerian Bar Association, 227
Nigerian Governors Forum, 229
Nigerian Labour Congress, 85
Nigerian Medical Association, 162
Nigerian National Alliance, 62
Nigerian National Democratic Party, 61,
  62, 63
Nigerian National Petroleum
  Company, 93
Nigerian People's Party, 72, 73,
  79, 112
Nkrumah, Kwame, 16, 140, 182, 184, 185,
  193, 194, 208
NLC, *See* National Liberation Council
NNA, *See* Nigerian National Alliance
Nnamani, Ken, 111, 235
NNDP, *See* Nigerian National
  Democratic Party
Northern Caucus, 232
Northern Consultative Group, 88
Northern Governors Forum, 110, 231
Northern Legislators Forum, 110
Northern People's Congress, 58, 59, 60, 61,
  62, 63, 65, 72, 76, 155, 156
Northern Political Leaders
  Forum, 233
Northern Senators Forum, 110
Northern Youth Alliance for
  Democracy, 110
NPC, *See* Northern People's Congress
NPN, *See* National Party of Nigeria
NPP, *See* Nigerian People's Party
NRC, *See* National Redemption Council;
  National Republican Congress
Nunumba, 190
Nyerere, Julius, 5, 263
Nzeogu, Chukwuma, 16
Nzeogwu, Chukwuma, 63, 64, 65, 82

O'Donnell, Guillermo, 41
Obama, Barack, 7, 182, 183, 194, 201
Obasanjo, Olusegun, 7, 25, 26, 28, 55, 63,
  64, 67, 69, 70, 71, 72, 77, 82, 85, 86,
  91, 95, 96, 97, 98, 99, 100, 101, 102,
  103, 104, 105, 106, 107, 108, 109,
  110, 111, 112, 117, 118, 141, 158,
  159, 166, 167, 168, 169, 170, 171,
  216, 220, 224, 225, 226, 230, 231,
  232, 233, 236
Ogun State, 67
Ohaneze, 100

Oil revenue, 2, 4, 12, 31, 51, 66, 67, 104,
    116t2.3, 137, 139, 140, 165, 169, 174,
    See also Resource curse
Ojukwu, Chukwumeka, 82
Okadigbo, Chuba, 100, 101
Okonjo-Iweala, Ngozi, 168
Olson, Mancur, 8
Ondo State, 76, 239
Oodu'a People's Congress, 233
Operation Feed Yourself, 188
Organization of Islamic Countries, 85, 87
Osaghae, Eghosa, 19
Oyo State, 76, 111

pan-Africanism, 186
patronage, 3, 4, 5, 11, 14, 26, 27, 28, 29,
    30, 34, 47, 48, 51, 53, 121, 122, 123,
    124, 135, 136, 139, 149, 151, 153,
    167, 171, 173, 174, 177, 181, 183,
    188, 197, 198, 199, 204, 205, 208,
    212, 213, 214, 215, 217, 218
PDP, *See* People's Democratic Party
People's Democratic Party, 95, 96, 100,
    101, 105, 107, 108, 109, 111, 117,
    225, 227, 231, 232, 233
People's National Party, 189
People's Redemption Party, 74
Perón, Juan, 222
Philippines, 40
Pinochet, Augusto, 7, 37, 38, 223
Plato, 16, 19
PNDC, *See* Provisional National Defense
    Council
PNP, *See* People's National Party
Political Bureau, 82, 83, 87, 235
post-colonialism, 3, 16, 19, 20, 135, 140,
    194, 234
power shift, 109, 111, 118, 231, 232, 233,
    234, 236
power-sharing, 21, 30, 100, 178, 182,
    195, 201, 202, 203, 204, 205, 206,
    207, 209
PRC, *See* Provisional Ruling Council
prebendalism, 14
presidentialism, 214
property rights, 8, 12, 28, 29, 71, 122, 127,
    128, 129, 130, 137, 145, 147, 156,
    158, 159, 162, 173, 174, 212, 215,
    216, 239
Provisional National Defence Council, 190,
    191, 192, 193, 208

Provisional Ruling Council, 89, 90, 91, 92,
    94, 112
PRP, *See* People's Redemption Party
public goods theory, 9, 14, 28, 47, 121,
    123, 126, 131, 134, 144, 148, 211

Ranger, Terrance, 204
rational choice theory, 220
Rawlings, Jerry, 178, 183, 189, 190, 191,
    193, 194, 223
resource curse, 3, 5, 8, 11, 31, 104, 139, 194
    rentier state, 25, 140, 151
Rivers State, 59, 76
Rothchild, Donald, 223
Russia, 93, 201
Rustow, W. W., 7
Rwanda, 6, 10, 13

Sachs, Jeffrey, 6
Salazar, António de Oliveira, 222
Sani, Ahmed, 98
Saro-Wiwa, Ken, 93
Save Nigeria Group, 230, 233
Second Republic, Nigeria, 72, 96, 162,
    172, 215, 235
selectorate theory, 48, 51, 122, 144,
    152, 215
Senate President, Nigeria, 72, 74, 86, 100,
    101, 102, 108, 111, 235
Senate, Nigeria, 64, 72, 73, 74, 75, 76, 86,
    93, 98, 99, 100, 101, 102, 103, 105,
    106, 108, 111, 161, 166, 200, 225,
    227, 229, 230
Senegal, 16, 196
Shagari, Shehu, 72, 73, 76, 78, 95, 98, 159,
    160, 162
Sharia, 76, 78, 87, 98, 99, 106, 168
Shell, 93
Shell Petroleum, 228
Shonekan, Ernest, 88, 143, 164
Singapore, 17
Sklar, Richard, 99
SMC, *See* Supreme Military Council
Smith, Adam, 50, 131
SNG, 230, *See* Save Nigeria Group
Social Democratic Party, 90, 91
Sokoto, 64
    Sultan of, 64
Sokoto caliphate, 90
Sokoto State, 79, 87
    Sultan of, 79, 87

South Africa, 71
South African Development
    Community, 201
Sovereign National Conference, 106
Soviet Union, 40
Speaker of the House, Nigeria, 73, 100,
    101, 132, 226
State Security Service, 231
Strøm, Kaare, 36, 37, 209
structural adjustment, 85, 115t2.3, 135,
    141, 163, 191, 197, 198, 209, 213
Supreme Court, 72, 95, 98, 104, 105, 108,
    129, 159, 229, 231, 239
Supreme Military Council, 65, 66, 67,
    68, 69, 70, 71, 77, 78, 79, 83, 112,
    161, 188
Supreme Military Council (Ghana), 189

Tanzania, 5, 6
Tekere, Edgar, 197
Tendi, Miles, 181
Third Republic, Nigeria, 83, 88
third term, 109
Togo, 11, 196
transaction costs, 36, 44, 49, 50, 51, 53,
    118, 122, 128, 144, 153, 173, 177,
    214, 215, 222
Transition Monitoring Group, 225
transitions, 56
    Ghana, 183
    Ghana 1969, 187
    Ghana 1993, 16, 178, 183, 191, 208
    in democratization literature, 8, 11
    Nigeria 1979, 25, 70, 71, 72, 97, 159
    Nigeria 1999, 2, 12, 15, 17, 24, 26,
        28, 95, 97, 111, 144, 166, 167, 229,
        232, 235
    transition plans, Ghana, 189
    transition plans, Nigeria, 65, 69, 71, 80,
        82, 83, 84, 86, 87, 88, 89, 90, 92, 94,
        95, 112, 118, 164, 165, 214
Transparency International, 2, 96
Tsebelis, George, 20, 34, 35, 37, 38, 45, 46,
    47, 222
Tsikata, Kwaku, 17
Tsvangirai, Morgan, 195, 198, 199, 200,
    201, 202, 204

UBE, *See* Universal Basic Education
Uganda, 6, 10, 120, 222
Umar, Abubakar Dangiwa, 90

Unions, 22, 62, 75, 84, 101, 105, 163, 166,
    177, 184, 186, 187, 189, 190, 191,
    192, 193, 194, 198, 199, 204, 206, 208
United Grand Progressive Alliance, 62
United Nations, 2, 131
United Nations Children's Education
    Fund, 176
United Nations Development
    Programme, 174
United Party of Nigeria, 76, 79
United Progressive Grand Alliance, 63
United States, 43, 45, 72, 93, 231,
    234, 235
Universal Basic Education, 132, 160, 167
University of Ibadan, 239
UPGA, *See* United Progressive Grand
    Alliance
UPN, *See* United Party of Nigeria

Valenzuela, Arturo, 38
veto player theory, *See* veto players
veto players, 3, 4, 20, 21, 22, 25, 27, 28,
    29, 30, 33, 34, 35, 36, 37, 38, 39, 40,
    41, 42, 43, 44, 45, 46, 47, 48, 49, 50,
    51, 52, 53, 55, 56, 58, 61, 66, 72,
    73, 75, 77, 78, 81, 83, 84, 89, 106,
    109, 112, 117, 118, 121, 122, 123,
    130, 134, 136, 137, 138, 139, 140,
    143, 144, 145, 146, 147, 148, 149,
    150, 151, 152, 153, 154, 155, 156,
    158, 159, 161, 163, 164, 165, 167,
    168, 169, 170, 171, 172, 173, 174,
    176, 177, 178, 179, 180, 181, 182,
    188, 195, 203, 204, 205, 209, 211,
    213, 214, 215, 216, 217, 218, 219,
    222, 224
veto players, types of
    collective, 35, 36, 45, 52, 55, 81, 83, 84,
        118, 177, 178, 214, 219
    individual, 20, 26, 27, 29, 33, 35, 36, 43,
        52, 55, 177, 178, 214, 215, 219
    institutional, 26, 29, 33, 36, 41, 43, 52,
        55, 57, 66, 72, 75, 96, 101, 106, 112,
        117, 161, 166, 174, 177, 178, 208,
        214, 219
    military factions, 3, 27, 28, 33, 40, 41,
        42, 43, 45, 52, 55, 57, 80, 81, 82,
        83, 84, 85, 89, 90, 91, 92, 95, 112,
        118, 134, 165, 177, 178, 182, 186,
        189, 192, 193, 204, 205, 208, 214,
        215, 219

veto players, types of (*cont.*)
　partisan, 27, 33, 36, 41, 42, 43, 52, 55,
　　57, 58, 72, 73, 75, 100, 112, 117, 155,
　　159, 204, 207, 214
　regional veto, 28, 33, 42, 43, 44,
　　52, 57, 64, 65, 85, 87, 88, 96,
　　98, 99, 106, 107, 112, 117, 118,
　　166, 215
Vietnam, 40
Volta region, 188

Waku, JKN, 95
War on Indiscipline, 79, 162, 163
Washington, George, 19
Weinstein, Jeremy, 180
Willowgate, 196
World Bank, 16, 94, 126, 128, 131,
　　138, 142, 156, 165, 169, 183, 190,
　　191, 201

Yar'Adua, Shehu Musa, 70, 71 82
Yar'Adua, Umaru Musa, 16, 31, 127, 170,
　　225, 227, 229, 230, 231, 232
Yobe State, 78
Yoruba, 57, 60, 61, 64, 65, 72, 75, 76, 78,
　　79, 80, 86, 90, 91, 92, 95, 96, 97, 99,
　　110, 111, 117, 233
Yoruba Council of Elders, 110
Yugoslavia, 13

Zamfara State, 98, 99, 106
ZANU, *See* Zimbabwe African
　　National Union

ZANU-PF, *See* Zimbabwe African National
　　Union-Patriotic Front
ZAPU, *See* Zimbabwe African
　　People's Union
Zaria, 64
　Emir of, 64
ZCTU, *See* Zimbabwe Congress of Trade
　　Unions
ZFTU, *See* Zimbabwe Federation of Trade
　　Unions
Zikist Movement, 64
Zimbabwe, 2, 10, 29, 30, 31, 175, 176,
　　177, 178, 179, 180, 181, 182, 194,
　　195, 196, 200, 203, 204, 205, 206,
　　207, 209, 217, 223, 251, 267
Zimbabwe African National Union,
　　196, 197
Zimbabwe African National Union-
　　Patriotic Front, 194, 195, 196, 197,
　　198, 199, 201, 202, 203, 204, 205,
　　206, 207
Zimbabwe African People's Union,
　　196, 203
Zimbabwe Congress of
　　Trade Unions, 198
Zimbabwe Federation of Trade
　　Unions, 199
Zimbabwe National Liberation War
　　Veterans Association, 197, 202
Zimbabwe Unity Movement, 197
ZNLWVA, *See* Zimbabwe
　　National Liberation War Veterans
　　Association

BOOKS IN THIS SERIES (*continued from page iii*)

1 *City Politics: A Study of Léopoldville, 1962–63*, J. S. La Fontaine
2 *Studies in Rural Capitalism in West Africa*, Polly Hill
3 *Land Policy in Buganda*, Henry W. West
4 *The Nigerian Military: A Sociological Analysis of Authority and Revolt, 1960–67*, Robin Luckham
5 *The Ghanaian Factory Worker: Industrial Man in Africa*, Margaret Peil
6 *Labour in the South African Gold Mines*, Francis Wilson
7 *The Price of Liberty: Personality and Politics in Colonial Nigeria*, Kenneth W. J. Post and George D. Jenkins
8 *Subsistence to Commercial Farming in Present Day Buganda: An Economic and Anthropological Survey*, Audrey I. Richards, Fort Sturrock, and Jean M. Fortt (eds.)
9 *Dependence and Opportunity: Political Change in Ahafo*, John Dunn and A. F. Robertson
10 *African Railwaymen: Solidarity and Opposition in an East African Labour Force*, R. D. Grillo
11 *Islam and Tribal Art in West Africa*, René A. Bravmann
12 *Modern and Traditional Elites in the Politics of Lagos*, P. D. Cole
13 *Asante in the Nineteenth Century: The Structure and Evolution of a Political Order*, Ivor Wilks
14 *Culture, Tradition and Society in the West African Novel*, Emmanuel Obiechina
15 *Saints and Politicians*, Donald B. Cruise O'Brien
16 *The Lions of Dagbon: Political Change in Northern Ghana*, Martin Staniland
17 *Politics of Decolonization: Kenya Europeans and the Land Issue 1960–1965*, Gary B. Wasserman
18 *Muslim Brotherhoods in Nineteenth-Century Africa*, B. G. Martin
19 *Warfare in the Sokoto Caliphate: Historical and Sociological Perspectives*, Joseph P. Smaldone
20 *Liberia and Sierra Leone: An Essay in Comparative Politics*, Christopher Clapham
21 *Adam Kok's Griquas: A Study in the Development of Stratification in South Africa*, Robert Ross
22 *Class, Power and Ideology in Ghana: The Railwaymen of Sekondi*, Richard Jeffries
23 *West African States: Failure and Promise*, John Dunn (ed.)
24 *Afrikaners of the Kalahari: White Minority in a Black State*, Margo Russell and Martin Russell
25 *A Modern History of Tanganyika*, John Iliffe
26 *A History of African Christianity 1950–1975*, Adrian Hastings
27 *Slaves, Peasants and Capitalists in Southern Angola, 1840–1926*, W. G. Clarence-Smith
28 *The Hidden Hippopotamus: Reappraised in African History: The Early Colonial Experience in Western Zambia*, Gwyn Prins

29 *Families Divided: The Impact of Migrant Labour in Lesotho*, Colin Murray

30 *Slavery, Colonialism and Economic Growth in Dahomey, 1640–1960*, Patrick Manning

31 *Kings, Commoners and Concessionaires: The Evolution and Dissolution of the Nineteenth-Century Swazi State*, Philip Bonner

32 *Oral Poetry and Somali Nationalism: The Case of Sayid Mahammad 'Abdille Hasan*, Said S. Samatar

33 *The Political Economy of Pondoland 1860–1930*, William Beinart

34 *Volkskapitalisme: Class, Capital and Ideology in the Development of Afrikaner Nationalism, 1934–1948*, Dan O'Meara

35 *The Settler Economies: Studies in the Economic History of Kenya and Rhodesia 1900–1963*, Paul Mosley

36 *Transformations in Slavery: A History of Slavery in Africa*, Paul E. Lovejoy

37 *Amilcar Cabral: Revolutionary Leadership and People's War*, Patrick Chabal

38 *Essays on the Political Economy of Rural Africa*, Robert H. Bates

39 *Ijeshas and Nigerians: The Incorporation of a Yoruba Kingdom, 1890s–1970s*, J. D. Y. Peel

40 *Black People and the South African War, 1899–1902*, Peter Warwick

41 *A History of Niger 1850–1960*, Finn Fuglestad

42 *Industrialisation and Trade Union Organization in South Africa, 1924–1955*, Stephen Ellis

43 *The Rising of the Red Shawls: A Revolt in Madagascar 1895–1899*, Stephen Ellis

44 *Slavery in Dutch South Africa*, Nigel Worden

45 *Law, Custom and Social Order: The Colonial Experience in Malawi and Zambia*, Martin Chanock

46 *Salt of the Desert Sun: A History of Salt Production and Trade in the Central Sudan*, Paul E. Lovejoy

47 *Marrying Well: Marriage, Status and Social Change among the Educated Elite in Colonial Lagos*, Kristin Mann

48 *Language and Colonial Power: The Appropriation of Swahili in the Former Belgian Congo, 1880–1938*, Johannes Fabian

49 *The Shell Money of the Slave Trade*, Jan Hogendorn and Marion Johnson

50 *Political Domination in Africa*, Patrick Chabal

51 *The Southern Marches of Imperial Ethiopia: Essays in History and Social Anthropology*, Donald Donham and Wendy James

52 *Islam and Urban Labor in Northern Nigeria: The Making of a Muslim Working Class*, Paul M. Lubeck

53 *Horn and Crescent: Cultural Change and Traditional Islam on the East African Coast, 1800–1900*, Randall L. Pouwels

54 *Capital and Labour on the Kimberley Diamond Fields, 1871–1890*, Robert Vicat Turrell

55 *National and Class Conflict in the Horn of Africa*, John Markakis

56 *Democracy and Prebendal Politics in Nigeria: The Rise and Fall of the Second Republic*, Richard A. Joseph

57 *Entrepreneurs and Parasites: The Struggle for Indigenous Capitalism in Zaïre*, Janet MacGaffey

58 *The African Poor: A History*, John Iliffe

59 *Palm Oil and Protest: An Economic History of the Ngwa Region, South-Eastern Nigeria, 1800–1980*, Susan M. Martin

60 *France and Islam in West Africa, 1860–1960*, Christopher Harrison

61 *Transformation and Continuity in Revolutionary Ethiopia*, Christopher Clapham

62 *Prelude to the Mahdiyya: Peasants and Traders in the Shendi Region, 1821–1885*, Anders Bjørkelo

63 *Wa and the Wala: Islam and Polity in Northwestern Ghana*, Ivor Wilks

64 *H. C. Bankole-Bright and Politics in Colonial Sierra Leone, 1919–1958*, Akintola Wyse

65 *Contemporary West African States*, Donald Cruise O'Brien, John Dunn, and Richard Rathbone (eds.)

66 *The Oromo of Ethiopia: A History, 1570–1860*, Mohammed Hassen

67 *Slavery and African Life: Occidental, Oriental, and African Slave Trades*, Patrick Manning

68 *Abraham Esau's War: A Black South African War in the Cape, 1899–1902*, Bill Nasson

69 *The Politics of Harmony: Land Dispute Strategies in Swaziland*, Laurel L. Rose

70 *Zimbabwe's Guerrilla War: Peasant Voices*, Norma J. Kriger

71 *Ethiopia: Power and Protest: Peasant Revolts in the Twentieth Century*, Gebru Tareke

72 *White Supremacy and Black Resistance in Pre-Industrial South Africa: The Making of the Colonial Order in the Eastern Cape, 1770–1865*, Clifton C. Crais

73 *The Elusive Granary: Herder, Farmer, and State in Northern Kenya*, Peter D. Little

74 *The Kanyok of Zaire: An Institutional and Ideological History to 1895*, John C. Yoder

75 *Pragmatism in the Age of Jihad: The Precolonial State of Bundu*, Michael A. Gomez

76 *Slow Death for Slavery: The Course of Abolition in Northern Nigeria, 1897–1936*, Paul E. Lovejoy and Jan S. Hogendorn

77 *West African Slavery and Atlantic Commerce: The Senegal River Valley, 1700–1860*, James F. Searing

78 *A South African Kingdom: The Pursuit of Security in Nineteenth-Century Lesotho*, Elizabeth A. Eldredge

79 *State and Society in Pre-colonial Asante*, T. C. McCaskie

80 *Islamic Society and State Power in Senegal: Disciples and Citizens in Fatick*, Leonardo A. Villalón

81 *Ethnic Pride and Racial Prejudice in Victorian Cape Town: Group Identity and Social Practice*, Vivian Bickford-Smith

82 *The Eritrean Struggle for Independence: Domination, Resistance and Nationalism, 1941–1993*, Ruth Iyob

83 *Corruption and State Politics in Sierra Leone*, William Reno

84 *The Culture of Politics in Modern Kenya*, Angelique Haugerud

85 *Africans: The History of a Continent*, John Iliffe
86 *From Slave Trade to "Legitimate" Commerce: The Commercial Transition in Nineteenth-Century West Africa*, Robin Law (ed.)
87 *Leisure and Society in Colonial Brazzaville*, Phyllis Martin
88 *Kingship and State: The Buganda Dynasty*, Christopher Wrigley
89 *Decolonization and African Life: The Labour Question in French and British Africa*, Frederick Cooper
90 *Misreading the African Landscape: Society and Ecology in an African Forest Savannah Mosaic*, James Fairhead and Melissa Leach
91 *Peasant Revolution in Ethiopia: The Tigray People's Liberation Front, 1975–1991*, John Young
92 *Senegambia and the Atlantic Slave Trade*, Boubacar Barry
93 *Commerce and Economic Change in West Africa: The Oil Trade in the Nineteenth Century*, Martin Lynn
94 *Slavery and French Colonial Rule in West Africa: Senegal, Guinea and Mali*, Martin A. Klein
95 *East African Doctors: A History of the Modern Profession*, John Iliffe
96 *Middlemen of the Cameroons Rivers: The Duala and Their Hinterland, c.1600–1960*, Ralph Derrick, Ralph A. Austen, and Jonathan Derrick
97 *Masters and Servants on the Cape Eastern Frontier, 1760–1803*, Susan Newton-King
98 *Status and Respectability in the Cape Colony, 1750–1870: A Tragedy of Manners*, Robert Ross
99 *Slaves, Freedmen and Indentured Laborers in Colonial Mauritius*, Richard B. Allen
100 *Transformations in Slavery: A History of Slavery in Africa*, 2nd Edition, Paul E. Lovejoy
101 *The Peasant Cotton Revolution in West Africa: Côte d'Ivoire, 1880–1995*, Thomas J. Bassett
102 *Re-Imagining Rwanda: Conflict, Survival and Disinformation in the Late Twentieth Century*, Johan Pottier
103 *The Politics of Evil: Magic, State Power and the Political Imagination in South Africa*, Clifton Crais
104 *Transforming Mozambique: The Politics of Privatization, 1975–2000*, M. Anne Pitcher
105 *Guerrilla Veterans in Post-war Zimbabwe: Symbolic and Violent Politics, 1980–1987*, Norma J. Kriger
106 *An Economic History of Imperial Madagascar, 1750–1895: The Rise and Fall of an Island Empire*, Gwyn Campbell
107 *Honour in African History*, John Iliffe
108 *Africans: History of a Continent*, 2nd Edition, John Iliffe
109 *Guns, Race, and Power in Colonial South Africa*, William Kelleher Storey
110 *Islam and Social Change in French West Africa: History of an Emancipatory Community*, Sean Hanretta
111 *Defeating Mau Mau, Creating Kenya: Counterinsurgency, Civil War, and Decolonization*, Daniel Branch
112 *Christianity and Genocide in Rwanda*, Timothy Longman

113 *From Africa to Brazil: Culture, Identity, and an African Slave Trade, 1600–1830*, Walter Hawthorne

114 *Africa in the Time of Cholera: A History of Pandemics from 1817 to the Present*, Myron Echenberg

115 *A History of Race in Muslim West Africa, 1600–1960*, Bruce S. Hall

116 *Witchcraft and Colonial Rule in Kenya, 1900–1955*, Katherine Luongo

117 *Transformations in Slavery: A History of Slavery in Africa*, 3rd edition, Paul E. Lovejoy

118 *The Rise of the Trans-Atlantic Slave Trade in Western Africa, 1300–1589*, Toby Green

119 *Party Politics and Economic Reform in Africa's Democracies*, M. Anne Pitcher

120 *Smugglers and Saints of the Sahara: Regional Connectivity in the Twentieth Century*, Judith Scheele

121 *Slaving and Cross-Cultural Trade in the Atlantic World: Angola and Brazil during the Era of the Slave Trade*, Roquinaldo Ferreira

122 *Ethnic Patriotism and the East African Revival*, Derek Peterson

123 *Black Morocco: A History of Slavery and Islam*, Chouki El Hamel

124 *An African Slaving Port and the Atlantic World: Benguela and Its Hinterland*, Mariana Candido

125 *Making Citizens in Africa: Ethnicity, Gender, and National Identity in Ethiopia*, Lahra Smith

126 *Slavery and Emancipation in Islamic East Africa: From Honor to Respectability*, Elisabeth McMahon

127 *A History of African Motherhood: The Case of Uganda, 700–1900*, Rhiannon Stephens

128 *The Borders of Race in Colonial South Africa: The Kat River Settlement, 1829–1856*, Robert Ross

129 *From Empires to NGOs in the West African Sahel: The Road to Nongovernmentality*, Gregory Mann

130 *Dictators and Democracy in African Development: The Political Economy of Good Governance in Nigeria*, A. Carl LeVan

CPSIA information can be obtained at www.ICGtesting.com
Printed in the USA
LVOW06*0806151215

466694LV00007B/65/P

BIG
BUSINESS
AND
PRESIDENTIAL
POWER